AGENCY

A PARTIAL HISTORY OF LIVE ART

FOREWORD

TWENTY YEARS AND COUNTING
LOIS KEIDAN 6

INTRODUCTION

THERON SCHMIDT 10

BODIES

INTRODUCTION 15

CONVERSATIONS

MARTIN O'BRIEN & KIRA O'REILLY 21

GEORGE CHAKRAVARTHI & MANUEL VASON 29

ALEXANDRINA HEMSLEY AND JAMILA JOHNSON-SMALL (PROJECT O) & SELINA THOMPSON 39

PROVOCATIONS

THOSE WHO HAVE SUFFERED UNDERSTAND SUFFERING: NOTES ON THE BODY (IN PAIN)
DOMINIC JOHNSON 47

AGENCY, HABITUS, EMBODIMENT
AMELIA JONES 57

SPACES

INTRODUCTION 71

CONVERSATIONS

TIM ETCHELLS & ANDY FIELD 79

LESLIE HILL AND HELEN PARIS (CURIOUS) & JOHANNA TUUKKANEN 89

REBECCA FRENCH AND ANDREW MOTTERSHEAD (FRENCH & MOTTERSHEAD) & HAYLEY NEWMAN 97

PROVOCATIONS

FROM A DISTANCE
HEIKE ROMS 107

THE GIFT OF PLACE
JOHN E. MCGRATH 115

INSTITUTIONS

INTRODUCTION 127

CONVERSATIONS

MARY PATERSON & JOSHUA SOFAER 135

ROSELEE GOLDBERG & CATHERINE WOOD 145

GARY ANDERSON AND LENA ŠIMIĆ (THE INSTITUTE FOR THE ART AND PRACTICE OF DISSENT AT HOME) & BRYAN BIGGS 155

PROVOCATIONS

STILL LIVE: THE FREE UNIVERSITY OF LIVERPOOL (2010–2013)
JANE TROWELL 165

INSTITUTIONAL CELEBRATION
JEN HARVIE 175

COMMUNITIES

INTRODUCTION 191

CONVERSATIONS

SIMON CASSON & THE VACUUM CLEANER 197

JORDAN MCKENZIE & RAJNI SHAH 205

ANNE BEAN & ALASTAIR MACLENNAN 215

PROVOCATIONS

PERFORMED COMMUNITIES: IMAGINING SOME RESEARCH WORTH DOING
ALAN READ 225

COMMUNITY—A CASE STUDY IN FOUR ACTS: THE BREWERY, THE CIRCUS, THE WICK, AND THE GREEN
LOIS WEAVER 233

ACTIONS

INTRODUCTION 249

CONVERSATIONS

KATHERINE ARANIELLO AND AARON WILLIAMSON (THE DISABLED AVANT-GARDE) & RICHARD DEDOMENICI 255

BARBY ASANTE & DAVID A. BAILEY 265

RON ATHEY & CASSILS 273

PROVOCATIONS

PERFORMING UTOPIAS: FOR A LIVE ART THAT LIVES AND LETS LIVE
JOHN JORDAN 283

'PHILOSOPHICAL TANTRUM' #10: ON ART, IMAGINATION, DEMOCRACY, CENSORSHIP, HOPE, ETC.
GUILLERMO GÓMEZ-PEÑA 291

TIMELINE 304

INDEX 313

WORKS CITED 316

ACKNOWLEDGEMENTS 320

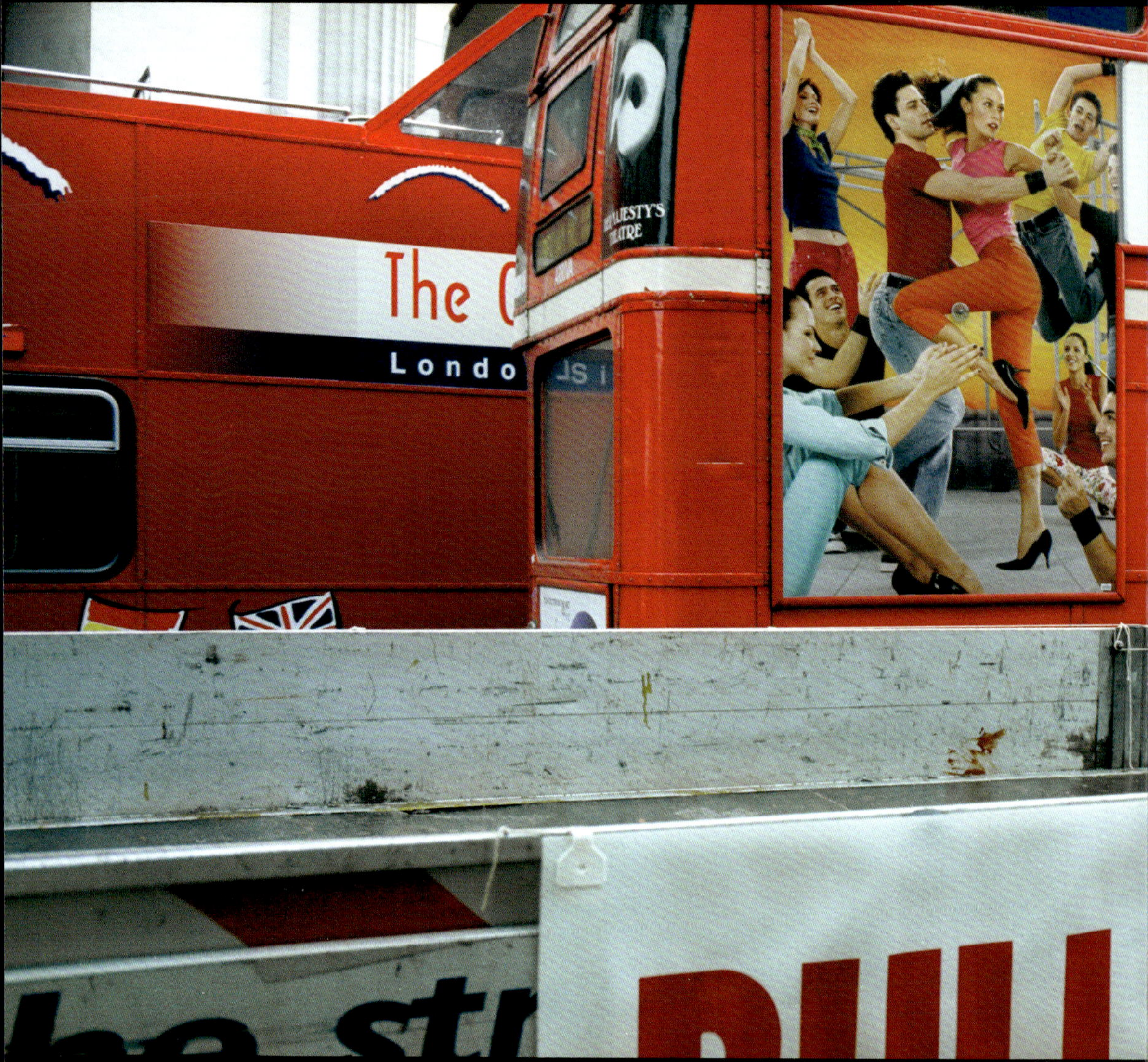
The
MAJESTY'S

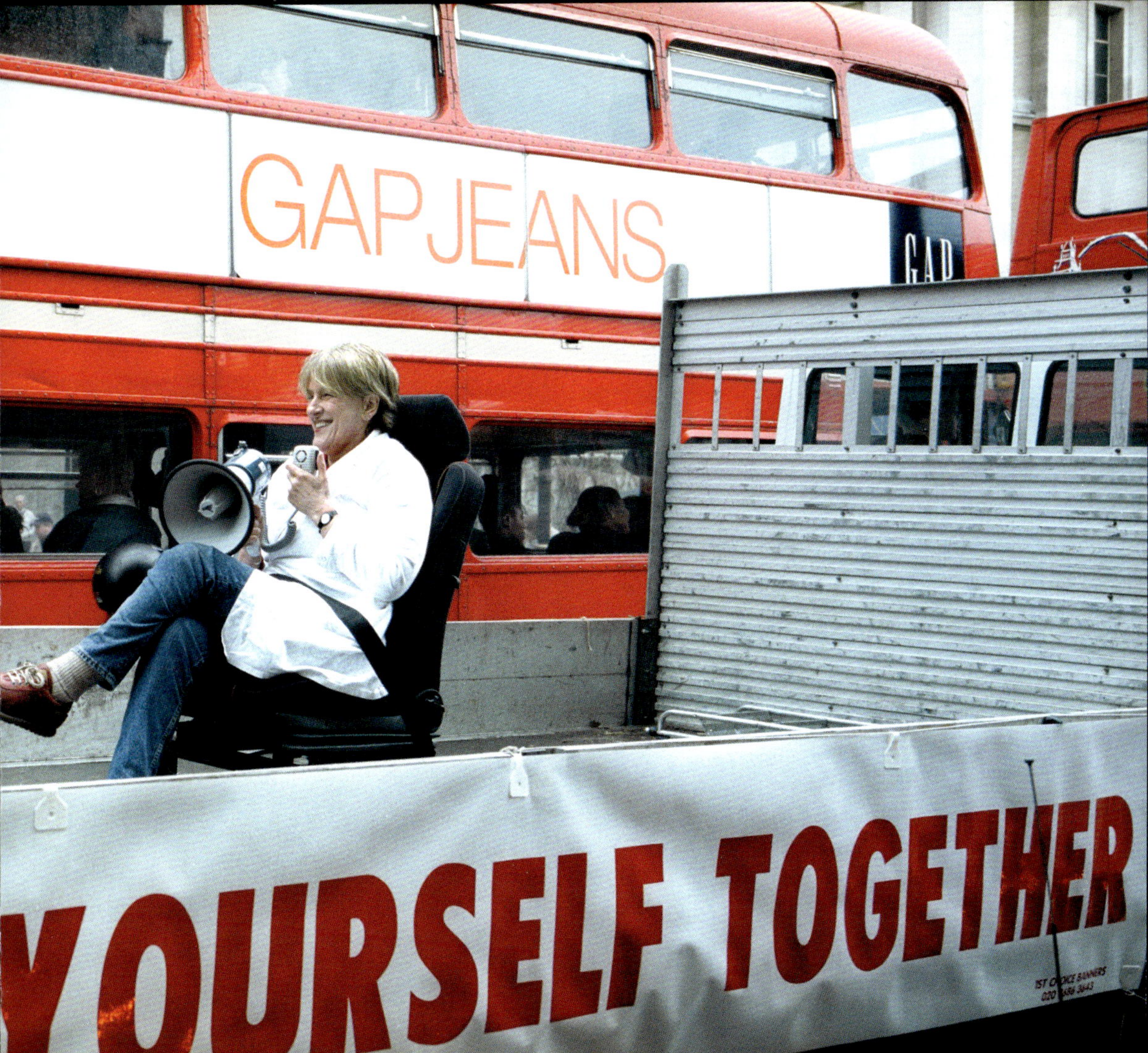
GAPJEANS
GAP
YOURSELF TOGETHER

FOREWORD: TWENTY YEARS AND COUNTING
LOIS KEIDAN

When Catherine Ugwu and I launched the Live Art Development Agency in January 1999 we had no idea it would still be going twenty years later. In truth I didn't imagine it would last beyond the term of our first Arts Council grant, let alone that LADA would grow from a two-man band based around a couple of desks, shelves and blank pieces of paper, to a six-person operation running a complex web of projects, resources, opportunities, and publishing.

The unexpected longevity and unimagined expansion of LADA in many ways speaks to advances in the profile, position, and possibilities of Live Art over the last twenty years. Some of those advances are reflected in this 'partial' collection of provocations and conversations curated by Theron Schmidt, which considers the agency of Live Art in relation to the big questions of Bodies, Spaces, Institutions, Communities, and Actions, and does so through the lens of LADA.

Published on the occasion of LADA's 20th anniversary in 2019, *AGENCY* is, for me at least, an opportunity to reflect on how the shifts and developments within Live Art have impacted on LADA's work, and in turn, on the ways in which what LADA does, and how it does it, have adapted and evolved.

Perhaps the biggest shift that has affected almost everyone involved with Live Art is technology. Developments in technologies allow us all to create and access online platforms to research, connect, share, catalogue, publish, and disseminate Live Art in unprecedented ways. Technology is a critical factor in the heightened level of interest and developments in the histories and archiving of Live Art and has enabled artists, scholars, and curators to both research, and create new contexts for, underrepresented artists and untold histories. Technology has been instrumental in shifts in the critical thinking and popular profile of Live Art, making it possible for artists, writers, and audiences to bypass the mainstream gatekeepers of culture. It's impossible to overestimate the impact of technology on the functionality of LADA—our capacity to document, archive, publish, and disperse Live Art through digital publications and online platforms such as Live Online and, through them, to reach and connect artists and thinkers across the globe and to go where Live Art hasn't gone before.

The institutional embrace of Live Art over the last twenty years is another hugely significant shift. When LADA started in 1999, Live Art was still very much the runt of the litter in the cultural life of the UK, ignored, trashed, or undervalued by most institutions. But the last twenty years has seen an unparalleled institutional engagement with experiential, experimental, and ephemeral practices, with many previously impenetrable museums, galleries, theatres, and festivals opening their doors to Live Art. Since LADA's *Live Culture* programme at Tate Modern in 2003, the 2012 opening of Tate Tanks (the world's first museum space dedicated to performance), and the extraordinary range of partnerships built by Live Art programmers and festivals across the UK, it's now tempting to count the institutions that *haven't* in some way embraced Live Art's ways of working rather than those that have.

The widespread teaching and study of Live Art within Higher Education is an equally catalytic development that has impacted on the increasing pervasiveness of Live Art and influenced the work of LADA. In 1999, only a handful of universities and art colleges had a commitment to such kinds of process-based artistic experimentation, or understandings of how it could contribute to scholarly research and discourse. The students who made it to LADA's office to see what was on our shelves—most of them rejects or refugees from more traditional disciplines—had invariably found us themselves, and not many artists we knew were employed to teach. LADA started at the same time as the artist Lois Weaver joined the Drama Department at Queen Mary University of London and one of our first collaborations was to set up an informal Live Art in Higher Education in London Forum. Every six months or so for a couple of years, a motley crew of academics would gather together to discuss the challenges of bringing the practices and approaches they were so passionate about into the academy. Today couldn't be more different—LADA's Study Room regularly welcomes students sent to us by their tutors, hosts scores of student groups from universities across the UK and beyond, many artists now hold teaching positions (albeit some more precariously than others), all kinds of Live Art related PhDs are being undertaken, and LADA works closely with a wide range of scholars and universities. *Performance Studies international:12, Performing Rights*, hosted by Queen Mary in 2006, with LADA as its cultural partner, was a pivotal moment for us in testing ways we could position artistic practices within research focused contexts, and vice versa. *Performance Matters* (2009-2013)—an Arts and Humanities Research Council funded research project in collaboration with Adrian Heathfield of University of Roehampton and Gavin Butt of Goldsmiths, University of London, considering the cultural value of Live Art—had a seismic impact on Live Art's, and indeed LADA's, role within research culture. And in 2018, LADA partnered with Queen Mary University of London on a new MA Live Art. From where I sit, Live Art in Higher Education has come a long way since 1999.

This institutional embrace and academic legitimacy should not in any way suggest that Live Art has somehow been tamed. Far from it. Live Art is still a fiercely politicised, provocative, and unruly area of practice. Live Art is all about difference—different ways of making and experiencing art; different ways of documenting and dispersing performance; different ways of being in, and seeing, the world; and different ways of occupying the institution and rethinking approaches to research and knowledge.

In 1999, the kinds of artists and practices LADA particularly championed were not only interested in the body as their site and subject, and in testing the nature, role, and experience of art, but were just as concerned with representations of cultural difference, with the construction and performance of identity, with giving visibility to the hidden and forbidden. For LADA, Live Art was more than a space to think about what art is and can do, it was a space to think about who has agency and what they can do with it.

Over the last twenty years, the embodied and subversive practices around the politics of the body that so characterised much Live Art in the late 1990s are still as vital and urgent as ever—but Live Art as a practice and an approach has also influenced a wider spectrum of process-based, experiential art, spanning all kinds of disciplines and subjectivities, and testing new forms of audience relationships. Since 2016, LADA has been working with the artist and researcher Sibylle Peters and Tate Early Years and Families Programme on projects inviting children and adults to look at the world together through Live Art. With these partners we have produced *PLAYING UP*, an intergenerational game based on historical Live Art works, and *KAPUTT*, a transgenerational academy of creative destruction, and, through them, contributed to debates and practices on what it is possible, and permissible, to *do* with kids, and on what that *doing* can *do*. Such radical and transgressive children's projects would have been inconceivable for either LADA or Tate in 1999 and reflect both the changes in societal attitudes to children and childhood and the evolving potential of Live Art itself.

One of the ways I've been looking back on LADA's history has been through location. In her essay in this collection (in the section on Communities), Lois Weaver writes beautifully about the different locations that LADA has occupied since 1999 across the East End of London and what those locations say about London and ideas of community. But as well as thinking about *where* we've been located, I've also been reflecting on *how* we've been located.

In 1999, with our desks and shelves holding a handful of books and VHS tapes, LADA was primarily an office, a base for us to go out into the world on an evangelical mission of Live Art conversion. In the early days we worked closely with Arts Council England on advocacy and strategic initiatives such as *Focus Live Art* (a kind of national audit of the scene) and establishing Live Art UK (a national network of promoters and facilitators, which continues to thrive); and with the British Council on projects flying the Live Art flag abroad (including Live Art exchanges between the UK and China, supported by *Connections Through Culture*). But as the world has caught the Live Art bug and younger organisations like Forest Fringe tour their exciting programming models internationally, LADA's approach has changed and become increasingly more about connecting with the world through the dispersal of ideas and things—digital platforms and projects, publications, and films. More importantly, with the expansion of our work into publishing and programming, and with those shelves growing into our Study Room (the world's largest open-access research facility for Live Art), we have found ourselves more and more bound to a place, a place we now think and talk about as a *Centre for Live Art*—a knowledge and research centre, a production centre for programmes and publications, and an online centre for experimentation and dissemination.

The phrase 'without whom' might have been written for the people without whom LADA would neither have started nor lasted. Paula Brown at London Arts Board who had the vision to make funds available for a Live Art Development Agency for London and whose wisdom and support guided us through the first ten years. Co-founder Catherine Ugwu for getting the show on the road before leaving to bring all her Live Art sensibilities to the opening and closing ceremonies of the London Olympic and Paralympic Games in 2012. Daniel Brine and CJ Mitchell who took LADA to other levels for how we work and what we are able to do. Everyone who has worked at, or with, LADA in whatever capacity, or undertaken an internship with us. And finally enormous gratitude is due to all LADA's Patrons and to everyone who has been a member of LADA's Board since 1999, and especially its Chair Cecilia Wee.

INTRODUCTION
THERON SCHMIDT

What is Live Art? As a relatively recent way of framing certain artistic practices, particularly championed within the UK contemporary art sector, Live Art is intentionally capacious in the range of pratices it can include: body art, performances for the stage, cabaret, interactions in public, site-responsive work, invisible interventions, overtly political actions, and many other ways of working. From its early usages as a term, its very breadth and inclusivity has been held up as its strength: 'Live Art represents a challenge to received ways of doing, thinking and seeing; a rejection of a single art form practice; a way of opening frontiers to any political, social or cultural agenda,' Lois Keidan wrote in a 1991 discussion document for the UK Arts Council 's National Arts and Media Strategy.[1] In Keidan's document, and in other documents advocating for Live Art, this theme recurs: Live Art is commonly defined as an opposition or challenge to received artistic, social, and political categories. As Jennie Klein notes, 'Part of the success of Keidan's report lay in its refusal to define live art, except insofar as what it was not—theatre, dance, music, or art objects.'[2] This refusal continues in Keidan's later 'Vision Statement' (2004) for the then newly formed Live Art UK network: 'Live Art cannot be placed within any singular history, be seen through a disciplinary lens, or be held in any cultural boundary or place.'[3] As Klein observes, this oppositional stance also celebrates a wilful marginality: 'For much of its short existence, performance/live art has existed purposefully on the margins of most art critical, pedagogical, and historical discourses.'[4] This 'outsider' positioning continues throughout the answer the Live Art Development Agency website gives to the question 'What is Live Art?': 'Disrupting borders, breaking rules, defying traditions, resisting definitions, asking awkward questions and activating audiences, Live Art breaks the rules about who is making art, how they are making it and who they are making it for.'[5]

However, this series of definitions over the 1990s and 2000s tracks a history not only of anti-establishment opposition, but also of solidification and development. Keidan's advocacy within the Arts Council was successful in increasing support for Live Art to such an extent that in 1998 Arts Council London made funds available to set up a 'Live Art Development Agency' (LADA), which Keidan and Catherine Ugwu founded in 1999. And the Live Art UK network launched by that Vision Statement has continued to grow, with a proliferation of organisations and initiatives of various kinds and sizes around the UK (even as others become unsupportable and disappear). And so, the aim of this book is to take the twenty-year anniversary of the establishment of LADA as an opportunity to reflect not only on what Live Art has been *against*, but also what it has been *for.* Rather than defining the practices that have gathered in relation to Live Art in oppositional terms—what they might be seeking to critique, reject, or disrupt—this collection sets out to reframe them in terms of the kinds of relations and commitments they might be seen to model or advocate. What kinds of care and recovery do they enable? What do they connect as well as reject? What do they make possible as they test the impossible? What ideas of success do they stand for as they risk failure?

At the heart of this project is an enquiry into agency: the capacity for new kinds of thoughts, actions, and energies as enacted by individual artists and groups. The concept of agency has been variously conceived, with the question of 'what *is* agency?' often shaped by one's answer to the question 'who or what *has* agency?' As Ellen Messer-Davidow notes from the midst of 1990s debates within feminist theory, agency has a chameleon-like quality: if one thinks of it as attached to an entity—an individual, a collective, or a social structure—it takes on the qualities of that entity.[6] In social theory, agency has typically been described in relation to actor/structure dualism: a tension between individuals' experiences as active agents, with the freedom to exercise their preferences, and the social and cultural conditions that shape, mediate, and even determine what it is possible to think, feel, and do. In relation to artistic practices, scholars such as Shannon Jackson and Jen Harvie have argued that there is no fixed distinction between a work of art and the support structure in which it develops: institutions and the value-structures they endorse, critical writing and the vocabulary it makes possible, subcultures and the oppressions they face, are all part of the conditions of possibility for works of art and other acts of agency—even as such actions might challenge or shatter those conditions.[7]

In this way we might think of agency as an emergent property, as a shape of encounter, as a relational quality, rather than something that belongs to someone (or something): agency is a *doing* rather than a *having*. Such a performative understanding of agency is put forward in the thinking of so-called 'new materialisms', which seek to collapse actor/structure dualism by focusing on the agency of *everything*: agency is not the exclusive domain of the human, but also nonhuman beings, networks, organic and inorganic matter, etc.[8] As Karen Barad puts it, 'agency is a matter of intra-acting; it is an enactment, not something that someone or something has.'[9] In other words, agency *is* Live Art: the possibility for new forms of living and being, manifest, for example, in the interplay between the lived experience of *bodies*, the value-structures of *institutions*, the capacities of different kinds of *spaces*, the movement and dispersal of *communities*, and the resonance and reverberation of *actions*. These five lenses form the framework for the conversations and provocations that have been gathered for this book—a set of lenses that are useful less for their specificity than in their multiplicity, indicating a range of cross-connecting (and intra-acting) nodes by which the theme of agency can be approached:

> BODIES: reimagining what the body can do; the exploration of body-based practices in relation to contexts of

medical frameworks, sexual and racial politics, and conventions of display; the establishment of regimes of training for Live Art practices, both within institutional contexts and also constituting the work itself for some practitioners.

SPACES: artists and projects engaging with specific places and histories as well as the conventions of different kinds of sites of encounter; the importance of physical spaces and resources for the development of individual and collective agency; the histories of particular locations and the communities associated with them; conceptual, imaginative, and temporary spaces of opposition; questions of locality, distance, and internationalism.

INSTITUTIONS: the effects of the institutionalisation of Live Art practices; the opportunities and compromises presented by working across and between cultural and political institutions; artists who reject or trash Live Art's own political claims or processes of institutionalisation; those who remain outside institutions, including the institution of Live Art, by choice or by exclusion; documentation, legacy, and the role of critical writing and publishing.

COMMUNITIES: artists working with Live Art strategies as ways of connecting with existing communities or the construction of new networks of long-term social relationship; the overlapping of artistic activities with marginalised or politicised communities; coming together to consider the conditions of artistic labour.

ACTIONS: interventions by individuals or groups within specific political contexts; personal and community transformation; questions of visibility and invisibility of individuals and groups; engagement with mainstream forms of spectacle; activism, protest, and revolution; what might be next.

As a history of Live Art, this collection sits alongside others, including Dominic Johnson's *Live Art in the UK* (2012) or Deirdre Heddon and Jennie Klein's *Histories and Practices of Live Art* (2012), which opens with Heddon's admission that 'Writing a history of live art is something of an impossible task.'[10] The contributors to Klein and Heddon's collection suggest various points of departure for considering a history of the term: Roddy Hunter and Judit Bodor begin with the 1966 *Destruction in Art Symposium*; Beth Hoffman cites Gilbert & George's *The Singing Sculpture* (1969);[11] and other commentators in this area point to the foundation of *Performance Magazine* and the establishment of the Performance Art Platform (later the National Review of Live Art), both in 1979, as a key moment in the history of Live Art. Other histories choose a temporal focus, as in Helena Goldwater's 'study room guide' to performance art in the 1970s,[12] or a geographical one, as in Áine Phillips's edited collection *Performance Art in Ireland: A History* (2015)[13] or Heike Roms' ongoing project *What's Welsh for Performance? (Beth yw 'performance' yn Gymraeg?).*[14]

In a similar way, although there are deliberate references to broader contexts and activities, this collection chooses to focus on a specific area of activity: the artists, projects, and initiatives connected to LADA during its first twenty years. As an enquiry into agency, it seems appropriate that this idea would be considered in relation to the history of one particular 'Agency'—LADA itself. In the world of international art and festivals, there are certainly larger and more visible organisations than LADA, but focusing on the history of this particular organisation enables close attention to the specific material circumstances within which it works: the kinds of support structures it has fostered, the strategic opportunism it has pursued, the personal as well as institutional relationships it has cultivated, and the social and cultural opportunities with which it has engaged. And despite its relatively small size, the timeline of projects, opportunities for artists, and publications that is included at the end of this book is testament to its diverse energies over twenty years. The biographical introductions to the contributors to this volume highlight their various relationships with LADA, and the photographs used throughout the book are for the most part related to LADA projects, initiatives, publications, screenings, or resources. This focus on LADA is one sense in which what is offered here is a *partial* history.

Furthermore, this collection is a partial history in that it is composed primarily of edited extracts from conversations between artists, thinkers, and curators working in this field, collected within the structure of overlapping themes or lenses described above, alongside invited provocations on those themes. This approach acknowledges the impossibility of any single 'History of Live Art'. Instead, it recognises that histories are always multiple, based on individual perspectives, and that they might well be remembered differently by different people. It proposes that what is important about any history will vary depending on who is speaking, and with whom, as well as when and where that conversation happens. And it is an invitation to learn from the radical intelligence of artists and makers as they navigate and transform the social, conceptual, and aesthetic contexts within which they work.

The contingency of these histories is further emphasised by the formal approach this collection takes of staging conversations between pairs of contributors—some of whom know each other very well, some of whom are meeting for the first time, but always having a conversation that might well have been different on a different day or with a different pairing. The participants in these conversations were chosen to represent a breadth of perspectives and diverse combinations of interlocuters, but could easily have been composed of countless others. They speak for themselves, and they stand in for many others working in relation to the term 'Live Art', who would, no doubt, have had other things to say. These conversations are grouped in each thematic section with short provocations that mostly come from a single voice—and here, too, the provocation authors were asked to draw on their own partiality: the kinds of things to which they are partial, and the experiences of which they were a part.

This assembly of views from multiple experiences, placed in relation to each other, is perhaps the best attempt to give a portrait of what 'Live Art' is, and what it might make possible. And *conversation* feels like an appropriate form for Live Art: both in its liveness and exposure, as a lived encounter unfolding in an unrehearsed present—and also in its art. The texts presented here all began as conversations that would generally last between one and two hours, and which have been edited, reworked, and recomposed (with the contributors' permission and amendments as desired) to create a different conversation for the page—one that aims to preserve the quality of spoken dialogue, but is not intended as a verbatim record.[15] In these final versions my own voice has been edited out to give more room to the speakers themselves, but I want to acknowledge that these conversations were framed within a particular format, and invited to respond to particular themes, which were ones that I imposed and are not intended to suggest anything about how the artists themselves might locate their work. I also introduce each thematic section with a brief overview of how LADA itself has grappled with these issues through its projects and initiatives.

Across all the contributions are explicit and implicit reflections on the question of agency—what it is that has enabled artists to make the work they want to make, and what that work has enabled for others—but these responses cannot be reduced to any singular theory or model of agency. Instead it is clear that one of the ways we find agency is in conversation with others—and this collection is dedicated to the hope that you, too, might find that agency unfolds in the encounters you have within these pages.

1. Lois Keidan, *Discussion Document: Live Art* (National Arts and Media Strategy Unit, Arts Council (UK), 1991), P218, Live Art Development Agency Study Room.

2. Jennie Klein, 'Developing Live Art', in *Histories and Practices of Live Art*, ed. by Deirdre Heddon and Jennie Klein (Basingstoke: Palgrave Macmillan, 2012), pp. 12–36 (p. 25).

3. Lois Keidan, *Vision Paper: A Question of Live Art* (Live Art UK, 2004), p. 9 <https://www.liveartuk.org/uploads/documents/Live_Art_UK_VISION_PAPER.pdf>.

4. Klein, p. 12.

5. Live Art Development Agency, 'What Is Live Art?' <http://www.thisisliveart.co.uk/about/what-is-live-art/>.

6. Ellen Messer-Davidow, 'Acting Otherwise', in *Provoking Agents: Gender and Agency in Theory and Practice*, ed. by Judith Kegan Gardiner (University of Illinois Press, 1995), pp. 23–51 (p. 29).

7. Shannon Jackson, *Social Works: Performing Art, Supporting Publics* (New York and London: Routledge, 2011); Jen Harvie, *Fair Play: Art, Performance and Neoliberalism* (Basingstoke: Palgrave Macmillan, 2013).

8. See, for example, Jane Bennett, *Vibrant Matter: A Political Ecology of Things* (Durham: Duke University Press, 2010); *New Materialisms: Ontology, Agency, and Politics*, ed. by Diana Coole and Samantha Frost (Durham: Duke University Press, 2010).

9. Karen Barad, *Meeting the Universe Halfway: Quantum Physics and the Entanglement of Matter and Meaning* (Durham: Duke University Press, 2007), p. 178.

10. *Live Art in the UK*, ed. by Dominic Johnson, special issue of *Contemporary Theatre Review*, 22.1 (2012); *Histories and Practices of Live Art*, ed. by Deirdre Heddon and Jennie Klein (Basingstoke: Palgrave Macmillan, 2012), p. 1.

11. Heddon and Klein, pp. 67ff., p. 41.

12. *Glimpses of Before: 1970s UK Performance Art*, ed. by Helena Goldwater <http://1970s.thisisliveart.co.uk/>.

13. *Performance Art in Ireland: A History*, ed. by Áine Phillips (London and Bristol: Live Art Development Agency and Intellect, 2015).

14. Heike Roms, *What's Welsh for Performance? Beth yw 'performance' yn Gymraeg?* <http://www.performance-wales.org/>; Heike Roms, *What's Welsh for Performance? An Oral History of Performance Art in Wales 1968–2008, Vol.1* (Cardiff: Samizdata, 2008).

15. A conversational form seems appropriate to the field, and others have used the form: a more strict approach to oral history is used in Roms' project described above and by Dominic Johnson in *The Art of Living: An Oral History of Performance Art* (Basingstoke: Palgrave Macmillan, 2015), and dialogue takes cinematic form in Adrian Heathfield and Hugo Glendinning's *Crossovers* films created as part of the *Performance Matters* project; see <http://www.thisisliveart.co.uk/projects/crossovers>.

BODIES

GEORGE CHAKRAVARTHI
ALEXANDRINA HEMSLEY
DOMINIC JOHNSON
JAMILA JOHNSON-SMALL
AMELIA JONES
MARTIN O'BRIEN
KIRA O'REILLY
SELINA THOMPSON
MANUEL VASON

BODIES

When one thinks about Live Art one thinks about bodies: extravagant, fierce, wounded, proud. It is the zero-point, the most basic material of Live Art: the body that is not (*but still is*) a depiction of a body, as in visual art, nor pretending to be a character, as in dramatic theatre. For many, the body—and perhaps more specifically the body in pain or under some duress—will be their point of entry into Live Art. That entry might even be through a photographic image rather than live encounter, but can still be powerful: in the conversation below, Martin O'Brien, recalling a time he thought he wanted to be an actor, remembers his 'little squeal' at flipping through Amelia Jones and Tracey Warr's *The Artist's Body* and encountering an image of Bob Flanagan. Others will encounter the extraordinary images created collaboratively by photographer Manuel Vason with Ernst Fischer, Franko B, Helen Spackman, Kira O'Reilly, and many others in collections such as *Encounters* and *Double Exposures* (a LADA co-publication):[1] the body splayed out, transformed, transfigured in its performance for camera.

As Dominic Johnson writes in his provocation for this section, the body in pain provides a challenge for representation: 'pain *provokes yet evades* full representation and communication.' Kira O'Reilly recalls her encounters in art school: 'There was always this push against representation: don't do a picture of that. *Make* it. Make it *alive*.' This is one sense of representation that is challenged by the centrality of the body in Live Art: the distinction between representation and actuality, and between image and liveness, always traversing the borders between these unstable categories.

But there is also another sense of representation that is challenged and tested: its political sense. The way that different values are ascribed to different kinds of bodies. The way that some bodies are allowed to appear and others disregarded. The way that bodies are disciplined under regimes of sexuality, ability, race, national status. It's into these regimes that George Chakravarthi describes himself intervening with his reimagining of *The Last Supper*, or his more recent project creating large-scale images for the Royal Shakespeare Company: 'this was about being brown and queer, about going in and saying that I can occupy this [institutional] space for a certain length of time.' And with regard to this political sense of representation, it is in the body that one might feel a denial of agency, as a 'sizzle', as Selina Thompson describes in her response to a work that she felt devalued Black bodies.

Live Art presents challenges to aesthetic representation, but it also exists within a system of political representation. These questions of inclusion and visibility have formed the basis for one of the most persistent strands of activity by the Live Art Development Agency, beginning with its pre-history: a 1990 report for the Arts Council (UK) by Michael McMillan raised questions around the Eurocentrism of performance art and its exclusion of Black and Asian artists, and Lois Keidan's 1991 discussion document for the Arts Council's National Arts and Media Strategy (NAMS) advocating for greater attention to Live Art drew extensively on McMillan's report.[2] When Keidan left the Arts Council to become Director of Live Arts at the Institute of Contemporary Arts (ICA), she and her colleague Catherine Ugwu programmed a number of events that addressed these questions of representation and the visibility and politicisation of certain kinds of bodies.[3]

After working at the ICA, Keidan and Ugwu co-founded the Live Art Development Agency in 1999, with Ugwu leaving in 2000 to work as an independent producer on large-scale pubic events. Over its history, LADA has undertaken a series of critical self-reflections about its own structures of inclusion and exclusion, under the name *Restock, Rethink, Reflect* (RRR), which set out to map and mark underrepresented artists and histories, and act as a corrective to these exclusions (including LADA's own blind spots).[4] These began with RRR1 on *Live Art and Race* (2006–2008), looking at the ways artists of colour were being written out of history, which culminated in the mixed-media publication *Documenting Live* (2008);[5] continued with RRR2 on *Live Art and Disability* (2009–2012), which led to a public programme and symposium (London 2011; New York 2014) and the subsequent publication *Access All Areas*;[6] RRR3 on *Live Art and Feminism* (2013–2015), that amongst many outputs included an online exhibition supported by Google Arts & Culture,[7] a Wikipedia edit-a-thon,[8] *Are We There Yet?*, a Study Room Guide edited by Lois Weaver and Eleanor Roberts, and the performance programme *Just Like A Woman* for City of Women Festival (Ljubljana, 2013, with other versions presented in London and New York, 2015). At the time of this collection, the current RRR4 project is on *Live Art and Privilege* (2016–2018), addressing exclusion and under-representation amongst the young, the old, the displaced, and those excluded through economic and social barriers.[9]

Having identified an area that needs addressing, LADA's approach is to invite artists and thinkers to work as collaborators, and to take advantage of opportunities that arise through these connections. Some of these projects are discussed by artists in this collection: it is through *Access All Areas* that Martin O'Brien first began the ongoing collaboration with Sheree Rose that he describes, for example, and in a later section The Disabled Avant-Garde (Katherine Araniello and Aaron Williamson) also refer to their participation in this event. Elsewhere in this book, Rajni Shah discusses *Documenting Live*, for which

Right: Project O, *Voodoo* (2017).
Image Jack Barraclough and Katarzyna Perlak.

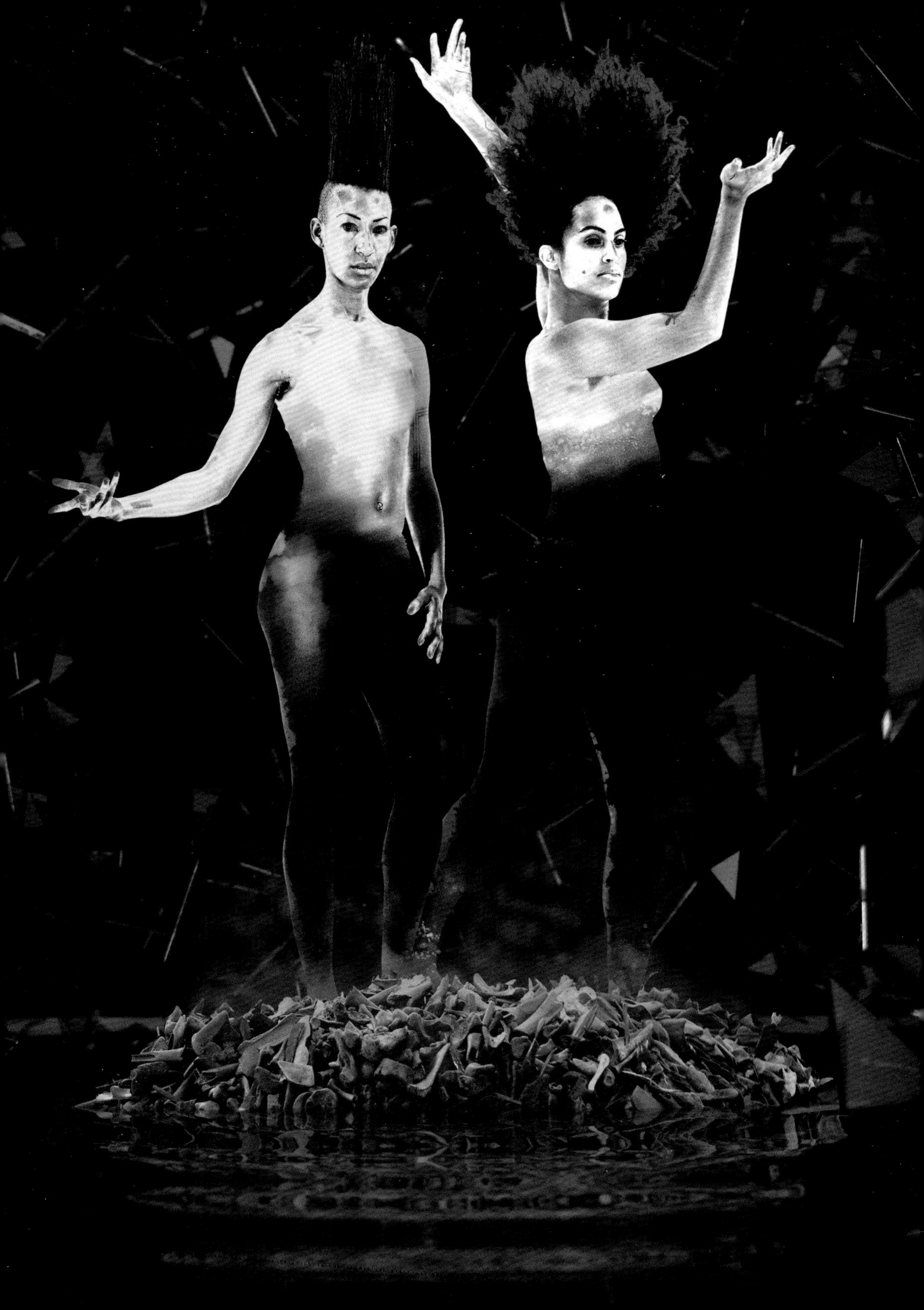

she was the project director, and Barby Asante was a contributor; and an image by Alexandrina Hemsley and Jamila Johnson-Small of Project O is on the front of the Google Arts & Culture online gallery on Live Art and Feminism. Keidan describes these projects as following a 'non-model': 'we don't know what needs to be done until we find out what needs to be done.'[10]

As such, RRR follows some of the approaches of Live Art practice itself: deliberately constructing a frame under which certain bodies appear, and testing the limits of that frame through provocation and experimentation. Alexandrina Hemsley puts it this way, describing Project O, her collaboration with Jamila Johnson-Small:

> The conditions outside the work are not in our favour. They are stacked against us; they are racist; they are dystopian; they are fucked. But we can go in the studio and really start our environment from scratch, construct our own terms, and enact them. And we can navigate the conundrums, the conflicts, the transformations through our bodies.

The agency of bodies is never singular, Amelia Jones suggests in her provocation: it is 'never about one body, one mind, or one "individual".' Bodies find agency in relation with others, in lived experience within a deliberately constructed frame of artistic practice—which is also a way of making a life.

1. *Manuel Vason: Encounters–Performance, Photography, Collaboration*, ed. by Dominic Johnson (Bristol: Arnolfini, 2007); *Manuel Vason: Double Exposures–Performance as Photography–Photography as Performance*, ed. by David Evans (London and Bristol: Live Art Development Agency and Intellect, 2015).

2. Michael McMillan, *Cultural Grounding: Live Art and Cultural Diversity: A Report for the Visual Arts Department of the Arts Council of Great Britain* (Arts Council of Great Britain, 1990), P1703, Live Art Development Agency Study Room; Keidan, *Discussion Document: Live Art*.

3. Examples include *Queer Bodies* (21-26 September 1993), co-curated with Gay Sweatshop, which presented work by US artists responding to the AIDS crisis; *More Respect* (7-28 September 1994), co-curated with Keith Khan, advertised as 'a season of new performance from a new wave of black artists'; or *Corpus Delecti*, curated by Coco Fusco (12-30 November 1996). Ugwu worked with David Bailey and INIVA to curate *Mirage: Enigmas of Race, Difference, and Desire* (12 May-16 July 1995), and edited the influential publication *Let's Get It On: The Politics of Black Performance* (London and Seattle: ICA and Bay Press, 1995). Live Art activities at the ICA (1993-1996) are archived as P2036 in the Live Art Development Agency Study Room.

4. See http://www.thisisliveart.co.uk/projects/restock-rethink-reflect.

5. *Documenting Live*, ed. by David A. Bailey, Lois Keidan, and Rajni Shah (London: Live Art Development Agency, 2008). Keidan describes this project as partly a response to venues saying they would programme more Black and Asian artists if they knew any; the publication and DVD was conceived to respond to this perceived absence of information.

6. *Access All Areas: Live Art and Disability*, ed. by Lois Keidan and CJ Mitchell (London: Live Art Development Agency, 2012).

7. Live Art Development Agency and Eleanor Roberts, 'Live Art and Feminism in the UK', *Google Arts & Culture* <https://artsandculture.google.com/exhibit/1gLSx6pobvq_Ig>.

8. Lois Weaver and others, 'Editing Ourselves into History: A Live Art and Feminism Wikipedia Edit-a-Thon', *Contemporary Theatre Review* [2015] <https://www.contemporarytheatrereview.org/2015/editing-ourselves-into-history/>.

9. See http://www.thisisliveart.co.uk/projects/restock-rethink-reflect-four-on-live-art-and-privilege/

10. In conversation with the author, 6 February 2018.

BODIES
CONVERSATION
MARTIN O'BRIEN
KIRA O'REILLY
DATE
31 DECEMBER 2015
PLACE
LONDON

Martin O'Brien's work considers existence with a severe chronic illness within our contemporary situation. Martin suffers from cystic fibrosis and his practice uses physical endurance, hardship and pain-based practices to challenge common representations of illness and examine what it means to be born with a life-threatening disease, in works such as *Mucus Factory* (2011–2014), *Regimes of Hardship* (2012), *Breathe For Me* (2012–2016). He also makes works that explore attitudes toward contamination, sometimes using the figure of the zombie, as in *Taste of Flesh/Bite Me I'm Yours* (2015) and *If It Were The Apocalypse I'd Eat You To Stay Alive* (2016). He was a contributor to LADA's RRR2 *Access All Areas* programme (2011), where he began a series of collaborations with Sheree Rose; has led several DIY projects including *For The Dead Travel Fast* (2017), part of the DIY+ series supported by the Jerwood Foundation. In 2018 LADA published *Survival of the Sickest: The Art of Martin O'Brien*.

Kira O'Reilly is an interdisciplinary artist whose work, as she discusses here, has moved through many phases. In the late 1990s and mid-2000s she made works that incorporated bloodletting and medical practices, including *Bad Humours / Affected* (1998), *Wet Cup* (1999–2001), *Succour* (2001–2002), and *Untitled Action for Bomb Shelter Kuopio* (2003); from the mid-2000s she made interspecies work (such as *inthewrongplacednesss* (2005–2009) and worked in bioart projects with SymbioticA and the University of Birmingham and others. Her practice has also been informed by combat sports and martial arts, and she led the LADA DIY project *Thinking Through the Body*. Combative Manifestos (2013). In 2018 LADA co-published *Untitled (Bodies): Kira O'Reilly*, edited by Harriet Curtis and Martin Hargreaves, as part of its Intellect Live series.

Martin and Kira shared a studio space with other artists in Deptford, South London. This conversation took place as they were preparing to vacate the space which had recently been sold for development, and Kira was soon to begin her new role leading the MA in Ecology and Contemporary Performance at University of the Arts Helsinki.

Kira: If we're going to talk about history, the first thing to say is that I can't talk for who I was from back then, because that person doesn't exist! I am not a continuous, uninterrupted being. This is something I talk about with Fiona Wright, who is a very important artist from my point of view and whose practice and friendship has influenced me massively. We're of a similar age, and every few weeks or few months we speak. We return to this idea that we're different people, and that the people used to be are dead, so to speak. So anything I say now is through the lens of someone who was called Kira O'Reilly on New Year's Eve 2015 [*when this conversation took place*].

I studied at University of Wales Institute, Cardiff, under Anthony Howell, Paul Granjon, Janice Howard and various visiting artists. I studied time-based art for three years, where my work was not separate from the practices and discourses of other time-based media such as video, writing, or technology. I felt like I was engaged in a sumptuous dance between ideas and not-ideas. And I worked with materiality and process.

Cardiff was incredibly important. We had an extraordinary peer group who would always push you. They would say, why do you want to *represent* that? Why don't you *do* it instead? There was always this push against representation: don't do a picture of that. *Make* it. Make it *alive*. I was having a conversation about working with leeches, and I was wanting to put leeches on flowers or lilies or something. And because of another student at the time, Bryony Watson, I realised that I needed to put them on my skin. So there was always this push toward: it needs to be actual, it needs to be real. And just after there was a show called *Body Radicals* that Gordana Vnuk curated in the theatre at Chapter Arts Centre, which had people like Ron Athey, Franko B, Annie Sprinkle, Stelarc, ORLAN—a lot of the work that Lois [Keidan] had curated at the ICA.

But I wasn't remotely interested in 'Live Art'! I really struggled with the term 'Live Art', and I still do. I'm an *artist*. 'Live Art' seemed like a wonderful idea for funding purposes, perhaps. In the early days when Lois and Daniel [Brine, LADA associate director, 2000–2008] would talk about it, it made a lot of sense as a way of getting work out there and supporting work. But it seemed like those kinds of art works had always existed—in my world anyway. And at the same time as the language around 'Live Art' was emerging there was also New Labour, and the talk about 'the sector' or 'the industry'. And I just think 'fuck off', you know? That sounds like something you learn at business school. I went to an extraordinary, wild, very un-politically correct degree in Cardiff on purpose. I wanted to be around mavericks, including mavericks who pissed me off at times.

I was also deeply affected by HIV/AIDS and hepatitis C, illnesses that were very present in the communities I was part of, seeing the bodies of friends affected and deaths. I felt that I had lived through wars. The fact that I was even alive was miraculous. I couldn't stand this language of economics and industry whilst making work that felt full of risk, viscerality and politics. I found the concretisation of institutional practices of curation, producing and programming and their gatekeeping functions difficult. It felt troubling to be in continual financial precarity, trying to make riskful work with one's body, one's substance, whilst the power dynamics with institutions felt so stacked against the artists making the art works these institutional practices relied on to some extent. That's why it's important what you are doing, Martin, as well as people like Franko B and Lee Adams, at places like the Flying Dutchman.[1]

Martin: I was frustrated by the kinds of restrictions in different places, and here was a space where they said you can do whatever you like. They don't even ask what you're going to do.

Kira: It's practical, as well, because it allows people to say 'I know what I'm doing' as opposed to 'I have to tell you what I'm doing'. It reminds me of a beautiful piece you did, Martin, at this conference they had at Dartington, where you had studied for your degree. And you performed by the bins where you used to go and meet boys—is that right?

Martin: Yes. I turned up to perform, and I had forgotten how small the gallery was. And then I saw the bins, which were just across the way, and where I used to go and make out with boys! The performance was called *It's Good to Breathe in (this Devon Air)*. It started with me rubbing alcohol gel onto my chest and then cutting the shape of lungs onto my chest. I laid on a wedge that I use for physiotherapy, so my head was lower than my feet, and I beat my chest to loosen mucus on the lungs. Then I spat the mucous into little pots and then started crawling as I carried the pot with my mouth. I did really shallow cuts on my chest so it's barely visible at first, but it started to bleed after the wound opened, and the line becomes more visible. Then at the end I crawled to the mucus and smeared it on my body and doused my hair with it, and allowed it to drip from my fingers into my mouth. Just playing with it, really. So that was interesting when you were talking about materials, Kira, because I was thinking about being led by materials. I came from a theatre background where the focus was different, and I certainly didn't have that upbringing of allowing materials to lead you. But where I've come to is a place where the materiality of my own flesh, and my own fluids, lead the work.

Kira: Well, materials have agency. I got very bored with performance studies. I'd go to science and technology studies conferences, or bioart conferences instead, where people would talk about materiality and materials and their performativity. That's cascaded into a million different very important conversations that are very relevant to now, about what's happening with our world at the moment.

For me, what became a very frustrating ghetto concept—in Live Art, anyway—was the idea of 'The Body' without that ever really being questioned, or only questioned in very tiny ways. Humans are so human-centric! That's why your work is such a great example for me, Martin, thinking about mucus and bacteria congregations. What do these ideas of 'the body' mean when we're a number of different biomes all at once? Of course there are artists who were working these ideas a long time ago, but it's not something that had apparently entered into performance practices or discourses. Instead it all seems to be about separating a body from an environment as opposed to being something that's more immersed—no, 'immersed' is not even the right word, because it suggests there's a 'you' that is immersed, as opposed to talking about bodies that are relational, constantly remaking, unmaking, and remaking.

But I was reading Nicola Triscott's blog about the work that you made for *Trust Me, I'm an Artist*, and her reservations around programming performance art, and she talks about how much health and safety is a massive part of it.[2]

Martin: I had this experience recently at another venue, where they came to me only a little while before the performance and said, 'Martin, we need to speak to you.' They said that they had spoken to their lawyers who advised them not to allow me to do certain sections of the performance, because they were classified as sex acts. There was a section where Sheree [Rose] was supposed to fuck me up the ass with a strap-on, and they said that they would need a sex license in order to be able to do it. And there was another section where I was supposed to put a butt plug into the ass of another performer, Zack McGuinness. In the end we had to change it so that he put it into himself, because it doesn't count as 'sex' if he does it himself!

This was part of an ongoing collaboration with Sheree Rose. The first time I saw Bob Flanagan and Sheree Rose's work was flicking through *The Artist's Body*, by Amelia Jones and Tracey Warr.[3] I was about 18, and I had no sense of performance or art as a place where any politics of identity could be explored—I was just interested in being a performer, like an actor! And I was flipping through this book of incredible images, and then there was this one image of a male groin sewn up and nailed to a plank of wood. The image caught my eye, and I think I let out a little squeal. I stopped at the image and read the description next to it, which said something about Bob Flanagan being an artist who uses S&M in his practice to explore cystic fibrosis and its relationship to the body.

'Cystic fibrosis.' My heart just stopped when I read those words, because I didn't know anybody else with cystic fibrosis. The nature of the disease is that they keep you

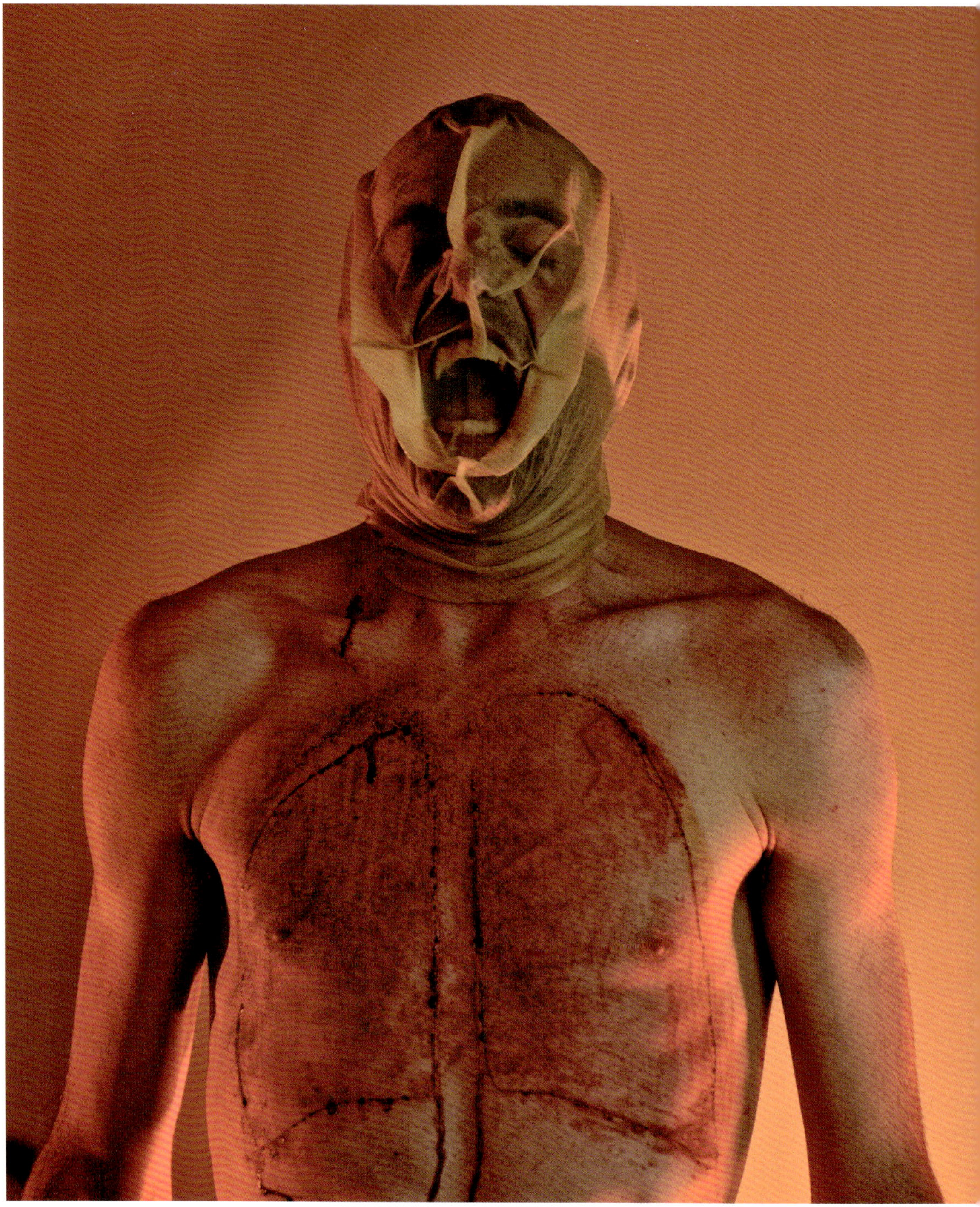

away from other people because of the risk of cross-infection, so it's a really solitary disease. And suddenly I felt this connection to a person, who's dead, but they're an artist… and I wasn't yet an artist, but starting to explore art. That's when I really started to think about art as a place where I could explore the politics of identity, or the conditions of existence, and what it means to live as somebody with a life-shortening chronic illness. What it means to be alive in this world under particular kinds of conditions. I started to explore that in my art, and eventually I started a whole relationship with Sheree, as well.

I wrote to her in 2009 or 2010—I found her on Facebook!—and just said, 'I really love your work, and can we start this dialogue?' Then we started a dialogue over months and months, where we'd write back and forth with questions for each other. Then the Live Art Development Agency, who had commissioned one of my pieces, *Mucus Factory*, asked me to do a project for *Access All Areas*, and they said they could bring Sheree over. I met her for the first time at Paddington, and the next day we performed the first piece we did together, a re-imagining of a video piece she made with Bob and Mike Kelley called *100 Reasons*, where she spanked me 100 times. The desire to work with her came out of trying to address their legacy and the way they influenced my work—and also because every time I did a performance, people would say, 'Oh, do you know Bob Flanagan?' I was getting so sick of this! But now we've become such good friends, and we have such a good relationship through making performances. It's become much more than trying to address something historical. It's about two people who want to collaborate.

Kira: You mess around with so many categories, as well, with your age differences. I saw Sheree recently at Royal Vauxhall Tavern and she was saying, 'Well, I'm like his mother except I play with his penis!'

Martin: It's a kind of caring relationship, a question of what care can be. There's this caring side to her. She might be beating the shit out of me, but it's with a kind of love for each other.

There was an interesting moment in one performance where I was chained up with my arms and legs, spread-eagled, with a butt plug in, and pegs on my nipples and testicles. I was blindfolded. There was a heater blasting right under me, and I just passed out in that position. The assistants got me down and laid me on a bed. And Sheree just stroked me and gave me water and cared for me in that more traditional sense of how one might think about care. And she brought me around, and once I was conscious, she went back to torturing me. The audience just sat there and watched all this go on. It just was part of the performance, part of the process.

Left: Martin O'Brien, *It's Good to Breathe in (this Venice Air)*, Venice International Performance Art Week (2016). Image Edward Smith.

A lot of the work I do has long durations, and one of the things I have struggled to articulate is about working over long durations in order to explore the idea of life and restricted duration. Firstly, that this extended duration has this strange relationship with the duration of a life which is somehow shortened or inhibited—like a constant feeling of death and life that somehow working over these long durations has allowed me to explore.

And secondly, back to materiality again: There's something about working over long durations with the body—and with my flesh, and the stuff that comes out of me, as material—that allows a process to change. The mucus actually changes texture over an hour. And also *I* become physically exhausted over 12 hours—I start to cough much more and wheeze, constantly spitting mucus. The physical effects of the disease become visible on my body over duration, and actually the disease becomes visible over a long period of time. Whereas I can walk down the street and nobody knows I have cystic fibrosis.

I was also wondering about the biological time of ageing, if that's something you're thinking about now, Kira.

Kira: Because I'm 48, you mean? [*laughs*]

Martin: You know, working with Sheree she's constantly thinking about death and ageing. Which was such a part of her work with Bob.

Kira: Well from the point of view of being a Buddhist, you can't practice as a Vajrayana Buddhist and not practice a death (and rebirth) all the time. It's a fundamental practice. That's to do with this idea of being continually flickering between death and rebirth. There are practices that can be done every night, of dissolution from waking state into the dream state that are also preparation for physical death.

When I was taking skin biopsies from freshly killed pigs during a residency at SymbioticA circa 2004, I learnt about the more ambiguous states of life and death enabled by biotechnology. If you take a biopsy of a mammal, a culture of cells can then be created. And if this is subjected to the right conditions those cells will continue to divide, up to about 40 times, despite the death of the host body, and you can keep cultivating them. If you freeze them, you can suspend that growth. Then later you can defrost those cells and they'll resume their growth. So that's really interesting: if you take a biopsy from you now and then you pass away, the chances are that we can grow your cells, that life will exceed you in some way. A body doesn't just 'die' unless it's something very sudden that consumes the entire body. We think death is this singular event, this one thing, but it's a process. It occurs over time—and within it life is implicit.

1. The Flying Dutchman is a fetish bar in London, which hosted an event series called *Discharge*, curated by Martin, and *Untouchable*, curated by Franko B.

2. Nicola Triscott, 'Trust and the Taste of Flesh: The Ethics of Martin O'Brien's Zombie Performance' [2015] <https://nicolatriscott.org/2015/12/15/trust-and-the-taste-of-flesh/>.

3. Tracey Warr and Amelia Jones, *The Artist's Body* (London: Phaidon, 2000).

BODIES

CONVERSATION

GEORGE CHAKRAVARTHI

MANUEL VASON

DATE

21 FEBRUARY 2016

PLACE

LONDON

George Chakravarthi is a multi-disciplinary artist whose work draws inspiration from a diverse range of cultures, histories and identities, often engaging with the Western art canon as in *Resurrection* (1998), *Olympia* (2003), and the commissions for the Royal Shakespeare Company that he discusses here. His self-portraits offer intimate access to his psyche through personas and alter-egos, eliciting the viewer's own revelations and conclusions through live, photographic and video works that include *Barflies* (2002), *Masking* (2009, commissioned by LADA), and *Negrophilia!* (2010-2014). Some of his early video portraits are collected in the DVD *UnSeen* which LADA released in 2009. With LADA he has also received a One-to-One Artist's Bursary, contributed to RRR1 / *Documenting Live* (2008) and RRR3/ *Just Like A Woman* (2013-2015), and as 'Maxx Shurley' was LADA Thinker in Residence (2004-2005) on curatorial approaches to cultural diversity.

Manuel Vason has been one of the most prolific photographers working in relation to Live Art, and his collaborations have produced some of its most iconic images. His work is collected in the volumes *Exposures* (2002), *Encounters* (2007), and *Double Encounters* (2015), along with collaborative publications such as Franko B's *Oh Lover Boy* (2001), the SPILL Performance Tarot pack (2009), and *Still Image Moving* (2010) with In Between Time Festival (2010). His work has been exhibited internationally, including in Berlin, Brussels, Chicago, Galway, Glasgow, London, Moscow, São Paulo, Singapore, Thessaloniki, and Venice. His work explores the relationship between photography and performance, presence and representation, and is an ongoing critical reflection on processes of collaboration. With LADA he has led the DIY projects *Becoming An Image* (2010) and *The Photo-Performer* (2014), which explored Manuel's idea of a hybrid mode that combines performer and photographer.

As they describe in this conversation, both George and Manuel have had very longstanding relationships with LADA, but have not collaborated with each other.

George: I didn't go to art school to get a job. I went to art school to be an artist. I was really hungry and desperate to make some work. So when I graduated, anyone who was going to give me £100 was a novelty. While you're at art school you have studio space, contacts, feedback, projects to do… but when I left I suddenly felt this incredible isolation. I had to build up a support network again. After graduating, Lois [Keidan] and Daniel [Brine, co-directors of LADA] were on my list of people that I should meet who might possibly help me, and they happened to be the only people who properly helped me. It really wasn't just about funding. It was about conversations and development, and planning what kind of work I wanted to do. They were able to talk about the work in particular ways. My first encounter was really positive and I always went back, no matter what I did, which is why we've had this ongoing relationship. I still see the Agency as being very supportive, open, and there's no agenda. And the other thing is there was no exploitation—because art is exploited all the time. In this period of time we're talking about, I had lots of experiences of feeling exploited, as well as feeling incredibly supported.

After I graduated, I took my degree show to the National Review of Live Art in Glasgow. The work was a live reconstruction of The Last Supper and four films called *Resurrection*.

Manuel: When was this?

George: 1998.

Manuel: I remember that! It was at the Arches. I arrived on Saturday, and I think your show opened Thursday, so I missed the live performance, but I remember seeing the prints.

George: Yes, they used the image on the publicity, and as somebody who has just come from art school, that was major. It gave me a push, a feeling that it's really possible to be an artist—and that I *had* to do it. I felt like I had an edge on a lot of work that was coming from performance, as I was drawing on lots of disciplines. My work was referencing painting, religion, 'Bollywood' cinema…. Sometimes that has been detrimental, because it makes the work complicated and people find it hard to pin me down. This is an ongoing issue with my work.

After the NRLA I was offered an MA at the Royal Academy. I had to do a formal interview, and they asked me to bring a portfolio. I said, 'Okay, I'll bring something,' and so I brought in this 12-foot by 5-foot photograph of the Last Supper [*Resurrection*], with me sitting on a chair. The panel was six or seven very intimidating, scholarly, RA-type people. It was a very British institution: a completely different world, a different language, different ways of feeling and receiving information. But they loved the quirkiness—that I would turn up with just one image, but the image needed six people to lift it into the room!

It was a hard place to study. We'd have these very long tutorials, and they were obviously very able to talk about painting and the references in my work, but as soon as I wanted to talk about any other kinds of work, or live performance, they were like: 'We'll see you tomorrow. Bring something else in.' They thought that I would just make the Last Supper type work, whereas I never wanted to limit myself.

I often keep a journal, and one of the things I was writing about at the time was transsexuals and this underground culture, this hidden world under the visible world. I remember going to a few places and finding them incredible, in terms of performance. There were a couple of people I met who I found really fascinating, and then I started dressing and going out myself. This is an aspect of my practice that is very precious to me, which is that I won't make work about or talk about anything that I don't know myself. I don't want to reinterpret somebody's manual, or people—often heterosexual academics—writing about sexual identities. It's really important for me to know it first-hand. So that became an obsession for me.

So I made *Barflies*, which was me in three different personas in three different bars. Manuel, you've photographed them, so you know. They *had* to be filmed in straight social spaces because I wanted to lift it out of the underworld and bring it to mainstream pubs. I loved the danger of it, the unknown of it. It was a huge learning experience of human behaviour and human fears, human fetishes, human disgust. My idea was to show an aspect of that vulnerability, but I didn't have to *perform* it, because once you're actually in that space and doing it, you are vulnerable. There's no performance.

Manuel: When I first met Lois and Daniel, I was very naïve, and very confused. I was working as an assistant of Nick Knight at Metro Studios, and I had two big studios and plenty of equipment available for my personal projects, when we were not shooting commercial stuff. And I had an infinite amount of 10x8 Polaroids left over from various photo sessions.

The first live artist I ever collaborated with was Ernst Fischer. I was asked by the curator of a program of performances at the ICA in London to make a series of images of the artists to be exhibited in the corridors of the institute. Ernst came to the studio and we spoke a little bit. He said he was going to do a kind of Butoh dance, and that he was going to cut his eyebrows as part of the dance. I said okay, let's do it. And then it looked like he went into a kind of trance, which was a Butoh method of rolling his eyes back. So already I was thinking: 'Man, I can't even speak to this guy!' And with the blood in his eyebrows I thought we better do these photographs quickly, or I'm going to have to call someone!

During the photo session, I was responding without really understanding what Ernst was doing. I mainly responded following aesthetic judgments with little parameters for comparison. We did a series of images where he was performing and I was following. I was completely disturbed and attracted. It was an interesting challenge, because normally with these big 10x8 plate cameras, the *photographer* doesn't move—you ask people to move for you. A lot of the images were blurred, and it was fantastic. I loved the blurriness. I loved the mess. I was testing some out-of-date film, and the outcome was stained by fingerprints, or had some kind of abnormalities or damages. And Ernst loved it, too. He said he would much rather identify his actions with those large out-of-date, blurry Polaroids than with clean and sharp film.

Then we did a series of images using fire, and at one point I could smell Ernst's hair and skin burning. I felt an intensity in my body that I had never felt before. It was a compelling feeling of engagement, a sense of responsibility. Once you've experienced something like this, you want more, and most of all you want to know why....

At that time I was searching. I was coming from a world of pure aesthetics and prescribed content, and I was searching for something more important to communicate. I was involved in the fashion world, where if you could discover a new lighting trick or a new technique to polish the result, you could turn it into a big pile of money. The content in fashion photography is constantly the same: 'if you buy this item you will feel as good and beautiful as the model depicted'—so how you deliver the message is everything. And I participated in this process, even though I was searching for something different to say. The making of the images was fantastic: very performative, challenging, and unusual.

But at first, as consequence of my fashion upbringing, the relationship with the subject was just a shake of hands. Just something like, 'Thank you very much for giving me this series of images and your twisted body language for my own portfolio.' I was thinking and behaving at that time purely as a photographer, giving more attention at the surface of things. I was the thief, the person that captures and appropriates. As photographer you gain the right to speak for others, at times, without having the knowledge or the permission. But there was a genuine passion and an intuitive attraction for diversity and the world of Live Art. And Lois and Daniel helped me to mature a completely different approach, to find a personal understanding

Overleaf: George Chakravarthi, *Negrophilia!* (2014). Image the artist.

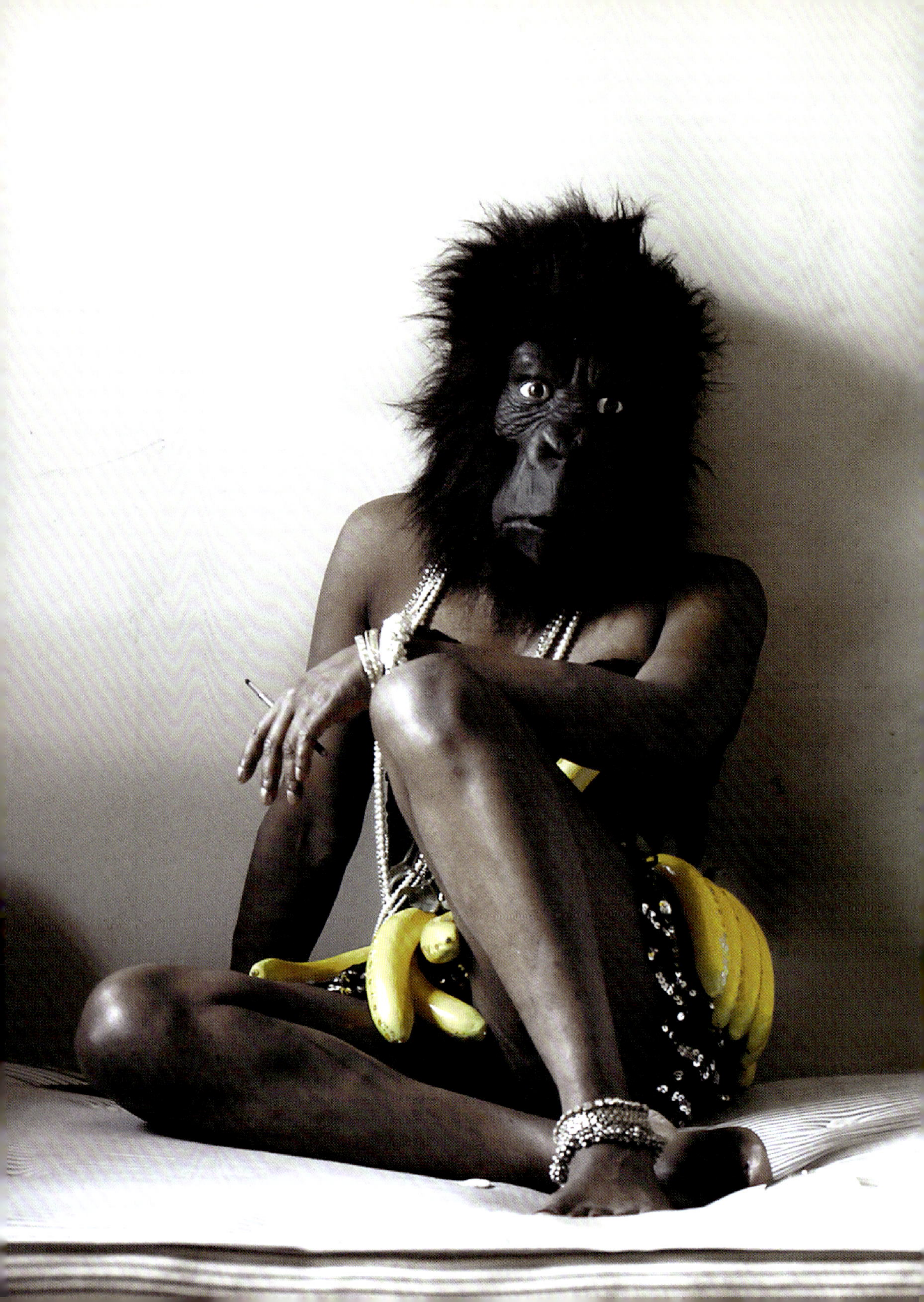

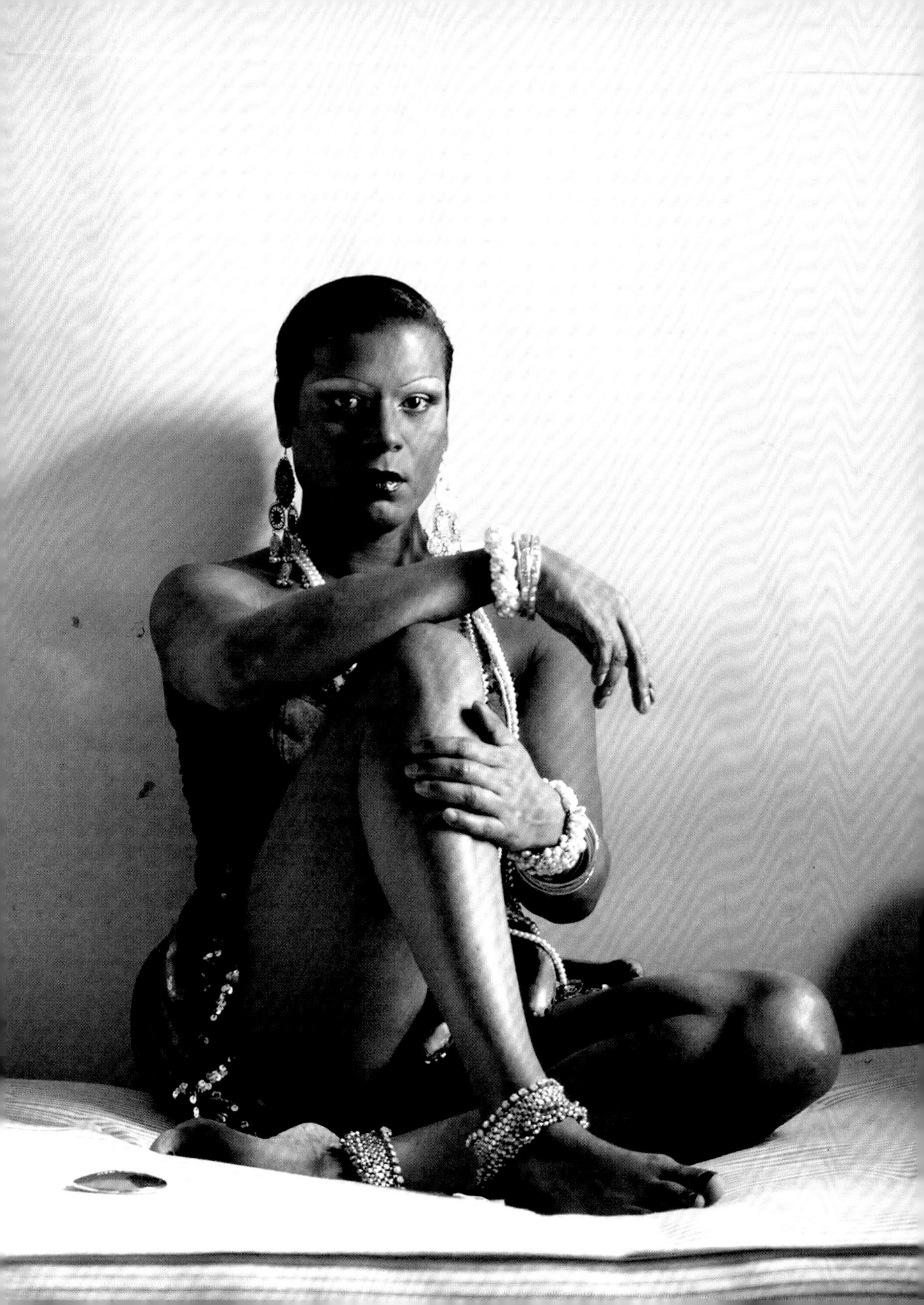

in the middle of that confused space between photography and performance. Specifically, this had to do with the relationship with the subject. I really didn't understand why they opened the door and actually offered me opportunities for collaborating. They must have smelled my genuine intention. Looking back, I think Lois totally understood that. She saw there was a project there, that as an outsider to the field of Live Art, and in total opposition in a way, I could actually bring something novel into the space. And she helped me to grow, to build an understanding, to shape a perspective, and to develop deeper relationships with the subjects.

George: I've had to become very aware of my own image, because it's so recurring in my work. It's why I have to create them myself. I'm really aware of how my images are read, and what they have to be in order to control that gaze. It's a really interesting thing, because the image is always looking back at you, too. The challenge is to control and guide the gaze, and also allow as much room for interpretation as possible.

There's an image I made as part of *Thirteen*—a series of images based on the thirteen suicides in Shakespeare's plays for the Royal Shakespeare Company—that was really problematic for lots of people. It's a naked image of me as Lady Macbeth in a red velvet cape, with a breast bodice made of leather that is very close to my skin colour, so they look like they're my breasts, and I've done a tuck. It's placed in this skyscape so it's kind of an angel image, but it's also quite fierce, like the goddess Kali. We talked and talked about this particular image, about censorship and religion, and I sat on it for a long time before I said to myself, yeah, I'm going to do it.

When I first got the call from the RSC, I thought, 'You do know what I do, don't you? Have you seen my work?' The reason I accepted it is because I am really interested in space, site, and heritage within different cultures. I thought that for *me* to be at the Royal Shakespeare Company—well, for me it's nothing but activism. A lot of my work has a sense of activism, and this was really about being brown and queer, about going in and saying that I can occupy this space for a certain length of time. And it happened, and I did it, and it was exhibited there and it was a major success—but what's really heartbreaking and revealing is when I read the comments book. It's amazing how much my race is referenced by people. But that's also why I'm so glad I did it.

Institutions comes with their institutionalised thinking, and once an artist is placed within an established institution your integrity is really challenged. I had to really assert my practice, my reasons and justifications, and literally prepare material to go in and speak about my work in a language written for the institution. All over an image! So that's the flipside, too—it really made me realise how *powerful* we are as artists.

Manuel: Our society has become so visual. I think that imagery has become almost too powerful.

George: Too powerful?

Manuel: It's overpowering the other mediums. There's always been a friction between the live and the document, but I've started thinking about how they are linked through the performative image.

George: Does the image become more powerful than the performance, or the performance become more powerful than the image?

Manuel: I think they're linked. You can think of the way that the image creates the live or how the live is memorised as image. There is this pleasure when you recognise an image, or even this kind of discomfort when you come across an image that doesn't fit in your mental archive, and you need to analyse it, assimilate it. I've become very critical about my own images. There's this drive for making imagery, analysing imagery, searching imagery, producing, collecting, archiving, sharing, discussing, hiding.... I really think we can call it pathological.

But if you look at images that have been created there is a lot of imitation and very little differentiation. The repertoire of controversial images or what can represent diversity is actually quite confined, because this is what society is trying to impose. It's trying to say, 'express yourself,' because if you don't do it, you're not free. So please *do* take off your clothes, and do something quite strange, or that crosses over gender. Please do it. But at the same time it says: these are the parameters or the models to copy. This is the society of well-being where freedom is a strategy of conformism and control.

And when I think about performance art and Live Art, it's literally playing with these restrictions, and just trying to push the flag an inch outside that. It's really important to be critical and question a system of imposed desires and behaviour. It's about how we can stretch these parameters, this 'yes' and 'no'. It's that experimentation, that willingness to follow your own intuition and engage (and disengage) with the main culture, that for me has been a very key aspect of Live Art and performance art. It's this subversive flirting, and at the same time trying to open some mechanisms, that stimulated me to participate and contribute.

George: What's interesting to me is that there seems to be something seductive for younger artists about being a live artist. Like it's something you zip into, like a costume.

Manuel: The question is how can we support our best artists? What is the relationship with universities and institutions? Do we really want to teach Live Art? Our most interesting artists have such an unusual upbringing and they found their practices out of necessity, away from protocols. It's more truthful than someone who has come from four years of reading in search of a job. It is too easy to do a bit of Franko B, a bit of Kira O'Reilly, a little bit of George and then put on a wig to make it queer. This work is very derivative, first of all, but more importantly, it doesn't have a necessity. Most students don't have the urgency to do art. Live Art cannot be taught as a job or a career. And this is why Live Art cannot grow where they are sterilising subversive thinking.

George: What's being lost is a consistency in seeing it through.

Manuel: My inspiration is people like Alastair MacLennan, to actually be there, at 75, and to still be excited, making new work at every occasion. The artwork of living and surviving.

Manuel: It shouldn't be called Live Art anymore, that's finished.

George: No, that is finished!

Manuel: I think we should call it survival art. Or necessity art. Or something different.

George: We're the lost. We're beyond what's going on now, because we are heart and soul, committed to it forever.

BODIES
CONVERSATION
ALEXANDRINA HEMSLEY AND JAMILA JOHNSON-SMALL (PROJECT O)
SELINA THOMPSON
DATE
21 AUGUST 2016
PLACE
LONDON & GRONINGEN

Working together as Project O, Alexandrina Hemsley and Jamila Johnson-Small make dance-based work that looks to the body as a site of politics in relation to legacies of colonialism and the tendency towards fetishisation, exoticisation and fear of the other. They have made dances for the stage (*O*, 2013), performative interventions in public space (*Be Your Black Girlfriend*, 2015), choreographies for bodies that are not their own (*SWAGGA*, 2015), a performance lecture (*Benz Punany*, 2014), a school (The New Empowering School, 2015), and an eight-hour looping immersive performance (*Voodoo*, 2017). Alexandrina led the DIY project *Present Histories* (2015) for artists of African heritage; and with Seke Chimutengwende, the DIY Progression project *Unfunky UFO: 2100AD* (2017), a retreat for artists of colour to explore how their work journeys in dialogue with futurity. LADA co-published Project O's book *A Contemporary Struggle* (2015).

Selina Thompson is an artist and performer based in Leeds. Her work is focused on the politics of identity and how this defines our bodies, lives and environments. Her work often clusters around themes: *The Job Centre Project* looking at work and unemployment; *Edible Women*, a body of work that explores the fat body, dieting, control around food, including the solo performance *Chewing the Fat* (2013); and *As Wide And As Deep As The Sea*, exploring Black British Identity, including *Dark & Lovely* (2014) about Black hair, *salt.* (2017), based on Selina's experience retracing one of the routes of the Transatlantic slave trade, and *Race Cards* (2016), an interactive installation and archive. *Race Cards* was the basis for the DIY project *Fine, We'll Answer Them* (2014), which Selina led at the Progress Festival in Toronto, and Selina was a LADA Resident in the Wellcome Collection Reading Room (2017).

This conversation took place over Skype while Selina was in the Netherlands.

Alexandrina: I think it's a little accidental that our work has been classified as Live Art. I even remember having a little resentment that 'Live Art' was more responsive to the work I was making than 'dance' was—because if I were to align myself with a genre at the time, it would have been contemporary dance. But there seemed to be more breadth of discourse within Live Art, and it was a lot more permissive in terms of how our work was seen. We could make references that were about dance, but also were about other structures, other perspectives. So I had to re-negotiate where I situated my practice for a while. For example, I tried to make a concertina book for my dance MA but was told that was a 'no-go' area: like, why would I want to use the form the essay took to convey any ideas? But then later, as Project O, Jamila and I were able to make a book and have it co-published by LADA.[1]

Jamila: For me there's something about the conflict with dance between athleticism—being the muse or vessel for someone else's idea—versus being an artist. In Live Art it's assumed that you are an artist. There is also the understanding that what you're making is coming from you or is related to *you*, rather than to a history of technique or to conventions of the dance genre.

Alexandrina: In dance school, virtuosity had a very distinct form. But there are many, many virtuosic performances within Live Art, and they all look different from one another.

Selina: In my third year at university we worked on avant-garde theatre, and we made this really awful piece. It was so bad! It had all the clichés: we were all naked, we got covered in hair gel, we were 'born' out of beanbags, we had a bath in some milk and there was choral music ... it was awful! But I really liked the *way* that we worked. Everything was allowed, and we made it and then explained it afterwards. So when I graduated, I very much took the label 'Live Artist' for myself, and my desire to make work that felt like that—where I could do what I wanted, and then worry about definitions and explanations afterwards.

And this also had to do with having come from a theatre background, where you find a play and there's a 'director' and there are 'actors' and there are 'designers'. And when the director comes into the room, they instruct everybody and they're always right. I knew I didn't want to work in that way. My mentors when I started out were a company called Invisible Flock. They made all kinds of work: they made apps, they made games that you could play backstage in a theatre, they made full on theatre shows... just whatever they wanted to do, they did it. And the three of them in the company were equal, and they were mates. The way that they worked seemed to be as much how they defined themselves as the work that they made. I thought: I could do that. I could work like that for a really long time.

Jamila: Working with Alexandrina as Project O has been great in terms of validating feelings or individual agendas. You can have an idea and wonder if maybe it is ridiculous or stupid, and the other one can say, yeah, that's a really great idea! So it's a lot easier to run with more extreme or ambitious ideas because we're two. Having a thing called Project O gives permissions to do more, be bigger, be louder.

Alexandrina: We're more solid because there are two of us. Also, the question of validation is particularly important because of the intersectional issues we work around including race and gender. I feel like I can be believed. I'll never forget early on in our friendship talking to Jamila about some racist thing that had happened, and she was like, 'Yeah, that happens, that happens to me too.' There is so much that is invisible, so much that wants to suppress the idea that racism is still an issue in the UK.

Selina: Until I was 18 I lived in an area of Birmingham were everybody was Black or Asian. And then I went to uni and I was like, 'Shit, everybody's white!' I wasn't really expecting that. It's because no one in my family had been to uni, so none of us anticipated what this would be like. My family didn't have the tools to help me navigate that. I was naïve. And I think I was naïve when I first came into art, as well. There was part of me that thought, 'It's art. Race isn't going to be an issue here.' I was quite violently shaken out of that, which needed to happen. But I'm aware of these instances of naivety in myself that keep being shaken.

Often when I'm making work, I feel like I'm jumping over the university bit of my life, the white bit, so I can connect with the kind of people that made up my life before. So in *Dark and Lovely*, I put myself in a hairdresser's and I'm surrounded by women who are my mum's age. There's a project I want to make on mental health where I'm going to be working with men my dad's age. The next project we're doing is working with lots of Black teenage girls, which connects back to school for me. I think there's always a part of me that's trying to bring these two things together: that teenage girl with her hair gelled down the side of her face, and the version of me now, sitting on this Skype from the Netherlands, drinking water infused with mint and lemon! How can these two people come together in my work?

Jamila: Can you talk more about why those people are separate? Because they make up 'you', right?

Selina: It took me a really long time to figure out this had happened. I don't think I figured it out until [the controversy around] *Exhibit B* happened,[2] when I was really angry and lots of people weren't. I saw *Exhibit B* in Edinburgh, and at that time—though I didn't have the language for it then—I knew that I wanted to make a show about the afterlife of slavery. So I saw this work, which was at a big international festival—and I was really horrified by it! Again, it's just naivety on my part. I'm sure other people would have looked at the copy

Right: Selina Thompson, *Chewing the Fat* (2013). Image Richard Davenport.

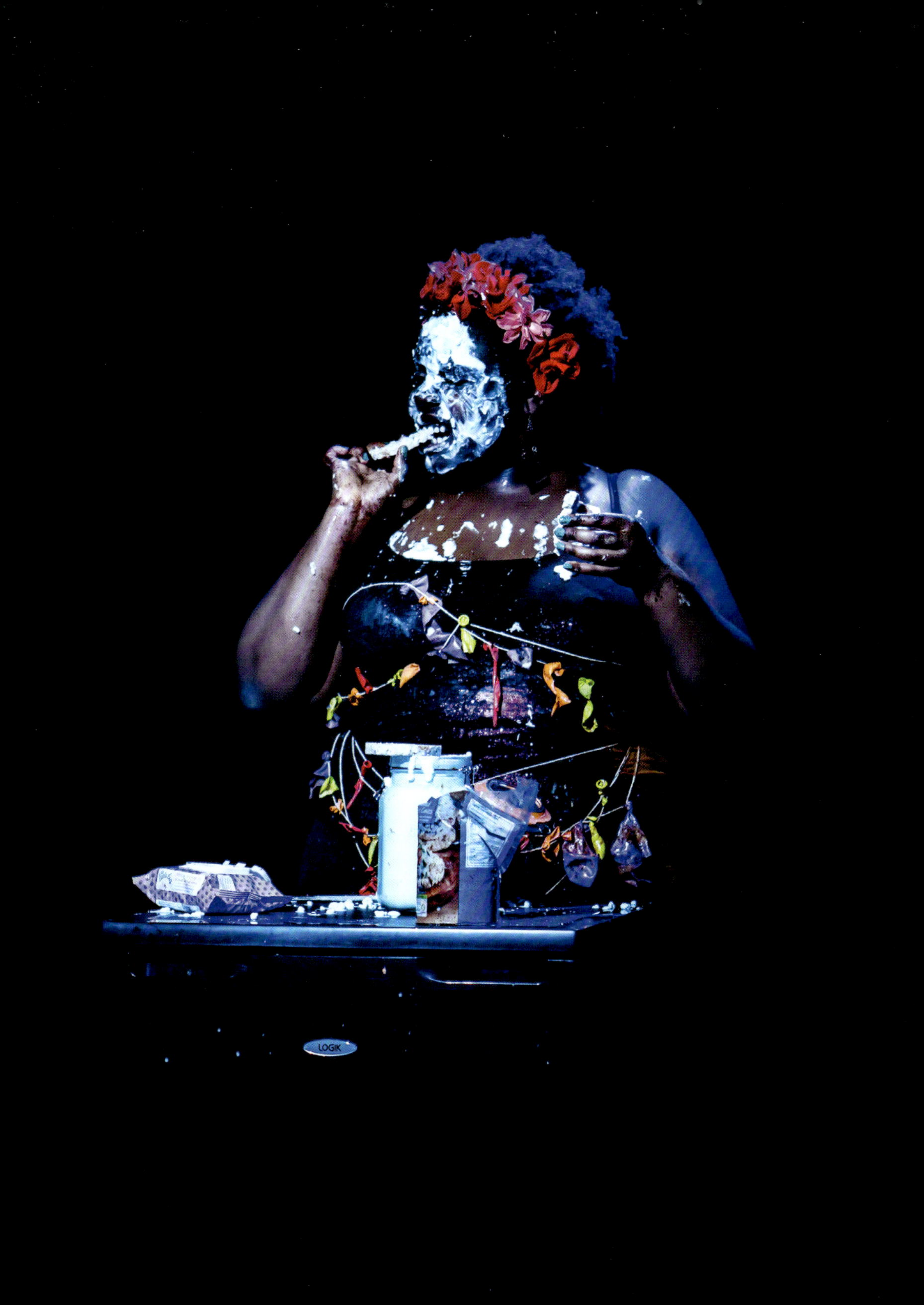
LOGIK

for it and decided it was trash and not gone to see it. But I didn't. I went to see it, and I was so angry. So angry. It was like this sizzle in my body.

So I wrote something about it for my blog.[3] I wrote it, and it was out of my body, so I didn't have to worry about it anymore—that's how I write. But then *Exhibit B* went to London, and it was protested and then withdrawn, and what I wrote got a lot more mileage than I ever anticipated. I ended up being forced into all of these conversations about it. All of these people who I really respected were saying things that I thought were so wrong. I thought: here you are, several decades older than me with the entirety of the internet at your fingertips, and what you say is so wrong. How have you been doing it with those assumptions in your heart and in your heads? It was like the scales falling off my eyes, and once you start to see that shit, you can't stop seeing it.

I don't know if I've answered your question, Jamila. It feels like I hacked great big parts of myself off so that I could fit into uni comfortably, and then *Exhibit B* happened with all this anger, which is horrible, but also cleansing. It's as if this person that I thought was destroyed is like 'Naah, I wasn't destroyed, I was here all along. Hello!' I feel that a lot: trying to navigate these different spaces. It's messy.

Jamila: It is messy. But it's also messy because those splits are so violent, and they happen when you're denied agency. You're not allowed to be full in a place that you're not represented, in a place where you can't meet yourself. It's not just about verbal acknowledgement—like someone saying, 'Selina, are you okay?' It's that the *structure* would have had to be less racist and then you would have been okay. You could be full, but you're not. You have to fragment yourself because the space itself is incredibly full of one particular form of violence.

Alexandrina: I can really relate to the process of splitting and the work it can take to bring parts of yourself back together and undo the silencing. I have this question in terms of this conversation, which is: did Live Art make *Exhibit B* happen? It didn't come out of nowhere, so who was supporting it? We're part of the world that supported that piece. Which agendas, modes of art production, spectatorship and consumption were being validated by this piece of artwork?

And this word 'naivety', and those moments where you get fucking shaken out of it.... There's a level of comfort—not innocence or safety, but maybe optimism and hope—and then every time there's something that disrupts that. I don't know if it happens more to people of colour. I don't like the internalised shame that thinks we have to then be accountable for our naivety. We have to somehow justify ourselves and say, 'We were so foolish, thinking that we could be accepted on our own terms.' Or believing (despite plentiful lived experiences) that someone else wasn't going to cross a boundary in an incredibly invasive way. Or that we're not going to experience work as more violent than our white peers and colleagues.

Jamila: I think the most telling thing about this kind of situation is having to learn to trust my feelings, my responses to things. My first response is 'Am I going crazy?' 'Am I being over-sensitive?' 'Do I have a personality problem?' It's as if I need to trust that I was actually having those feelings. I need to pay attention to them and I need to trust them because they are what is going on. That is the first thing, before 'schooling' others. Before 'Why do I need to tell you this?' The first thing is always self-doubt. The first thing is always, 'Is the problem me?'

And then beyond that, there's the feeling of being put in a position where you're being asked to explain something to someone, but it just doesn't work because they're not living that experience. They're hearing, but they can't understand; they can't comprehend what you're trying to say. You can exhaust yourself trying to explain going inside yourself, your deep, dark, horrible feelings that are all ragged and angry and nasty, bringing them up, trying to deliver them eloquently outside yourself to someone else who just doesn't have a fucking clue. That is horrible.

Selina: Jamila you wrote a blog about the right to be silent, the right not to have to comment. I remember having a stormy response to it at the time, but also feeling very envious, because at that point I didn't feel like I had a right to silent and not to comment. But increasingly I do. My feeling is that if you want to understand how this works, you'll go and find it out for yourself. People have been writing about this shit for decades. I'm not doing it. Because my energy is finite, and it's stopping my growth. Doing all of this schooling, and being in these conversations where I reiterated the same thing over and over and over again, was inhibiting my ability to expand and learn more and think more and do more. Fundamentally, I feel like my responsibility as an artist, and as person, is to grow.

Jamila: I think it's important to think about how and when we learn, and how people get access to experiences that they don't have. How do you understand a situation? How do you have empathy? I was speaking with Gillie Kleiman the other day and she said, 'You know, sometimes people just have to believe other people; they just have to take what they say as what something is because they will never know themselves.'

Selina: I remember how hard it was to write *Dark and Lovely*, the piece I made about hair. I thought, 'Maybe this has been done to death. Maybe everybody knows this already and no one needs to see it.' But then when we were touring it that wasn't the response. I remember doing it in Newcastle and there was one Black woman in the audience. Everybody else was white. It was like just me and her. She waited until everybody had left and then we spoke and both had a bit of a cry. And then she went home.

What am I trying to get at here? Maybe I don't have the language for it yet. I guess I would say that I'm always fundamentally making work for myself. And that if you're a Black person and sometimes you feel crazy, I just want you to come to my shows and know that sometimes I feel crazy, too—but we're not.

But I don't know if I still identify with 'Live Art' quite as strongly. The more work you see, and the more artists you get to know, and the more discourse you read, the more restrictive a label can feel in the making process. I feel like my work is more 'chatty' now, and sometimes I think this doesn't feel like 'Live Art', because it doesn't feel serious enough, or radical enough, or difficult enough.

Jamila: When we came up with this by-line 'Project O, a contemporary struggle' we were laughing away! We were really almost outraged that we could use such a line for our privileged dance work that we're making, with our Arts Council funding to dance around in the studio, when there are struggles happening on bodily levels where bits of bodies end up far away from other bits of that same body.

We are doing something incredibly joyous and fulfilling with our experience of the struggle, our part in this struggle. To be able to work with someone who is my friend in a space where I can grow, where we are growing together over time and simultaneously addressing all this horrible shit is such a gift. There are endless problems. There are endless barriers and walls and glass ceilings and doors closing. But we make dances. We dance. That is the way we can 'fight' with little—what do you call it?—inverted commas. I'm waggling my fingers.

Alexandrina: The conditions outside the work are not in our favour. They are stacked against us; they are racist; they are dystopian; they are fucked. But we can go in the studio and really start our environment from scratch, construct our own terms, and enact them. And we can navigate the conundrums, the conflicts, the transformations through our bodies.

Jamila: Maybe this is about self-realisation. This work is *talking* about things on a wider scale, but as we make it we're also *living* that thing that we're aspiring towards. That's kind of huge.

Alexandrina: The things I want to be in dialogue with an audience now are the same things I wanted then: I want everyone to be involved. I want everyone to know that we're all implicated in these oppressive systems that are actively in process (more than a colonial hangover!). They don't happen to other people that are outside of ourselves. They happen to all of us differently and we need to take notice. Make space. Allow experiences to be released from their silence.

1. Jamila Johnson-Small and Alexandrina Hemsley, *A Contemporary Struggle* (London: Live Art Development Agency and Project O, 2013).

2. *Exhibit B* was an installation-performance, created by South African artist Brett Bailey, that used the form of 19th and 20th-century ethnographic displays (or 'human zoos') to represent contemporary Black bodies (such as asylum seekers from African countries) in living dioramas. It was generally praised at European festivals, but controversy accompanied its Edinburgh version in 2014, and its subsequent version in London was cancelled following protests.

3. Selina Thompson, 'Exhibit B' [2014] <http://selinathompson.co.uk/exhibit-b/>.

BODIES

PROVOCATION

DOMINIC JOHNSON

TITLE

THOSE WHO HAVE SUFFERED UNDERSTAND SUFFERING: NOTES ON THE BODY (IN PAIN)

Dominic Johnson is a scholar of Live Art. He teaches Live Art at Queen Mary University of London. He writes about and collaborates with artists whose work has tended to be marginalised in institutional and critical histories of art and performance. In recent years, he has published books and chapters on the relations between Live Art and extremity and endurance, consensual self-injury, queer politics and HIV/AIDS, sabotage, one-to-one performance, the occult, crime, and pornography. His most recent book is *Unlimited Action: The Performance of Extremity in the 1970s* (2018). From 2005 to 2012, his frequently bloody performances were shown around the world, in festivals, galleries, museums, theatres and clubs, a commune, a dungeon, and a desert. He collaborates frequently with the Live Art Development Agency: he is a long-term member of its Board of Directors; he co-edits the book series Intellect Live with them; and co-designed MA Live Art—the first programme of its kind in the UK, which commenced in 2018 at Queen Mary in partnership with LADA.

In wood-panelled room—repurposed from its former usage as a place of reprimand for juvenile delinquents—Martin O'Brien stands naked before us and pulls needles from his scrotum (*If It Were The Apocalypse I'd Eat You Alive*, Toynbee Studios, London, 2015). Sheree Rose had placed them there with expert roughness minutes earlier, while he lay mummified in duct tape, after having been force-fed noxious liquids through a chrome funnel. As O'Brien leverages the needles from his body, the courtroom is shaken by a loud thud and some commotion: someone has fainted flat out onto the bags and jackets stacked at the back of the room. The room is hot and the atmosphere is loaded with images of pain and endurance. A helper attends to the fallen, and O'Brien soldiers on. Subsequently, O'Brien is spanked, has his hands nailed to a table (by me, as it happens), suffocates himself in a latex hood, and drags a scalpel round the skin of his chest to sketch the shape of his ravaged lungs in a hieroglyph of blood.

My brief recollection of *If It Were The Apocalypse* stages the messy, approximate transferal of our own imagined (or remembered) experience of a similar kind of pain, from one's own contingent body (his) to another's (yours). That sex is foregrounded in O'Brien's work—in the specific accoutrements of sadomasochism—only adds to the confusion of how we think we feel, what we might make of it (say, in meaning), and what we think we know about his pain (and/or his pleasure).

We will all know pain, both physical and emotional. We will know it from the minor twinge of the stubbed toe to the full ruin of devastating injury or illness; from the temporary sting of a personal insult, to the enduring crisis of emotional or psychic desolation. The lucky among us may live our lives in relative freedom from the more portentous end of these continuums. Yet none of us is saved from the fact of pain, as a physiological phenomenon that accompanies having a sensate body and a sympathetic mind, joined as vectors of our situation in the world.

As the performance-poet Patti Smith sings, 'those who have suffered, understand suffering'. Smith means that the nature of pain cannot be properly explained; we struggle to put our pain into words, to give it a shape that would manifest, authenticate, or record it. Yet having pain, we know pain. Our knowing gives it—and our lives at large—its own authenticity, with or without the reality or grace that words might allow our pain in the perception of others. Our attempt to pass on this knowledge to others is—constitutively—a troubled venture. In our cries, screams, gasps, as in our more measured statements and representations, we struggle to stage the particularity of our hurt.

'Those who have suffered, understand suffering, and *thereby extend their hand'*, Smith intones, suggesting another key point about pain: the full reality of pain is incommunicable, and beyond representation, but this fact precipitates or enables *a culture of pain*, a commitment to creating or styling the attempt to communicate our pain to others. The obstacles to representing pain itself—beyond showing its superficial signs, like a gash in the skin, or a scream in the mouth—do not prevent us from listening intently to how another tries to make her pain known.

Making an object of one's pain has been a frequent and persistent project for historical and contemporary art: from paintings presenting great duress; to graphic documents of war or personal suffering; to performance art that attempts to harness self-injury as a formal technique. This essay introduces some key works in Live Art and performance art and asks how artists deal with the constitutive manner in which pain *provokes yet evades* full representation and communication. I also explore the historically divisive place of pain in art and aesthetics, which extends differently into the present.

Historical depictions of pain—especially those showing the mortification of flesh—also sought to *stay* the full horror of suffering, from the medieval period until at least the nineteenth century. Decorum was compulsory, as it prevented the subjugation of beauty to pain, and saved pleasure from dissolving in disgust. The classic Greek sculpture, *Laocoön and his Sons*, is a visceral image of suffering; in a treatise on the sculpture, the eighteenth-century philosopher Gotthold Lessing celebrates how 'a passive courage of endurance' is retained in the facial and physical comportment of Laocoön, despite the emotional and physical ordeal Laocoön is trapped within.[1] For Lessing, Laocoön's face is transcendent, and not distorted by pain, despite the serpent that bites his naked loin, and the imminent death of his sons by strangulation. For orthodox aesthetics, allowing the tortured priest to scream would subordinate the ideal beauty of the human body to external reality (to the horror of what it would entail to be devoured by snakes). Allowing Laocoön his pain would 'degrade' the sculpture, regardless of its topic.[2] If a work of art demands a visceral response, a pained one, or a feeling of disgust, it therefore shakes the foundations by which art is held separate from everyday life.

As if by some effect of sympathetic magic, we may therefore intuit pain in the experience of an other, and may approximate it in our own sweaty palms, tightness in the stomach, fretful alertness, heartbeat racing. Our desiring investment might embody similar symptoms—it's not always clear what we are feeling in such moments of alarm. Neither is it clear what the other feels, in terms of the molecular specificity or density of her or his pain. At the same time, the veracity of another's pain cannot be discounted. How, then, do contemporary performances and their documentation produce or reproduce pain, including through pain's avatar, the wound? And who or what is challenged by the production or representation of pain, wounds, and hardship in performance?

The history of performance art since the 1960s has often privileged the spectacle of the body in pain, in part to bring art to bear more fully upon life, and vice versa—think, for example, of Marina Abramović and Ulay slamming into walls or each other; ORLAN submitting herself to choreographed situations of invasive cosmetic surgery; William Pope.L dragging himself across arduous cities on his hands and knees; Kira O'Reilly mapping the gridded contours of her body in scalpel nicks; or He Yunchang asking an audience to vote on whether he should or shouldn't cut a one-metre gash in his side (they voted in favour, so he did). Performance art typically involves the use of performance as distinct from the perceived falsehoods and fakeries of theatre. Emerging from histories of fine art, or otherwise in counterpoint to theatre, performance art rejects the conventional modes of training, skill, and virtuosity associated with the performing arts, and it repudiates the impersonation, characterisation, and repetition required by acting. As an effect of these refusals, therefore, pain or ordeal has often been trafficked centre-stage (as it were); performance artists have sought to manifest or take advantage of the body as a material for the production of un-simulated, unrepeatable, and seemingly unmediated performances. In great part, pain is provoked as the ground for the playing out of an action; or else it emerges as a side-effect—an inevitable or even unfortunate consequence—of a greater formal project, including that of appropriating one's own body as raw material for the production of an image. (Dance or circus or bodybuilding is also prone to the latter.)

Pain plays a part in a litany of performance works after 1960, with effects that are sometimes shocking, sometimes banal, possibly funny, and generally difficult or even terrifying for the viewer. The artist makes an object of her or his pain, to instrumentalise, control, or heighten it, and therefore to comment on major themes in contemporary life: like consent, pleasure, technique, technology, biomedicine, repetition, relationships, ethics, or our tacit culpability with non-consensual suffering in war. Others dismiss pain as a useful idea, despite the extremity of their actions—not least because the critical emphasis on pain may condemn the artist and the work of art to charges of sadomasochism, pathology, self-harm, narcissism, or nihilism.

Overleaf: Martin O'Brien and Sheree Rose, action at *Access All Areas*, London (2011). Image Manuel Vason.

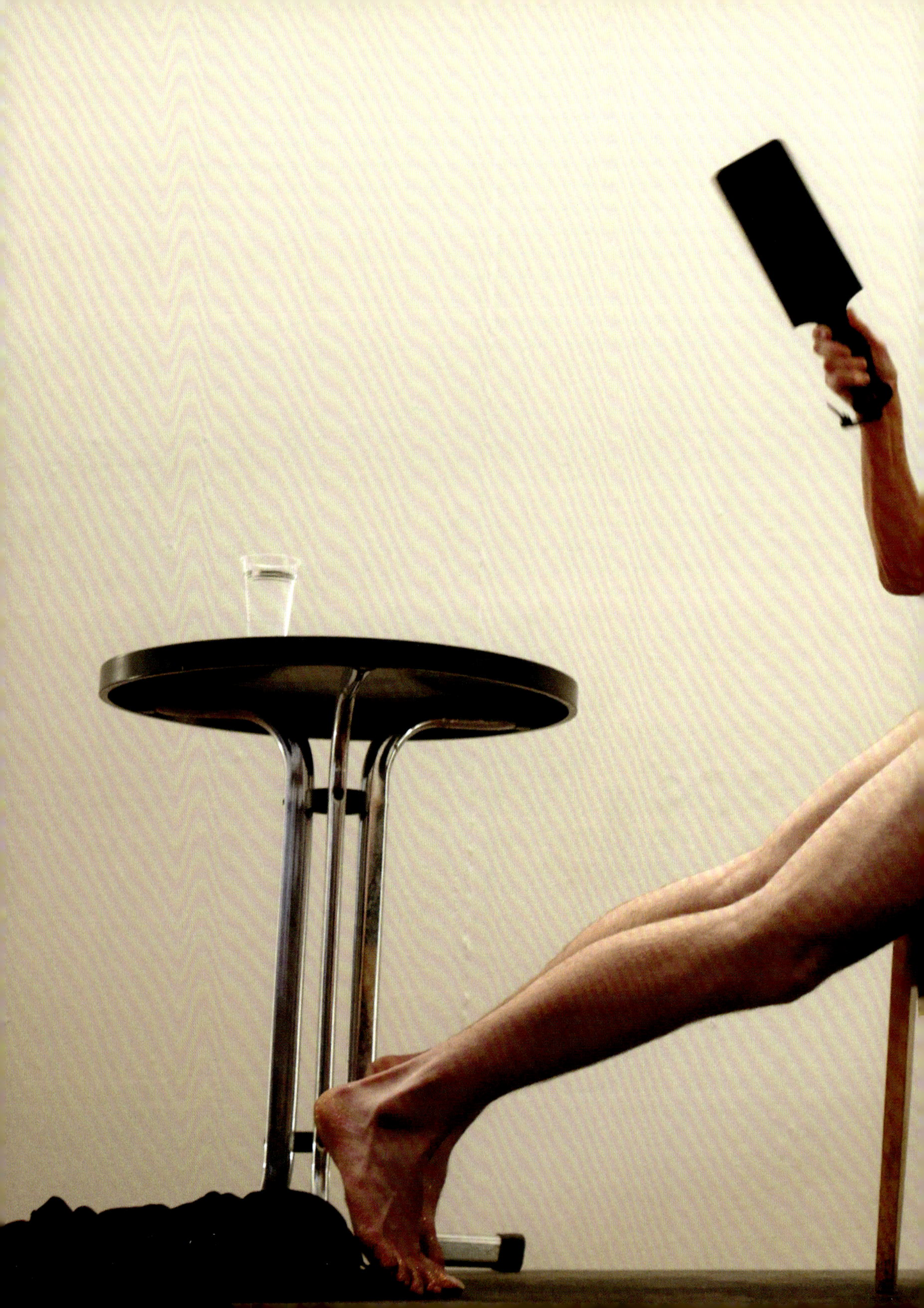

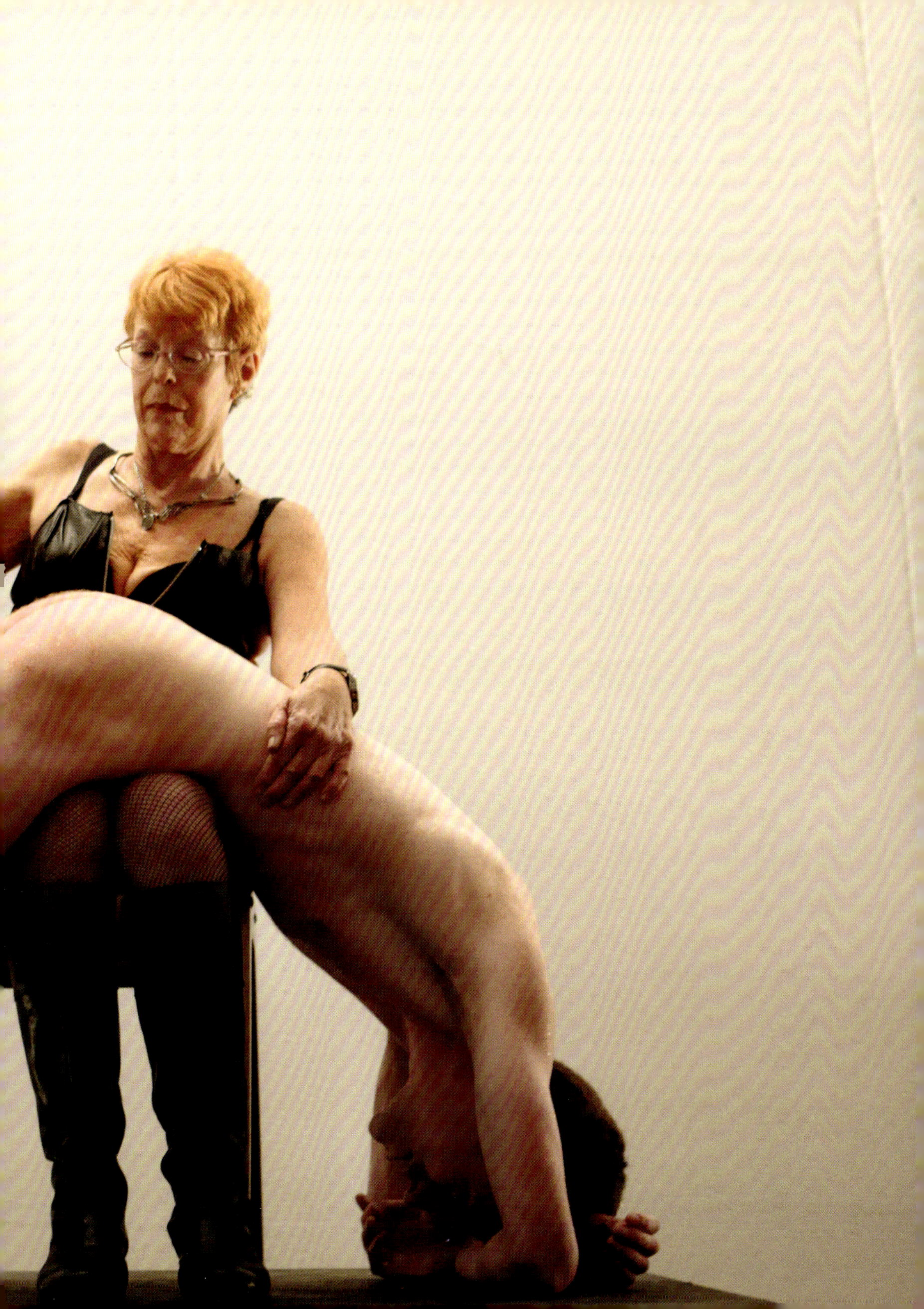

Artists who inflict pain or duress upon their own bodies are sometimes hailed by critics as heroes, triumphing over adversity or fate. Other critics take issue with the valorisation of pain and risk as alibis for machismo or narcissism, mental illness or self-abuse. Historically, women and gay men have been particularly susceptible to the latter charges. Critics have often resorted to questioning the motives of artists, or doubting their sanity, when to cater to the disconcerting power of an image is perhaps too difficult, too worrying, or too horrible. Such artists, we are told, are pretentious, attention seeking, headline grabbing, politically naïve, or insane.

For example, in the *Guardian*, Sam Wollaston writes of Kira O'Reilly's use of outmoded medical techniques: 'I'm no expert, but that just seems to be about personal fetishes, and not much to do with art.'[3] In *The Times*, the artist Grayson Perry condones this view, ridiculing Ron Athey's work as the heedless spectacle of 'someone pump[ing] a couple of litres of saline into their scrotal sac': 'One suspicion I have of a lot of performance art, particularly body art,' he continues, 'is that it is a handy arena for exhibitionists.'[4] (Perry doesn't mean it kindly in his caricatures of Athey and other artists including Bob Flanagan, Vito Acconci, and Rebecca Horn). Such readings objectify a critic's personal suspicion about an artist's motives, and replace an opportunity for critical acuity with a pernicious kind of moralism. Neither Wollaston nor Perry spends the time to think about the historical, cultural, or formal specificity of performance art. In the case of O'Reilly's work, for example, neither account can begin to allow a reader to address her use of wet-cupping or leeches for bloodletting, her intense training towards painful actions like falling in slow motion down a flight of stairs, or the complex ethical demands for live audiences, who consent to and sometimes participate in her performances. We miss the fact that O'Reilly never seems to articulate or stage her hurt, such that the physical activity of wounding or marking—while looking painful—is always formally distinct from the projections we might like to make (I have never seen her cry or scream in performance; I struggle even to remember her grimacing).

If strategies of ridicule and stigmatisation are commonplace in popular accounts, similar practices of containment also contaminate serious scholarship on Live Art.[5] Such criticism may inhibit the political and other effects of performance—by way of charges of exhibitionism, or self-harm, or naïveté. Some may do so out of good will, care, or self-preservation, prompted by their own horror at the lengths to which an artist seems to feel she must go to make an image. As Tanya Augsburg writes, 'While the typical question asked by spectators, "Do you feel pain?" is more benign than the critic's question, "Is she mad?" both types of questions aim at discrediting [the artist's] ability to think for herself, to be rational, and to make decisions about her own

Right: Franko B and Manuel Vason, *Collaboration #5* (2002). Image Manuel Vason.

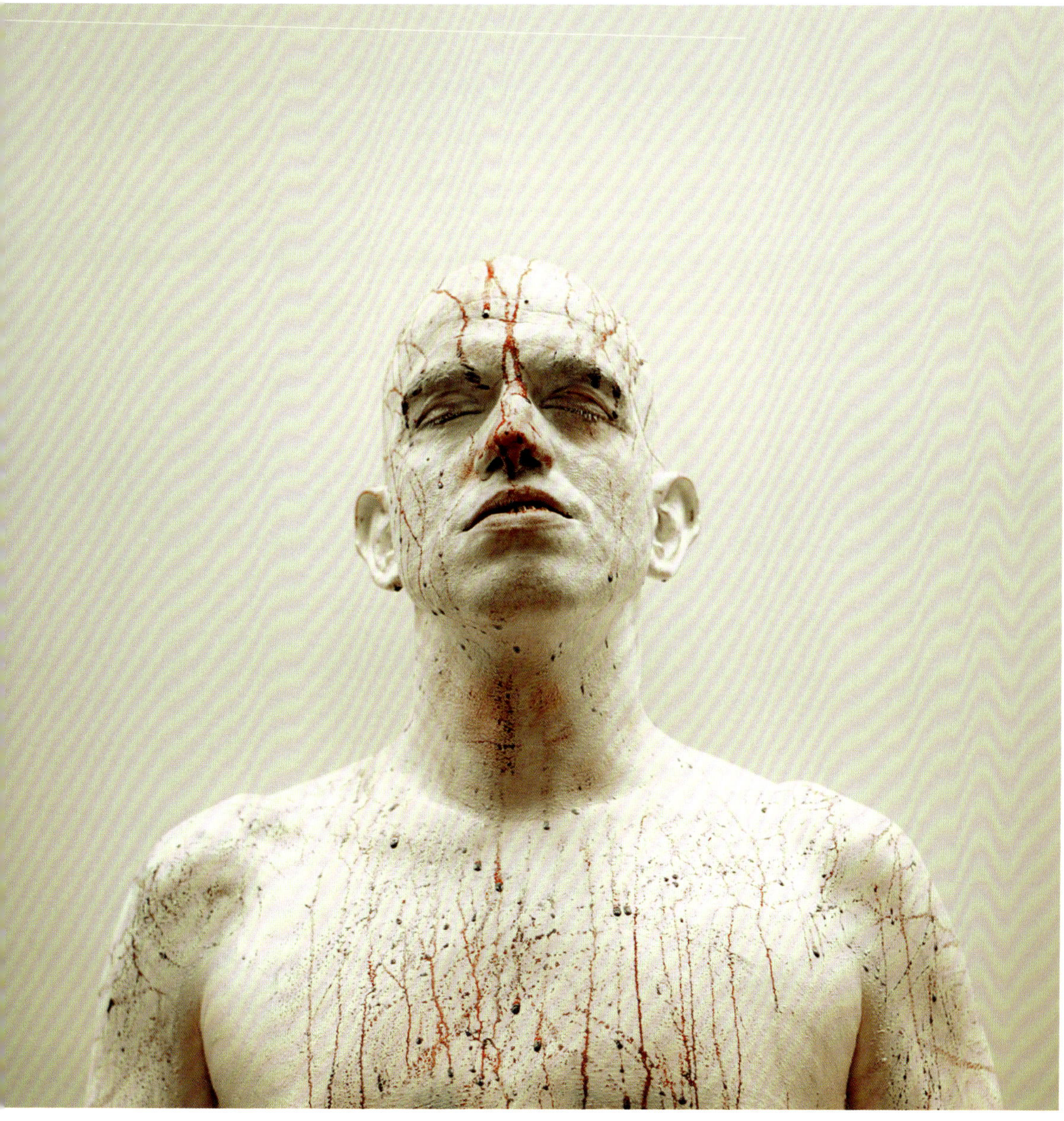

body.'[6] Focusing on pain prompts difficult questions—and sometimes provides distorting frames. The problem of pain may both sharpen and blunt the critical tools with which seek to understand art and performance.

When Franko B sits or lays bleeding on an illuminated bed in *Still Life* (2004), or walks up and down a catwalk with blood dripping from cannulae inserted into the crooks of his elbows, in *I Miss You!* (2000), his performance strikes me as by turns delicate, romantic, pathetic, and deliberately monstrous. Or when Rocío Boliver puts acrylic threads through her skin and tears them free with screams of pain and anguish, and turns the tide on our grief by playing her vagina as a trombone with a bike pump, in various manifestations of her series *Between Menopause and Old Age* (2012–present), we are gripped between emotional highs and lows, and I lose track of my handle on what my body feels, and the sense of all decorum about what one should or can feel in the space of art is left in tatters. The effects are shattering in the wake of a performance by such artists, just as the costs for the artists may sometimes be drastic. Franko B notes as much when he writes, 'if a monster is that which shows itself as much as it is seen by you, then let me be a monster'.[7] In its destitution and its pain, the body in pain—as a kind of self-created monster—is subjected to a physical disaster, violently separated from the myth of a common, natural human body, and burdened with profound and multiple meanings and affects. We gasp in front of it, feel squeamish, cry, or faint, and call into question the sensible limits of our conception of the human, the good, and the right—the limits of what can be lived, or survived. The cultural historian David Morris writes, 'Pain not only hurts but more often than not frustrates, baffles, and resists us. It seems we cannot simply suffer pain but almost always are compelled to make sense of it'.[8] That is to say: this image or this action—it hurts. We know this much. We reach for the language through which our experience can be made sense of. *Those who have suffered understand suffering, and thereby extend their hand.*

1. Gotthold Ephraim Lessing, *Laocoön: An Essay upon the Limits of Painting and Poetry*, trans. by Edward Allen McCormick (Baltimore: Johns Hopkins University Press, 1954), pp. 8–9.

2. Lessing, p. 15.

3. Sam Wollaston, 'Last Night's TV', *Guardian*, 15 March 2006 <http://www.theguardian.com/media/2006/mar/15/broadcasting.tvandradio>.

4. Grayson Perry, 'Yes, Performance Art Is Extreme and Silly, but It Does Have a Point', *The Times* (UK), 22 March 2006, p. 16.

5. For a critique of the scholarly distortions and pathologisations of ORLAN's surgical performances of the 1990s, for example, see Dominic Johnson, 'Psychic Weight: The Pains and Pleasures of Performance', in *ORLAN: A Hybrid Body of Artworks*, ed. by Simon Donger and Simon Shepherd (New York and London: Taylor and Francis, 2010), pp. 84–99.

6. Tanya Augsburg, 'Orlan's Performative Transformations of Subjectivity', in *The Ends of Performance*, ed. by Peggy Phelan and Jill Lane (New York: New York University Press, 1998), pp. 285–314 (p. 307).

7. Franko B, 'I Feel Empty', in *Live: Art and Performance*, ed. by Adrian Heathfield (London: Tate, 2004), p. 226.

8. David B. Morris, *The Culture of Pain* (Berkeley: University of California Press, 1991).

BODIES

PROVOCATION

AMELIA JONES

TITLE

AGENCY, HABITUS, EMBODIMENT

Amelia Jones is the Robert A. Day Professor and Vice Dean of Research at the Roski School of Art and Design at University of Southern California. A feminist curator and a theorist and historian of art and performance, her recent publications include *Seeing Differently: A History and Theory of Identification and the Visual Arts* (2012); *Perform Repeat Record: Live Art in History* (2012), co-edited with Adrian Heathfield and co-published by LADA; the edited volume *Sexuality* (2014); and, co-edited with Erin Silver, *Otherwise: Imagining Queer Feminist Art Histories* (2016). Her exhibition *Material Traces: Time and the Gesture in Contemporary Art* took place in 2013 in Montreal and she programmed the events *Trans-Montréal* (2015) in that city, followed by a related publication 'On Trans/Performance', a special issue of *Performance Research* (2016). Her *Live Artists Live* performance and conference program took place at USC in 2016. Amelia is currently working on a retrospective of the work of Ron Athey (*Queer Communion/ Ron Athey*) and a book entitled *In Between Subjects: A Critical Genealogy of Queer Performance* on press at NYU Press in the 'Sexual Cultures' series.

Slowly, slowly, ever so excruciatingly slowly.... a body tumbles in slow-motion down an ornate Victorian stairway. This body is completely bare, unprotected, vulnerable to hurts and bruises, its musculature straining and evident as it gyrates, pulled downward by the inexorable force of gravity. Seemingly random, in fact nothing could be more purposeful. The body is resisting the pull downward. The muscles, trained and engaged, are activated to prevent the cascade of rapid movements that would normally beset a body falling unwittingly down the stairs. The action is choreographed. The piece is a dance, not a headlong crash of limbs. I feel it in my bones and muscles, which clutch and strain in empathetic, kinesthetic response.

I was there, watching Kira O'Reilly's *Stair Falling* at the Whitworth Art Gallery (University of Manchester) in 2009.[1]

What *Stair Falling* communicates and even insists upon in its live experience is the hinge between the body (which has its own 'life' of needs, wants, pulses, fluctuations, gestures) and the agency that propels or restrains it. This is not the age-old division between body and mind that Descartes famously solidified in his mid seventeenth-century proclamation 'I think therefore I am' (followed by an even more decisive assertion: 'This "I", that is to say, the mind by which I am what I am, is entirely distinct from the body, ... it is easier to know than the body....').[2] Rather, *Stair Falling* exemplifies a careful kind of performance art that thoughtfully and painstakingly enacts a mode of conceptual embodiment that refuses the Cartesian split, focusing on exploring the interrelation between body and agential force (or, in phenomenological terms, 'intentional arc'[3]). O'Reilly's piece is brilliant not only because it is beautiful and spare in its address and exploration of the particular space it inhabits, as well as the forces that condition those spaces and our bodies. It is brilliant as well precisely because it insistently *shows* that the body is always already agentially driven, the mind always embodied. She opens up the hinge (or 'chiasmus') between inside and out of the embodied subject.[4]

Furthermore, O'Reilly's piece makes witnesses of the work aware that this agency is not singular. My description above makes clear the adjustments I was making as I viewed the work in 2009 (due to my state of mind and body at the time), an experience I have access to only through memories (aided or distorted by the photographs of the event), memories that are in turn conditioned by my current state of mind and interests.

To this end, I must insist—as performances such as this make it crystal clear—that agency is never lodged in a single place or with/within a single body. It is rarely admitted (although phenomenologists such as Maurice Merleau-Ponty understood this) that the question of agency (which is also always a question of meaning and value, particularly obviously when one is assuming value to be attached to social or political effect) is never about one body, one mind, or one 'individual.' Whether scholars or everyday witnesses of performance art care to admit it or not, the most profound performances (such as O'Reilly's) have a way of insistently reminding us that the gesturing, moving, breathing, or otherwise *articulating* body of performance is always already connecting to others (connect-*ing*, not connect-*ed*: the relationality is always in motion). It has no value as a performing body without those others. So thinking about the 'agency' of the performing body demands thinking at the very least also about the other bodies performing, participating, and/or engaging with that body.[5]

Thinking about agency and the body also requires pondering how we get from thoughts in our head to movements of our body—bringing to bear the question of intentionality in the phenomenological, philosophical, or psychological senses. In turn, addressing the question of intentionality—assumed and naturalised by most art historians and ignored by most performance studies scholars—is actually central to exploring how and why we produce or watch (engage with) performance. Whether we admit it or not, any work we view or engage with as performance 'art' we assume to be motivated by some kind of 'intentional' agency (this is the case even if, as with myself, we consider ourselves poststructuralists and suspicious of simplistic ideas of intentionality).[6] Without succumbing to the latter—as with many art historians who claim not to be lapsing into psycho-biography, claim to be eschewing intentional accounts all together, while failing to acknowledge their assumptions surrounding the artists' putative motivations for her/his choices—I insist that we need to acknowledge our beliefs and desires in assigning such motivations as we view and experience performance art in particular.

To this end, one of the most interesting contributions performance makes to the visual arts' situation, I have long argued, is precisely this way in which it activates such questions, putting them out in the open. If our desire to assign motivation or intention to what we are seeing is being suppressed or veiled, as it so often is in art historical discourse and particularly in art criticism, then performance at least troubles this. My favourite examples have always been those moments in the development of performance art in which an artist flagrantly enacts herself in ways that (precisely) disallow this suppression of their viewers' self-interest and desire: viz., Yoko Ono's *Cut Piece* (1964–1965), VALIE EXPORT's *Tap and Touch Cinema* (1968), Adrian Piper's *Catalysis* works (1973–1974), or Carolee Schneemann's *Interior Scroll* (1975).

Right: Kira O'Reilly, *Stair Falling*, Whitworth Art Gallery, Manchester (2009). Image Marco Anelli.

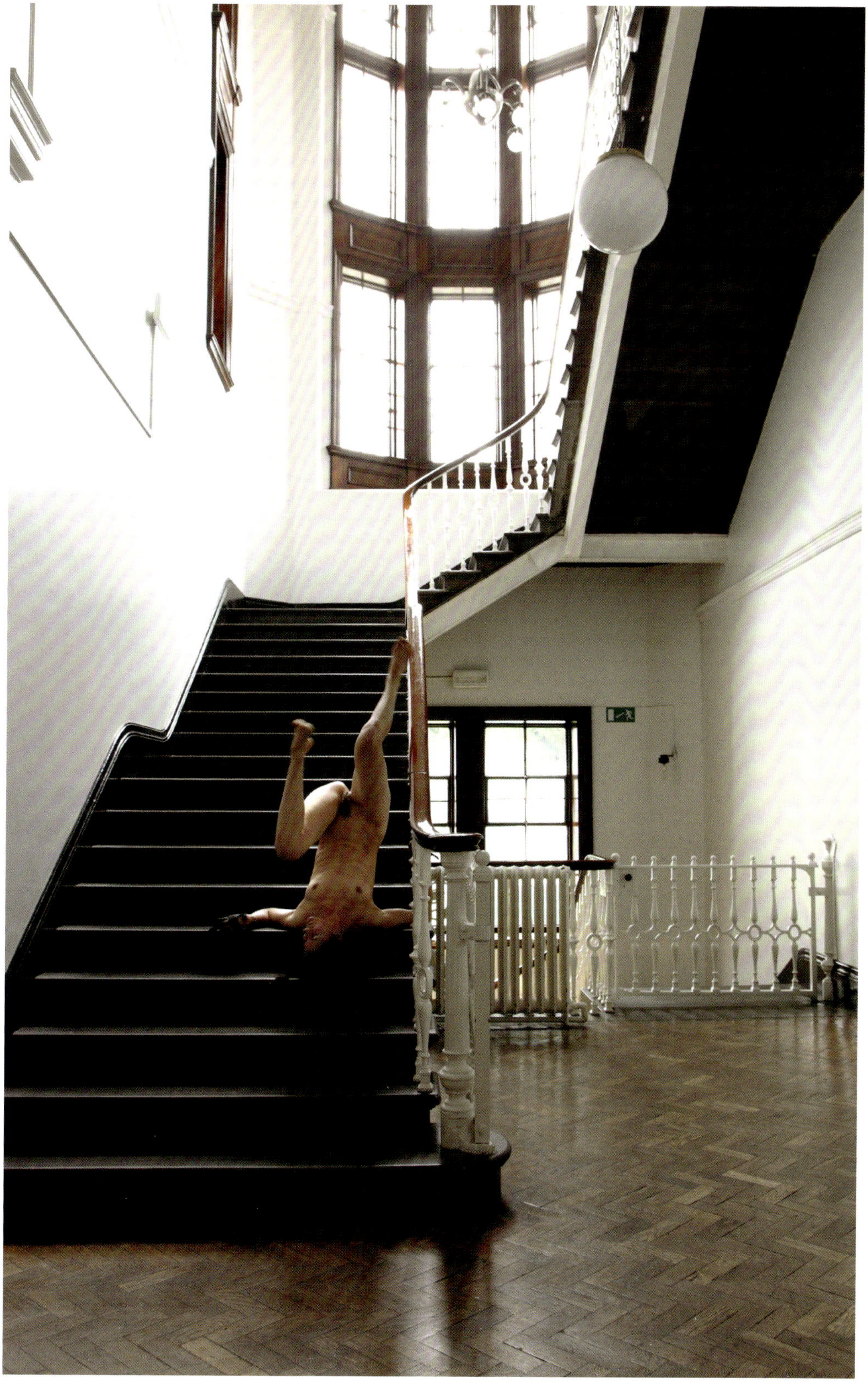

Examining the question of agency and embodiment is crucial if we are to understand anything about how particular art practices mean and have value, but also—more importantly—about how art *works* in general. The concept of the habitus provides one way of thinking these things through. Anthropologist Marcel Mauss in 1934 described the habitus in terms of 'bodily techniques' of habitual training and constraint—providing a model to understand the normative choreographing of everyday bodies, enacted in relation to repetitive codes of behaviour linked to class, gender, sexuality, race, ethnicity, chosen occupation, and other modes through which we position ourselves in the world.[7] For Mauss, the training of the body for any kind of specialised sport or art activity is a locus of the joining of the social with the biological or 'natural'; he uses this point of joining (or *hinge*) to explore the limits of bodily training as these are faithfully reiterated, and negotiated or in certain cases ruptured by performing bodies in various kinds of bodily activity—just as we might do in relation to various kinds of performance.

We might also look beyond Mauss to more recent theories of embodiment and performance. In his 1980 study *Le sens pratique* (translated into English in 1990 as *The Logic of Practice*), Pierre Bourdieu redefines habitus as the inexorable set of inscribed bodily practices through which we are always already immersed in ideology, in social structures. He notes:

> the *habitus* tends to favor experiences likely to reinforce it .... Through the systematic 'choices' it makes [or allows us to make] among the places, events, and people that might be frequented, the *habitus* tends to protect itself from crises and critical challenges by providing itself with a milieu to which it is as pre-adapted as possible, that is, a relatively constant universe of situations tending to reinforce its dispositions by offering the market most favourable to its products.[8]

I would argue that, given the possibility of failure and the nuances of ephemerality in live performance (the act that can never be repeated in exactly the same way twice, no matter how closely choreographed), it makes the repetition of habitual, inscribed modes of being (or, as Bourdieu might put it, the ideological dimension of our behaviours and identifications) evident—whether the performance reiterates or challenges them or both. One example of how this works is the piece *Judas Cradle* (2004–2005) by Ron Athey with the collaboration of professional opera singer Julianna Snapper. While Athey wilfully torments himself by placing his anus on the sharp point of a 'judas cradle' (a pyramid-shaped torture device from the middle ages) and fails in singing opera properly (meshing the singing with a kind of hybrid speaking-in-tongues), Snapper deliberately dehabituates her opera-trained body by hanging upside down on a rack. Her diaphragm pushing downward into her lungs, her voice becomes strangled.

She suffers a kind of martyrdom to her body, which drips downward like the flayed flesh of Marsyas, gulping and howling like a strangled dog. Athey's extreme manipulations and violations of the male body (the habitus of which is, at the very least, that it be kept impenetrable) and Snapper's dehabituating of the opera body by turning it into a performance artist's body (upside down, unable to sing properly) foreground for the viewer/participant our own habitual bodily and psychic constraints and resistances.

Attention to the habitus, then, might foreground live performance as the point where the 'implicit' body becomes evident. The explicit body is, as performance theorist Rebecca Schneider has argued, the radically denaturalised female body presented publicly in feminist performance to elicit politicised responses; she is referring in particular to the subversion of norms that occurs by definition when a woman artist enacts herself in 'explosive literality' as an agential force of performance art (as with my examples of feminist performances above).[9] In this way, the implicit body might be said to be the disciplined body, the body constrained by its habitus, the body that repetitively reinscribes dispositions, inclinations, and social norms, often, particularly in everyday life, without recourse to self-reflexivity on the part of the subject who enacts it.

Focussing on the habitus allows us to look more closely at the hinge between explicit and implicit embodiment—between a body constrained by habit, disciplines, techniques, or regulatory practices and one driven to expose, violate, trouble, parody, or shatter these constraints. And as such the joining between body and agency. At the very least, this focus shows a range of differences among disparate forms of performative media, with opera and dance—so dependent on formalised movement and pre-mapped choreographies—occupying the far end of the spectrum where the habitus (disciplined body) reigns, and radical performance art (perhaps) occupies the other pole—its conceit often being that it overthrows all norms, often through violent, sexual, or otherwise excessive or unpredictable behaviour.

It may be (surely is) impossible fully to overturn our various forms of habitus, no matter whether sexual, professional, or otherwise. And yet Athey's extreme actions and Snapper's distorted opera body suggest that the context of performance *art* offers possible ways of refusing what Bourdieu called our expected 'conditions of existence,' through embracing the missed timing of 'dispositions ill-adjusted' to existing bodily forms and existing environments.[10] Breaking habits might be one of the most interesting ways to misbehave, producing potentially new modes of embodiment that—at least momentarily—escape the constrictions of the habitus.

O'Reilly's body, in a simpler and far more spare way than the gloriously melodramatic dehabituations enacted in *Judas Cradle*, reminds us of our own 'dispositions ill-adjusted,' in their severe limits and constraints. In these ways, performance art foregrounds embodiment in frameworks that, by definition, dehabituate its movements (there can be nothing 'natural' about even the most mundane or simple action performed under the guise of 'performance art,' particularly not the act of falling in slow motion, naked, down a Victorian stairway at a performance event). By doing so the most evocative of these works reminds us of the most important question that underlies all art making, viewing, and participating: that of how agential forces ripple across and through bodies and spaces to render, in always complex and undecidable ways, meanings and values that can never be fully contained.

1. For those who did not witness the live work, one gets a different, but also interesting, effect and affect from the work by viewing the exquisite photographs by Marco Anelli that were taken during the action. See *Kira O'Reilly: Untitled (Bodies)*, ed. by Harriet Curtis and Martin Hargreaves (London and Bristol: Live Art Development Agency and Intellect, 2018), pp. 10, 136–38; other versions of the piece are also documented (see pp. 140-41).

2. René Descartes, 'Discourse 4', *Discourse on Method and The Meditations*, trans. by F. E. Sutcliffe (Harmondsworth: Penguin, 1998), p. 54.

3. This is Maurice Merleau-Ponty's term for understanding how agency moves through embodiment. See *Phenomenology of Perception* [1945], trans. by Colin Smith (New York and London: Routledge, 2002).

4. See Merleau-Ponty, 'The Intertwining–The Chiasm', in *The Visible and the Invisible* [1964], ed. by Claude Lefort, trans. by Alphonso Lingis (Evanston, IL: Northwestern University Press, 1968), pp. 130–55.

5. Not the least, in this particular case, the overwhelming and megalomaniacal personality of Marina Abramović looming over the Whitworth performance, which was part of Manchester International Festival's *Marina Abramović Presents* at this venue. I write about this problem of subdued, distorted, or oppressed agency (simply put: Abramović dominated the physical experience of the work, as well as the performances of a dozen other major internationally known performance artists included in it because of the framing of it and the fact that she led a 'bootcamp' before one was allowed to see it; correlatively, she also dominates the press accounts and documentation preserving it in history). See my article '"The Artist Is Present": Artistic Re-Enactments and the Impossibility of Presence', *TDR/The Drama Review*, 55.1 (2011), 16–45.

6. On this point, see my book *Seeing Differently: A History and Theory of Identification and the Visual Arts* (New York and London: Routledge, 2012).

7. Marcel Mauss, 'Techniques of the Body' [1934], *Economy and Society*, 2.1 (1973), 70–88. This section on the habitus repeats some of my arguments from 'Habits are hard to break: The habitus and performance,' in the special section co-authored with Marin Blažević in collaboration with soprano Vlatka Oršanić, 'The Voice of Death, Rupturing the Habitus', *Performance Research*, 19.3 (2014), 140–43.

8. Pierre Bourdieu, 'Structures, *Habitus*, Practices' [1980], in *The Logic of Practice*, trans. by Richard Nice (Stanford: Stanford University Press, 1990), pp. 52–65 (p. 61).

9. Rebecca Schneider, *The Explicit Body in Performance* (New York and London: Routledge, 1997), p. 2.

10. Bourdieu, p. 62.

Right: Ron Athey, *Judas Cradle* (2004). Image Manuel Vason.

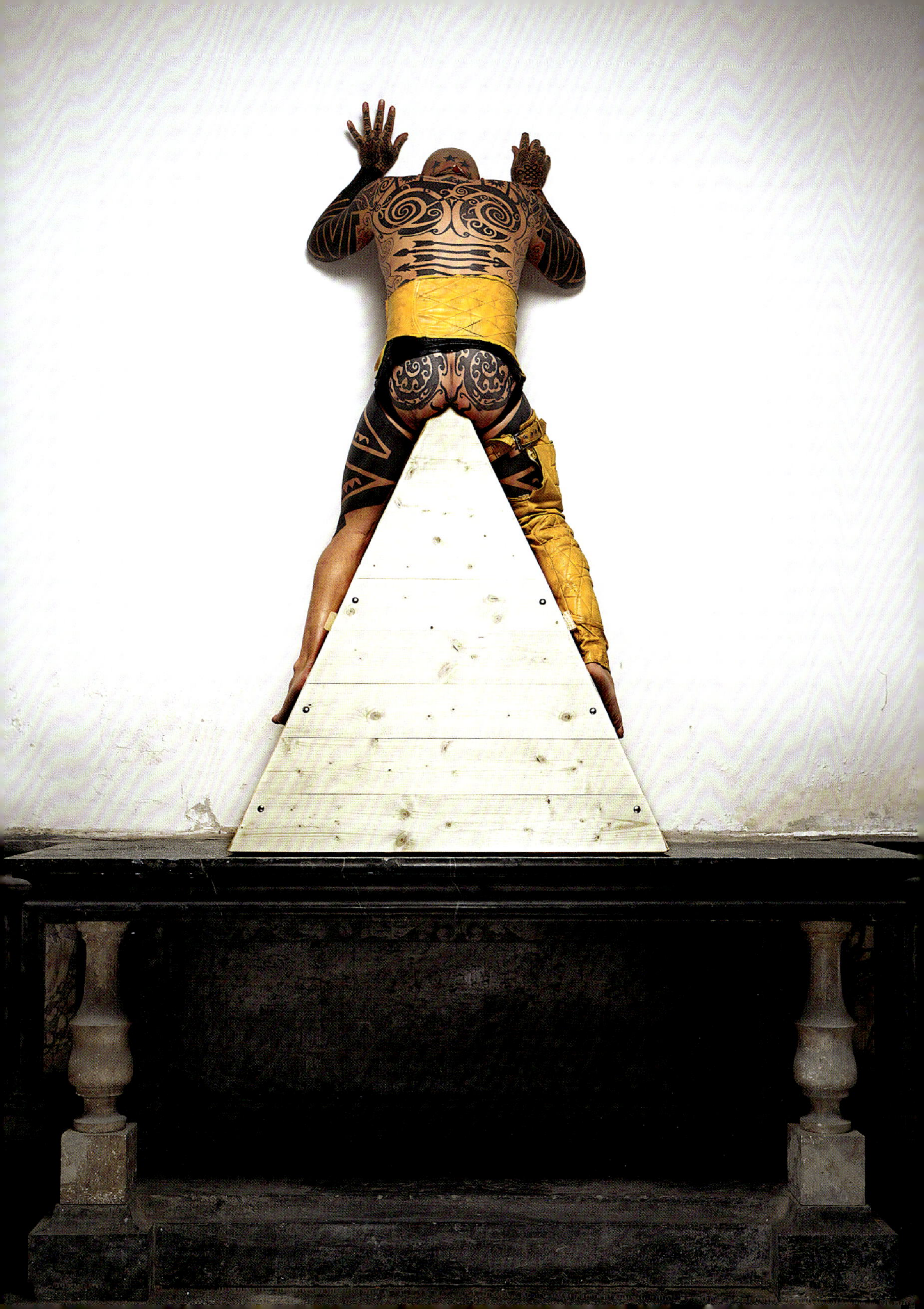

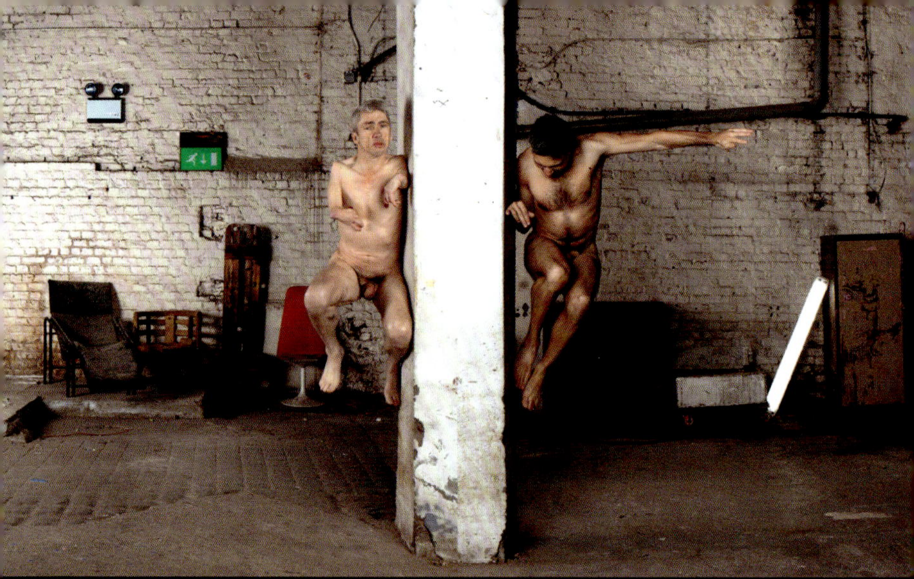

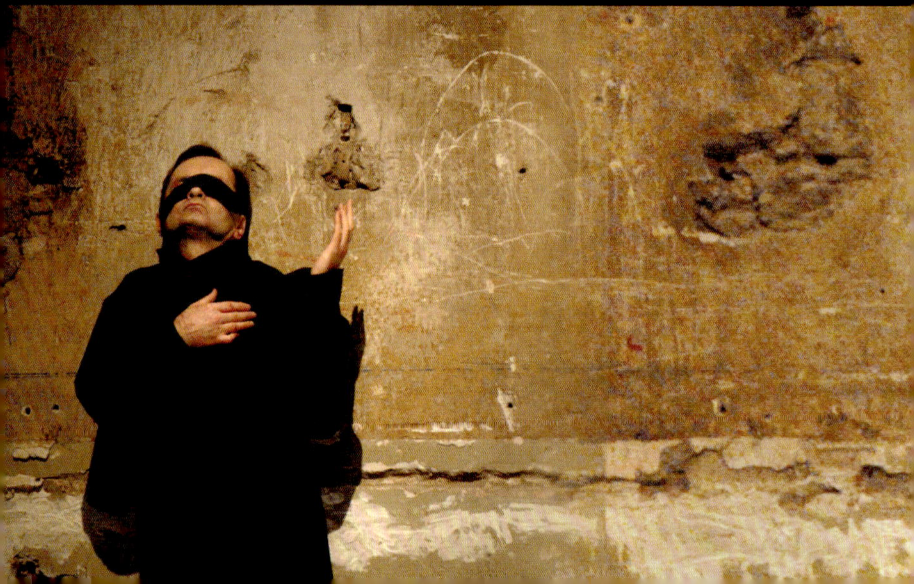

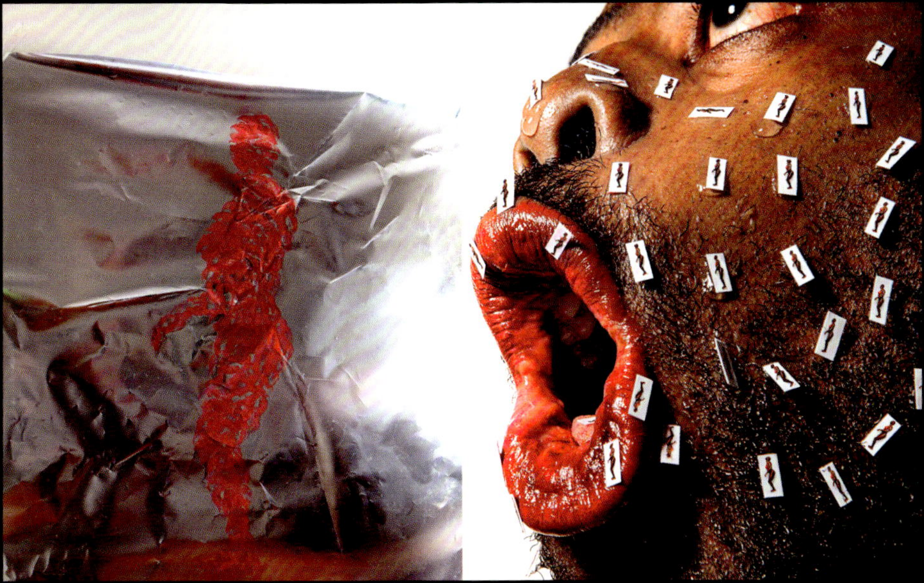

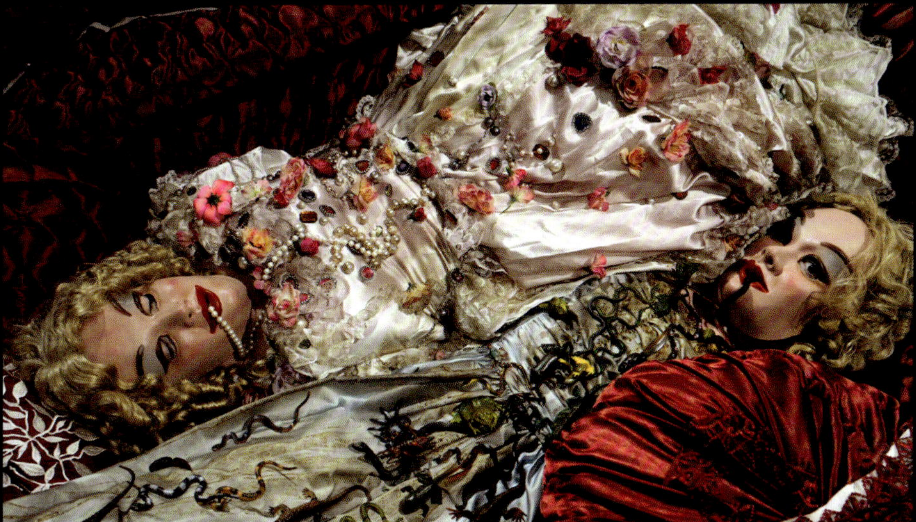

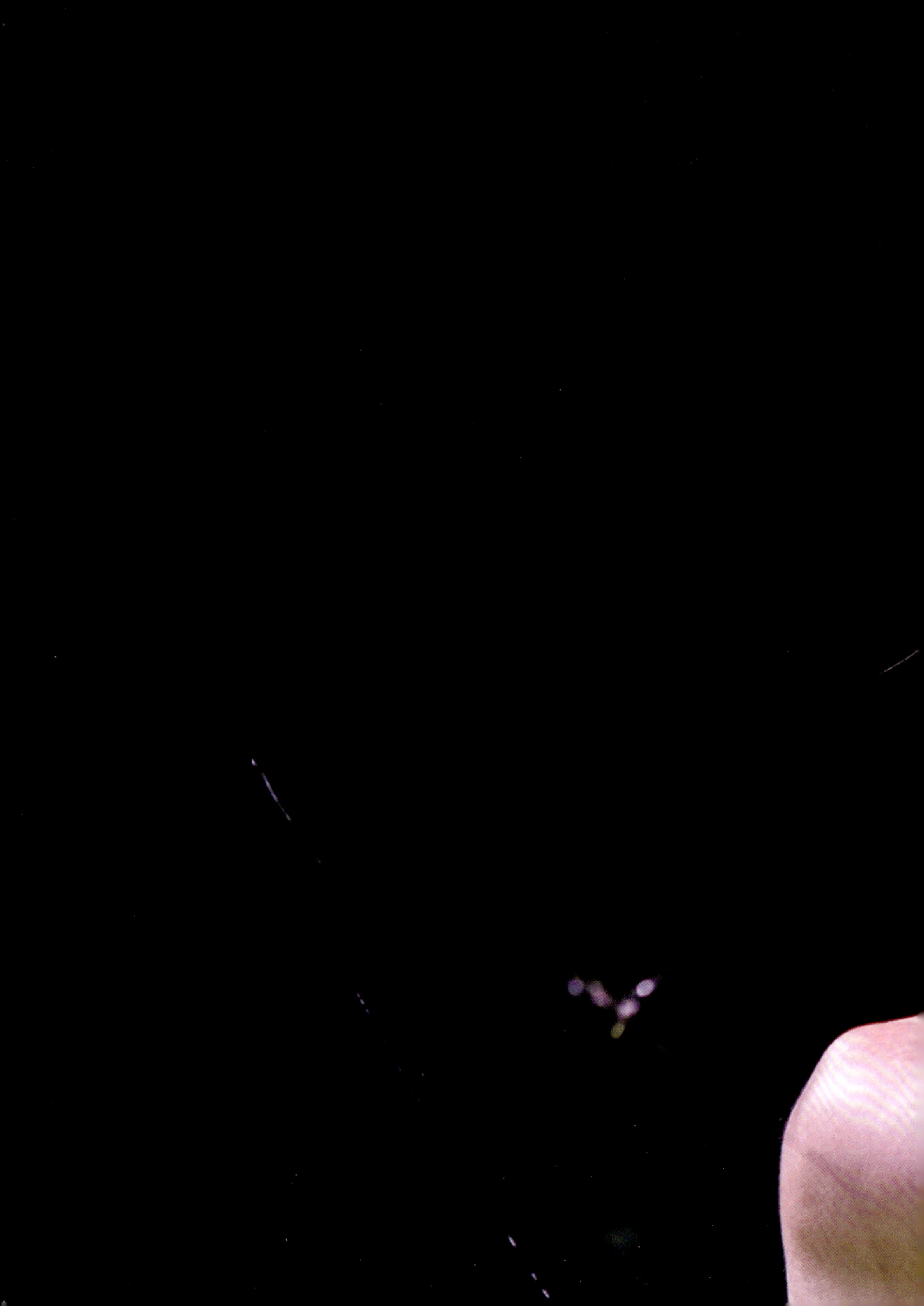

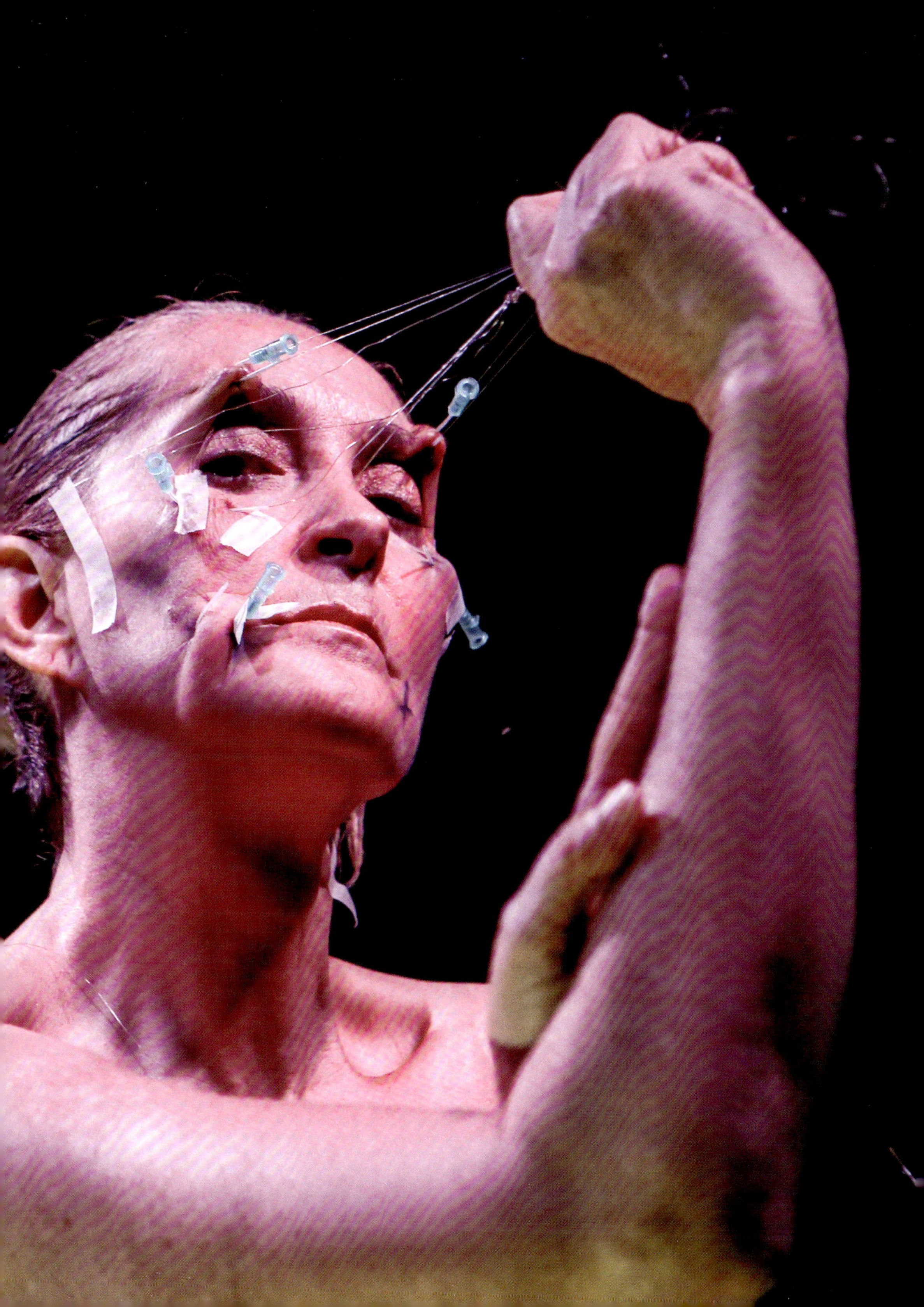

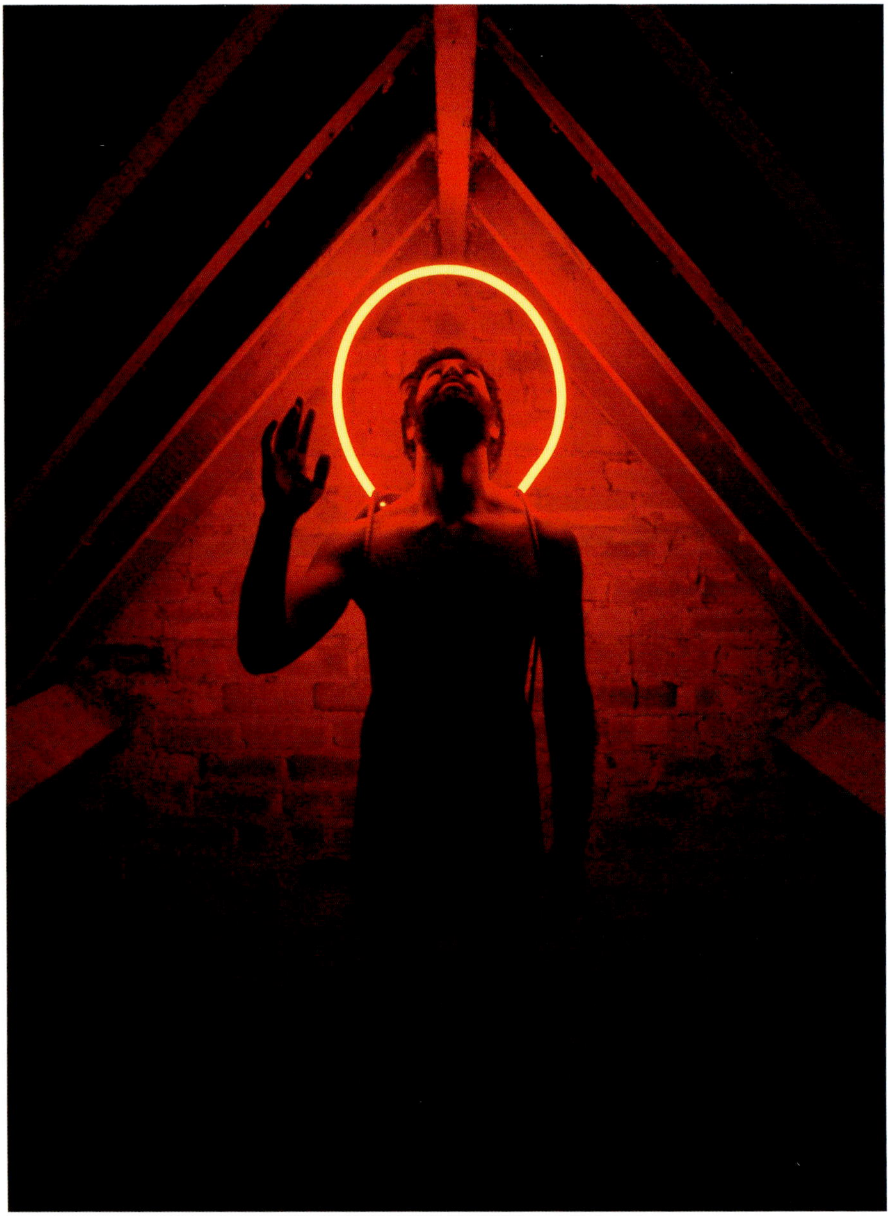

Harminder Singh Judge, *Halo (Prototype)* (2007). Image Charlie Levine.

SPACES

TIM ETCHELLS
ANDY FIELD
REBECCA FRENCH
LESLIE HILL
JOHN E. MCGRATH
ANDREW MOTTERSHEAD
HAYLEY NEWMAN
HELEN PARIS
HEIKE ROMS
JOHANNA TUUKKANEN

SPACES

If you want to look at the 'root' of LADA's radicality, suggests Hayley Newman in one of the following conversations, it is in the theatre: literally, LADA emerged from the theatre space at the ICA (Institute of Contemporary Arts). Lois Keidan and Catherine Ugwu's time at the ICA in the 1990s, along with Alan Read running its Talks programme, was a rich period of artistic activity, as Helen Paris and Leslie Hill recall, with the ICA providing a centre for sharing and finding solidarity with like-minded artists. In making a move out of theatre—and out of the gallery—Live Art enacts a dislocation that is conceptual as well as physical, re-inscribing itself into other environments, communities, and economies.

For some, this move out of conventional spaces is a liberating one: in this section, Andy Field describes the way that Forest Fringe's separation from the existing mechanics of the Edinburgh Festival Fringe 'allowed us to exist outside of the financial, and also the aesthetic, conventions of the Fringe.' But, he continues, no space is empty of 'meaning, politics, and history.' John McGrath expands this point in his provocation: 'no space is neutral … the power dynamics running through any space will always be part of the meaning of an event that happens in that space.'

Several of the artists in this section describe their approaches to the challenge of responding to these new circumstances: 'each form, each context, each location means you have to think differently,' remarks Tim Etchells. Sometimes these are subtle, almost invisible insinuations, as with French & Mottershead's 'microperformances', or they are ambiguous provocations, as with Etchells' neon signs that might appear in public spaces. Others are more forceful interventions, such as Guillermo Gómez-Peña's unsettling presence in a regional airport in Finland (as part of Johanna Tuukkanen's ANTI festival); or the occupation of the Turbine Hall in Tate Modern by Liberate Tate (described by Hayley Newman), one of a series of actions that contributed to oil company BP ending their branding/sponsorship agreement with the Tate.

One way of tracking Live Art's relationship to spaces and places is through the literal itinerary of the Live Art Development Agency itself, through the four different premises it has occupied in the twenty years of its existence.[1] Keidan and Ugwu's 1998 proposal for funding to the Arts Council cited director Ritsaert ten Cate's declaration that 'Theatrical space begins in the mind,' and they quoted his call for 'a space, and a climate, for creativity.'[2] Upon receiving funding, LADA's first incarnation was nothing more than an office with a desk in the former Truman's Brewery, located off Brick Lane in London's East End. After Ugwu left and Daniel Brine joined Keidan as Associate Director, they quickly outgrew this space, particularly as a result of beginning to collect materials donated by artists. These materials formed the beginnings of LADA's Study Room, a dedicated space made possible by the Agency's move to the former Rochelle School on Arnold Circus. The landlord's vision for this site was to create a cultural hub, such that LADA shared the location with fashion and graphic designers, but after twelve years they were priced out of the increasingly fashionable location.[3]

The 2012 Olympic Games in London, and the concurrent re-development of the Hackney Wick/Stratford area of London, were the backdrop for LADA's next move, to The White Building, a strategic development run by Space Studios under the auspices of the London Legacy Development Corporation (LLDC). Up against the Lea River, this felt like the frontier of gentrification, initially abundant with independent galleries, artist squats and studios—for a time, a nearby warehouse was home to the fiercely uncompromising]performance s p a c e[. Again facing rising rents, in 2017 LADA moved nearer to its original, more central location at The Garrett Centre in Bethnal Green, renting from the Unitarian foundation. This present location makes for an unusual alliance, but Keidan describes a feeling of shared progressive values with LADA's new landlord, and depicts their partnership as symptomatic of the kinds of surprising alliances made necessary by times of crisis.[4] Its vaulted ceilings and stained-glass windows provide a striking setting for LADA's collection of large-print photographs of radical bodies, and there is increased room for the ever-growing Study Room collection. Significantly, in recent years LADA has started describing itself as 'A Centre for Live Art', and there is something of a consolidation of resources, as well as a return from the city's margins, that this move represents.

At the same time as LADA has been circling around East London, Live Art has circulated around the UK and beyond. The National Review of Live Art—which began in Nottingham in 1979 as Performance Platform, and moved to Glasgow from 1986 until its final iteration in 2011[5]—made Glasgow a (nearly) annual site of activity, as many of the contributors to this collection recall. Other centres of activity have included Dartington College of Arts in Devon; Fierce in Birmingham; In Between Time and the Arnolfini in Bristol; Chapter Arts Centre in Cardiff; SPILL Festival of Performance, initially in London before establishing residency in Ipswich; Forest Fringe, initially based in Edinburgh but increasingly working internationally;

Opposite clockwise from top left: Trumans Brewery, Brick Lane. Rochelle School. Image Dreamstime and A Foundation; The White Building, Hackney Wick. Image Will Pryce; The Garrett Centre. Image Amy Poole.

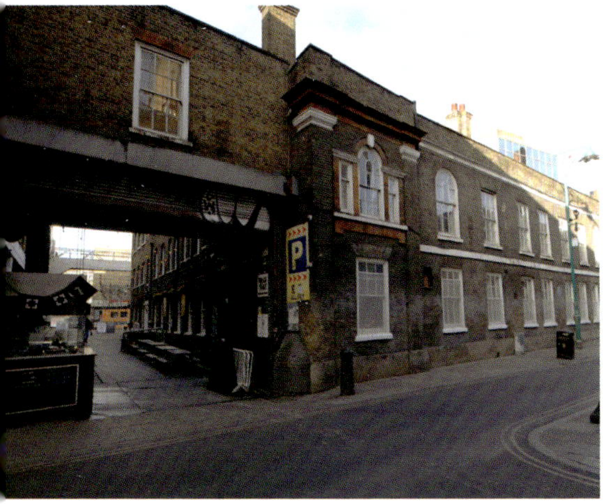

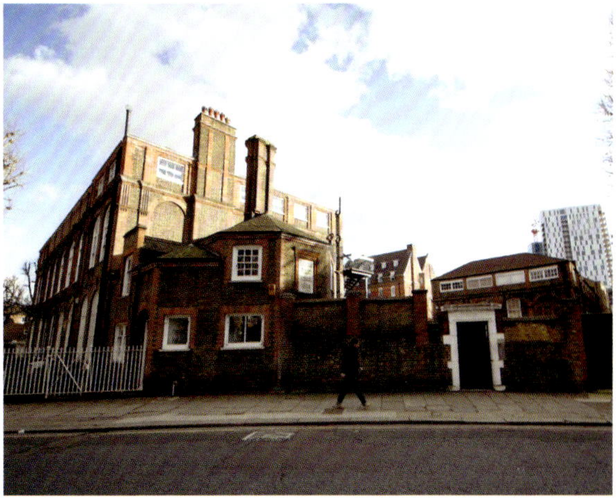

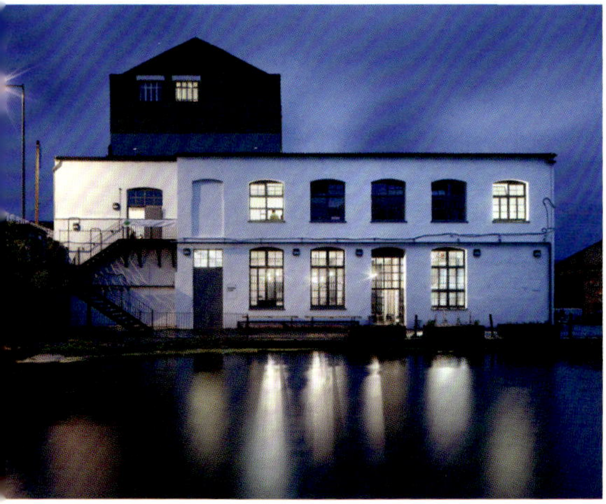

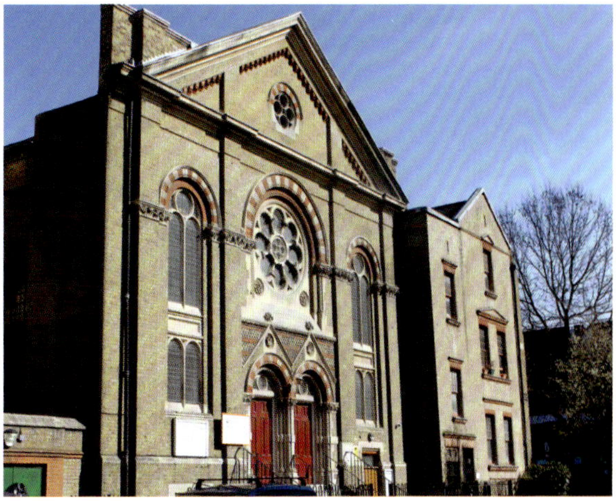

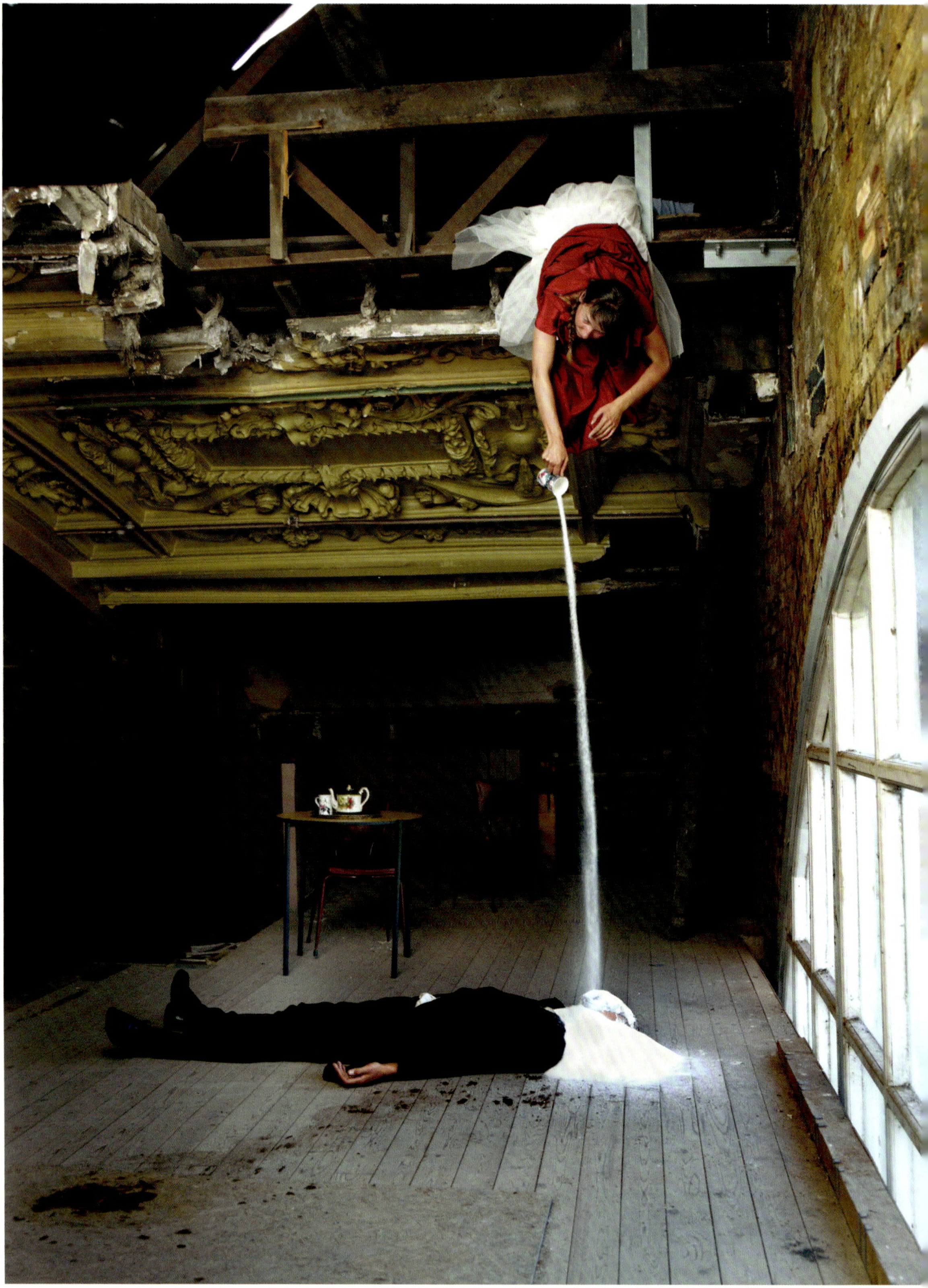

National Theatre Wales; Contact, hÅb, and Manchester International Festival in Manchester; Bluecoat (Liverpool); Colchester Arts Centre; Lancaster Arts; Compass Live Art and Live Art Bistro in Leeds; Wunderbar in Newcastle;]performance s p a c e[in Folkestone; BUZZCUT in Glasgow; and in London, Artsadmin, Steakhouse Live, Battersea Arts Centre, Duckie/Royal Vauxhall Tavern, LIFT; and others that continue to emerge.

Many of these organisations are part of the Live Art UK network, formed in 2003 and coordinated by LADA, which has facilitated links between different parts of the country. Individual members of Live Art UK have also undertaken initiatives that are concerned with supporting places and spaces for Live Art: LADA's publication *Programme Notes* (2007) compiled 'case studies of locating experimental theatre'; Lancaster Arts convened a 2012 symposium that strategised approaches to touring Live Art practices; and, building on the multinational collaboration Up To Nature, In Between Time explored questions of Live Art in the public realm.[6] These initiatives have resulted in Live Art practices that have manifest far from the centres of culture and power: a collaboration between LADA and Disability Arts in Shropshire (DASH) led to the *M21* weekend in the medieval town of Much Wenlock, a London 2012 Cultural Olympiad commission that included, amongst other things, The Disabled Avant Garde appearing as their satirical versions of the Olympic mascots;[7] and LADA also facilitated a Live Art programme as part of Heart of Glass, a ten-year project for St Helens, one of the most disadvantaged areas in the UK.[8] Beyond these strategic partnerships have been countless initiatives by individual artists responding to site, landscape, and environment. Supported by LADA's DIY workshop scheme (discussed more fully in the 'Communities' section of this collection), for example, Zierle & Carter took participants to the very edge of Cornwall; French & Mottershead led a Live Art camping trip; and artists such as Richard Layzell, Lorena Rivero de Beer, and Rajni Shah took peripatetic explorations of urban spaces.[9]

But at the same time as Live Art practices have sought inspiration and intervention in dispersal and dislocation—'a sense of critical distance', as Heike Roms describes in her provocation—there has been an interest in returning to sites of power. This is a challenge Tim Etchells poses to the Forest Fringe generation in his conversation with Andy Field: the ambition to occupy significant cultural spaces. LADA's *Live Culture* programme for Tate Modern (2003) (discussed in the next section on 'Institutions') remains a touchstone example of this, with its iconic images of Oleg Kulik's human mirror ball, or Franko B's painted and bleeding body, rewriting the rules of what kinds of actions happen in

Left: Paul Carter, Alexandra Zierle and Manuel Vason, *Becoming An Image* (2010). Image Manuel Vason.

one of London's most visited public spaces. This spirit continues in more recent LADA projects at the Tate, such as collaborations with Sibylle Peters in *Playing Up* (2016), a Live Art game launched with a three-day 'Play-In' in Tate Modern's Turbine Hall that re-imagined Live Art works as ways to bring together children and adults, and *KAPUTT: The Academy of Destruction* (2017) that assembled transgenerational teams of investigators to explore the theme of destruction in art;[10] or in artist residencies in the Reading Room of the popular Wellcome Collection.[11] Live Art is no longer only found in the most radical spaces, but is finding ways to occupy the most mainstream of places as well. As the conversations in this collection address, this shift might feel radical, welcome, subversive, or simply inevitable.

1. This is a journey that Lois Weaver traces very evocatively in her contribution to the later section of this collection on 'Communities'.

2. Ritsaert ten Cate, 'A Home for Working and Living', in *Theaterschrift*, 2 ('The Written Space'), ed. by Vertaalbureau Deceuninck and Martine Bom (1992), 48–57 (p. 48). Original LADA funding proposal provided to the author.

3. *Frieze* magazine moved into the complex just before LADA left, and Keidan recalls the nearby grand opening of the cynically named Avantgarde Tower, an uninspiring 25-storey property development (where a 2-bedroom flat recently sold for £1.75 million), the same day that LADA moved out of Shoreditch.

4. Keidan says, 'In a way, we do similar things but in very different ways. Ultimately, LADA are all about supporting underrepresented artists, practices and histories, looking at the dispossessed and the disempowered. And the Unitarians are really pioneering in terms of feminism, social justice and gay rights.' Lydia Ashman, 'Live Art Development Agency: New Space Provides a Context for Collaboration', *a-n The Artists Information Company* [2017] <https://www.a-n.co.uk/news/live-art-development-agency-new-space-provides-context-collaboration>.

5. See Deirdre Heddon, 'National Review of Live Art: The 30th Edition', *Contemporary Theatre Review*, 20.3 (2010), 386–88; *The National Review of Live Art 1979–2010: A Personal History (Essays, Anecdotes, Drawings and Images)*, ed. by Deirdre Heddon, Jennie Klein, and Nikki Milican (Glasgow: New Moves International, 2010).

6. *Programme Notes: Case Studies for Locating Experimental Theatre*, ed. by Daniel Brine and Lois Keidan (London: Live Art Development Agency, 2007); *Getting It Out There: The Future of Touring and Distribution for Contemporary Theatre and Live Art*, ed. by Mary Paterson and Theron Schmidt (Lancaster and London: Live at LICA and Live Art UK, 2013) <http://www.liveartuk.org/uploads/documents/giot.pdf>; *I See a Fake Moon Rising: Live Art in the Public Realm*, ed. by Maddy Costa (Bristol: Live Art UK and In Between Time, 2013) <http://www.liveartuk.org/uploads/documents/ibt_lauk_publication_website.pdf>.

7. DASH (Disability Arts in Shropshire) and Live Art Development Agency, *M21: From the Medieval to the 21st Century* (London: Live Art Development Agency, 2012).

8. See *Praxis Vol 1: Of People, Place & Time*, ed. by Chrissie Tiller and Patrick Fox (St Helens and London: Heart of Glass and Live Art Development Agency, 2017).

9. Zierle and Carter, 'At the edge of the land, of practice, and of knowing' [2012], <http://www.thisisliveart.co.uk/opportunities/at-the-edge-of-the-land-of-practice-and-of-knowing/>; FrenchMottershead, 'Live Art Campers!' [2007], <http://www.thisisliveart.co.uk/opportunities/diy-4-live-art-campers-north-west/>; Richard Layzell, 'Deprivation and Overload' [2002], <http://www.thisisliveart.co.uk/opportunities/diy-2002-call-for-participant>; Lorena Rivero de Beer, 'Exercises to Activate the Political Imagination of the City Wanderer' [2009], <http://www.thisisliveart.co.uk/opportunities/diy-6-lorena-rivero-de-beer-exercises-to-activate-the-political-imagination/>; Rajni Shah, 'Not Knowing' [2009], <http://www.thisisliveart.co.uk/opportunities/diy-6-rajni-shah-not-knowing/>.

10. Sibylle Peters, *Playing Up: A Live Art Game for Kids and Adults* (London: Live Art Development Agency, 2016). See also <http://www.thisisliveart.co.uk/projects/playing-up-live-art-for-kids-adults/>.

11. See <http://www.thisisliveart.co.uk/projects/the-residents/>.

SPACES
CONVERSATION
TIM ETCHELLS
ANDY FIELD
DATE
23 DECEMBER 2015
PLACE
LONDON

Tim Etchells has worked in a wide variety of contexts, notably as leader of the world-renowned performance group Forced Entertainment and in collaboration with a range of visual artists, choreographers, and photographers. His work spans performance, video, photography, text projects, installation and fiction. Some of the projects that are referenced in this conversation include *Quizoola!* (1996), a durational performance by Forced Entertainment (lasting six or twenty-four hours, depending on its presentation), in which performers take turns interrogating each other from a stack of some 2000 questions ranging from the banal to the deeply personal; and Etchells' ongoing series of neon sign works, displayed in interior and exterior sites, that consist of ambiguous phrases such as 'Wait here I have gone to get help' (*Wait Here*, 1996), 'We wanted to be the sky' appearing on the London skyline (*We Wanted*, 2011), or 'All we have is words / All we have is worlds' (*All We Have (Double Line)*, Athens 2016). Tim is one of LADA's Patrons and has contributed to numerous LADA projects throughout the years. From 2008–2013 he was one of the recipients (along with Anne Bean) of the LADA/Tate *Legacy: Thinker In Residence* awards, out of which he created the publication *While You Are With Us Here Tonight* (2013), published by LADA.

Andy Field is one of the directors of Forest Fringe, founded by Deborah Pearson in 2007, which created an alternative performance space in the context of the Edinburgh Festival Fringe, as Andy discusses here. Forest Fringe has since helped produce events throughout the UK and internationally, including events in Beijing, Guangzhou, Hong Kong, Jakarta, Melbourne, Seoul Shanghai, and Toronto, and is a member of the Live Art UK network. With Forest Fringe, Andy and Deborah created *Paper Stages* (LADA and Live Art UK, 2013), a set of instructions for action described as 'a festival of performance contained within the pages of a beautifully designed book'. The book cannot be purchased with money; instead, readers are asked to donate an hour of their time. Under his own name, Andy also creates interactive, site-responsive projects for theatres, warehouses, carparks, and streets. Andy led the DIY workshop *STEAL THIS WORKSHOP* (2014).

Tim: I think everybody builds up their own repertoire of pieces that are, in a sense, a map of the territory, a way of steering their own practice. Certain works stay with you as a kind of touchstone: an object you carry with you to remind yourself of what's possible, what might be at the core of something, what the sharpest articulation of something might be. I can think of performances I saw in the 1980s and 1990s, but also things that I didn't see: Chris Burden's *Shoot* or Tehching Hsieh's work. When I think about works like these, or Alastair MacLennan's work or Ron Athey's work, they have a kind of core simplicity or extremity within them. They are a reminder of how powerful something can be when you go right to the heart of something.

But I also did an interview with Gary Stevens in the 1980s, and I remember he talked about different kinds of risk. He said there's the risk of nailing yourself to a Volkswagen, but there's the risk of making work that involves playing with cuddly toys, which he'd just done in a piece called *Animal*. The risk was that you look ridiculous. That has stayed with me as a reminder that not everything has to be pain and suffering, and that there might be other ways to get to the heart of something!

With Forced Entertainment, we began as a theatre company in the unusual position that we didn't really like theatre, and have had little to do with the culture of 'plays' and 'playwriting'. The connection we had was more to other forms of live entertainment—cabaret, stand-up, music, or residual forms like vaudeville , and the way those things had been articulated into television in the 1970s and 1980s. We were also gripped by other public performance forms—media events like the press conference or public enquiries. Of course we're not the only people who were busy with these kinds of things, and this approach—through dislodging the play—has become a prevalent way of thinking about what a live practice might be. Thinking away from theatre proper gives you access to different kinds of structures, or ways of thinking about composition. But also it allows a different relation to audience. A different kind of contact.

Andy: Different forms can pluralise the potential meanings of what's happening on stage. I've been thinking about [Forced Entertainment's] *Quizoola!*, and how it's possible—not only possible, but quite interesting—to watch two people on a stage asking each other questions for six hours. Although their positions are relatively static, the meanings of their relationship, and our relationship to them, are constantly rotating—from quiz show, to police interrogation, to just Tim and Terry

[O'Connor] asking each other questions. It's like you're watching a ballet of different circumstances and situations taking place within just the tone or inflection of someone's voice. That's only possible because you've manifested this space where the meaning of a person on stage has all of these possibilities latent within it.

And I think about the same thing when I see work that bears that influence. It doesn't need to be explicitly influenced by cabaret, vaudeville, or any of those forms of popular entertainment, but I see that slipperiness, that plurality of possible meanings, in Deborah Pearson's *The Future Show*, for example, or Christopher Brett-Bailey's work. It feels like they're able to do something really interesting because they are the inheritors of the space you've created for them—and other artists working in similar ways.

Tim: At the same time, we weren't making stand-up or making vaudeville, but we were also influenced by epic European theatre—sometimes directly, but usually by a kind of rumour or broken telephone process. I don't think we'd ever seen Pina Bausch, for example, except for one videotape—but we had seen Impact Theatre, and *they'd* seen Pina Bausch. So it was a meeting of cultural forms, and our ambition was to draw on one to make the other.

Andy: My own reference point was when I was 18 years old and went to see the National Student Drama Festival, which seems like it should be an unlikely place to have your first encounter with Live Art. But someone there was a big fan of Dartington, and so there was this regular trickle of Dartington work that used to appear alongside, say, Leeds University doing *Macbeth*. While I was there I saw a company called Deer Park, which was Augusto Corrieri, Sven Steinhauser, and others. I'd never seen anything like this. I had no frame of reference for how to watch it, but amidst all these conventions of narrative theatre, this seemed, as you were saying, to be getting to the heart of something—even if I couldn't quite articulate what it was.

Then I ended up doing the MA in Text and Performance with Alan Read at King's College London the first year that he ran it. And everything that Alan did felt like it was trying to transcend the notion that you had to set yourself in opposition to institutions, and instead seemed to be about occupying and insinuating yourself into the place of the other—a kind of [Michel] de Certeau approach. So Alan had us literally squatting in the disused Anatomy Theatre at King's. They said you couldn't use it, and we had a classroom assigned to us somewhere else in the building, but he taught the classes there anyway. And the same thing could be said of the relationship he intended us to have with RADA [*the MA was a joint offering between King's and RADA*]. Alan seemed to be providing us with the necessary tools to be able to engage with the totems of the theatre world from within, to queer them and transform them, rather than having to define ourselves in opposition.

Forest Fringe emerged directly out of that course, because the first year of Forest Fringe in 2007 was Debbie's [*Forest Fringe founder Deborah Pearson's*] final project for that MA. And you can see Alan's influence in a very real and direct sense: in the same way that we were almost squatting in King's, or insinuating ourselves into the conventions and structures of somewhere like RADA, we arrived at the Edinburgh Festival with a similar approach. Not an opposition, but that we're going to try to get inside of this thing and see what we can do from there. Having our own space allowed us to exist outside of the financial, and also the aesthetic, conventions of the Fringe. The space really demanded it, because it was such a gloriously unwieldy, very visible space. You couldn't operate under the illusion that this space was empty. It was full of meaning, politics, and history, and also full of the people who were there watching, and you couldn't escape from them.

Tim: Within the work of Forced Entertainment, there's always been an interest in the established theatrical relation of auditorium and stage, and we've done so much to explore that as an experience, as a mechanism, as a structure. But alongside that there have been strands of our work that were trying to challenge that theatrical bottom-line, particularly in terms of time. From 1993 we did the first durational piece, twelve hours of *12am: Awake & Looking Down* at the ICA in London. And that piece emerged directly from our having seen artists like Alastair MacLennan at the National Review of Live Art, where he was doing 36-hour pieces in the gallery. Seeing that work shifted the ground for us.

So within the company's work there were always projects that tried, in a way, to step outside of the usual theatre economy. And alongside that, as a solo maker, I have always been working in different media—writing, or making photos or video works, or making posters and neon signs. The desire in all of that work is to invent another relation to audience, as you were saying. The nice thing about installing a neon text-work in a street, is that it demands a different kind of attention from the viewer. Those works intersect with daily life. They interrupt the city, speak into public space. I really like the idea of any cultural artefact—a text in a book, a poster, a neon sign, a video—as an object that can construct a relation with you. That process doesn't involve the live presence of performers, but it does activate the viewer in a way that's analogous to the processes that go on in a performance. There's a triangulation, a negotiation between the object of the performance and the audience, and a negotiation between the diverse people gathered in a particular audience. For me, a written text in a book does a similar thing to a reader—there's an active performative moment in reading, the same with a neon piece in the street or a video.

So making work in the frame of visual art has been an opportunity to step outside of the economy that I've normally been working in.

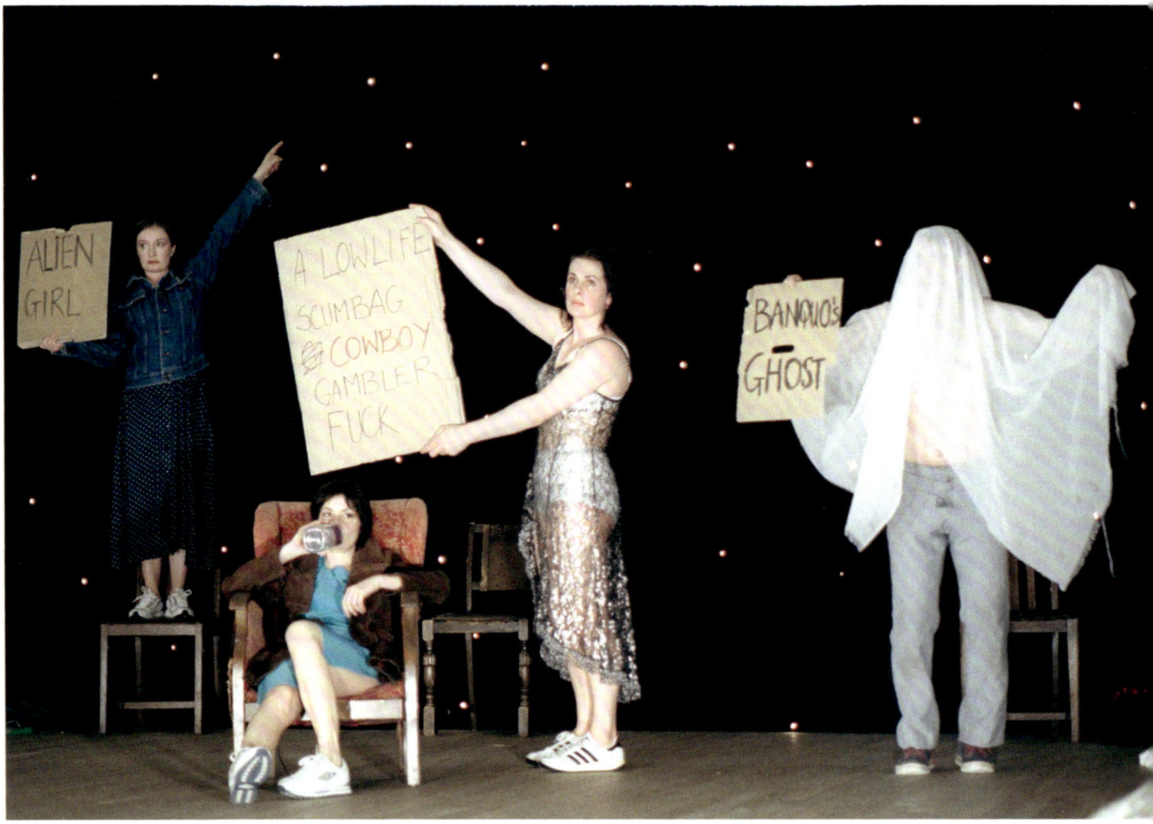
ALIEN
GIRL
A LOWLIFE
SCUMBAG
COWBOY
GAMBLER
FUCK
BANQUO'S
GHOST

I guess the other important thing to say about that work—differentiating it from theatre practice—is to say that it doesn't involve the circulation of human beings. Forced Entertainment has been touring its work since 1984—30-plus years of constantly being on a bus or a plane or a train. What we always say about performances is that we get paid for not being at home! There's no money in being at home: what we can earn from performances in Sheffield we can live on for a couple of days! So as much as people talk about Forced Entertainment's relationship to Sheffield, which is obviously very important in terms of the works, we're an itinerant group at heart. We're migrant workers, basically. Travellers.

Andy: Rachel Chavkin from the TEAM calls their process 'aggressively inefficient'. And I suppose one of the things that interested me in the book project *Paper Stages* was an interest in what the meaning of a book might be in an era where that's no longer the most efficient way of sharing information. What does a book mean? What does the physical object mean? It's similar to the aggressive inefficiency of theatre and performance, where the inefficiencies or restrictions that are implicit are part of its virtue. I think the same is true for a book.

I describe *Paper Stages* as 'a festival disguised as a book,' and it consists of scores or instructions for its reader to perform. But even before you open it, another thing I was trying to do was undermine the notion of exchange. For example, we say 'this book costs one hour', in the same way you might say this book costs £10—but once you to start to unpick it, the whole thing unravels, because we're not checking that you've done your hour. The exchange that's necessitated you to get the book appears to be a monetary exchange, but reveals itself actually to be an act of performance. It's an invitation, a provocation. So before you've even started to read the book, you've been gulled into participating in its circulation of performances.

Left: Forced Entertainment, *12am: Awake & Looking Down* (2003). Image Hugo Glendinning.

Tim: I think this thing about pulling people into an act of participation of a certain kind is really critical. As Forced Entertainment, it's something that we've worked with a lot in the space of performance. And much of the work that I've done alone works on a similar principle. If you read the neon sign, 'Wait here I have gone to get help,' you're immediately in a narrative. Who is this 'I' who has gone to get help? Where have they gone? Will I wait?

Andy: One of the things I've taken from Live Art and performance art, and from Alan, is the very opposite of Peter Brook, in some ways. He says, 'All you need is an empty space,' but actually, you need the very opposite of an empty space. For me, pulling people into those acts of theatre is at its most effective when it doesn't happen in these kind of autonomous, restricted spaces, but when it happens at unexpected moments, when it feels like it's not constrained.

Tim: I have a positive relation to restriction. To me, making any art work, any communication is about understanding (or trying to understand) the nature of the restrictions that are in operation. What is a book? What can a book do? What can't a book do? That set of conditions are restrictive, because the book is not a car, and it's not a park or a performance. But if you understand what a book is, could be, has been, then maybe you can bend it or open the form out in a different way.

I think the same about theatre with its hugely problematic spaces, and all their histories and politics and assumptions. Those things are a hideous restriction—and at the same time, they are the things you have to work with when you're working in theatre. The gallery is the same to me. It's a frame. It's a set of expectations, conditions, and so on. A café is also something different and a bus is something different, and each form, each context, each location means you have to think differently. In a way it's a quite performative understanding of what anything is, which is to say as a performer one's instincts to understand a space are to stand in it and to try to physically feel what the dynamics of the room are. Where in this room do you want to stand? If you want to be watched, where do you need to be? How do you focus attention in this space?

Andy: That sense of pragmatism, trying to understand the conditions and constraints expectations that you're working in, has been really essential to the way that Forest Fringe has started to travel around the world. We've done a lot of work in Asia recently, in China, Japan, Korea, Hong Kong, and Bangkok. Probably it's just luck, with one gig leading to another. But I've also been trying to think about why it is that our work is invited there specifically. I think there is something to do with the currency of the immediacy of the encounter, and the scale. A lot of the things we are doing are operating on a more intimate, low-fi mode of production, a kind of anti-spectacle.

We were in Shanghai, where there is an architectural scale that seems almost deliberately designed to disenfranchise you, to make you feel insignificant. And within that, because of the fact that we're placing so much care and value on such seemingly insignificant activities, there's a sense in which perhaps we are nurturing an agency, an alternative means of production. We're imbuing intimacy with a cultural value that perhaps acts in opposition to the currency of spectacle and scale that seems to be so prevalent in those places.

Tim: That's interesting. What interests me is how you can work within a big, significant cultural space, and still do that work with attention and focus. Can you

Right: Tim Etchells, *Look Away* (lino cut print), work for LADA 15th Anniversary Editions (2014).

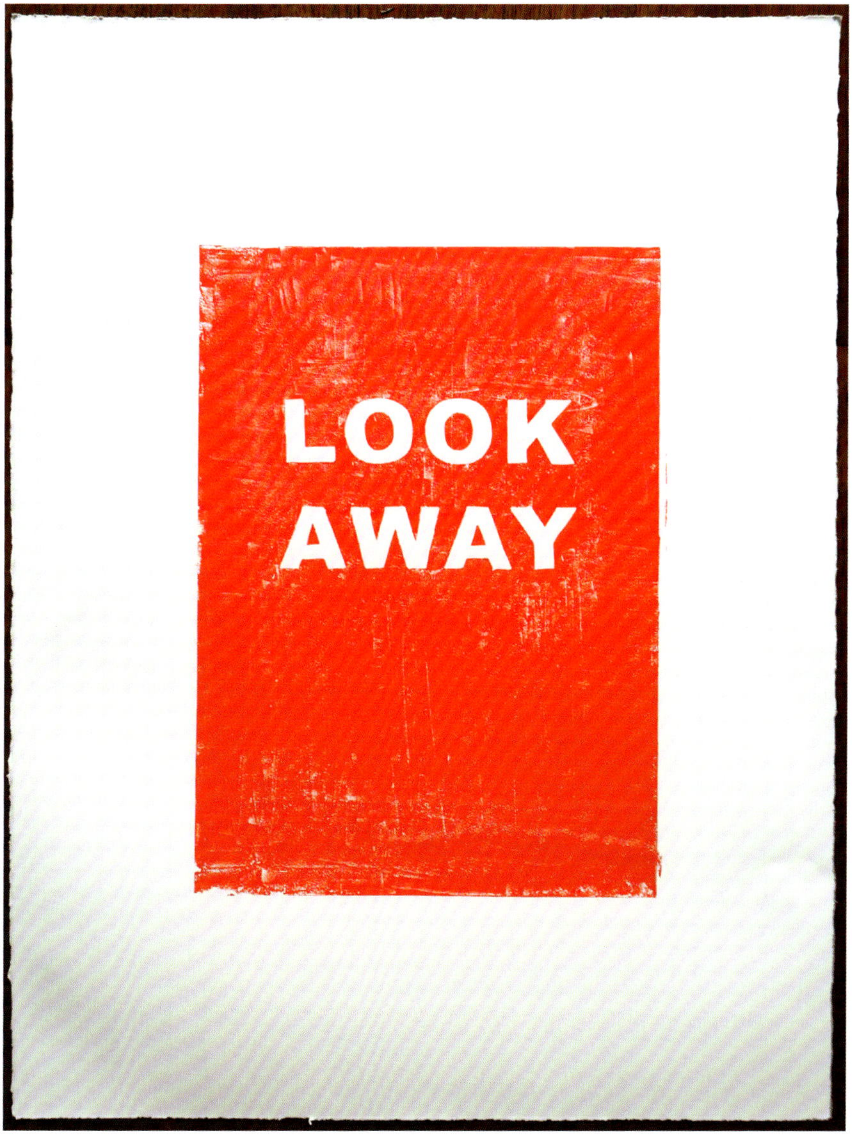
LOOK
AWAY

work in an opera house and still be working in this sort of way? It's a generational question for me, because I grew up seeing work on big stages, whereas with the Forest Fringe generation, I wonder, where is that ambition?

The other thing that's possible, of course, is that, from a radical point of view, perhaps these big cultural spaces are finished. Because they're too much in this zone of spectacle. But I'm curious if there's way of being in such spaces that reinvents them, or approaches them in a different way?

Andy: Maybe it's the same as with books—that publishing becomes interesting at the moment at which it feels like it's totally redundant, and has to be imbued with new meanings. Maybe these huge spaces, at their point of redundancy, are ready to be reimagined and to have new meanings attached to them.

SPACES

CONVERSATION

LESLIE HILL AND
HELEN PARIS (CURIOUS)

JOHANNA TUUKKANEN

DATE

01 FEBRUARY 2016

PLACE

CALIFORNIA & KUOPIO

Creating performance together as Curious, Leslie Hill and Helen Paris have produced over 50 projects in a range of disciplines including performance, installation, publication, and film. Their projects are often research-led and involve collaborations that draw on experts in various areas, as well as the lived experiences of participants and audiences, including: truckstop waitresses, biological scientists, political refugees, occularists, nuclear weapons experts, sex workers, old folks' social groups, and lost property workers. Their project *On the Scent* (2003), which they describe here, approached the relationship between smell and memory from a variety of perspectives, and has toured to 14 different countries (including the ANTI festival in Kuopio). Both Leslie and Helen were recipients of One-to-One Artist Bursaries, and Curious has had a very long relationship with LADA, including contributions to East End Collaborations; *Live Culture* at the Tate (where Leslie gave a plenary address); *Performing Rights*; and the DIY workshops *Autobiology* (2008) and *Private Keep Out* (2016), the latter of which led to the publication *The Artist's Borderpanic Compendium* (LADA, 2018) supported by a DIY Progression grant.

As she describes here, Johanna Tuukkanen founded the ANTI Festival in Kuopio, Finland, in 2002. Dedicated exclusively to work presented in public space, ANTI has become one of the key opportunities for artists working in Live Art, site-responsive work, and other forms of experimental practice. ANTI Festival has also participated in international collaborations for presenting site-responsive work, including *A Space for Live Art* (with New Moves International, Glasgow; Les Halles, Brussels; Les Subsistances, Lyon; Kampnagel, Hamburg; City of Women, Ljubljana; and Accion Mad, Madrid); *Up To Nature* (with Black Box Teater, Oslo; brut wien, Vienna; In Between Time, Bristol; and Maska, Ljubljana); and *Future DiverCities—Creativity in an Urban Context* (2016–2020). In 2014 ANTI launched the ANTI Festival International Prize for Live Art, the only international prize for Live Art.

Helen: I want to start by thinking about agency before the Live Art Development Agency—that is, the agency being offered to Live Art and live artists by Lois Keidan through her work at the ICA [Institute of Contemporary Arts, London]. So much of my own education around Live Art came through showing and seeing work at the ICA—seeing my UK contemporaries like Marisa Carnesky, and international artists like Karen Finley. Like Annie Sprinkle. Like Leslie Hill. In fact, that is how Leslie and I met.

Leslie: As an artist on the ground in the mid-1990s, the ICA is where everybody wanted to show work and went to see work. They also had great commissions, which had ripple effects, so that they were supporting 'emerging artists' before the Arts Council had so many schemes for emerging artists.

Helen: And there was the interconnectedness of the talks programme...

Leslie: ... Because Alan Read was doing the talks and events programme, it was such an exciting space. After Alan left, and Lois shortly afterwards, it felt like a huge hole. We no longer had that place to see work, to show work. And *then* you really saw site-specific work. Not that there wasn't site-specific work before then, but after Lois didn't have a venue where she could program work, I think there was a lot more site work because there wasn't *the* space anymore for live work.

Helen: There was also the significant role that festivals had in providing different *kinds* of spaces, which enabled more site-sympathetic or site-specific work. In the UK, Fierce, for example, and In Between Time, and of course the work that Johanna has done with ANTI in Finland.

Johanna: ANTI began in 2002, when I was working for the Regional Arts Council of North Savo, as regional artist covering all the performing arts, and our head office was in Kuopio. I had produced some smaller events and there were quite strong art institutions already, but it seemed like the city was yearning for something new, something more experimental, something more contemporary. At the same time as I was working at the Arts Council, a new regional artist for visual arts joined the team. He had produced a kind of environmental art project along one of our highways, Highway 5, which runs through Kuopio. When he joined the team, we started to talk about how we could combine our budgets to do something bigger. How to make city spaces more inviting, but also how to programme different kinds of works to activate different sites in the city—both the well-known, 'nice' places, but also the hidden and forgotten places in the city. From these conversations, ANTI Festival came out.

From very early on, it was also clear to us that we wanted to make this an international festival. This was partly about bringing new ideas to the existing art community, because the existing infrastructure was not very experimental. But when we did the first festival, it was really an experiment. We didn't know if it would continue. I remember waiting at the Kuopio airport for an international artist, I don't remember who it was, but the Kuopio airport is so tiny and I was like, 'Oh my god, what have I done?' But even from that first year, we were amazed by the number of proposals we got from our open call. And then in the second year it was triple the amount, and so on. So it felt like there was a need from the international artist community to find structures for site-based work.

Helen: The way you talk about setting up ANTI, Johanna, you make it sound almost easy. But it must have been a challenge to activate all those myriad sites in the city, and to get people interested—not just in theatre, but in a particular *kind* of theatre. A big undertaking, but one that elicits rich rewards, both for audiences and artists. Working with venues can sometimes be understandably prescriptive: they need to bring in a certain number of audience, the gig has to be in the evening, in a black box space etc. What festivals like Fierce and ANTI offered was a literal thinking outside the box.

I'm also thinking of the more non-prescriptive funding opportunities such as Artsadmin's bursary or LADA's one-to-one scheme. Through the Artsadmin bursary, for example, we made *Vena Amoris* which was just for one audience member at a time. There wasn't a pressure to bring in a certain box office amount, or to be in a theatre space. In fact, I had the whole building [*Toynbee Studios, where Artsadmin is located*] open to me: from the café, to unused corridors, to unused cubby holes in those unused corridors. That freedom facilitated all kinds of ideas and enabled rich experimentation.

Leslie: On the Scent was specifically commissioned for Fierce. We first performed it with Lois Weaver in a house in West Bromwich. We thought it was going to be one weekend only, and that would be it. But it ended up going to a lot of international festivals, and ANTI was one of them. Conceptually, the piece was about smell and memory, and about the evocation of place and space. And doing that project in homes all around the world opened up my way of thinking about the relationship of smell and memory because we ended up with this repository of thousands smell memories from audience members from Finland, Europe, North America, South America, Australia, Asia.... I have a really different picture of the world than I had before. Theatres are kind of the same everywhere, but being in people's homes or apartments around the world is a really different insight into a place.

Helen: Yes, we ended up performing it hundreds of times for over a decade. It was a festival-friendly piece. If a festival was restricted in what kinds of venues they could offer, all they needed was an accommodating home owner.

Johanna: On the Scent is an example of a concept that is site-specific, but easily adaptable to new places. When we program the festival, there are various ways that works can respond to sites and places, and to the city of Kuopio. We are quite open and flexible; we don't have a singular idea of how the work needs to relate to a site or a place. Sometimes artists have a global idea of site, as opposed to a physical space, or the people who are inhabiting or using the site. And sometimes it's the other way around, with artists who work more with the people who inhabit the site, or who pass by or work there. Sometimes we have roaming works that take over the whole city, or work more with placelessness or *flâneur*ing in the city.

I'm also thinking about Guillermo Gómez-Peña, when he worked with a group of artists making different kind of interactions in the streets of Kuopio, and the Finnish white city that Kuopio is. He and Roberto [Sifuentes] were obviously *misplaced*, or questioning their relationship to the city and the place. They performed in different sites over the four or five days, and one of the places was the airport. Guillermo was sitting in a wheelchair in a corridor between two sliding doors at the exit from the airport. And I remember this woman walking through the corridor and just *screaming*. Guillermo was just sitting there. He was scaring her to death just by his beautiful presence.

Helen: When I think about ANTI, I think about the piece that Kira O'Reilly did in a bomb shelter. When I see the image of that piece—and particularly that image of you and her, Johanna, of you holding her—I see the work, but I also see the imprint of the *place* in the work, of Kuopio and the festival. All those things are layered into it and become part of the history of the performance.

Leslie: How does it work? Do you have locals who are like, 'You've got to use my bomb shelter!'?

Johanna: Yes, sometimes we have that! In the first five or six years, we pre-selected all the sites. But in more recent years, working with Gregg Whelan as co-director of the festival, we've opened that up more—sometimes we work with themes, or with conversations with the artists. I think we've opened the structure of the festival as it has developed.

I'm personally really interested in dialogical aesthetics and dialogical theory of art—where the site and what happens there, and the people who participate in the process, are as important as the artist and the artist's intention. In recent years, this

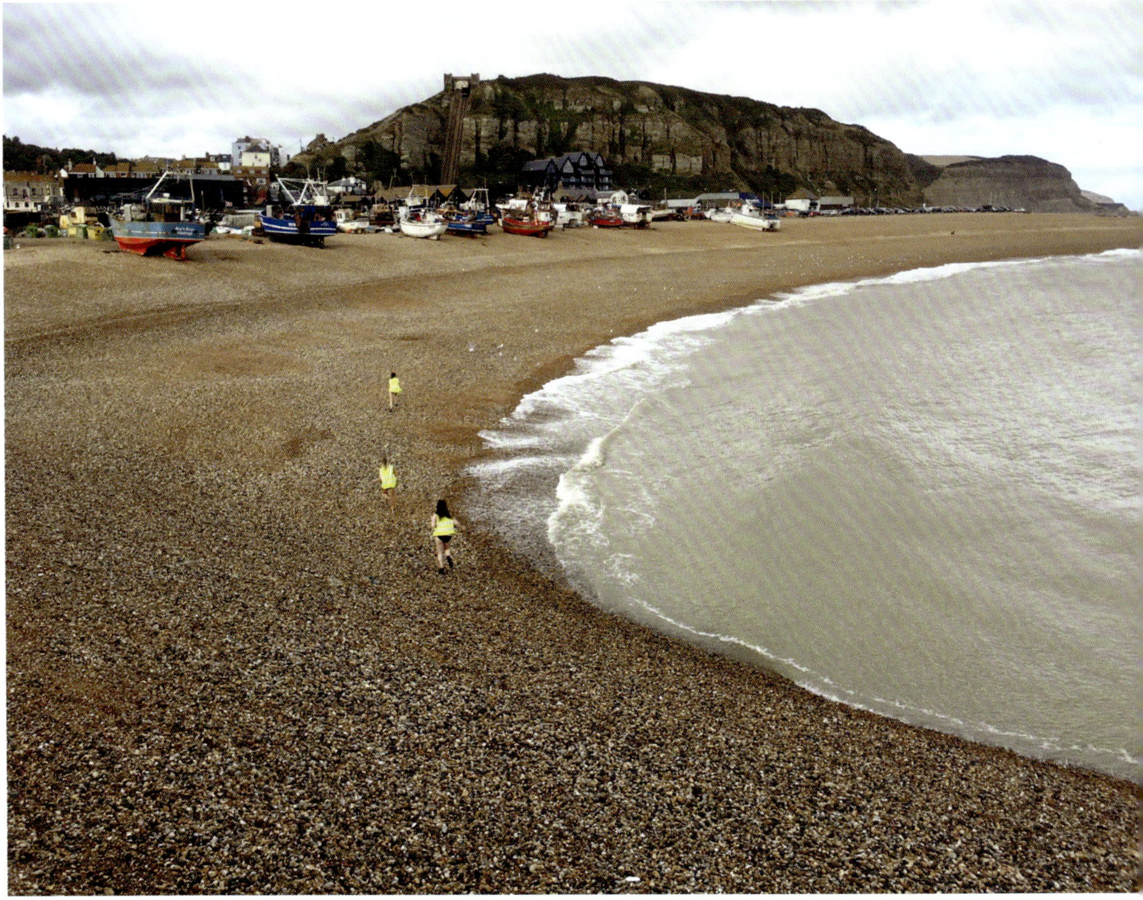

dialogical, collaborative way of working seems very much to have been at the core of what artists have been interested in doing at ANTI—as opposed to a more 'audience participation' approach some years ago.

We have worked in hundreds of different sites in the city over the years, from a hairdresser or a post office or a bank to the parks and streets in Kuopio. I always find it quite amazing that when we approach people who normally never have anything to do with artists, let alone performance art or Live Art, they're quite open and willing to become part of the festival, and to give their venues, and sometimes facilities and staff, to be used for the festival.

For me, it means that they see the value that the work has and want to support it, and they possibly see some impact it would have in their community. Often people say that contemporary art and performance is so difficult, and you don't understand anything about it, blah blah blah. I totally disagree. We talk and negotiate very openly with people: what is going to happen and what the artist's intentions are and what they're going to do. And on a very grassroots level, I feel like it changes how people think about art and artists. They see that artists are actually quite amazing people who really want to have a collaborative, dialogical way of working, and it's not just about themselves and their work.

Left: Curious, *Private Keep Out,* DIY (2016). Image the artists.

Helen: Much of the work we've made as Curious has intentionally sought interaction and conversation. When we have explored a particular curiosity—such as the relationship between smell and memory, or what gut feelings are—we have asked others to be part of the inquiry. That's always been part of the work: the agency that's inherent in that very simple act of conversation with audiences and communities, both local and global.

Leslie: We had to think a lot about agency with a project we did called *(be)longing*. The Women's Library, who wanted to do something for the hundredth anniversary of the social reformer Josephine Butler, offered us a commission to make a project that engaged with sex workers. Butler was an important figure in first-wave feminism, one of the first middle- or upper-class women to come out publicly and lead campaigns to repeal the Contagious Diseases Act, which was designed to punish prostitutes—women—but not their clients—men. The Library thought we would be a good match as artists who often worked with community groups on socially engaged projects. That was probably the strangest beginning we've had to a project! I don't think we've ever had content imposed in quite that way.

We thought about it, and we said we would work on the project as long as the Women's Library understood that we were never going to ask them explicitly about sex work. We *would* talk with them about other things—so we came up with the theme of longing and belonging. If they wanted to talk with us about sex work, they could; but in fact they never did, because that's all people ever talk to them about! I never noticed before, but these communities are really hounded by journalists to get salacious interviews. We worked in Soho, where we just did cold-calling at brothels. We worked with Open Doors, which is a NHS (National Health Service) group that go out and give condoms and sandwiches and health advice and have a health drop-in clinic once a week. And we worked with a homeless group because prostitution isn't uncommon amongst homeless women.

We had to think about agency a lot in terms of what work we tried to make accessible to the public or not, because the Women's Library wanted something that they could have as part of their exhibition as a public outcome. With the more vulnerable groups, we produced things that were just shown in-house for those groups. Whereas the Open Doors group were teenage girls in school; they did not have drug addictions; they knew what they were doing; and they had two social workers with them who had their backs at all times. There was a really strong sense that they had agency, that they knew their own minds, and wanted to do something political. We made a film with them, and their dream was for people from the Home Office to come and see it. So Emmy Minton, who we worked with, made that happen, and Emmy stayed connected with the group for years afterward.

Johanna: I believe in this very social theory of space that everything that happens produces space. And, not only for me but for others as well, this opens the question of how you might want to see your city. Not only during the festival, but every day: what kind of things would you like to see? What would you like to happen there? And how can you be active or be part of that?

I really like this commitment to the city, the relationship and the conversation and dialogue with the city—what ANTI means for Kuopio and how it partly *produces* what Kuopio is. One thing I always say is how the festival has entirely changed the map of Kuopio for me. This is not my home town, I'm not from here, and I don't have a specific love for Kuopio. The festival has definitely brought me into sites and places that I would have never gone to otherwise. But also, all those encounters in the city have completely changed the way I experience the city. That's the corner where I was lifted across the street by Tryst's *Assisted Street Crossing*; in this park I saw a group of school kids playing with and having a conversation with each other through the megaphones of Madeleine Flynn and Tim Humphrey; this is the car park in which Cassils performed *The Powers That Be (210 Kilometers)* addressing Kuopio's proximity to Russia, a country where queer and trans lives are acutely vulnerable and under siege, lacking any protection under civil law; and this island I was rowed to by Simon Whitehead and brought a piece of wood from the wood panel of my house as a contribution to *BURN*.... The festival has created a personal map for the city for me.

SPACES

CONVERSATION

REBECCA FRENCH AND
ANDREW MOTTERSHEAD
(FRENCH & MOTTERSHEAD)

HAYLEY NEWMAN

DATE

29 JANUARY 2016

PLACE

LONDON

As French & Mottershead, Rebecca and Andrew have created socially-engaged, visual, and participatory projects in site-specific contexts and locations. The roles of participants are frequently directed and framed, inviting them to become active collaborators in artworks that disturb and develop their sense of self. They have also shown work in galleries across the UK and internationally, including Tate Modern; The Photographers Gallery; Salt, Istanbul; Centro Cultural São Paulo; and Perth Institute of Contemporary Art (PiCA). As they discuss, they've had a long relationship with LADA, including leading the DIY projects *Live Art Campers!* (2007) and *Living Archives* (2014); contributing to East End Collaborations; creating a Study Room guide on participation and socially-engaged practice; creating a custom 'microperformance' for the Live Art GALA (2014); working as LADA Thinkers in Residence in 2006/2007; and creating the film *Pearls of Wisdom* (2009) for LADA's tenth anniversary, compiling all the advice they had been given in meetings at LADA with Lois Keidan, Daniel Brine, and Andrew Mitchelson.

Hayley Newman creates performances, interventions, music and texts that explore humour, subjectivity, documentary practices and fiction. Her work *Connotations–Performance Images 1994–98* (1998), which she describes here, claims to present photographs of a series of performance actions carried out over several years, but was actually created during a single week. She has increasingly made work that responds to social, economic, and ecological crises, including the novel *Common* (2011), which arose out of her self-declared role as artist-in-residence in the City of London; her collaboration The Gluts, an 'eco-electric girl band' who took their musical *Café Carbon* to the Copenhagen Climate Summit in 2009; and her participation in the art/activist group Liberate Tate. *Connotations* was presented as part of *Live Culture* (LADA/Tate, 2003), and LADA has released a DVD of The Gluts and collaborated with Liberate Tate on *Take the Money and Run?* (2015). Hayley was also a recipient of a One-to-One Artist's Bursary.

Hayley: The thing about being an artist is that you are always being selected to be in something or out of something.

Rebecca: Yeah, it can feel like that!

Hayley: And there isn't any power in that. How do you get to show your work? Someone has to open the gates to let you do that. Somehow you have to learn that you're actually *not* completely disempowered in that situation.

Andrew: I remember going to have a meeting with Lois [Keidan] and Daniel [Brine] at their first office in Truman Brewery, because we had an idea we called 'microperformance' and we were making work, but we didn't have any support for it. It was a key turning point for us.

Rebecca: They were very encouraging. I remember sitting in my studio after that and at awkward moments when I felt a bit down, I would rally myself by saying, 'Lois Keidan thinks our work is interesting and we should pursue it!'

Andrew: They were able to show you a way that you could navigate the different support structures that were around, and the people at the heart of them. There were different agencies at that time, like New Work Network, which was very useful for putting artists in contact with each other and developing artists' voices.

Rebecca: We used to put on our work ourselves: find a space, make art and invite people. Whereas when you're doing it within some kind of institution or funding structure, there's a feeling that you're building a career. But you need a different strategy to build a reputation when you're not doing it within an institution.

Andrew: I remember looking around and saying, 'We don't like 'doing' performance! We don't want to be on stage.' But in the Live Art scene at that time, cabaret was one of the main forms.

Hayley: I think it relates to the beginnings of the Live Art Development Agency, and how Lois came out of the theatre department at the ICA. If you think about their radicality, their 'root', that is the root of their radicalism. At the beginning, I felt quite alienated from that, as well. I didn't want to make work in that space. I understood its importance, but also wanted to challenge it. I think that performers found other places to work—and that once LADA was formed it was responsive to those moves.

Andrew: We're really passionate about using interventionism as part of our practice. For the first couple of years, we were doing these projects where we worked with local community members and trained them to be micro-performers in events that would happen in their space. For example, with the West Indian Ex-Services Association in Clapham, we worked with their members to put on a night that would bring a London art world to them.

Rebecca: The performers were drawn from the art world *and* from the Association. And the audience was also from the art world and the club—so there was a melding together of two different worlds. But within that, there was this layer of people who were doing microperformances, and no one knew who they were or what they were doing. So it created this environment of suspicion and intrigue of wondering who was doing what. Like, 'What if I can't stop blinking? Will people think I'm a performer because I keep blinking?!'

Andrew: And following from that, we did an event with the City of London opposite the Stock Exchange, working with people in the City, but also art world people, too. These were enlightening experiences, but training and working with thirty people took months, a lot of energy, and was hit and miss. And that led to a realisation that we didn't necessarily have to go through the process of workshops in order to activate an audience in the way that we wanted. And we resolved it by creating these microperformance instructions called The People Series that we could create in two or three days and deliver into people's hands.

Rebecca: They layer on top of an existing social context, whether that's a private view in a gallery, a festival, a conference. They try to reveal the unconscious performances that take place in the context. For example, we did it at the re-opening of the Arnolfini Gallery after its refurbishment, when all the UK 'art-eratti' were there. We visited the space and pulled out architectural details, and we went to some posh private views and watched how people perform, how they touch each other and interact. Then we wrote subversive instructions to break that down, which we gave to people as they came in.

They don't have to do the performance, of course. But the fact of us inviting everybody who entered the space to take a card means that everybody knows what's going on, and so it creates a perceptual shift—wondering what is and isn't a performance.

Andrew: I like the thought that Nick Serota [then Director of the Tate], who was there, could have picked up the instruction 'Rim your glass.'

Rebecca: He was nice, and was interested. He came back and asked for another card, didn't he?

Andrew: I think the way to establish a practice is to learn by *doing* it. Rather than copying or aligning yourself with the canon. To explore it through the actual process of doing. We had to do it by flying by the seats of our pants, through the experience of failure and testing.

Hayley: Those points of disorientation are really important, and they are something that I really rely on. The thing I can identify in my key works is that there was always a sense of being completely lost within them. There was no roadmap for any of them, no way out of the creative predicament of being lost while making something.

Connotations was like that. I didn't know what was happening when making it. Casey Orr (the photographer) was only around for a week, so we had to run it like a film shoot, and I was coordinating everyone involved: all the costumes, all the hair changes. But more than that, I felt like I was working in the dark, and had to figure it out as the work was being made. I think that *Connotations* was a hunch that came out of a desire to answer historians and canon-makers as an artist. I wanted to reply to their writings, but didn't quite know how, and felt I had to do so in my own language: a pre-lingual form that moves into something verbal. So it was challenging, both in terms of logistics but also at an emotional level. I think that's something I've always worked with: both operating within critique and activating a political sphere, while also connecting with emotion and expression.

And [the book] *Common* was like that, too.[1] I wrote it in six weeks, because although there was no fee for the work, I had a contract to deliver it by a certain date. So I just went into the City of London and wrote. I'm very interested in working processes where there's no perspective, where I'm in something and there's no point from which to see. I had to use all my brain power and faculties to think through what was happening. I'm here. I'm trying to physically make sense of the City through my body. Gathering information through my senses. And the [2011 London] riots were happening at that time. I was originally compelled to write *Common* out of a sense of injustice, and those events further compounded that. People who were protesting were arrested and criminalised, whereas the bankers and other forms of criminality weren't confronted. It was a very interesting time to be there.

Andrew: Your experience of engaging with the City reminds me of these 'micro-classes' we ran with City workers to make *My Word is My Bond*. We would get up in front of these groups and ask them, 'Would you like to come with us to learn how you can perform differently?' We also had money jobs working in the City ourselves, doing desktop publishing in banks. Working closely with bankers gave us a sense of how their language was depersonalised, and how it could be a very sexualised environment.

Overleaf: French & Mottershead, *Spiceland (Asian & Afro Caribbean Food & Groceries), 11.15am, 9 June 2007, Norwich, UK.* From *The Shops Project*. Image French & Mottershead and Barbara Laws.

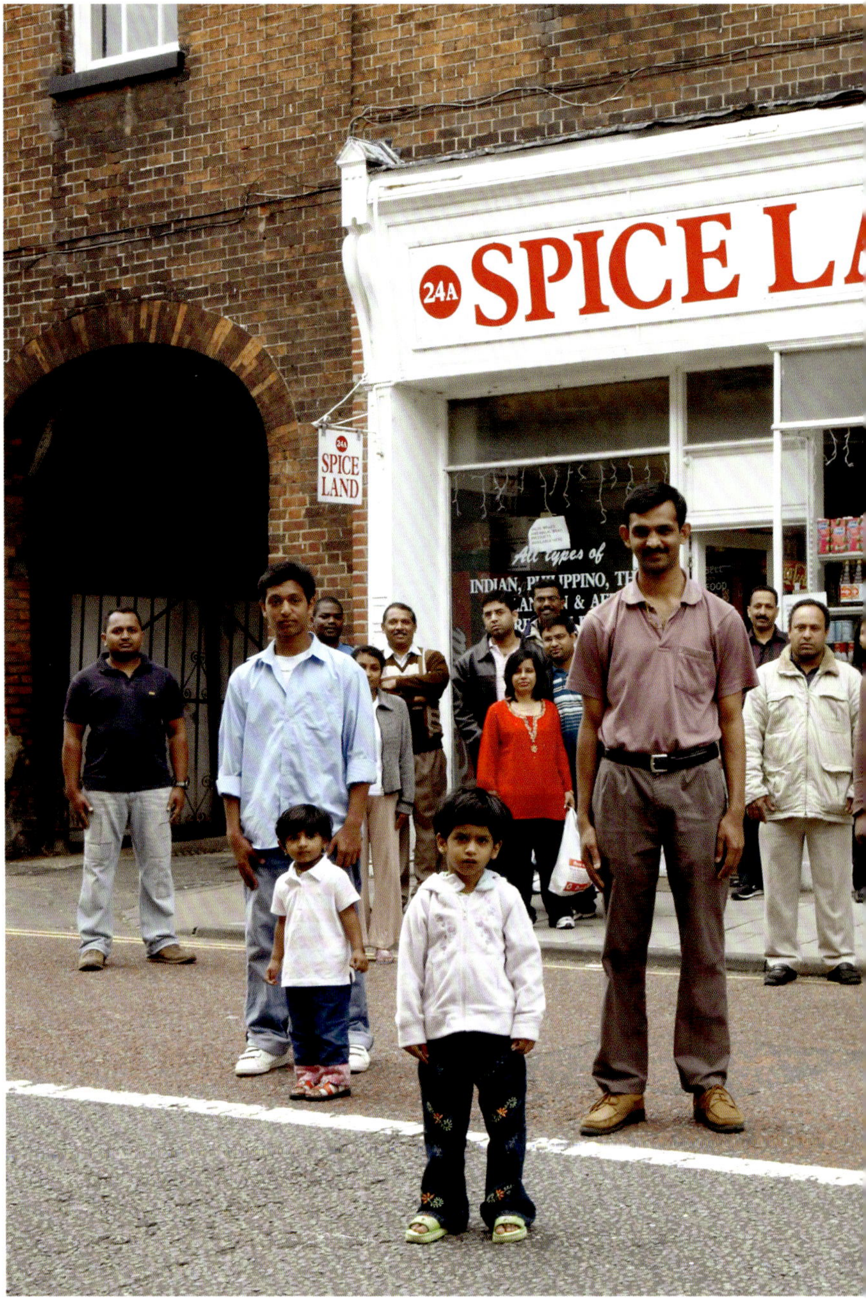

SHOPS
FRENCH|MOTTERSHEAD
NORWICH-EAST 2007
PHOTO: BARBARA LAWS

Rice
Toor dal
Urad dal
Coconut oil
Turmeric powder

Chilli powder
mustard seed.
vegetables

Rice

Fish
meat
Palm oil
pepper

Vegetables, Grocery Oil, Ghee

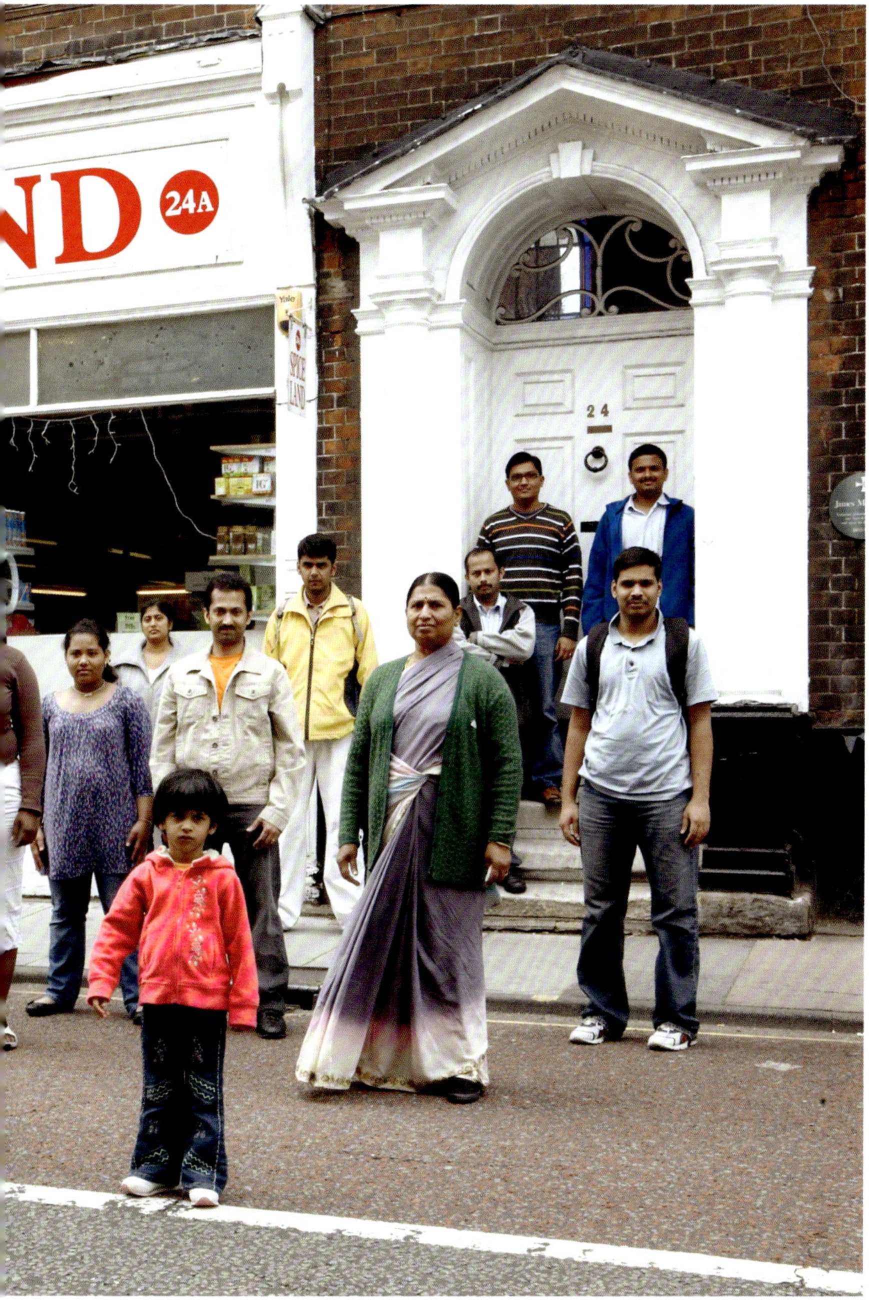

nda
-
meat

Bread
Chappthi
chapathi
Parota
fish Rice

Chilly Powder
Vegitable
Fisch
Cocanat.

Rice,
Beans
Basmati Rice
Longgrain Rice
egusi SPice
garri Plaintain.

2. SPICELAND
9 JUNE 2007
11.15AM

Rebecca: We started taking our work internationally because of the ANTI Festival. We wanted to make work outside London and become glamorous international artists! [*laughs*] And ANTI was a good fit for us, because it was programming work outside gallery spaces and engaging people.

Andrew: Back then, when they announced their call they published twenty sites across the town, and you were invited to make proposals for those particular sites. That particular year there were five shops, and each photograph of a shop was empty of people—they just showed the space like an architectural photograph. So it triggered the thoughts, 'What is the connection between each shop and its people? What are the identities of these places?'

Rebecca: We were thinking about all those transactions, that there's a transaction of money for goods. But there's also a whole level of social transaction.

Andrew: We wanted to work with the shopkeepers to twist that exchange, so they would distribute these invitations to ask customers if they wanted to be part of a group photograph of the shop's customers.

Rebecca: It was quite interesting how different shops participated. The record shop owner obviously had a tight community who probably hang around his shop as well as buy music, so he invited everyone personally and enthusiastically. But with the bakery, the owner who agreed to the project was not the person serving the customers. So those staff just stuffed our flyers in the customers' bags. The staff weren't sufficiently empowered within the decision to participate in the artwork to get behind it.

Andrew: What we really loved about the pictures is that they're so tribal. The way that the people look and how they perform relate to their identity, and they're next to each other in that shop. People who go to the heavy metal record shop look different from the people who buy fish.

Rebecca: That was in 2005, and then we went off all over the place to explore social relationships around commerce in different ways. It could be international traders in China or a vendor in Brazil who sells vegetables off the back of a donkey.

Hayley: I want to ask you, what do you think the people you work with get out of what you do?

Rebecca: It depends on the individual. I think in some cases it's as basic as someone being pleased that we are interested in putting our lens on them and their life, like when we worked with a local butcher in Istanbul. It's that 'somebody wants to talk to me about my shop and my social and commercial relationships, and finds that interesting enough to make me the focus of something'. There's such a spectrum between an artist who decides 'I'm doing this project and I just need these people to be in it,' and something that is more of a collaborative co-creation. Our work tries to be the latter. From the participants' point of view, it's been more successful when we have been able to engage them and their ideas in the process, and they can see that they're making something *with* us.

Andrew: In the work we're doing at the moment, *Afterlife*, we're writing a series of audio narratives that describe the decomposition of the human body and the influence of a particular environment on its transformation: a woodland, water, an art museum, a home. We've been writing them with forensic anthropologists, conservators, ecologists, and transforming the scientific information into a narrative the listener can *feel*. The idea is to tap into a listener's familiar references and bodily sensations, so they 'live through' what is being described as if it were their own body decomposing. It's like a conversation with their imagination, one that honours *them* or *their* body and *their* relationship to a place, or a site or their life, and punctures a fear of the unknown.

Rebecca: It's been a more empowering process as an artist hasn't it? Because with participatory works, you can have a brilliant idea, but if the person you're working with doesn't want to represent themselves in that way, then you can't make the work. You're constrained by the boundaries of how people like to see themselves. It has a way of 'nice-ificating' your practice.

Hayley: I find institutional arm-twisting anxiety-making....

Rebecca: It's like a kind of grooming sometimes, isn't it? It's almost like you're grooming people to take part in your work! Or when an institution says, 'We can "get" you 50 people.' And it's like, 'No thanks, we don't want you to "get" us anyone!'

Andrew: And what do you want from your work, Hayley? You're creating a situation where you're engaging with people and you want them to get something out of it, and it could be argued that it's a similar situation to what we're setting up—but we call it 'participatory' and you don't.

Hayley: Maybe something transformative. Some way of seeing the world differently—like a swerve ball that knocks your vision in a different direction. We're all *in* our lives, but at what point do we get leverage on them? Through The Gluts and with Liberate Tate, I became interested in stakeholder intervention—but at a local level, a kind of proximity. The works aren't just interventions because they are a bit like conversations: they make arguments and open up space for change.

With Liberate Tate, my experience is that our relationship with the Tate has been with the security. It's not Nick Serota. It's not the curators. It's the security, because they're on the ground. With *Time Piece*, we occupied the Turbine Hall of Tate Modern for 25 hours. In the morning we walked in carrying food and sustenance and materials for a compost toilet, and we set up camp at the bottom of the slope. We began writing passages from books on art and activism in charcoal on the floor of the Turbine Hall, like a tide of words that were creeping up the floor.

Then at the end of the day the Tate security said, 'If you're not out by 10:40 we will ring the police.' At that point the camp was reconfigured, and we had worked out who we thought would be arrested and who wouldn't. When the police came we were still writing, and they said, 'We're going to do whatever Tate wants us to, and Tate says you can stay.' At that point the Tate sealed us off, we installed our own toilet under a black tent, and slept through the night. In the morning a Liberate Tate member was speaking to one of the security guards and saying, 'I'm really, really sorry that you've had to stay up all night.' The security guard said, 'Don't worry, we did it together.'

Andrew: It sounds like an enormous piece. But I also find myself drawing comparisons just on a personal level, which is the level we work more on, about the effect that these interventions can have. You don't necessarily know what's going to happen. Last year we got an email from someone that said, 'Thank you very much.' Ten years ago at the NRLA [National Review of Live Art] in Glasgow we had distributed microperformance instructions, and this guy got one that said, 'Tell someone that you think they're pretty.' So he approached a woman and said, 'I think you're pretty.' In subsequent years they've moved from Glasgow to New York to the West Coast, survived cancer, had children and got married. He wrote to us and said, 'All this happened because you distributed this little instruction.'

Rebecca: Actually, it was probably giving him permission to do something he'd like to have done anyway. But the microperformance instruction meant he could do it as 'art'.

Hayley: It's about giving yourself permission to do something. That's what I've learned from Liberate Tate, too. You just take the permission and do something.

1. Hayley Newman, *Common* (Isle of Wight: Copy Press, 2013).

SPACES
PROVOCATION
HEIKE ROMS
TITLE
FROM A DISTANCE

Heike Roms is Professor in Theatre and Performance at the University of Exeter, and was previously based in Aberystwyth, Wales, for twelve years, where she led the multi-layered research project *What's Welsh for Performance? Beth yw 'performance' yn Gymraeg?* As she describes here, this project draws on oral history, performance reconstruction, and interconnected histories to trace the emergence of performance art and Live Art in Wales. She also has an interest in destructivist art, and was a key contributor to the intergenerational project *KAPUTT: The Academy of Destruction* (2017) at Tate Modern, directed by Sibylle Peter and co-produced by LADA. Heike is co-editor of *Contesting Performance: Global Sites of Research* (2010) and *Thinking through Theatre and Performance* (2019).

My relationship with the Live Art Development Agency has for the most part been a long-distance love affair. I have enjoyed the occasional intimate face-to-face encounter over the years: I have spoken at some of LADA's events, and most recently I participated in Sibylle Peters' intergenerational *KAPUTT: The Academy of Destruction* (2017) at Tate Modern. *KAPUTT*, like all of the projects LADA produces, was precise about its location, in this case an institution at the very heart of Britain's art establishment, where the 'kid academicians' not only tested out different approaches to destructiveness but also examined their place within what counts as contemporary art. But the majority of LADA's activities I have experienced at one remove, browsing announcements and reading reflections, listening to accounts and perusing the website. Having lived and worked in Wales since the mid-1990s, I have never even visited LADA's Study Room in East London. And yet I count LADA among the strongest influences on my work. Its efforts to give a diverse field of artistic practices a sense of community have always included those of us who study and write about it and have encouraged me to engage with the lesser-known histories of the field. Having been invited to write a reflection on the relation between place, performance and agency, I will briefly consider this relation through the lens of 'distance'. How does Live Art perform across distance, whether geographical or temporal? How does distance form communities? How does distance provide agency? And what value do we attach to the notion of distance itself?

The Death of Distance?

We have become accustomed to considering questions such as these as indicative of the very opposite of distance: it is more common now to think about the fact that we are in touch with and touched by events that happen a long way away as a sign of our ever-growing nearness, facilitated by digital communication and social media exchanges that produce a sense of intimacy. Already in 1997, journalist Frances Cairncross proclaimed the very 'Death of Distance': tethered to a digital web of virtual proximity, the geographical distances between us would become irrelevant, she argued. And proximity would lead to a rise in empathy and care: 'Bonded together by the invisible strands of global communications, *humanity may find that peace and prosperity are fostered by the death of distance*', concludes Cairncross' analysis.[1] In an age where digitally-mediated access often breeds vicious trolling we may now scoff at such cheery optimism. But the underlying assumption that associates distance with indifference and proximity with engagement pervades much of our contemporary thinking. Distance has become something we have to overcome. Debates on place and space, for example, often celebrate the virtues of immersing oneself in the specificity of a particular location, being on the ground and in the thick of it, experiencing a place through one's immediate senses, particularly that of touch. A politics of proximity is widely considered a key strategy with which to offset our modern alienation from and exploitation of the environment. In the wider field of performance too, theatre has moved out of its traditional middle distance from the spectator into a relationship of proximity that equates experience and participation with immersion.

Driving this move toward proximity has been the desire—wholly justified, I should add—to offer a corrective to traditional Western epistemologies that for so long considered distance a prerequisite for knowledge, and that cemented ideals of disinterestedness and objectivity at the cost of more intimate, embodied forms of knowing. These days, though, as geographer John Wylie has observed, practice-based, performative, and creative approaches to knowledge are more likely to be distinguished by an 'ethos which most often emphasises proximity to the objects of inquiry as a key path to insight. If distance *is* maintained, it is perhaps more usually through a kind of recoil movement in which criticality, a sense of *critical distance*, is re-introduced at the point of reflection and writing.'[2] Wylie instead argues for the reintroduction of a certain critical distance directly into our inquiries and the way we undertake them to counter what he considers simplified and regressive conceptions of locatedness and belonging.

I don't have the space to really engage with Wylie's sophisticated argument here, which is geared toward a radical rethinking of landscape as a 'mode of experience, imagination, and presentation'. I would merely like to propose that it might also be productive to rethink the particular mode of experience, imagination, and presentation that is Live Art through the lens of distance—like turning a telescope around and peering through the wrong end, so that things that had been brought closer are moved further away again for a fresh look. Thus, when theatre scholar Alan Read characterises performance as 'modest acts of up-scaling that materially reduce the distance between things, bring things closer together in order that we might perceive them in the same place at the same time',[3] we might consider such relationships of proximity in performance (whether to things or to people) as in effect finely calibrated distances.

Distant Readings

My own work as a researcher of performance histories is seemingly deeply invested in the very opposite of distance. For the past ten years I have been charting the emergence and early development in the 1960s and 1970s of those art practices we have come to call performance or Live Art. And I have done so in the context of Wales, a small, bilingual country of around three million people situated on the western edge of the British Isles. I have tracked numerous examples of such work, covering the years between 1965 and 1979: from an early Happening in Cardiff in the mid-1960s; via destruction art events in Swansea; conceptual performed photography in Newport; improvised music events in Anglesey; to a performance art festival in Wrexham in the late 1970s (for those of you unfamiliar with Wales' geography, this means events happening all over the country).[4] Why, though, draw a geographical boundary around the history of an art practice that often transcended such boundaries in its aesthetic or political aspirations? Because, I want to propose, there is one aspect that only really comes into view if we keep our attention focused on the long-term developments that occur in a specific locality: namely how the history of performance art is more than the sum of individual events of performance. Such events can no longer be kept discrete: they begin to show their connections to performances that came before and after; they expose their interactions with documents and documentation; they point to the histories of the bodies, objects, and buildings involved; and they reveal their enmeshments in networks, organisational practices, and institutional structures of various kinds. As a critical strategy, is this then not the very embodiment of close reading?

In fact, this shifting of attention away from exceptional events to the larger scene of activity of which they were a part has many parallels with what Italian literary scholar Franco Moretti has called 'distant reading'.[5] The close reading practices—the careful, sustained interpretation of texts—that have for so long defined the study of literature, so Moretti argues, have led to a very small canon of books that are continuously re-evaluated. Instead, he advocates taking up a distance from these texts in order to understand the development of literature by aggregating and analysing greater amounts of data, such as the number of all the books published in a certain period, for example. I have some problems with Moretti's predominantly quantitative research approach (art practices are not easily squeezed into quasi-scientific patterns)—although I admit I do find the sheer number of performance works that were made in Wales in the 1960s and 1970s illuminating (over 800, created over fifteen years, are currently documented in my project). The number itself can be taken as a useful indicator of how profoundly and broadly art-making changed under the influence of the performance-based approaches to artistic experimentation that emerged during the latter half of the twentieth century, 'even' beyond the established centres of the avant-garde in what is assumed to have been marginal cultural contexts, such as that of Wales.

More useful to me than number-crunching, however, has been Moretti's notion that 'distance is [...] not an obstacle, but a

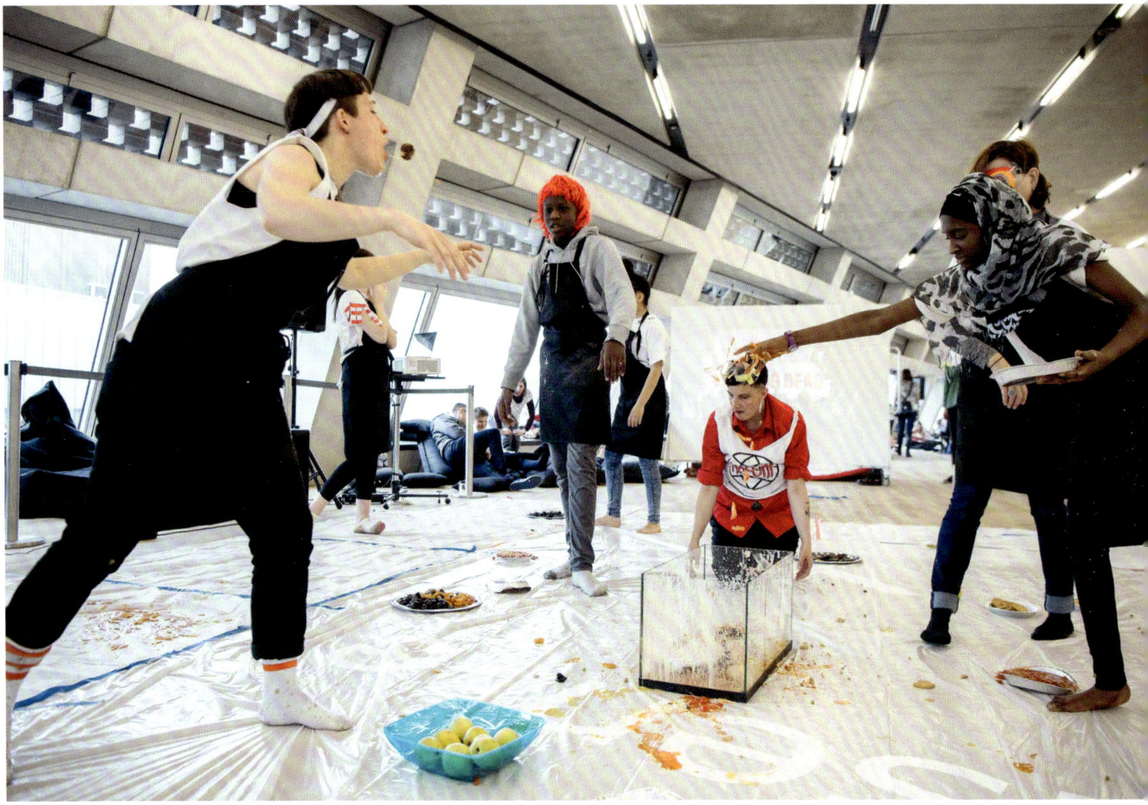

specific form of knowledge: fewer elements, hence a sharper sense of their overall interconnection'.[6] My work may be committed to a highly located approach to inquiry, which has immersed itself deeply in the performance history of a specific place. But at the same time I have held individual works of performance at a certain critical distance rather than subject them to close reading, so that the interrelatedness (personal, material, institutional, affective, thematic) between these works in this place and beyond, across distances or space or time, may come into sharper focus.

Distances in Space and Intervals in Time

Consequently, my research is devoted to the early history of 'performance art in Wales', and not principally of 'Welsh performance art'. The difference is subtle but important: it is not my primary aim to unearth a Welsh manifestation of performance art that was somehow aesthetically distinct from developments elsewhere. Rather, my interest is the interrelation of work made in Wales with transnational artistic practices and their channels and networks of exchange, on the one hand, and the local conditions of making, on the other. Historians of Live Art have frequently identified spatial proximity as the very condition that made the emergence of performance possible. RoseLee Goldberg, for example, has written about the 'meeting place of unusual minds—be it in a café in Milan, in Zürich or in New York, where ideas were fermented and from where actions fanned out to intimate theatres such as the Salle Gaveau in 1920s Paris, innovative art schools such as the Bauhaus in Germany after the First World War and Black Mountain College in the United States after the Second, or the lofts and 'alternative spaces' of downtown Manhattan in the 1960s and 1970s'.[7] Such places of encounter feature in the history of Live Art in Britain too: university arts festivals, artist-run venues, art colleges, performance platforms all offered invaluable opportunities for artists to hang out together and develop work as a result. But distance has always been equally influential on the emergence of performance work: articles read in magazines about happenings in other cities; exchanging writings or scores with artists in different parts of the world; or mere rumours and hearsay of events in far-flung places—geographical distance was often experienced in a very material way and worked on strategically by artists, through forms of documentation, publication and networking. LADA's dissemination strategies owe much to this long-standing tradition.

And distance is not merely a spatial phenomenon, but a temporal one, too. An interval of time opens between a past event of performance and our response to it in our present time. Art historians have long sought to fill this interval by seeking

Left: Sibylle Peters, *KAPUTT: The Academy of Destruction*, Tate Modern (2017). Image Katherina Duve.

evidence for direct influences between artists or works—history is thus seen as being set in motion by original, singular, and unrepeatable artistic gestures, which then impact on others. Feminist scholars have pointed out how the concepts of influence and importance that underlie this form of historical account have tended to perpetuate a (predominantly male / straight / white) canon. In the face of the many absences, gaps, and exclusions that mar such accounts, they have instead begun to theorise what a historiography of performance may look like that thinks differently about the temporal distance that opens between an event in the past and us in the present: as an interval that is filled with recurrent (but not necessarily continuous) engagements with the event. Whether they conceptualise such engagements as the affective transmission of ideas and feelings (Kristine Stiles);[8] as the cross-mappings of shared themes and concerns (Elisabeth Bronfen);[9] or as the gesture of the 'hail', as a call and response for which there is no real origin (Rebecca Schneider),[10] these historiographies offer alternative models for how Live Art practice has persisted and developed across a distance of time that is itself filled with many live encounters with the work.

Peering through the wrong end of the telescope

It has not been my ambition to provide a coherent theory of distance in this brief reflection—rather, to sketch out some of the ways in which the issue of distance could figure for Live Art, its present, pasts, and possible futures: how in performance we are often brought together by being apart, share our labour by working in remote places, are touched across intervals of time, are connected by being located, and may find agency in distance.

1. Frances Cairncross, *The Death of Distance: How the Communications Revolution Will Change Our Lives* (Boston: Harvard Business School Press, 1997), p. 279.

2. John Wylie, 'The Distant: Thinking toward Renewed Senses of Landscape and Distance', *Environment, Space, Place*, 9.1 (2017), 1–20 (p. 5).

3. Alan Read, *Theatre in the Expanded Field: Seven Approaches to Performance* (London: Bloomsbury, 2013), p. 86.

4. See my website, http://www.performance-wales.org/

5. Franco Moretti, *Distant Reading* (New York and London: Verso, 2013).

6. Franco Moretti, *Graphs, Maps, Trees: Abstract Models for a Literary History* (New York and London: Verso, 2005), p. 1.

7. RoseLee Goldberg, 'Hidden from History: Performance Art and the Imagination', in *Art, Lies and Videotape: Exposing Performance*, ed. by Adrian George (London: Tate, 2003), pp. 20–24 (p. 21).

8. Kristine Stiles, 'The Story of the Destruction in Art Symposium and the "DIAS Affect"', in *Gustav Metzger: History History*, ed. by Sabine Breitwieser (Vienna and Ostfildern-Ruit: Generali Foundation and Hatje Cantz, 2005), pp. 41–65.

9. Elisabeth Bronfen, *Crossmappings: Essays Zur Visuellen Kultur* (Zürich: Scheidegger & Spiess, 2009).

10. Rebecca Schneider and Lucia Ruprecht, 'In Our Hands: An Ethics of Gestural Response-Ability. Rebecca Schneider in Conversation with Lucia Ruprecht', *Performance Philosophy*, 3.1 (2017), 108–25.

SPACES

PROVOCATION

JOHN E. MCGRATH

TITLE

THE GIFT OF PLACE

John E. McGrath is Artistic Director of the Manchester International Festival. He was previously artistic director of Contact in Manchester (a Live Art UK network member), which places young people at the heart of both its artistic work and its organisational processes; and John was the founding artistic director of National Theatre Wales, which, as he describes here, has produced work for a wide range of sites and spaces, including village halls, beaches, army ranges, and walks through sheep pastures. Across these very different scales ranging from the local to the international, John has supported artist-led experimental practices that disrupt and reimagine the relationships between community and place.

On the 8th of May 2015, I stood in a car park outside the Labour Club in Merthyr Tydfil. The night before the Conservative Party had won an unexpected majority in the UK elections, and we had opened a production of Brecht's *Mother Courage*, with a cast entirely of women from South Wales, using the club as a site. At the climactic scene of the show, in the moment when Katrin beats the drum to alert the nearby town to danger, and is shot down from the roof of a peasant's house, veteran Welsh actress Sharon Morgan (cast like all the performers with no regard to age) clambered onto the roof of the Labour Club, beating an old bin with a beam of wood—and across the town bells could be heard—the tune of the Red Flag.

It wasn't, to be perfectly honest, our most popular show with some of the critics, who found the call to arms out of tune with the (pre-Corbyn) political times, and the karaoke-infused atmosphere of the club too literal for their Brechtian tastes. However, for me it was a significant piece on many levels. I knew at that point that it would be the last show I would direct for National Theatre Wales, after a seven-year journey setting up, launching, and developing the company: an initiative which had explicitly framed its mission as an exploration of nation and theatre through deep engagement with place. It had also been a show in which I'd had the privilege of working with a large cast of women, professional and non-professional, exploring this ever-resonant play. But perhaps more than anything, I had spent a lot of time in Merthyr Tydfil, hearing about its history and working with and alongside its people. I'd learned a lot: that the town was the first place in the world in which the Red Flag was raised in a political protest (hence that final scene); that many families and communities were held together by heroic women; that people argued a lot about immigration, welfare, austerity; that this had once been one of the most vibrant, dynamic towns in the world, a place of experiment and risk, feared by the powers that be. I had learnt that people hated establishment figures, but were open to anyone willing to spend time to talk. A year later when Brexit happened and Merthyr briefly became notorious as a 'Brexit heartland' (having voted resoundingly to leave despite being the beneficiary of EU subsidies), I was angry, not with the people of Merthyr, but with the ways in which mainstream attempts to understand what had happened erased all of the town's history and complexity.

Such experiences were common at National Theatre Wales—revelations gifted by places, through the process of performance:

The moment in Mike Pearson and Mike Brookes ' staging of Aeschylus's *The Persians*, in an army range in the wilds of the Brecon Beacons, when young soldiers, on their way to night manoeuvres and soon to ship out to Afghanistan, stood watching a play about the defeat of the world's greatest army. Beside them, other audience members remembered the families moved off those hillsides when the army took possession half a century ago.

Sheep—often there were sheep—moving complacently down the hillside to join the audience as we reached the final stages of Louise Wilson and Gillian Clarke 's *The Gathering*, a poetic, performative walk across Snowdon—the result of years spent in research with the shepherds who were now gently driving the sheep towards us in an act of extraordinary community.

The tension and then explosion of emotion in the school hall in Haverford West, where a teenage Bradley (now Chelsea) Manning had gone to school, and where Manning's life in military jail, in the Iraqi desert, and online was now being re-enacted to a first night audience including her mother and those who had attended the same high school.

The people of Laugharne, Dylan Thomas 's adopted home town, telling stories too tall even for the poet himself, revealing their own lives in very unexpected ways to the tourists and literary buffs scouring the town for signs of the great man.

And, most famously, a beach in Port Talbot, where a man emerges out of the crowd claiming to be a teacher. He is both a Hollywood star and a religious icon—Michael Sheen 's secular Jesus—retelling the story of a town that was 'passed over' by history, Port Talbot, a town full of pride and potential, but ignored even by its neighbours. Over a three-day performance, that town's voice rings out to the world and something really does change for good.

Every one of these pieces at NTW, and many more, shared one factor among their many differences: they were based on a very deep level of engagement with the places in which they were performed. Some pieces were made largely with local performers, but most were made with a core of professional actors and artists, who would move to that location for the rehearsal period—becoming temporary, in some ways disruptive, members of the community where the work was being made.

Taking this approach to national theatre—performance as an exploration of place, of specifics not national generalities—begged, perhaps, a question of wider community. How do such localised interventions join up into a larger narrative? Where is the national in a theatre of places? At NTW, a range of networks provided this connection—an online community, where anyone could post ideas, thoughts, responses—about NTW's work, or about their own; NTW TEAM, an open group of individuals throughout the country who would set up their own activities with NTW's support—and with the help of their peers; WalesLab , a programme for artists across Wales, supporting new ideas. In all of these examples and more, the principle of lateral networks was key—the support that members of networks could provide for each other far outweighed the direct input of NTW's small core team.

Resonant, localised artistic interventions, brought into a whole by lateral, self-supporting networks. Within all this, the role for artists was clear and urgent. The artists involved in each of NTW's works were provocateurs, individuals, disruptive creative forces. This was not the kind of community-based work that prioritises process and local voice only. Nor were the artists consistent in their approaches. Drawing on many diverse histories of Live Art, theatre, and performance, each artist took a very different relationship to place—ranging from deep, archival research, to the choice to physically relocate and live for many months in a community, to a more socially-focussed process of community recruitment. These were opinionated interventions: active, even argumentative, debates with the communities of which the artists had, for a time at least, become a part.

A bit like any good night out in Merthyr Tydfil.

When Brexit happened, there was a rush, among many in the arts world, to listen to the 'Brexit heartlands', to understand. But often that attempt at understanding became purely passive, or perhaps even passive aggressive. We're listening now—go on and justify yourselves! For a company like NTW the conversation had been going on a lot longer, and was intrinsically many-sided. If you really spend time in a place, you need to talk as well as listen.

By the time that vote happened though, I had moved on, back to Manchester, where I used to run Contact Theatre, to lead Manchester International Festival , as it took on a huge new initiative—The Factory—an ambitious building project in the heart of the city, dedicated to the making of large-scale, interdisciplinary art. What happens to all this politics of the local when you return to the city centre?

In fact, the politics and practice of NTW was rooted in the work pioneered at Contact a decade and a half earlier. A theatre venue on the edge of Manchester University's campus, Contact had, after a period of closure in the late 1990s, established itself in the early 2000s as a venue where young people from Manchester's many differing communities, and particularly from the culturally diverse neighbourhoods surrounding the university, were placed at the centre of all decision-making. The practice of place at NTW grew from an understanding, developed at Contact, that the question 'Who is here?' can be fundamental to performance-making. The place where the work is to be made—in Contact's case an eccentrically redeveloped 1970s building—and the vectors of people flowing through, or past, that place, become a fundamental question in that making. This does not mean the art becomes about the place: if theatre-makers were to create work largely about theatre buildings we would bore even ourselves. Rather, it implies that no space is neutral (or empty), and that the power dynamics running through any space will always be part of the meaning of an event that happens in that space: whether that meaning is recognised or ignored. At Contact, by placing young people from diverse backgrounds at the heart of decision-making, an environment was created where the work made—or even simply presented on tour—always, to differing degrees, became part of a conversation with those young people about the meaning and impact of that work.

Contact was and is a member of Live Art UK, a network of venues committed to supporting Live Art. Through this network, LADA was crucial in helping bring experimental performance to Contact , and supporting the idea that Live Art could thrive outside of its 'specialist' environment. It was always exciting to find some of the most radical Live Art and experimental performance gaining an audience at Contact, experienced alongside other very different work. As ever at Contact, the space of reception became part of the meaning, and often this radical work felt particularly open to such re-articulation by place.

Likewise, in Merthyr Tydfil, and throughout Wales, the recognition of place and communities in the making of work, determined a conversation, a dialogue, and argument sometimes, about the values, and the aesthetics, of life in and beyond that place.

Perhaps we could say that, at its best, work that engages deeply with place puts its location at the centre of a debate about the world.

Returning to Manchester, I find myself in a place that has explicitly recognised the importance of culture to the life and future of the city. At Manchester International Festival , I inherited an organisation with an enviable reputation for attracting major international artists to present entirely new work in Manchester's venues and found spaces. The city council, despite the national doctrine of austerity, has put support of the arts at the heart of its strategies for the city's future. None of these policies and practices are without issues, but overall the progressive commitment to culture as part of daily life is deeply impressive. As the latest bold initiative, The Factory, emerges on the horizon, the future of the city is being defined, at least in part, through the making of art.

How will the nature of artistic experiment be defined by the specifics of this new space: its significant scale, its encouragement of interdisciplinarity, its openness to an ideal of cultural democracy? We are yet to discover the qualities of the work that will be made at The Factory, but if we do our job right, the space itself, and the city in which it is grounded, will contribute to those qualities.

By inviting artists from across the globe to make new work in the landscape of Manchester, and by resourcing that work properly, an exploration is potentially opened up which is global but not globalised, which lives in and with the communities among which it is located, while making an invitation to the world.

And who are our guides on this journey? Artists—the more provocative the better—and the communities into which they sometimes step, and which sometimes gather around them: disruptive, argumentative, frustrating, inspiring communities of ordinary/extraordinary people, demonstrating that in the difficulties of the local lie the creative potentials of the social.

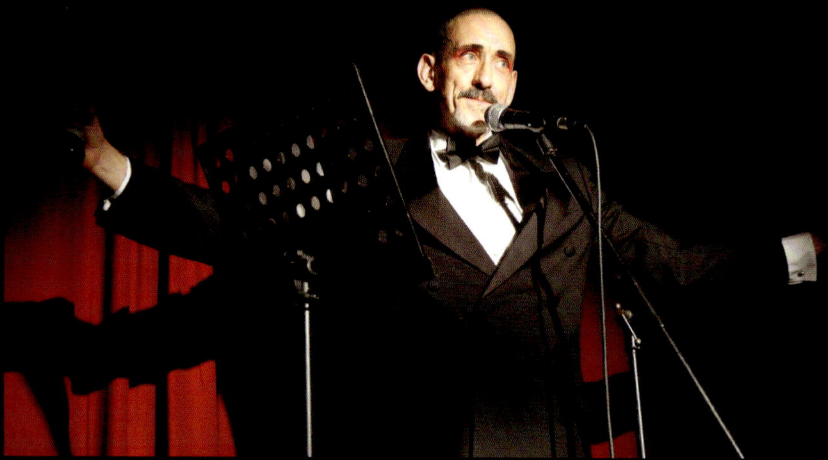

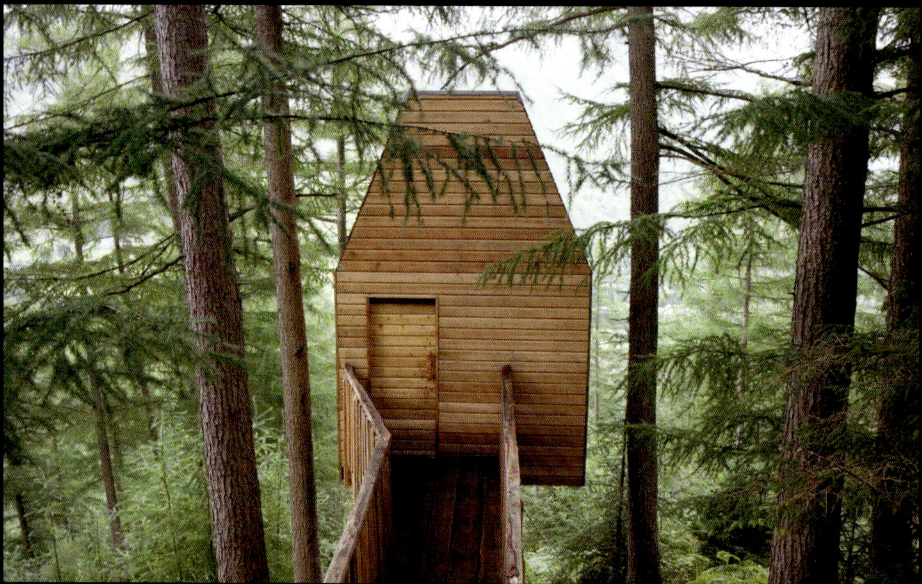

Top: Neil Bartlett, *ALAG: A Live Art Gala* (2014). Image Holly Revell.

Bottom: London Fieldworks (Bruce Gilchrist and Jo Joelson), *Remote Performances at Outlandia* (2014). Image the artists.

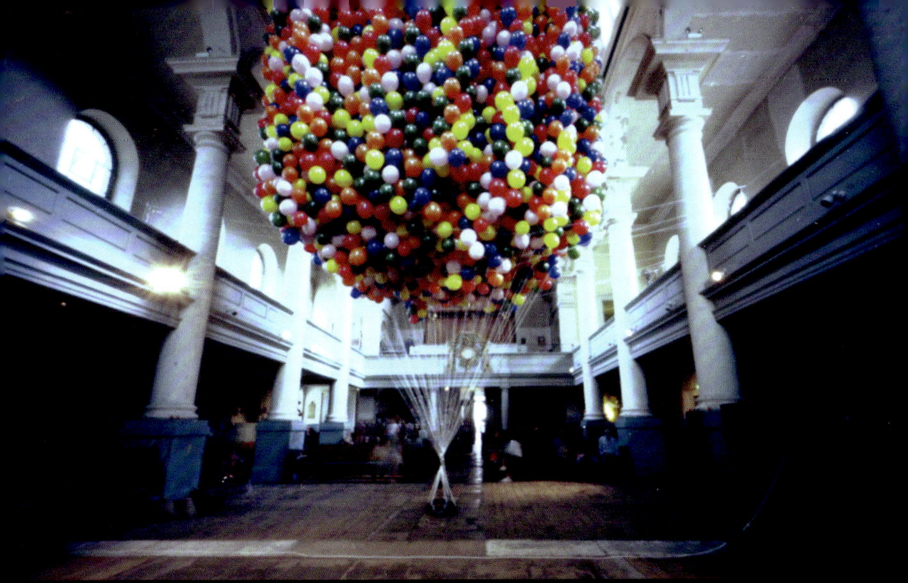

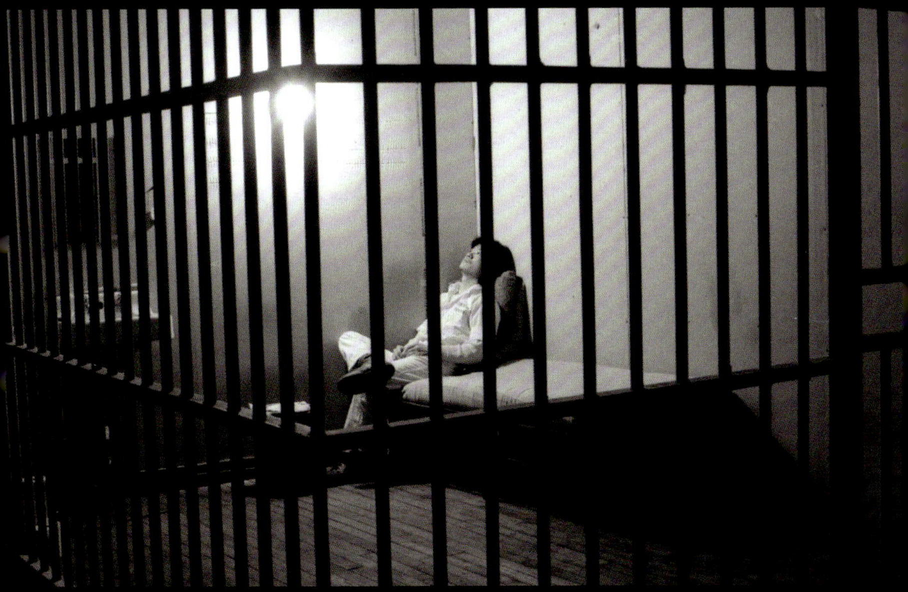

Top: Noëmi Lakmaier, *Cherophobia*, Unlimited Festival, London (2016). Image Tina Rowe.

Bottom: Tehching Hsieh, *One Year Performance* (1978–1979), New York
Image Cheng Wei Kuong © Tehching Hsieh.

Overleaf: Liberate Tate, *Time Piece*, Tate Modern (2015). Image Martin LeSanto-Smith.

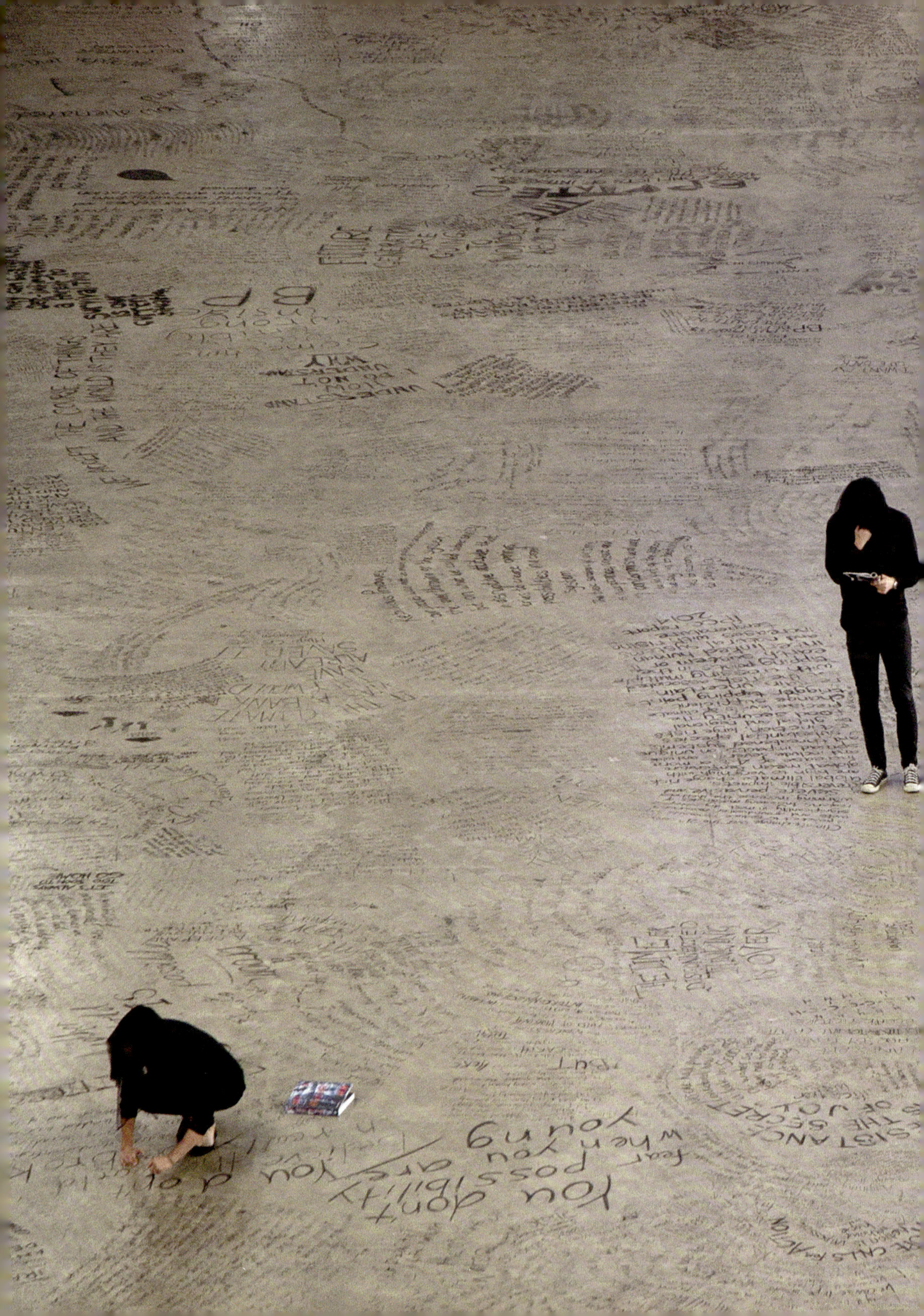

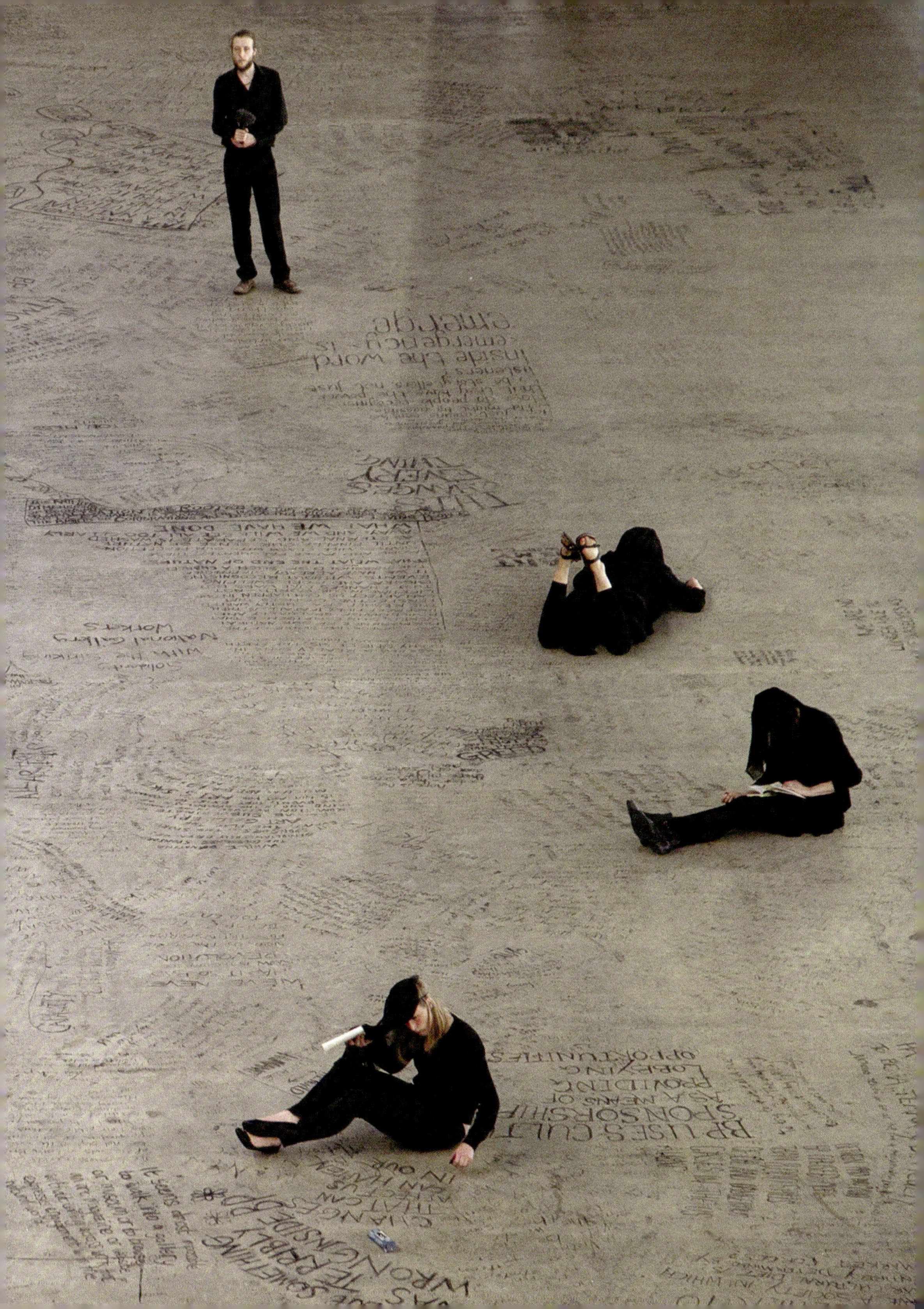

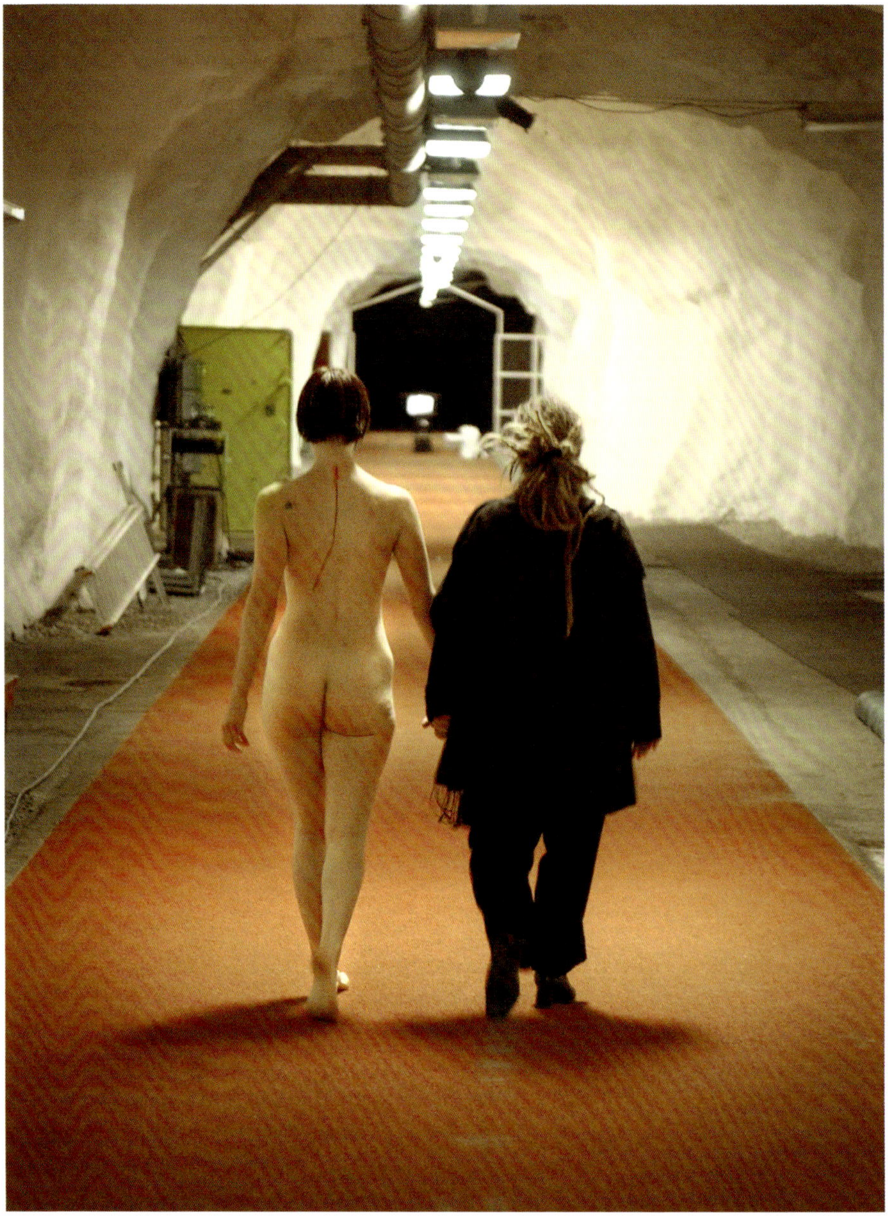

Kira O'Reilly, *Untitled bomb shelter action for Kuopio*, ANTI–Contemporary Art Festival (2003).
Image Pekka Mäkinen.

INSTITUTIONS

GARY ANDERSON
BRYAN BIGGS
ROSELEE GOLDBERG
JEN HARVIE
MARY PATERSON
LENA ŠIMIĆ
JOSHUA SOFAER
JANE TROWELL
CATHERINE WOOD

INSTITUTIONS

'Almost everyone I know under 30 is doing a PhD,' observes Mary Paterson in her conversation with Joshua Sofaer, which she attributes to the changing economic circumstances that affect the support available to artists—but she also identifies the knock-on effects that these individual strategic decisions have on artistic, curatorial, and critical practices. In RoseLee Goldberg's conversation with Tate curator Catherine Wood, they note that there is still a lot of work to be done for performance and Live Art to be fully valued within art historical narratives and the curatorial practices of major galleries; but they also observe the ways in which that work is well underway: performance is no longer an 'after-hours' event but part of the curatorial scheme of the Tate; and a festival like Goldberg's Performa in New York, which she describes as a 'museum without walls', gives status and visibility to Live Art and performance.

So Live Art is no longer a marginalised form, outside the institutions of major galleries and higher education, but finding ways to live with and within them. And LADA has played a key role in this institutionalisation of Live Art—indeed, as Paterson and Sofaer discuss (along with others in this collection, such as O'Reilly), even the term 'Live Art' is an institutional strategy, a term deployed for funding purposes and emerging out of Keidan's dexterity and experience with Arts Council and other funding structures.[1] *Live Culture* (2003), LADA's four-day takeover of many of Tate's prominent spaces that is the starting point for Goldberg and Wood's conversation, represents a key early intervention within institutional structures—as do the publications emerging out of it, such as Adrian Heathfield's richly illustrated collection *Live: Art and Performance*, or Joshua Sofaer's *The Performance Pack*, a self-contained kit that anyone can use to deliver an interactive lecture on performance.[2]

As Lois Weaver describes in a later section of this book, LADA has also carefully cultivated close working relationships with higher education. From its first year, LADA worked with Weaver at Queen Mary University of London to run East End Collaborations from 1999–2009 (renamed Fresh AiR from 2010), a performance platform for emerging artists.[3] The idea of 'platform' itself establishes a structure for progression of artists, but also somewhat institutionalises the pathway;[4] and a number of these platforms have proliferated throughout the sector for many years, from the hugely influential Platform, later 'Elevator', programme at the

National Review of Live Art to the 'National Platform' (now 'SPILL OPEN') at the SPILL Festival of Performance. At the time of writing, LADA's relationship with Queen Mary is continuing through collaboration on a new postgraduate MA Live Art—again, a development that both creates a structure for support and training, and is also a marker of professionalisation and institutional legitimation.[5]

These questions of the impact of institutionalisation of performance and Live Art were addressed, suitably enough, through an institutional collaboration. From 2009–2014, LADA partnered with Goldsmiths and University of Roehampton on the creative research project *Performance Matters*, funded by the UK Arts and Humanities Research Council, and directed by Gavin Butt, Lois Keidan, and Adrian Heathfield.[6] Amongst many activities, this project included two large-scale symposia (*Performing Idea*, 2010, and *Trashing Performance*, 2011) and funding for two full-time doctoral researchers, who convened a third public sharing (*Potentials of Performance*, 2012).[7] In a reflective conversation that took place near the end of the project, Butt frames the project in relation to the increasing visibility of Live Art within major institutions: 'The increased inclusion of performance and Live Art in museum and gallery programmes ... appeared to signal a change in the status of performance from a relatively minor and marginal practice to an increasingly valorised and visible cultural form,' he observes. 'Fast forwarding to now, ... it is clear to me that the institutional embrace of performance has moved on apace in the intervening years.'[8]

However, as all three project leaders address, this process of institutionalisation tends to reproduce the tendencies and ways of working of the institution itself: 'the institutions are doing it on their terms, and what they tend to ignore is the ecosystem and the culture that surrounds performance, that's been really hard fought for and carefully developed over a long period of time,' Keidan replies.[9] For this reason, it was important that *Performance Matters* collaborated not only with Tate Modern and the Whitechapel Gallery, but also the Bethnal Green Working Men's Club and LADA's then neighbours in Hackney Wick, The Yard and]performance s p a c e[. And alongside the inclusion of different kinds of contributors—including those who might be interested in 'trashing performance,' as in the theme of the second year of the project—there was also an emphasis on the generation of an alternative archive through publication and documentation. For example, a key output of the project was the production of *Crossovers*, a series of seven artist films, documentaries, and dialogues.[10]

Indeed, support for the dissemination of documents, critical writing, and artist voices has been one of the major

Right top: Lois Weaver, *FeMUSEum*, *Performance Matters* (2011). Image Christa Holka.

Right bottom: The Disabled Avant-Grade, *Backstage Drama*, *Performance Matters* (2011). Image Christa Holka.

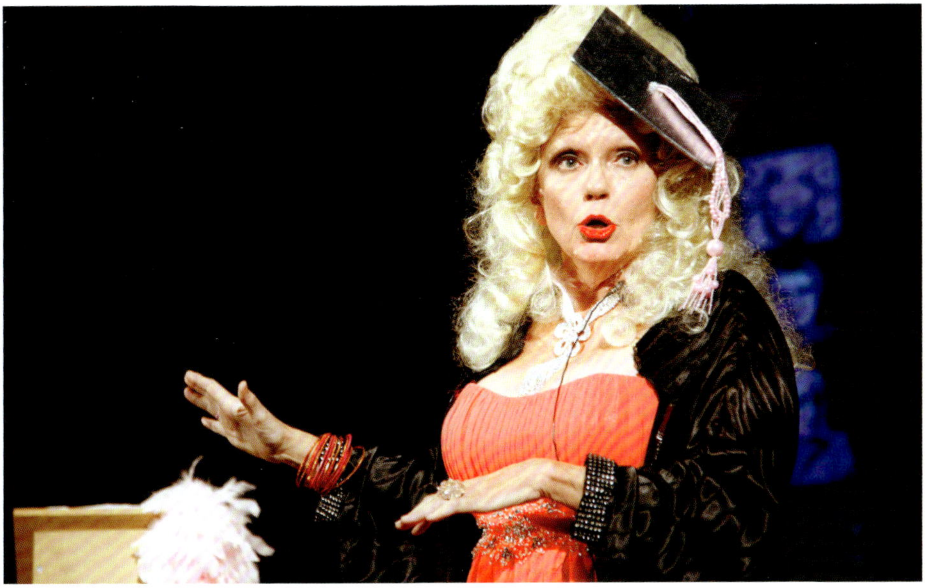

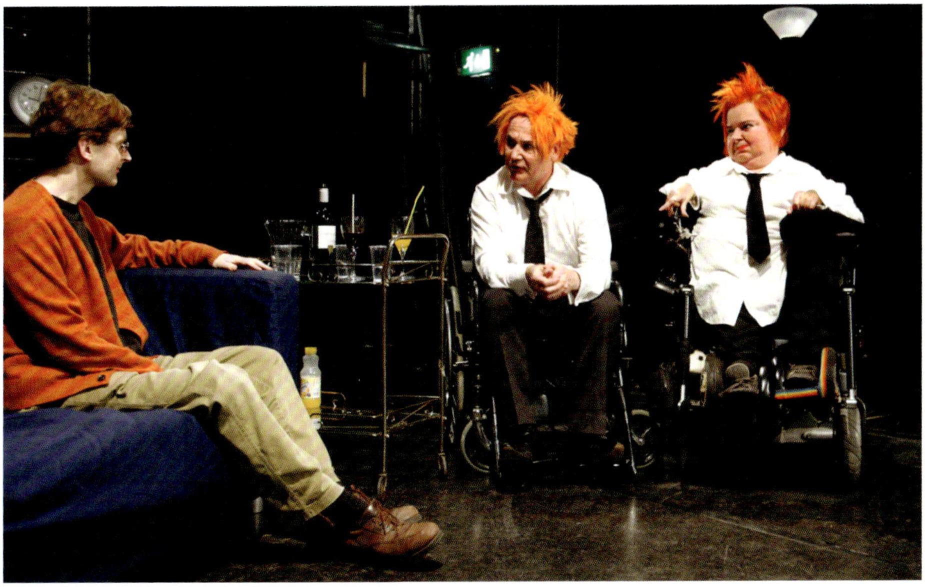

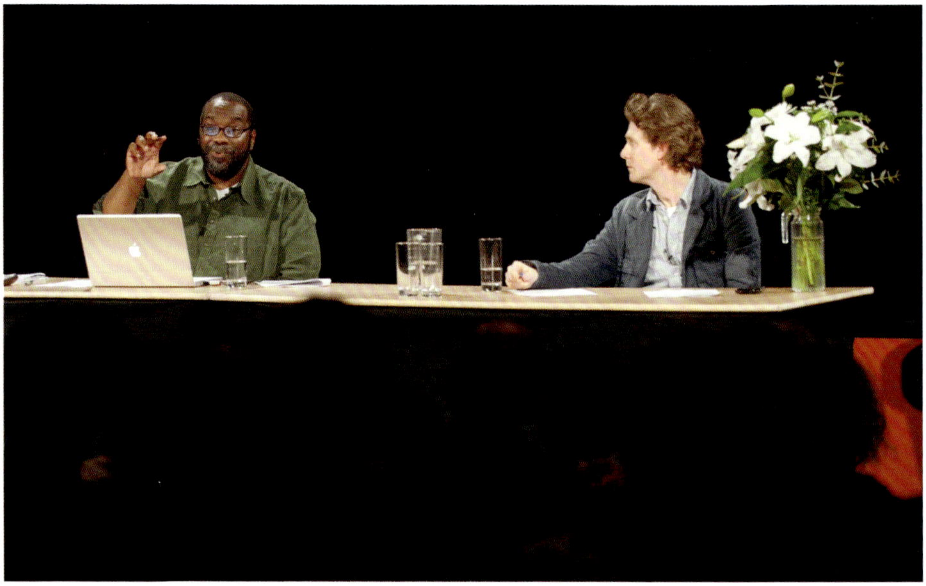

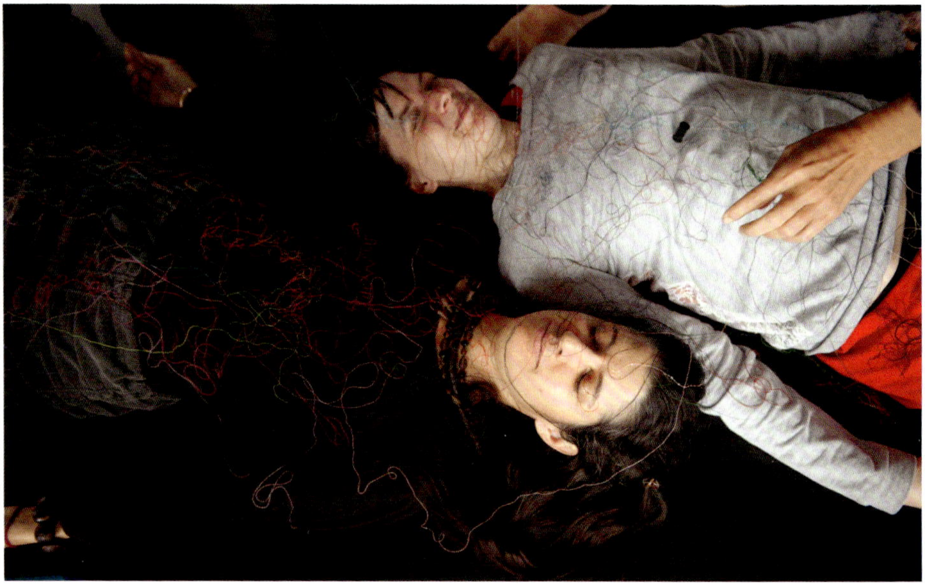

contributions of LADA and Live Art UK. As Mary Paterson describes in her conversation in this section, this support began with Live Art UK's *Writing from Live Art* (2006–2008), a mentoring project led by Joshua Sofaer to support new writers and new ways of writing about Live Art.[11] This was followed by the first *Live Art Almanac*, a collection of diverse writings around Live Art that took advantage of the ease of access to publication enabled by print-on-demand;[12] as well as an increase in online writing, particularly around festivals, pioneered by Paterson and her collaborator Rachel Lois Clapham. From that first *Live Art Almanac*, LADA has gone on to support an ever-increasing range of publications and co-publications, now at over 80 books and DVDs, with bespoke titles distributed through LADA's specialist online bookshop Unbound.[13] As Paterson writes elsewhere, 'The generic freedom of Live Art … rubs off on the texts that are written about it,'[14] and these publications have taken many forms, from custom artist publications[15] to substantial volumes co-published with academic and gallery presses and major publishing houses.[16] One of the distinctive elements of these initiatives has been the Intellect Live series, a partnership between LADA and Intellect Books, which assembles the first substantial monograph on significant artists in a series that so far includes Ron Athey, Raimund Hoghe, Lois Weaver, Adrian Howells, Kira O'Reilly, and Anne Bean.[17]

Left top: Fred Moten and Adrian Heathfield, *Other Durations*, *Performance Matters* (2010). Image Hugo Glendinning.

Left bottom: Janine Antoni Workshop, *Performance Matters* (2010). Image Hugo Glendinning.

Over twenty years, LADA's Study Room has also grown from a handful of donated artefacts to one of the world's largest publicly accessible reference collections of Live Art documentation and related publications, with over 7,000 catalogued items—many of which are unique donations from artists' private collections. As the collection has grown, LADA has commissioned 'Study Room Guides' on themes ranging from disability to food to motherhood, many of which function not merely as guides to other resources but as provocative interventions in their own right—such as John Jordan's collection of footnotes towards an 'insurrectionary imagination', Rachel Lois Clapham's formally inventive guide to performance writing, Rachel Zerihan's pioneering collection on 'one-to-one performance' that preceded most scholarship on this form, and, appropriately for this section, Johanna Linsley's guide on engaging with—and challenging—institutions.[18] 'What kind of stance can a radical politics take towards institutions in these times?' Linsley asks. 'It doesn't seem sufficient to be simply anti-institution, however coercive or obstructing some institutions can be. How can new models for institutions be achieved?'

Like the contributors to this section, LADA has found agency in collaborating *with* institutions—in a 'strategically interdisciplinary' way, as Paterson and Sofaer discuss—but also in *becoming* institution, which, as seen with examples such as the Institute for the Art and Practice of Dissent at Home or the Free Liverpool of University, can itself be a form of resistance: messy, wilfully naive, bold, and alive.

1. Jennie Klein describes LADA's emergence as both symptomatic of, and opportunistic with, the emphasis on 'innovation', 'risk', and 'experiment' in the policies of the 'New Labour' government of the early 1990s. See Klein, p. 29.

2. *Live: Art and Performance*, ed. by Adrian Heathfield (London: Tate, 2004); Joshua Sofaer, *The Performance Pack*, numbered edition (London: Live Art Development Agency, 2004).

3. See <http://www.thisisliveart.co.uk/projects/east-end-collaborations<.

4. In a conversation later in this collection, James Leadbitter describes the sense of legitimacy he felt when being invited–and paid–to contribute to EEC.

5. See <http://www.sed.qmul.ac.uk/drama/postgraduate/liveart/>.

6. See <http://www.thisisperformancematters.co.uk/>.

7. See <http://www.thisisliveart.co.uk/projects/crossovers>.

8. Gavin Butt, Adrian Heathfield and Lois Keidan, 'Performance Matters: Gavin Butt, Lois Keidan and Adrian Heathfield in Conversation', *Contemporary Theatre Review*, 24.1 (2014), 102–14 (p. 105).

9. Butt, Heathfield, and Keidan, p. 106.

10. See <http://www.thisisliveart.co.uk/projects/crossovers>.

11. See <http://www.liveartuk.org/activities/writing-from-live-art/>.

12. *The Live Art Almanac*, ed. by Daniel Brine (London: Live Art Development Agency, 2008).

13. See <http://thisisliveart.co.uk/publishing/category/all>; <https://www.thisisunbound.co.uk/>.

14. *In Time: A Collection of Live Art Case Studies*, ed. by Live Art Development Agency (London: Live Art Development Agency and Live Art UK, 2010), p. 144 <https://www.liveartuk.org/uploads/documents/In_Time_complete.pdf>.

15. For example, artist-led projects referenced in the present collection include *Aaron Williamson: Performance / Video / Collaboration*, ed. by Aaron Williamson and Oriana Fox (London: Live Art Development Agency and KIOSK, 2008); Becky Edmunds and others, *Dear Stranger, I Love You: The Ethics of Community in Rajni Shah Projects' Glorious* (London and Lancaster: Live Art Development Agency and Lancaster University, 2013); Jamila Johnson-Small and Alexandrina Hemsley, *A Contemporary Struggle* (London: Live Art Development Agency and Project O, 2013); *Survival of the Sickest: The Art of Martin O'Brien*, ed. by Martin O'Brien and David MacDiarmid (London: Live Art Development Agency, 2018).

16. Significant scholarly co-publications include Adrian Heathfield and Tehching Hsieh, *Out of Now: The Lifeworks of Tehching Hsieh* (Cambridge, MA, and London: MIT Press and Live Art Development Agency, 2009); *Perform Repeat Record: Live Art in History*, ed. by Amelia Jones and Adrian Heathfield (London and Bristol: Live Art Development Agency and Intellect, 2012); *Performance Art in Ireland: A History*, ed. by Áine Phillips (London and Bristol: Live Art Development Agency and Intellect, 2015)..

17. *Pleading in the Blood: The Art and Performances of Ron Athey*, ed. by Dominic Johnson (London and Bristol: Live Art Development Agency and Intellect, 2013); *Throwing the Body into the Fight: A Portrait of Raimund Hoghe*, ed. by Mary Kate Connolly (London and Bristol: Live Art Development Agency and Intellect, 2013); *The Only Way Home Is Through the Show: Performance Work of Lois Weaver*, ed. by Jen Harvie and Lois Weaver (London and Bristol: Live Art Development Agency and Intellect, 2015); *It's All Allowed: The Performances of Adrian Howells*, ed. by Deirdre Heddon and Dominic Johnson (London and Bristol: Live Art Development Agency and Intellect, 2016); *Kira O'Reilly: Untitled (Bodies)*, ed. by Harriet Curtis and Martin Hargreaves (London and Bristol: Live Art Development Agency and Intellect, 2018); *Anne Bean: Self Etc.*, ed. by Rob La Frenais (London and Bristol: Live Art Development Agency and Intellect, 2018).

18. John Jordan, *In the Footnotes of Library Angels: A Bi(bli)ography of Insurrectionary Imagination* (London: Live Art Development Agency, 2006) <http://www.thisisliveart.co.uk/resources/catalogue/study-room-guide-in-the-footnotes-of-library-angels-a-bibliography-of-insur>; *(W)reading Performance Writing : A Study Room Guide*, ed. by Rachel Lois Clapham (London: Live Art Development Agency, 2010) <http://www.thisisliveart.co.uk/resources/catalogue/wreading-performance-writing-a-study-room-guide-2010-by-rachel-lois-clapham>; *Live Art Development Agency Study Room Guide on One to One Performance*, ed. by Rachel Zerihan (London: Live Art Development Agency, 2009) <http://www.thisisliveart.co.uk/resources/catalogue/rachel-zerihans-study-room-guide>; *Dreams for an Institution: A Study Room Guide on Engaging & Challenging Institutions*, ed. by Johanna Linsley (London: Live Art Development Agency, 2013) <http://www.thisisliveart.co.uk/resources/catalogue/dreams-for-an-institution-a-study-room-guide>. For an index of all Study Room guides see <http://www.thisisliveart.co.uk/resources/study-room/study-room-guides>.

INSTITUTIONS
CONVERSATION
MARY PATERSON
JOSHUA SOFAER
DATE
20 DECEMBER 2015
PLACE
LONDON

Mary Paterson is a writer, artist, and producer. She is frequently commissioned by LADA and Live Art UK to write about Live Art practices, in works such as *In Time* (2010), *Access All Areas* (2012), *Getting It Out There* (2013), and commissioned responses to LADA projects such as *ALAG: A Live Art Gala* (2014), *Take the Money and Run?* (2015), *Through the Looking Glass* for Heart of Glass (2016), *Awkward Bastards 2* (2016), and *KAPUTT: The Academy of Destruction* at Tate Modern (2017). As 2009/2010 LADA Thinker in Residence, she wrote the hypertext document *a navigation through unbound*, and with Rajni Shah Projects she compiled *The Glorious Storybook* as part of *Dear Stranger, I love you* (LADA/Lancaster University 2013). As she describes here, she has also developed numerous collaborative writing projects that challenge the conventional forms and hierarchies of writing practice, including Open Dialogues with Rachel Lois Clapham, and Something Other and The Department of Feminist Conversations, both with Maddy Costa and Diana Damian Martin.

Joshua Sofaer works primarily with modes of collaboration and participation, which he explores through social sculpture, performance, installation, exhibition, and publication. He has created collaborations with institutions of various kinds, including *Scavengers*, a scavenger hunt for various galleries including Tate Modern (2005) and SFMOMA (2006); *Object Retrieval* (2009) with University College London (UCL), in which a single object from the UCL Pathology Collection was rigorously analysed by experts from various fields and members of the public; *Name in Lights* (2007), a national competition for the City of Birmingham to create a giant illuminated name of a single individual in the city's Centenary Square; and, described here, *The Rubbish Collection* (2014) for Science Museum London and a new staged version of Bach's St Matthew Passion for Folkoperan in Stockholm (2014). His 'infotainment' lecture *What is Live Art?* (2003) was presented as part of *Live Culture*, and with LADA he created the interactive, self-guided lectures *The Performance Pack* (2003) and *The Many-Headed Monster* (2009), as well as *Life Lecture* (2011), an online resource that structures and directs an audience to deliver a lecture to themselves about themselves. With Karen Christopher, Joshua led the DIY project *This Will Never Happen* (2015) as part of Heart of Glass for St Helens, Merseyside, that supported artists in working imaginatively with the form of the project proposal.

Joshua led the programme *Writing from Live Art* (2006–2008), of which Mary was a participant, and Mary is co-editor with Roberta Mock of *Joshua Sofaer: Performance | Objects | Participation* (LADA/Intellect Live, 2019).

Joshua: What the category of Live Art does for me—and I would assert for other artists—is to offer itself as a permissive category, one that not just allows but *actively promotes* thinking across different art forms *and* with different institutions. So as an artist, it offers me the permission and affords me the confidence, to work in or with institutions as diverse as an opera house, an art gallery, a science museum, a community association, a municipal rubbish dump, and so on.

Fifteen years ago, I would describe myself as a 'live artist'—but I really only did so for a couple of years, because I found it unhelpful. People didn't know what it meant. I think its pertinence and urgency as a term is in its use within institutional frames and as a lobbying tool for work that sits outside of subject specialisms. After a while of making work for Live Art audiences, I became frustrated. I became uninterested in seeing the same audiences at the work all the time—these audiences of experts that were talking to themselves. I still love going to see that work, but in my practice, I rejected those contexts for making my own work.

Mary: Was your frustration with Live Art audiences, or with a particular kind of academic emphasis?

Joshua: In a way they were the same thing for me. It seemed to me that the discourse around contemporary performance practice was only happening in the academy—and that was a real problem. That's why *Writing from Live Art* seemed necessary, and why I responded so well to your writing, Mary, because it seemed to address other readers than those in the academy. It was still dealing with difficult concepts, but didn't require expert vocabulary or a history of engagement with that kind of work.

Mary: Writing from Live Art was my introduction to Live Art, because I'd only even *heard* about performance art about six months earlier. I was coming to the end of a Masters where I'd come across Hannah Wilke and other feminist performance artists. I remember saying to one of my tutors, 'I think I've been waiting for feminist performance all my life.' She just said something like, 'Oh, that's nice, dear.' (It was a really awful environment!) But I was starting to have this feeling that was something like: 'I don't know what's going on, but I have the *right* to think about it.' And it seemed to me that I could take my cue from the permissiveness of the work itself. I think there's a definition on the LADA website that says Live Art is 'strategically interdisciplinary', which I always find very, very useful. It's about an approach, not a form. I felt I could take my cue from that approach.

At first I had a very common response to Live Art, which is that I saw it as ad hoc, as intervention; and I underestimated the amount of thinking behind it—all the theory that goes into it. As I got more involved, I became interested in the histories of the work, and how it works on different levels. But there's a huge freedom in that first approach: you feel like you have a right to respond. That's not something you get from, say, 19th century painting.

Then we did *We Need to Talk about Live Art* at the National Review of Live Art, which felt like this response to the immediacy of the event. We were printing things out, tearing things up and giving them out—blogging before blogging was a thing. And again there's that misunderstanding: the work itself isn't actually immediate—it's often very deliberate and has spent a long time in development—but it's the *reception* to the work that is immediate. And it's that reception that we were responding to. From there I've become more and more interested in how writing can translate and represent an experience that you might have in relation to a work of art, rather than trying to write about or explain the work itself: understanding how writing does not represent experience, but acts on it. And that is a kind of freedom from the academic model.

Having said that, I don't think the problem that you and LADA were addressing with *Writing from Live Art* has been solved. I don't think that there are avenues for accessible writing about performance art and Live Art. In fact, one thing that has happened over the time that I have been writing is that a lot of the magazines and journals where I used to publish—and be *paid*—have folded: *Dance Theatre Journal*, *Total Theatre*, *AN Magazine*. Now there are lots of places to publish, like *Exeunt* and so on, but none of them pay. And at the same time, lots and lots of young artists are doing PhDs—so many more than ten years ago. Almost everyone I know under 30 is doing a PhD, because that's a good way to sustain yourself.

Joshua: And what do you think is the result of the fact that artists are doing PhDs?

Mary: There are a few results. One is that it perpetuates the culture of not being paid for writing. Another is that it perpetuates the division between academic writing and performative writing. I acknowledge that I have a chip on my shoulder about this! I ran some workshops with LADA earlier this year, along with Maddy Costa and Diana Damian. Diana invited lots of people who write for *Exeunt* [where she is editor] and worked with her on SPILL writing,[1] and Maddy has worked in newspaper criticism, so she invited lots of theatre critics.

And *everyone* was doing a PhD or had done one recently. As a result, none of them expect to get paid for anything. They don't think that writing on a blog or in a magazine has the same value as an academic paper. And they don't think that the academy is the place to experiment with writing. Now, I think this is probably going to shift at some point, as all these practice-based PhDs are going to change the academic world. But from my perspective outside that world, at the moment it feels like these PhDs are a means for academic culture to encroach on practice, rather than the other way around.

I was shocked that these writers, who are younger than me, seem grateful for the opportunity to publish a 400-word review somewhere for free. You have a PhD! Why are you grateful? I read that as a form of academic culture, as part of the institution of academic culture, that sense of hierarchy and 'knowing your place'. And for me, the whole thing about Live Art is *nobody* has to know their place.

Joshua: Yes, that's true, and so as an artist coming from that kind of permissive culture, it is interesting to enter into institutional frames where a set hierarchy exists. Last year I was working with Folkoperan in Stockholm on a staged version of Bach's St Matthew Passion. Never in my life have I encountered such a strict procedure toward the making of a production than in an opera house: the soloists rehearse separately from the orchestra, who rehearse separately from the choir, and then they are all brought together at the last minute. That just absolutely couldn't work for me. I needed absolutely everyone on equal footing right from the beginning. In a way, *not* having possession of the knowledge of the standard procedure was liberating, because I could say, well, that won't work, can we do it like this instead?

And more explicitly than that would be *The Rubbish Collection*, the project I did at the Science Museum in 2014, where we engaged with all levels of the institution: right from the directorate level, who had to be actively involved, to the porterage staff, who had to be actively involved. The project was to sort and photograph every single thing that was thrown out by the Science Museum and its over 250,000 visitors over the course of 30 days. That included waste from the offices and from any acquisitions and museum objects, building materials from the building projects around the building, café waste from one of the seven cafes that they have, and waste thrown out by the public. Everyone has got waste. There were letters from the Prime Minister to the Directorate, for example, alongside love letters that had been written by kids on scrappy bits of paper. We then followed it on its route to recycling or incineration, and brought it back for an exhibition.

The project forced a kind of opening out of the institution. One thing that it demonstrated clearly was that, almost without exception, the curatorial staff are white and the porterage staff are black. The porterage staff, who are subcontractors, became visible because we were working

Overleaf: Joshua Sofaer, *The Rubbish Collection*, Science Museum, London (2014). Image Jennie Hills.

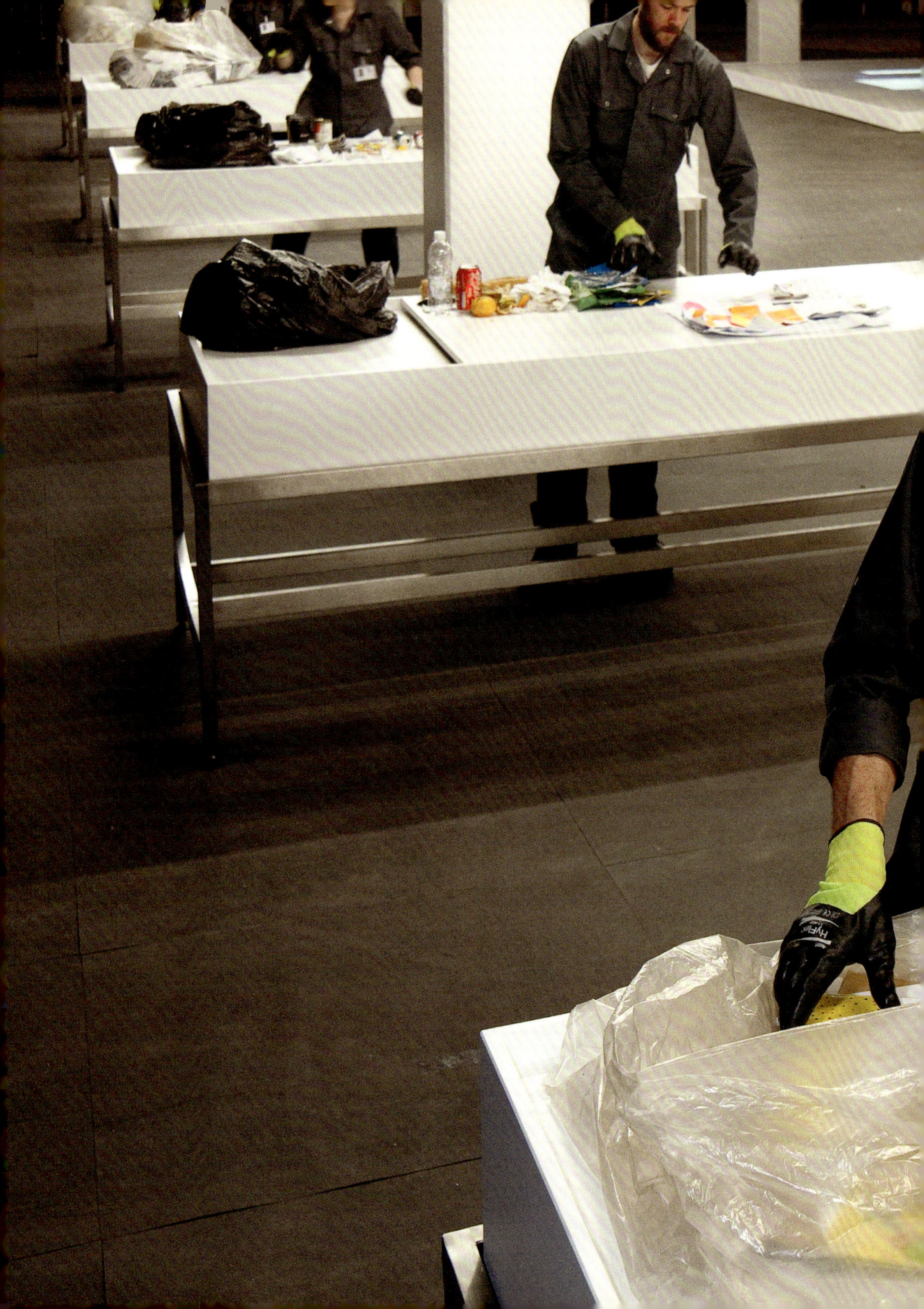
HyFlex

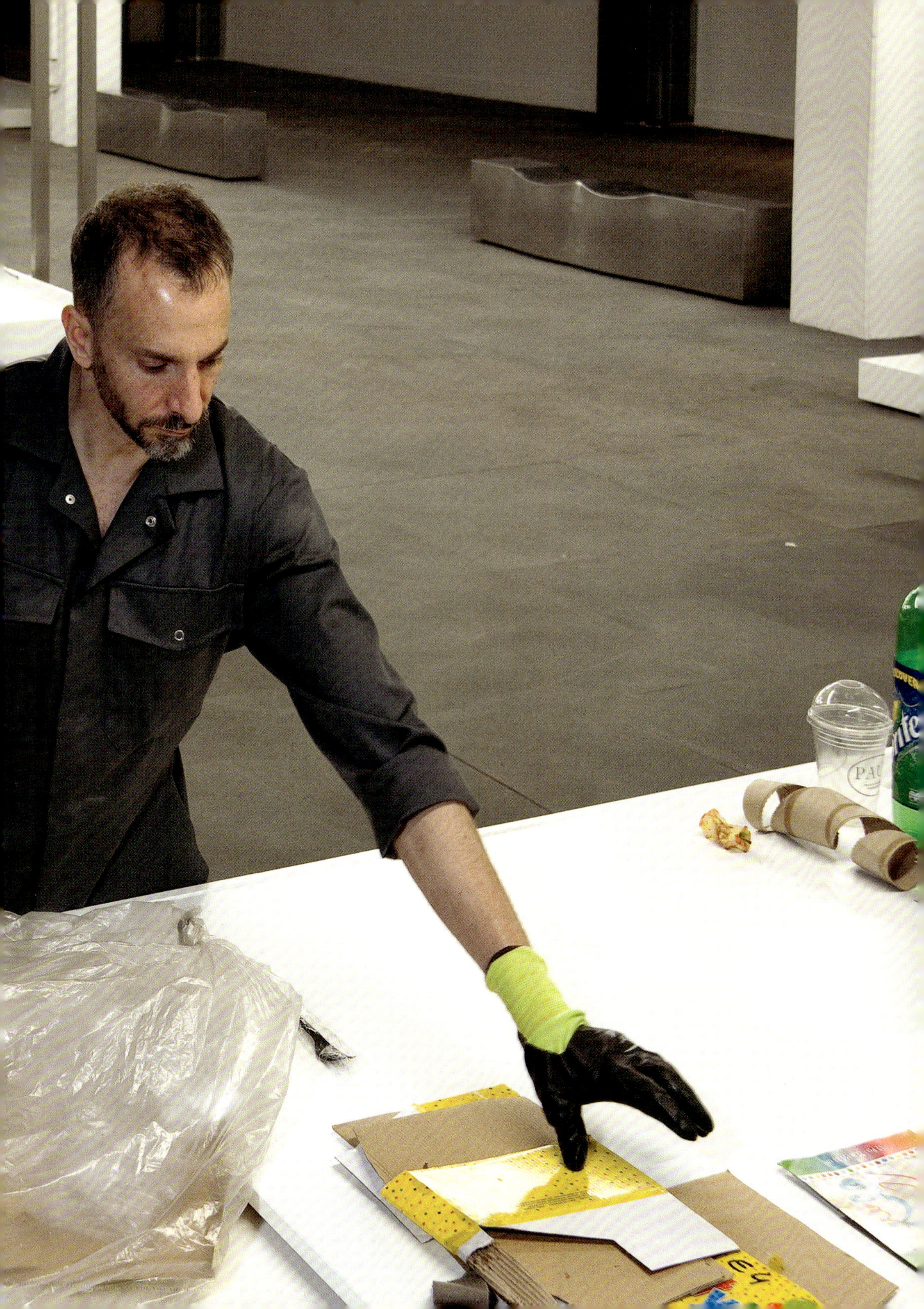

with them all the time because they were literally physically bringing the rubbish to us. Normally nobody even talks to them, and suddenly they're an integral part of this quite problematic exhibition that's happening over the course of three months. This kind of flattening of a hierarchy is a challenge for the institution because it's not how they normally work. The Science Museum had to be very brave in order to do that, because it literally brought the shit to the surface! [*laughs*] We even displayed the shit; the Science Museum displayed the excrement of its staff and visitors.

The project also resulted in an institutional shift—for example, changes in how they contract the café and the portering staff, and new regulations that they've implemented.

Mary: The work you've been doing with specific institutions—actual buildings and infrastructures—is fascinating. As a writer, I've also been thinking about more abstract structures we live within. Years ago I read a book about feminism that described the pernicious power of misogyny lying in the fact that it is institutionally un-institutional: its institution is its universalism. This does not mean that it is outside the institution, but rather that its institution is so powerful, that there isn't really an outside.

I thought about this working with Rajni Shah Projects on the project *Glorious*. As a process, I think *Glorious* intervened in lots of institutionally un-institutionalised cultural practices, and one of them was the idea of an authored, vouched-for, art historically positioned text that anchors the work in time and justifies it in history. This function of writing in relation to art is so deeply implicit in cultural 'unstitutions' that writing that tries to do something else often gets tied up in knots (and nots) explaining itself before it can even begin! How do you represent collaboration in the form of a book, with all its associations with authorship and authority?

With *Dear Stranger, I Love You* (LADA/ Lancaster University, 2013), the answer we found was partly to do with process: having a writer embedded in the project, as part of the company; an ongoing series of blogs and open invitations to others to take part; and a collaborative and generous relationship between Rajni and the company as a whole. It was partly to do with written form: short essays which draw on criticism, fiction, and poetry to evoke a sense of performance rather than document it. And partly to do with physical format: the publication included a 'Storybook' in a personalised box-set alongside a more formal evaluation and a DVD of films (by Becky Edmunds).

This question of de-institutionalising authorship as feminist practice drives my interest in collaborations: with Rachel Lois Clapham as Open Dialogues, where we would do things like record a conversation and edit it so that you can tell there's more than one person speaking, but you can't tell where they start or stop or how many people there are. And with Something

Other with Maddy Costa and Diana Damian, where we've pursued a series of collaborations between artists and technologists to think about how writing and performance exist online.

But the power dynamics here are complicated. Writing is powerful, and part of its power comes from its ability to communicate over time and distance. Writerly conventions are not just oppressive tools, but also compromises and shared frameworks designed for people who don't know each other. In my experience, many artists and curators interested in testing institutional boundaries in their practice are nevertheless most interested in writing that promises access to traditional hierarchies of knowledge—via the academy or the mainstream press. In this context, a de-authored approach is a challenge to power that might also feel like an obstruction.

Joshua: Yes, I agree, and perhaps I would add that in terms of artistic production, sometimes it's useful for work to have a named artist, someone who will take responsibility for the project. *The Rubbish Collection* at the Science Museum could never have happened without that. Of course, it's completely unimportant that it was *my* name, but nevertheless it needed a named artist. And sometimes it's not important that a name is visible at all, or that it is understood as an artist project.

This comes back to the 'strategically interdisciplinary,' nature of Live Art, as you said. You have to know when to use that hierarchical system to your advantage, and when to open a platform for others. I have to say that a completely open, democratic process completely fails for art-making. You just end up with beige!

One of the things I did in 2011 or 2012 was to train as a coach in Relational Dynamics, precisely because I wanted a way of eliciting responses from people that didn't include me bringing *my* language, but nevertheless could incorporate people on all levels into a project, whatever it might be. I have found that extremely useful in all kinds of contexts. I have a working methodology with people to engage participative response.

I've used coaching directly in my art. For example, I'm working on a project now called *Opera Helps*, where opera singers go into people's homes and are trained using Relational Dynamics techniques to listen to a problem that the person shares. The singer then selects an aria that they think pertains to the problem and sing it directly to the person in their home. My hunch was that if you make the *problem* the reason for people meeting, then paradoxically people will listen to the music more acutely.

Opera is my guilty secret. I mostly find theatre very difficult; but opera makes theatre so extreme that I somehow no longer worry about 'the theatrical'. I can be really shaken by opera. Not everybody has access to that, and in a way I think it is a form of reception for which you need to have a kind of education—not education in the sense of expert knowledge—but rather a certain kind of familiarity, or even just the permission, that this darkened red velvet auditorium might be for you

Mary: I think there's a parallel with Live Art: it's paradoxically something that can be extremely affecting, and something you need to be educated about. I had this hilarious, awful dinner party recently, where the kids were running around pulling books of the shelves. One of them was Rebecca Schneider's *The Explicit Body in Performance*, and a friend's husband was laughing at it because he saw it as pornography. So I tried to have a conversation, but it was impossible because everyone was giggling and going, 'Oh, look, it's a vagina!' And I was reminded of how a lot of the things that we take as read are really not, that they're quite specialist interests.

Joshua: Can I challenge that? Because it's precisely that socialised reaction to the body, that response of 'Oh, it's a vagina,' that drives the power of Live Art. Thinking about institutionalisation again, one can think of the family, or the community, or the government as a kind of institution, and the way in which we are conditioned to respond—in this case to a vagina. But, you know, young children do not have that response. If you show Live Art or performance art—quite hard, difficult work—to children, they do not have a problem with it. It's a socially conditioned response. The way in which children respond to that work is very much what we might a few minutes ago have called an 'educated' response, in as much as they are completely open to the consideration of that work.

1. SPILL is a festival of Live Art, which invites artists and writers to respond to its programme, following a model of embedded criticism first developed by Open Dialogues for SPILL's inaugural festival in 2007.

INSTITUTIONS

CONVERSATION

ROSELEE GOLDBERG

CATHERINE WOOD

DATE

26 JANUARY 2016

PLACE

NEW YORK & LONDON

RoseLee Goldberg is an art historian, curator, and critic whose book *Performance Art: From Futurism to the Present* (1979), now in its third edition and translated into fourteen languages, pioneered the study of performance art. She is also the author of *Performance Since the 1960s* (1997), *Laurie Anderson* (2000) and *Performance Now: Live Art for the Twenty-First Century* (2018). Known for her innovative curating and producing of performance as part of overall contemporary art exhibitions since her years as director of the Royal College of Art Gallery in London (1972–1975), with a program that included Christian Boltanski, Anne Bean, the Kipper Kids, Anthony McCall, and Marina Abramović, and in New York at the Kitchen in the late seventies, where her program included Brian Eno and Laurie Anderson, and the first one person exhibitions of Cindy Sherman, Robert Longo, Sherri Levine, and Jack Goldstein in the Kitchen Gallery. She also curated a performance series for 'High and Low: Modern Art and Popular Culture' (1999) at MoMA. In 2004, she founded Performa, the first biennial dedicated to visual art performance, committed to researching and presenting the history of performance throughout the 20th century and to commissioning new work for the 21st century. Performa Commissions include Isaac Julien, Shirin Neshat, Rashid Johnson, William Kentridge, Barbara Kruger, Adam Pendleton, Julie Mehretu, Laurie Simmons, Elmgreen and Dragset, Omar Fast, Candice Breitz, and many more. Goldberg has taught at New York University since 1987.

Catherine Wood is Senior Curator, International Art at Tate Modern, where she specialises in performance. She works on performance projects, exhibitions, collection acquisitions and displays, as well as being actively engaged in research. Catherine was instrumental in founding the performance programme at Tate in 2003 and since then has programmed more than two hundred live works by artists including Mark Leckey, Tania Bruguera, Trisha Brown, Katerina Šedá, Otobong Nkange, Ei Arakawa and others, both at Tate and within the online space Performance Room that she initiated in 2011. Catherine has curated *The World as a Stage* (2007, with Jessica Morgan), and *A Bigger Splash: Painting After Performance* (2012), and co-curated the Robert Rauschenberg retrospective with Achim Borchardt-Hume in 2017. She is author of *Yvonne Rainer: The Mind is a Muscle* (2007) and *Performance in Contemporary Art* (2018).

Catherine: The *Live Culture* event happened in 2003, just after I had joined Tate to begin devising a performance programme in 2002. I wasn't involved in organising or inviting *Live Culture*, as it was already planned, so I was there as an audience. What I liked about the form of the event was how it occupied the exhibition galleries and the Turbine Hall. The suite of galleries where Forced Entertainment, La Ribot, and everything else was installed was quite a big step, formally—not to be after dark or after hours, hidden somewhere else.

RoseLee: It was a terrific presentation—I especially loved the way that the visitor meandered through a range of different galleries and spaces throughout the museum.

Catherine: But what I found problematic was the way it was ring-fenced as a separate 'event', not part of the so-called 'core programme'. This was part of the problem that I was trying to address with what I then started to do at Tate, supported and encouraged by Sheena Wagstaff who was running the curatorial department. Until then, live performance had come into the museum on an opportunistic basis, often through the education programme. And *Live Culture* came in as an entity unto itself, and was important for supporting marginalised practice. But in a way, it also emphasised its marginalised status by remaining separate. Although it was *in* the institution, it wasn't *really* getting in there.

RoseLee: That's been my experience, too. Over the past several years, when I've been invited to present performance at a museum, I was inevitably put in touch with the education department—even though I pointed out that it would be preferable to talk to the curatorial department, that performance is best understood within the contemporary art conversation. It has been very important that you started in the curatorial department, Catherine, and that you've made your position clear since the beginning.

Catherine: My mission was to reflect the way in which artists were working with Live Art and performance as a continuation of making painting, sculpture, installation, video, and so on—so that it could naturally co-exist with the main exhibition and commission programme—rather than thinking about 'liveness' mainly in terms of bodily presence as the primary driver, as perhaps the Live Art Development Agency has done. But that's also why it was valuable to have had that *Live Culture* event at Tate, as part of the history of the field of practice, and also to test these different approaches against each other.

Of course, your book [*Performance Art: From Futurism to the Present* (1979)] was fundamental to setting out an art historical narrative that helped justify what I was trying to do. I knew that some of the most interesting contemporary visual artists—of my generation—were using performance as a medium as part of a wider practice. But your book demonstrated a back history, relating it to Constructivism, Futurism, and everything else.[1]

RoseLee: I felt the need to write a revisionist art history, to rewrite the twentieth century and to insert performance into its rightful place in that time-line. Because from the very beginning it has been a multimedia century. The work of Dada, or Futurist or Surrealist artists, was essentially activist, performance linked. In fact, there were a lot fewer solid objects—painting or sculpture—to speak of regarding these movements. Art historians had a hard time explaining it. Performance has been ongoing, but never understood as part of the language and materials that those artists were working with.

For me, examining performance is also a kind of study of the sociology of artists. It brings us much closer to the way that artists live, think, and work in their respective environments and context.

Catherine: Absolutely. From my perspective working in a museum, I feel like I have a different view from my colleagues because I look at things through the lens of performance—and so I somehow see all the objects, as [Robert] Rauschenberg put it, 'as the leftover of some activity.' He actually said that this was how he did *not* want his own work to feel, and so he tried to keep his work alive with kinetic and technological features. But his painting and sculpture was heavily influenced by his collaborations with performance and dance. I think you could put photographs of performative activity next to almost everything in our collection and understand its live basis. Art objects are more like fetish items that should be understood within a social ritual, and within a particular iteration of a community at a given time, but we've kind of forgotten about the social ritual part in the Modernist quest for universality.

RoseLee: Even more than being leftovers or fetishised objects, I go back to a very early comment of mine that performance was the avant-avant-garde. Often it would be the actual breakthrough that would help create the changes that we later see in the realisation of a form. For example, if Rauschenberg makes his white paintings and hangs them from the roof for a Black Mountain College event, which comes first? I think the action comes first. It radicalised the idea of what that object could be, the object followed the event.

Given the chance, I could go through MoMA and show you that the history of performance is actually there, in the collection, as is. It's been separated into

Right: La Pocha Nostra, *Ex-Centris (A Living Diorama of Fetish-ized Others)*, *Live Culture* (2003). Image Manuel Vason.

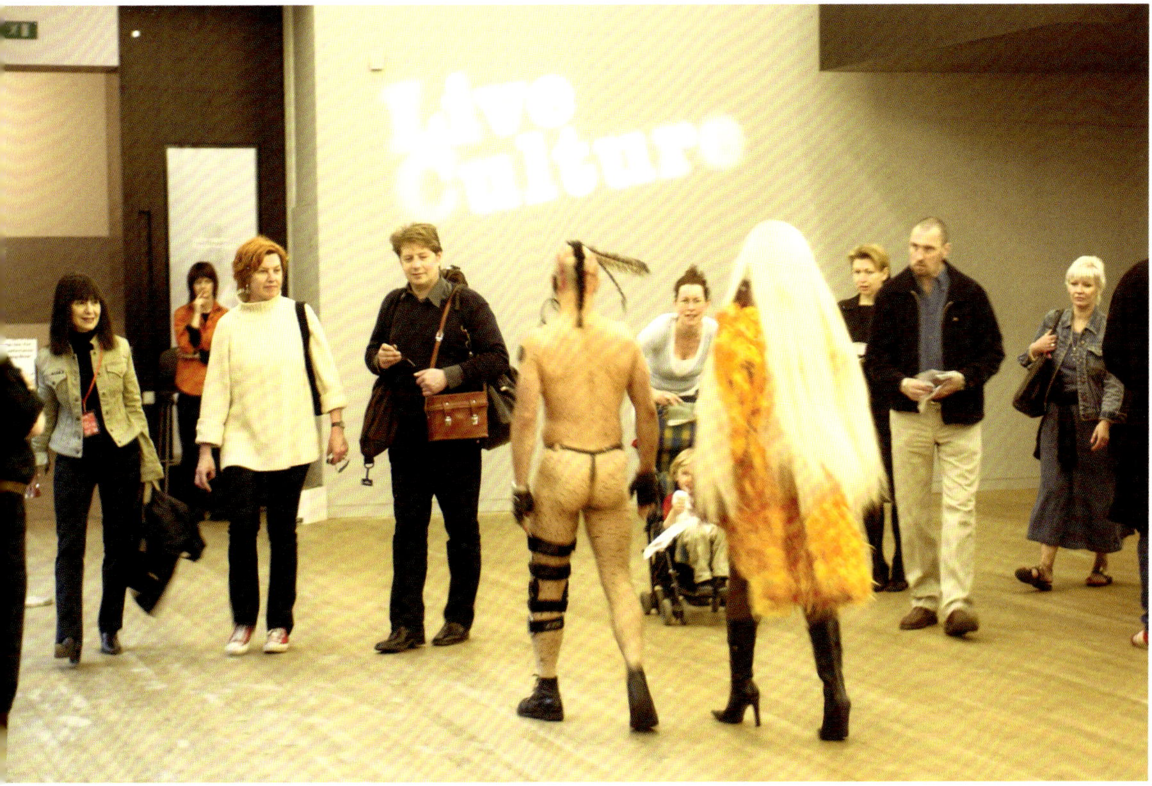
Live
Culture

different departments: Futurist manifestos and drawings tend to end up in the drawing department; a Joan Jonas video is in the video department; a Yoko Ono film is in the film department; Rauschenberg or [Claes] Oldenburg's events are so often left out of the story until relatively recently. In just about every decade you will find the history of performance right there staring at you. Performance is already *in* the collection; it's hiding in plain sight.

Catherine: It's an obvious point, but I think anything you put in a museum loses its original context and takes on a new meaning in relation to the things it's juxtaposed with. And I think that's the point of a museum, as a space for creating conversations between works that would not otherwise occur simultaneously in space and time. To not have performance in that conversation would be a huge loss in understanding the painting, sculpture and installation that was made in the twentieth century.

But when we opened the Tanks in 2012 at Tate, I remember journalists in the audience saying things like, 'Performance isn't supposed to be in the museum.' Or 'I remember in 1970-something traipsing to a field to see an Anthony McCall Happening, and *that's* what it's meant to be all about.' I think it's true: the texture of the work changes when it's put into a museum. But I think the power that's triggered by the imaginative encounter, even with documentation, is very strong. Through reading your book, for example, many of those images were absolutely burned into my mind and underwrite how I understand the contemporary work I see. Even the documentary fragments definitely fire the imagination of young artists who treat that as material.

I had an interesting conversation with Joan Jonas about looking at photographs of Jack Smith's performances. She was saying something like: 'These photographs are just nothing like it was to be there at the time in his loft. He'd turn up late. There were only ten of us. It went on for hours. It smelt like this. It was the atmosphere,' and so on. It was incredible to hear her testimony. But at the same time, I've spent *hours* looking at those photos and imagining it. They trigger an idea, which may be inaccurate, but it would be a tragedy not to have it represented at all, I think, just because it's not the 'real original'.

RoseLee: The question of the radical work in an institution is always interesting. I think the same concerns come up about performance in the museum with as other radical moments in art history—but so much of art history (and work in the museum) is the record of 'breakthroughs' of radical moments. They are no less radical for being recognised as an important moment in history. So, no, I don't feel that putting a work inside the museum deprives it of its radicality.

There is this fixation with the radical 60s. Yes, performance in the 1960s had a very different character, when so much artwork was about protest. There is a general perception that performance must always be 'radical'—that it's always provocative or disturbing. But that was about a particular timeframe, and it misses this entire history of how change occurs in society, as well as in art, and what comes on either side of that particular moment. It would be like saying 'painting' is only about the 60s, or it's just about Pop Art. No one would say that about painting, but they do about performance—and that by putting it in an institution you're taking the sting out of it.

Catherine: There's a big difference between taking a historical performance that was originally radical in, say, an artist-run space, or in the street, and trying to restage that in a museum, and the experience like I had with Mark Leckey, for example. I'd seen him doing performances in artist-run spaces, pubs, and nightclubs in the early 2000s with his band DonAteller. He always did things in a low-fi, almost grungy way, and so I was wondering how it was going to work when I invited him to do something at Tate. But he chose the most grand space in Tate Britain, which was the domed octagon, and he chose one of the most famous works from the collection, Jacob Epstein's *Jacob and the Angel*, and he played this serenade-cum-attack using a combination of sample Dadaist music and classical music. So he set up this very grand situation that was absolutely responding to the museum context, and it was equally radical because of the way that he reconfigured the elements of the museum's grand institutionalism. I think it's a case of how the artist can make a space inside the institution.

RoseLee: I think we could actually say that these kinds of performance—and you might also think of how Hans Haacke at the Guggenheim, or Jon Hendricks at MoMA, and many other protest events in and around institutions—have forced museums to rethink their role in contemporary culture. I remember in the old days, museums were like cathedrals or libraries, quiet and solemn, and contemporary art had very little place in them. The events and activism of the 1960s and 70s actually forced museums to rethink their roles.

Catherine: I think the current generation often have quite a different attitude, and a number of key artists that I've worked with have all worked in ways that are specifically to do with reimagining the institution inside the institution in really productive ways. It's not necessarily about critique in a deconstructive way. It's a constructive idea of how can we build a space together that might expand, shift or stretch what the given institutional format is. That can be a performative ambition of the work.

It can be about moving back and forth between the outside spaces, almost dragging the outside in, in order to generate possibilities for the institutional space like in Leckey's *Big Box Statue Action* that I just described, Boris Charmatz's *If Tate Modern was Musée de la danse*, Isabel Lewis's hosting of her *Occasion* in the Tanks in 2017, or Suzanne Lacy's re-make of *The*

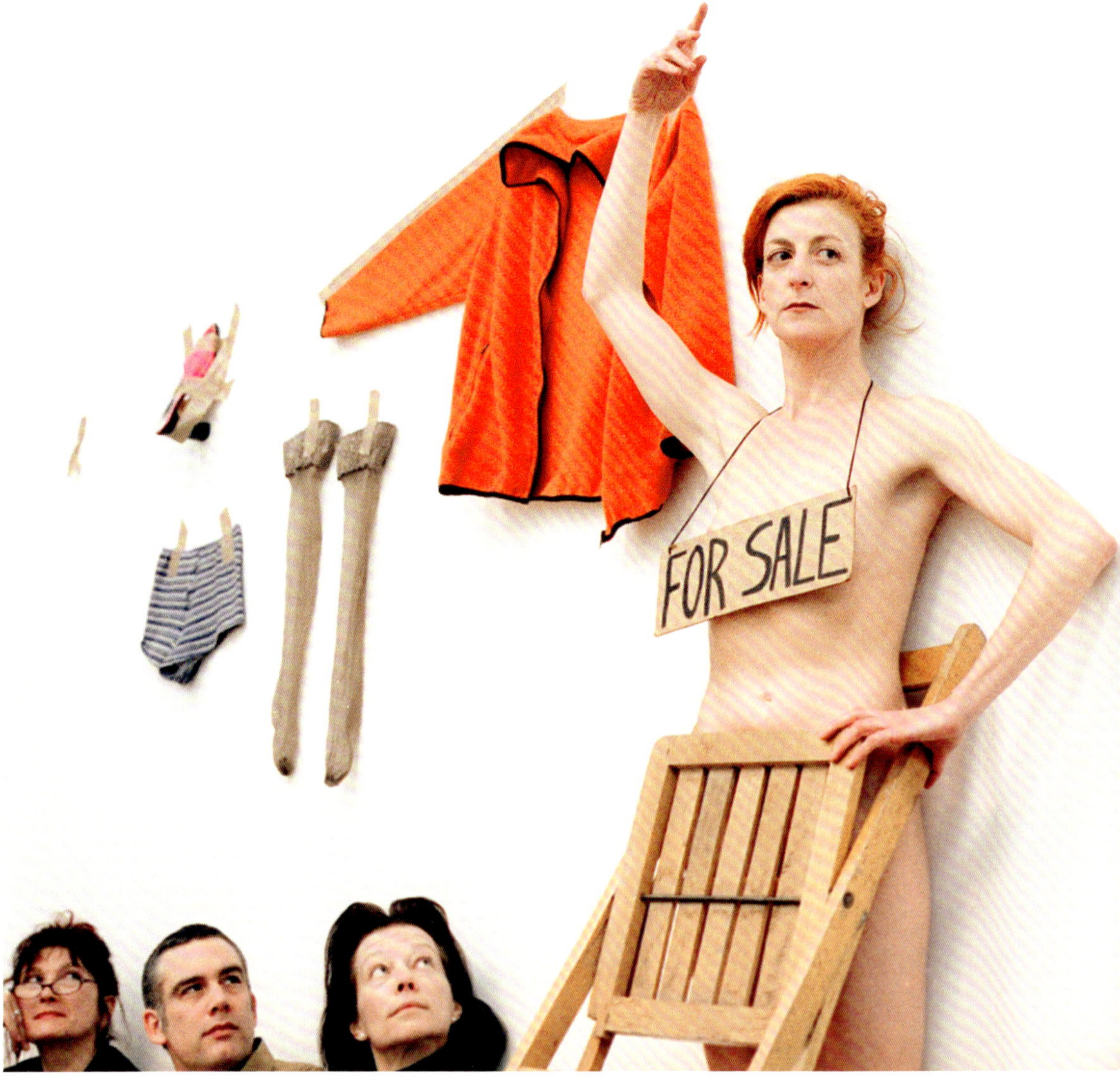
FOR SALE

Crystal Quilt (1985) as *Silver Action* in 2013. I think they all stretched and expanded the possibilities for what the museum could be and created these temporary situations where you would collectively experience it differently. I don't see the current generation as less radical because they want to compromise. I think it's an understanding that's built on the building blocks of 1960s and 70s performance and the ground that they broke. It's an understanding that institutions are just collections of people doing things in certain ways according to certain protocols and certain kinds of behaviour, and that they are performative structures in themselves—and therefore that they can be performed differently.

I don't know how many performances we've done at Tate in the past twelve years—maybe 250 or more. And every single thing we've done has put pressure on the institutional procedures and habits, our ways of doing things and ways of having conversations, and how we use the space. They have created this sequence of continuing micro-adjustments to what the institution is as a living organism. Whether that's about using the art-handling lift or the workshop that's meant to be for objects, which has been a big issue, for example. Or how to turn the lights down. And I would say each thing has set a new template in some way that has then grown into the habit of the institution. It becomes imprinted into institutional memory that we *did* that, and therefore we could do that again. It becomes part of the capacity of the institution—rather than saying that we don't really do that because we're here for putting displays on walls and things.

Left: La Ribot, *Panoramix*, *Live Culture* (2003). Image Hugo Glendinning.

RoseLee: Going back to the issue of rewriting art history, I felt that I had to start Performa in order for us to tackle that history in the most visible way, on a level that even contemporary curatorial departments don't have the capacity to do. I've been banging that drum ever since I wrote my first book 30-plus years ago, and it's taken creating Performa to show this history in all its complexity. I think of Performa as a 'museum without walls'. Without a building, we also have the flexibility to reinvent ourselves. We have to! Every year, we ask ourselves what issues are uppermost, how artists are describing the worlds in which we live, what means will they use. And how we can help artists develop and produce their ideas with the most support we can provide for them on every level.

All this adds enormous risk to everything we do; we must find spaces that will work for each artist's ideas, find separate funding, and reach audiences in unexpected ways. But the results have always been remarkable. Working with someone like Nathalie Djurberg, for example, to sit and watch her films in a small theatre and have her perform a live soundtrack is to see an artist work in a way she's never done before or since.

Yet it is an incredibly memorable piece that I think remains one of her strongest. Or Rashid Johnson staging *Dutchman (by Amira Baraka)* in the Turkish baths on 10th Street in New York, which sounds almost absurd, and yet was absolutely logical—and anyone who saw it was moved, disturbed, and powerfully heated up—literally and figuratively. The response we get from artists (to a Performa Commission) is the sense that they are being allowed to experiment in a way that is very different from working in a museum context, and they like it.

Catherine: I think London misses having something like Performa, as a commissioning festival. I think that's what the Live Art Development Agency does, or SPILL in the past, or what Louise O'Kelly and her team is trying to do with the Block Universe festival. Within the institution we can only do so much—and it is still an exhibition- and collection-driven place where performance is still finding its place. But the museum holds great potential as a space of encounter between different kinds of work and between people, in public space. I believe it is important to let performance work its way into the collection's DNA: not just as representation, but as a live attitude. Yet the ecology of different producers in a city is really important. We need each other!

RoseLee: We absolutely do! Partnerships are critical to what we do. That's the continuity of Performa. It has to exist as a citywide, international project that's larger than any of our individual efforts or organisations. There's extraordinary brain power, inside museums and outside, and extraordinary artists that one connects with around the world, who using performance as one medium amongst many. Performance provides connective tissue in ways that a 'solid' medium, cannot, because it is about connecting people, actions, conversations. It is a transmitter.

1. RoseLee Goldberg, *Performance Art: From Futurism to the Present* [1979], revised edn (London: Thames & Hudson, 2001).

INSTITUTIONS

CONVERSATION

GARY ANDERSON
AND LENA ŠIMIĆ
(THE INSTITUTE FOR THE
ART AND PRACTICE
OF DISSENT AT HOME)

BRYAN BIGGS

DATE

21 JANUARY 2016

PLACE

LIVERPOOL

As they discuss here, Gary Anderson and Lena Šimić created The Institute for the Art and Practice of Dissent at Home in 2007 as a space of dissent in response to Liverpool 08 European Capital of Culture. Based in their own home, the Institute hosts events, residencies, and conversations, and now houses the LADA Study Room in Exile. Committed to financial transparency, the Institute is currently funded by 10% of the combined household income (two lectureship salaries, some freelance work, child benefit), and if traveling to present their work, will make the financial arrangements for travel (or outsourcing of their presentations) part of the content of their work. They led the 2008 DIY project *First Retreat then Advance!*, which was where the banner they describe in this conversation was created, and were co-creators of The Free University of Liverpool, initially supported by a DIY project (2011).

Bryan Biggs is Artistic Director of Bluecoat, Liverpool's centre for the contemporary arts, has a long track record as exhibitions curator and commissioner of live art and interdisciplinary work. He collaborated with LADA in curating live art programmes for the 2002, 2004, and 2006 Liverpool Biennials. He continues to write and edit publications and is currently leading on an extensive archive project and editing a book charting Bluecoat's 300-year history.

This conversation took place at Bluecoat, where in 2010 Gary and Lena and their children participated in *Bed-In at the Bluecoat* with a response to the UK government cuts to social services (that also included a re-staging of Yoko Ono's *Cut Piece*).

Bryan: I've been researching the history of Bluecoat, which is 300 years old, and has been an arts centre for about a third of that time. I've been trying to get to the heart of why and how an arts centre became embedded in it, and why people supported it. In 1907, a group of art students moved in to set themselves up as an independent arts school. Over time, they bought the building—it wasn't just artists, but art lovers and Liverpool's enlightened bourgeoisie, who had money. As the first arts centre in the UK it was pioneering, but the working classes weren't part of the equation. However, they would invite other people to the centre, and in the early years of the century we know that trade union leaders and anarchists met progressive artists at Bluecoat. Liverpool had then an international mix because of the port, and this little institution had interesting connections—for example, they brought Roger Fry's First Post-Impressionist exhibition here in 1911 (including works by Picasso and Matisse). So, there was an appetite, if you like, for doing something a bit different. It was not what you would describe as a Live Art scene, but they liked to party!

Lena: At the same time as you had the beginnings of the Bluecoat you had the Liverpool Anarchist Communist Sunday School, which was set up in 1908 for educating children. It's interesting that it was happening at the same time.

Bryan: Then if we move forward to where the Live Art story really begins it is in the late 1960s when Yoko Ono performed here in what was our performance space. It was an early Fluxus piece. She was still with her husband, and had only just met John Lennon, so the audience came not because of Lennon but because they were interested in this stuff. We have to give credit for that to Adrian Henri, the Liverpool artist who did the first happenings in the UK in 1962—before London—inspired by what Allan Kaprow was doing in New York.

Adrian wrote a book in 1974 called *Environments and Happenings*, which was published in America as *Total Art*.[1] I've used that phrase a lot because I think 'total art' is a really useful way of describing this practice: it's not just painting, it's not just writing, it's not just performance. He was going to these marginal places—either countries you wouldn't associate with performance art, or marginal parts of the UK. He was saying that, at that time, Yorkshire was where all the interesting performance art was happening in Britain. Because it was! He really believed that if you had a really deep engagement with a place and it informs what you do, you don't need to go anywhere else.

Gary: I remember talking to Steve Higginson, who wrote a book called *Edgy Cities*, when Liverpool was European Capital of Culture in 2008.[2] He says that what makes Liverpool special is the open-ended nature of the city: that it's a port, that it's not a place to stay, it's a place to move through. But what's special about the particular groups of immigrants that settle here is that they're all running from something, and they're bringing an anti-authoritarian worldview because of what they were running away from. And that then gets spread through the culture. So in Steve's view, to be Scouse is to be against authority. To be somebody who likes dissenting. There's a kind of dissenting anarcho-arrogance about Scousers that I think is quite healthy.

Bryan: After Yoko Ono's performance in 1967, we can jump forward another fifteen or twenty years to when I was running the gallery. In the 1980s and 90s, most of the Live Art we were doing was coming out of visual art—not theatre. Sometimes it would be a performance in the gallery, but mostly it would happen outside of the building: billboard projects, installations, site-specific work, people doing poster projects in dodgy parts of the city and at night.... But over time we started to get applications for performance pieces in a theatre context. We booked groups like Forced Entertainment and Blast Theory, who were very much theatre-based, and needed to perform indoors—so Live Art came back inside.

Lena: When I came to live in Liverpool in 2000, I came from 'proper' theatre, because I was trained at drama schools in Bratislava and London. But because I had a baby, I realised I couldn't go to the theatre, so I mostly walked around galleries, like the Tate [Liverpool] and the Bluecoat. Then I saw an advert, I think from the Arts Council newsletter, that said to apply if you would like to do 'a Live Art piece' at the Bluecoat. And I thought, maybe I could do Live Art! That's how Gary and I first came to perform here.

Gary: We were like refugees from film and theatre! But for us things really started to happen when Liverpool was made European Capital of Culture in 2008. That came at exactly the wrong moment. We were already on the boil with critical feeling, because we were coming to the end of our PhDs and we were really wound up with critical art practices. And the link between 'culture', so conceived, and capitalism, couldn't have been clearer. What's the relationship between spiders climbing walls [*a reference to* La Princesse, *a giant mechanical spider created by French company La Machine as the highlight of the city's European Capital of Culture celebrations*] and the fact that the city council chose to sell off 42 public rights-of-way in the city centre to the Duke of Westminster's Grosvenor Corporation? Even if it's just coincidental, surely the Capital of Culture needs to reflect critically on its position?

So for us, we were asking ourselves whether working with institutions opens up the possibility that we're complicit with the capitalisms of culture. And what is 'culture'? We took a quote from Félix Guattari, who said 'The concept of culture is deeply reactionary,' and we made a big red banner and tied it between two trees on top of Everton Park which overlooks the whole city. That's what sticks in my mind about the Capital of Culture: that moment where we can have some distance from the city, visually and critically. A small gesture, token maybe, of 'the Capital of Culture is deeply reactionary'.

Lena: It was so apparent, that connection between capitalism and culture, because suddenly lots of money was available for institutions and there's a wonderful programme... and then it was gone.

Bryan: That's where I disagree, because I think it was a good thing. It bucked the trend of previous Capitals of Culture by going beyond being dominated by major institutions and high profile programmes. The city took it seriously, analysing the evidence for the impact of culture in a study called *Impacts 08*, which started two years before and finished two years after 2008.[3] It's a really strong piece of work about this impact. Of course, ultimately it was about attracting investment, and it sometimes felt as if the City Council didn't grasp the real value of the city's culture beyond being an effective marketing tool. But a lot of arts organisations were formed, and many of them—not all of them—continued after 2008. We've lost some of the edginess that we talked about before, and the capacity to just take things on in a very DIY way. But I think you probably still can—you've just got to be a bit more canny about how you do it.

Lena: It's an opportunity to be critical, as well. You can observe what's happening and do performances about it. There was a wonderful performance by one of my students, Tom Shephard, which was a walking tour around the Liverpool ONE shopping centre, showing the actual boundary of what was public and what was private land.[4]

Bryan: And we had a project with Richard DeDomenici, which was on the weekend that Liverpool ONE opened. He went into the new retail development with loads of black balloons that had the words 'Bored of Shopping' printed on them, and gave them out. And it was incredible—everyone just said, 'Yeah, great.' People didn't get the irony. The kids wanted them, and the parents wanted them, and the security guards let him do it. And then the next day he came here, to Bluecoat, and did the same thing with balloons that said 'Bored of Art'. The intention was that it was all part of consumerist desire, whether art or goods—it's all the same sham.

Overleaf: The Institute for the Art and Practice of Dissent at Home, *The Concept of Culture is Deeply Reactionary (Felix Guattari)* banner, *First Retreat, Then Advance!*, DIY (2008). Image the artists.

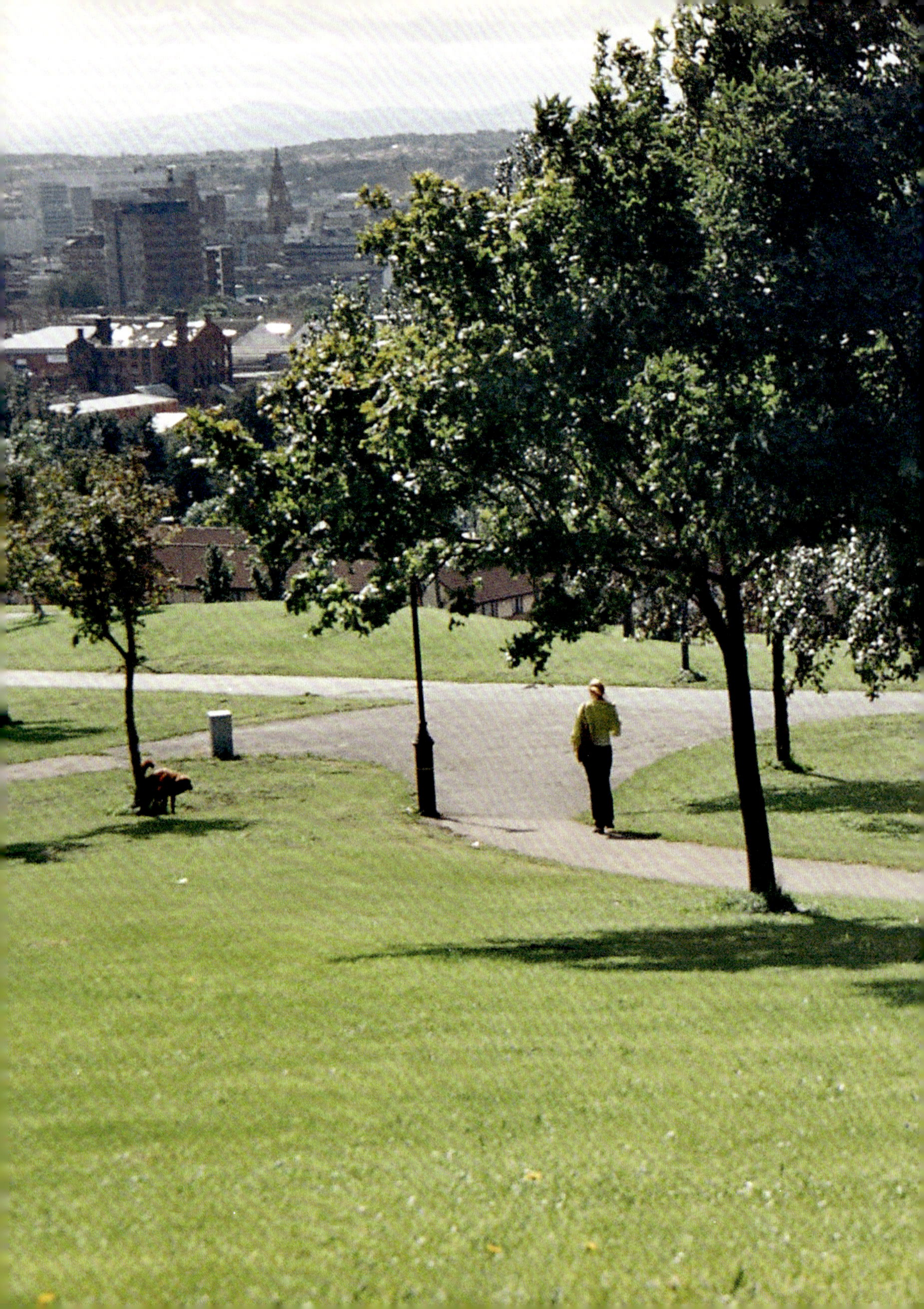

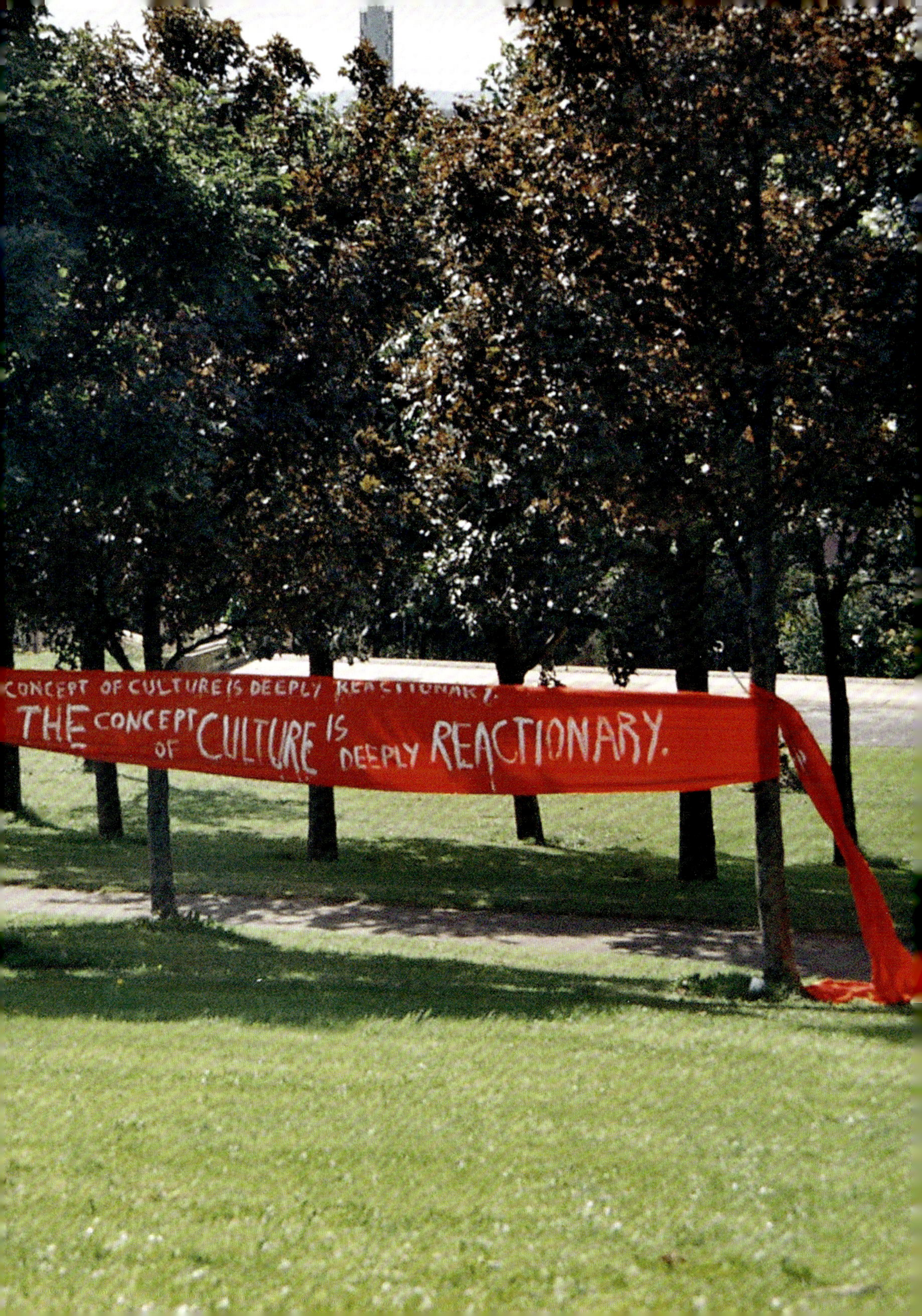
CONCEPT OF CULTURE IS DEEPLY REACTIONARY.
THE CONCEPT OF CULTURE IS DEEPLY REACTIONARY.

Gary: All the debate about culturally-led urban regeneration was fascinating to us. We were looking at what we could do from our tiny, small space. And that maybe in bringing in our everyday lives, and looking at our limits—because we've got little kids and can't do that much—maybe *that* can be the site of our maximum emancipation. So we decided, 'Let's just set up our own institution.' It was always a bit tongue in cheek, because the 'Institute' was just us, was just a family—and of course 'the family' is an institution. So we started layering our work in that way, thinking that there might be some agency in it somewhere.

Lena: It really came out of limitations, because with small children and having to pay for a babysitter, it was not possible to go out. We wanted to bring the world to us, to bring the world to our home. We already had a number of friends coming over engaging in critical dialogue. So we thought about formalising this, and also inviting people we didn't know, too. And the act of naming something... just by giving it a name meant it could start having a life of its own. And it did. We thought, let's give this thing a really long and difficult name: 'The Institute for the Art and Practice of Dissent at Home'.

Gary: We wrote it on the back of an envelope, and I remember one of the first things we said was that it had to be fun.

Lena: Yeah, fun. You always want fun!

Gary: But I also think it was because there was nothing else for us—unless we were prepared to go to the institutions and try to slot ourselves in. We felt it might be more interesting to be counter-institutional by semi-ironically setting up our own institution on the basis of things we didn't like about other institutions—like that they weren't necessarily financially transparent.

Lena: It was at the same time that we got our first academic jobs, 0.5 job each, and so we said we would fund the Institute with 10 percent of our salary—which was £256 per month. This was the money we could *actually* work with. And we would be transparent about it, so artists would know exactly what was available.

Gary: And because it was ostensibly a private space, our own home, we hoped that we would blur boundaries between private and public.

Lena: Our first event was private, a video recording of the painting of my pregnant belly. It was painted with the flags of different nationalities that my unborn child could be. Then we advertised our first public event, which was called *Pack-it-Up 08*—where we paid people to help us move to our new house, and we would all drive together as a kind of tour from South to North Liverpool. It was not a passive audience, as with an audience that has to pay. But instead we would pay the audience to participate.

Gary: It seemed to us to be a more honest relationship to an audience, because we wanted them more than they wanted us!

Lena: You were in one of the performances we did that year at the Institute, Bryan—*Miss Julie in Utopia*. We decided to rewrite the misogynistic play by August Strindberg. Instead of the domestic servant Christina, I became the Marxist revolutionary Tina inciting Jean and Julie to join me. We sang the Internationale together. We turned the play into a revolutionary party. At one point we asked the audience to unscrew all the doors of the rooms in the house and place them in the garden.

Gary: The house was wrapped in a big red banner, and I remember the police driving by really slowly, probably thinking: 'What the fuck is going on here?' Not asking for permission is part and parcel of a DIY aesthetic.

Lena: The Free University of Liverpool was like this as well. We set it up with Lorena Rivero de Beer, at a time when we were working in an institution which made it possible for us to dream things up because we had the privilege of income and security. It was a funny, bold thing to do, to say we are the Free University of Liverpool, and to have all these people on board as guest artists and teachers.

Bryan: It makes me think about Mandy Romero who appointed herself Queen of Culture for the Capital of Culture year. She would go along to events wearing a big sash and crown—and the city could easily have embraced her, but instead there was no official endorsement, so she had to do it herself. And thinking about convoluted titles of creative institutions, there was a Liverpool School of Language, Music, Dream and Pun in Mathew Street in the 1970s. It was inspired by a dream Carl Gustav Jung had in 1927, where he dreamt of Liverpool as the 'pool of life', and a local visionary, Peter O'Halligan, latched onto this. He drove to Switzerland to where Jung lived, and returned with a large heavy stone, from which a local craftsman carved a bust of Jung that was then displayed outside the school. He built this whole geometric mythology around the site, the idea that Liverpool was a sacred place where ley lines were converging on this street—Mathew Street, which had also housed music venues Eric's and The Cavern—and that only from here could The Beatles have emerged. It's typically Liverpool—mad but brilliant. It's individuals like him, and Mandy, and you, who don't readily fit into conventional structures, so you have to create your own thing.

Lena: But one of the things I worry about is how you can be resistant to structure, as a form of dissent, and also create an alternative at the same time. Our name sometimes worries me, The Institute for the Art and Practice of Dissent at Home, that it might be stuck in resisting those structures, through dissent, rather than projecting toward something else. Or resisting and at the same time creating something else. You don't want to be spending all your time fighting power.

Gary: We've done loads of thinking about that—how even though we're fighting capitalism, it's so deep in our heads that we're actually just reproducing capitalism by setting up some stupid institute in our home. Because we get lots of cultural capital from that—for example, here we are sitting with you having been chosen to be interviewed!

Lena: And it's not just institutions. I don't think I spend my time fighting institutions per se. I feel like I spend more time trying to fight capitalism. I think that's a much bigger oppressor than any kind of art institution.

Gary: And institutions—at least the ones I'm familiar with—have a latent utopianism in them somewhere, don't they? That's how I've always thought of the Bluecoat—as a failed utopian project.

Lena: That's the interesting question: how do you recover that initial impulse, that first desire to create something?

Bryan: I started off talking about the radical origins of this institution. But the people who set up the Bluecoat were essentially bourgeois, and, so long as they didn't die in the First World War, had the security of guaranteed work. But in 1927, when they bought the building, they established a constitution, which committed them to being custodians of the building and maintaining it as an arts centre, a place where all people could enjoy the arts. And that remains our mission.

It's always been a series of compromises, however, because it isn't just any old building: it's the oldest in the city centre, Grade One Listed. So, recognising that as a constraint (but also an opportunity for artists interested in interrogating our heritage), we have to work within that and ask: what can we do to keep the arts at the heart of what we do? That's what we try to do.

1. Adrian Henri, *Total Art: Environments, Happenings and Performance* (New York: Thames & Hudson, 1974).

2. Steve Higginson and Tony Wailey, *Edgy Cities* (Liverpool: Northern Lights, 2006).

3. University of Liverpool and Liverpool John Moores University, *IMPACTS 08: European Capital of Culture Research Programme* [2010] <https://www.liverpool.ac.uk/impacts08/>.

4. Liverpool ONE is a private, retail-led commercial development, owned by the Duke of Westminster's Grosvenor Corporation. Opening during the Capital of Culture year, it radically transformed the geography of the city centre.

INSTITUTIONS

PROVOCATION

JANE TROWELL

TITLE

STILL LIVE:
THE FREE UNIVERSITY
OF LIVERPOOL, 2010–2013

Jane Trowell is a member of Platform, a collective that brings together artists, activists, researchers and campaigners who collaborate to make work on social and ecological justice. In recent years, Platform has worked with Art Not Oil and Liberate Tate to successfully campaign for an end to oil company sponsorship in the arts, and, together with LADA, Artsadmin, and Home Live Art, hosted the event *Take the Money and Run?* (2015) which looked at wider questions of ethics, funding, and art. Jane has an ongoing interest in radical pedagogy in and through the arts. In 2011, Platform proposed the LADA DIY 7 project *Ethics will be the aesthetics of the Future*. The Free University of Liverpool (FUL) was chosen to respond to it. FUL ran for three years 2010 to 2013, both a protest against UK government attacks on higher education and a living experiment towards an alternative future. FUL embraced contradiction and disagreement as much as community and shared vision, evidenced in the multi-voiced reflection that Jane has assembled here.

> 'We were outraged and angry and somewhat energized by the injustice. We can do it, of course we can. A sense of capacity, possibly an arrogance to take it into our own hands. The Free University of Liverpool was born quickly, in an instant.'
>
> 'Everything moved too fast. In this metaphorical relationship, the sex might have been incredible and the other person might have been utterly fascinating, but… there's little chance that that heady start can be maintained and things turn sour really quickly.'
>
> 'The bits that make me feel ill to think about, the sordid, bitter arguments that I engaged in—my fault of course! Whatever! Oh, honestly shut the fuck up and piss off!'

What follows is not an essay. After this introduction, you will read a curated collage of excited, puzzled, and painful testimony from eight artist-participants (including me) from the Free University of Liverpool (FUL), collected three and a half years after FUL closed itself down.

All the artists are engaged with Live Art practices, activism, and education, involved in questions of how we devise a way to work together; how we resolve differences and learn from conflict; how we overcome disappointment.

FUL was started as a confrontation with the state—as one of many protests across England in autumn 2010 against draconian cuts to Higher Education. Within weeks, FUL attracted a phenomenal amount of support from progressive artists and academics.

It was in September 2011, during a LADA DIY project, that FUL engaged in DIY Curriculum Making. The Committee of FUL had made a proposal in response to Platform's DIY 'Ethics will be the Aesthetics of the Future' (V.I. Lenin).[1] After two weekends of DIY odyssey we arrived at a framework: F for filosophy (meta-thinking); U for utility (practical work); and L for location (place, belonging, and Liverpool). This genius fusion of praxis and place became the structure for the year-long FUL Foundation course.[2] FUL then evolved as a rich programme of art interventions, workshops, reading groups, skillshares and Liverpool-based work. It also developed a PhD, short for Project of Hope and Desire. Soon, FUL's participants were frequently invited to speak and perform about the university.[3]

When a group of us ended FUL, many observers were surprised but remained inspired. However, many regular FUL participants felt mixed, while others nursed wounds.

So what happened? FUL was activist in intent. FUL was intended to increase agency to act and educate—together and singly. FUL was intended as embodied, as 'live'—living art as urgent protest. It's not unusual for activism to burn brightly and then burn out, but FUL sustained its momentum for three years, as you can see from FUL's website.[4]

My questions here are: what are the impacts on FUL participants now? How was our agency affected, our belief in our capacity to change society? What can we learn for the wider movement, as creative activists and arts educators?

Here's my email to twenty FUL-ers on 15 February 2017:

> I'm really interested in ... what stays, what falls away.
>
> What now makes us laugh, that then made us cry. What still enrages.
>
> What has changed our lives for the better, for the different... What never got resolved. What is living in us from FUL, right now...

Although aware of FUL's ups and downs, I was struck by the tumult in the responses. It's clear that the impacts of FUL's practices will evolve long beyond the timescales of conventional 'evaluation'. As one participant wrote: 'feel free to take what you need/want from [my testimony], without having to satisfy "my truth"—which is changing anyway'. I've arranged responses through six themes: Politics, Ecstasy, Criticism, Ambivalence, Impacts, Learning. In Rancière's style, I won't explicate, leaving you to draw conclusions.[5]

Politics

FUL was born out of rage and protest and a beautifully naïve belief we could do something big in the light of the increase of tuition fees... FUL was born as a part of a political intent and a certain moment, to be a part of a social movement.

FUL was so exciting... It was during a moment when things seemed alive and people were trying to realise hope. There were a number of alternative academic, beyond-academic, against-academic-politico-intellectual projects being set up at the time… FUL looked actually like one of the most promising in terms of longevity.

I wish we would have done more to connect all the Free University projects to earlier free universities, to initiate ourselves into that longer history.

Some confusion about the political goals: outraged talk of youth in Liverpool, talk of class and race, getting a property and physically setting up an alternative university. Doing it.

But FUL started and remained all white people (I think?), and mainly, but not only graduates. Big problematic question: who didn't we know, didn't we reach, couldn't we speak to/with? Did we mean it? Who was 'we'?

I wonder now, in thinking about it, with FUL continuing as a force in my mind, what it does mean to protest against—what?

As always in my work… a tension between the anarchist and the socialist, creating autonomous mutual aid-based systems and fighting for the state to provide certain things like health and education that should be the core function of a state.

… the political agenda of FUL wasn't in the foreground throughout our weekly meetings

First of all it failed as a protest as it wasn't a part of a social movement, and secondly, it didn't even become the Frankfurt School (joke).

I think when engaging in creative and political work together, groups benefit from something to hang on to, practices and systems to help work through challenges

Ecstasy

FUL addressed something that was and is vitally important, and it brought together a group of people who I admire and value and miss being with as a collective.

Those early months of FUL were incredible… In many ways though it was like a relationship where everything moved too fast.

There was a powerful energy. FUL acted to channel a lot of frustration.

It was incredible to feel we could challenge institutional power and dream of replacing it with a better one.

Meeting underground at the News from Nowhere bookshop: the food was great, the vibe was electric and exciting.

A sense of 'we're going to make this up, and, guess what, we can'. Oh my God the liberation. A sense that it mattered to me that the people at the core of proposing FUL were from live art, performance, theatre. But I didn't know how or why.

I loved Deleuze's Abécédaire video sessions and us making our own video responses to it. However, I also enjoyed 'Conspiracy in the Hour of the Wolf' six weeks online writing workshop I devised for night-time online encounters . I loved the Merz Barn trip and I remember us on the top of some Lake District hill, screaming.[6]

I experienced a kind of ecstasy with FUL. We fostered new ways of learning and sharing insights together, new ways of performing 'education', new ways of exploring the complexity of art, education, politics and activism, confrontations with power (including our power), and how to (and how not to) organise ourselves. It was rare.

My guided meander: because I learnt stuff about Liverpool that might or might not be true, it doesn't matter, it was a very creative venture anyway.

It was awesome. Bauhaus eat your heart out.

The proposed PhD programme—Project of Hope and Desire. Absolute liberation.

But I loved being in the free space with people trying to be free, and children, and hope and play.

FUL was an incredible opportunity to explore power... Power as empowering and dis-empowering, as sharing and taking from... And what is it that makes it possible to look at ourselves in our relationship to power and what makes it impossible.

The final session... I was in front of everyone breastfeeding my new-born baby and saying something about FUL... I remember feeling vulnerable, frustrated and sad, grateful and able to be who I was at the moment in front of everyone... For me that was amazing...

It liberates me right here and right now as I sit at my desk at work, writing this email to you with new superhuman understandings of what is possible in the everyday.

Criticism

...the relationship was definitely all-consuming; after a couple of months there's little chance that that heady start can be maintained and things turn sour really quickly.

The lasting shaaaaaaame of it all. OMG. Whenever I think about it it feels like neural toothache, a nasty soft deadly pulse.

FUL of sickness.

I remember feeling very uncomfortable about the social dynamics that were in operation at a meeting in which we were supposed to be dealing with problems in the social dynamics.

...there was also something damaging about FUL (I nearly wrote the word poisonous)... some really unpleasant memories; people were hurt.

FUL was fraught with difficulties and unequal distribution of labour, time, and commitments. Group dynamics were difficult. There were favourites. There were slackers. There were careerists. There were silent accusations. There was an uncomfortable atmosphere. I remember a moment when FUL library was to be gifted to all of us, and everyone started grabbing the books as if it was wartime. I wouldn't do it again.

Somehow it felt that new forms of intolerance and rigidity emerged within all of us... and then so much regret at not being able to fulfil the impossible demand...

Everything became understood in terms of power relations, which is exhausting and disabling. FUL's fake horizontal politics made me much more disinterested in participation.

... there was a sense of dishonesty that I struggle(d) with.

FUL produced a great amount of sadness and decreased my power of action. Within its context, FUL robbed me of originality and singularity.

The closure of the group; losing contact with those people, the group. Still looking for something inspiring now, where do I live now to get that level of inspirational participation?

Final destruction, conclusion with no conclusion.

Ambivalence

I am genuinely torn down the middle about FUL.

The first FUL weekend I attended... was both very exciting and very uncomfortable for me. Many people there were artists and

I felt inadequately creative. I thought it was interesting to toss books into random piles as an interruption to the library but in my view libraries have been so important to revolutions, so I felt torn.

For me FUL was about accelerated learning, reading and discussions... I wasn't as interested in its playful aspect and performance/live art workshops; I had enough of those through my ... career as an artist.

Maybe the FUL project and in particular its image (its idea/its fantasy) was bigger than what we could hold. I think it's relatively easy to make claims for it, and make it sound much better than it was.

There was quite a remove between how we were perceived in the wider world (by those who thought positively of us and invited us to talk at places, etc.) and the reality of what we did.

I never felt that our actions just spoke for themselves—rather they were presented / perceived in such a way that made them something more significant than they were. How bad a thing that is, I don't know. People need symbols to rally around—and symbols inherently never perfectly capture what they represent...

Whether that less public damage outweighs whatever good we might have done in the wider world, I don't know. I'm not sure that that kind of maths is even possible.

And then, when I look back I think that it felt unsustainable because the replacement (FUL) was not really wanted, was somehow too open, too unsafe...

Being underground in News from Nowhere was inevitably darkish, a bit airless, a bit self-consciously secret? Were we 'performing' some kind of direct action plotting, cell, or radicalism? Hmm.

Impact

FUL of memories that refuse to dissipate—some gorgeous, some shameful.

The whole heavy neoliberal bureaucratization of my life in HE [higher education] is eclipsed with a single light thought from FUL.

my careworn, decent colleagues' beleaguered speeches at departmental meetings about which feedback form to use, whilst I race off on a Rancière solar-powered motorbike-of-the-mind.

I think—because of FUL—I'm less idealistic and more careful about what I'll commit to.

Now I do a PhD in a formal academic institution, but with 'Project of Hope and Desire' tattooed on my ethics and soul.

The Rancière reading group. I did it by Skype from work. That felt very cheeky.

I don't know if my current projects would have emerged without FUL. My thinking is more rigorous.

It changed the direction of my work. It made it clear that I wanted to train as a psychoanalyst, to find a way to understand what is it about our/my nature that made it so difficult to follow the dream that FUL represented further.

The highlight for me was someone explaining how inaccessible I sounded, so from that point forward I have been trying to understand the politics of my own language and presence in any space. It has been a big gift, but also about three years of self-silencing. That's been a lot of work and still is.

Gives me a reference point for the value of my creative acts.... I am on the move, looking for an inspirational place/event/people/cause/reason.

Learning

What I find hard ... is that I just presumed that the interpersonal aspect would be ok... That might have been naivety on my behalf..., but to fail in an area that I hadn't even considered as a possible site of failure feels more painful.

I think that a lesson of FUL was to learn about the probability of implosion when something consumes too much of too many people's energies.

Often—at least for me—failure feels like it's about not getting to the destination that we bought the ticket for. ... Failure might be about having a look at where it is that we have arrived at and deciding that, though it's not where we thought we were going to, there might also be something of beauty, interest, or value going on there.

And that maybe its ephemeral and disappointing nature was intrinsic to it, necessary.

I see some of what the FUL was doing in the Free Home University,[7] and long to make something like this doable in a sustainable way in this country.

One thing that is exciting is that the embodied questioning of our collaborative practices has so many quantifiable and non-quantifiable outputs.

FUL still hurts, but it still gives, gives, gives.

Live locally. Otherwise, it was what it was, warts and all.

I learnt that you need energy, mutuality, and focus. If you have that you can do anything.

1. See <http://www.thisisliveart.co.uk/opportunities/the-committee-the-free-university-of-liverpool/>.

2. See <https://thefreeuniversityofliverpool.wordpress.com/foundation-degree-2/diy-curriculum-making/>.

3. To read more, see The Free University of Liverpool, *Foundations* (Liverpool: FUL Press, 2012) <https://www.thisisunbound.co.uk/products/foundations>.

4. The Free University of Liverpool <https://thefreeuniversityofliverpool.wordpress.com/>.

5. With FUL we read Jacques Rancière, *The Ignorant Schoolmaster: Five Lessons in Intellectual Emancipation* [1987] (Stanford: Stanford University Press, 1991), where he critiques the role of educator as 'explicator'.

6. <https://www.youtube.com/watch?v=w9xMpWWRRdA>.

7. Free Home University <https://musagetes.ca/project/free-home-university/>.

INSTITUTIONS

PROVOCATION

JEN HARVIE

TITLE

INSTITUTIONAL CELEBRATION

Jen Harvie is a writer, editor, and teacher. Her work focuses on the cultural politics of contemporary theatre and performance, and on artists' practices of making work in particular social, cultural, and material conditions. In *Fair Play—Art, Performance and Neoliberalism* (2013), she explores the decline of social democracy and the ascendance of neoliberal capitalism in the UK, and the ways art and performance are affected, but also how they respond and resist. She has edited two collections with LADA on queer artists' work: *The Only Way Home Is Through the Show: Performance Work of Lois Weaver* (2015, co-edited with Weaver) and *Scottee: I Made It* (2018). Other work on and with artists includes *Making Contemporary Theatre: International Rehearsal Processes* (co-edited with Andy Lavender, 2010) and her podcast of interviews with performance makers, *Stage Left with Jen Harvie* (https://soundcloud.com/stage_left). She is co-editor of Palgrave Macmillan's series Theatre & (with Dan Rebellato), teaches at Queen Mary University of London (QMUL), and was one of the organisers of the 2006 conference co-run by LADA and QMUL, *Performance Studies international #12: Performing Rights*.

> Working to support those who make, watch, research, study, teach, produce, present and write about Live Art in the UK and internationally, and to create the conditions in which diversity, innovation and risk can thrive.
> The Live Art Development Agency (LADA)[1]

> DON'T LET MUSEUMS reduce art to the small numbers of artists who have won a popularity contest among big-time dealers, curators and collectors. If museums don't show art as DIVERSE as the cultures they claim to represent, TELL THEM they're not showing the history of art, they are just preserving the history of wealth & power.
> Guerrilla Girls (2017)[2]

Institutions have a bad rap. With good reason. Too often, they are exclusive, elitist, conservative, turgid, self-serving, and wasteful. Despite all that, I want to celebrate them, at least in parts. In this short essay, I review why institutions are so reviled and often rejected, especially within art worlds since the rise of institutional critique. I then explore some of the collateral damage that can emerge both from rejecting institutions and from parallel practices that anti-institutionalism is related to, such as neoliberal deregulation, though that connection may at first appear counter-intuitive. I explore some of the potential benefits of institutions. And I conclude with a little institutional celebration, by examining what can be and what is done by a good, self-reflexive, responsive institution, specifically LADA.

Institutional critique

Why do institutions have a bad reputation, and why specifically have they been repudiated by so many artists and arts organisations, famously including Hans Haacke, Daniel Buren, Mierle Laderman Ukeles, Andrea Fraser, and the Guerrilla Girls? The art practices of institutional critique that took hold in the late 1960s censure institutions for the ways they exercise their overwhelming power. Across decades of work in this area, artists have focused on various problems with how this power is deployed. I'll focus on three here, relating to bureaucracy, self-interest, and exclusivity.

The critique of institutions as bureaucratic sees them as unimaginative, organisationally obstructive, and unaccountable, even corrupt. In this view, they are cumbersome, stagnant, unresponsive to both social change and requests to change, and staunch defenders of the conservative status quo. Their prioritisation of management and other would-be 'support' services is perceived as a waste of money which prevents funds from going directly towards the institution's key purpose—to support art and, implicitly, artists.

A second line of critique addresses the ways institutions sometimes exploitatively serve themselves at the expense of artists, and even in conflict with their own stated principles and ethics. One strand of this critique focuses on institutions' acceptance of funding regardless of its origins and connections. Activist groups Art Not Oil Coalition, BP or Not BP, and Platform, for example, campaign to discourage institutions such as the UK's Tate and Royal Shakespeare Company from accepting funds from companies with histories of ecological vandalism such as BP.[3] LADA, Platform, Home Live Art, and Artsadmin co-ran an excellent day of discussion on this topic in 2015, titled *Take the Money and Run?*[4] A second strand of this critique relates to the risk that institutions might exploit or appropriate artists, instrumentalising them by taking credit for their work or identities without having earned the credit. For example, when a gallery or venue shows diverse artists' work in order to claim a commitment to diversity, it needs to go beyond mere tokenism to properly support the artists and to make the kinds of structural changes that will enduringly ensure diversity across its artists, audiences, and beyond. A third strand in this context is the charge that institutions reap not only reputational benefits from artists but also a disproportionate share of the profits of their labour. *Artquest* journalist Medeia Cohan-Petrolino observes that art galleries 'often add on anywhere between 33% and 100% to [the artist's] price as their commission, [and] commission on work sold through boutique shops or specialist stores may reach as much as 250%, or more.' This makes the artist's 'final selling price two and a half times more than what [they're] earning from the sale'.[5] And this is before work is re-sold at even greater profit by collector-institutions, as when Charles Saatchi sold Tracey Emin's *My Bed* for £2.54 million in 2014, having bought it for £150,000 in 2000.[6]

By far the greatest criticism put forward by many artists, including the Guerrilla Girls quoted in the second epigraph above, highlights the profound exclusivity of arts institutions, which tend to reproduce their own—often unexamined—values. As art historian Linda Nochlin wrote in 1971,

> [T]hings as they are and as they have been, in the arts as in a hundred other areas, are stultifying, oppressive, and discouraging to all those, women among them, who did not have the good fortune to be born white,

> preferably middle class and, above all, male. The fault lies not in our stars, our hormones, our menstrual cycles [...] but in our institutions and our education [...].[7]

Institutional exclusivity, or gate-keeping, excludes diverse artists but also diverse audiences, diverse arts practices, and so creativity. It is authoritarian, dictating which people can be artists as well as what artists can do, from the forms their work should take to its size, media, and subjects. Institutional meaning potentially overwhelms whatever appears within its frame. Institutions' oppressive restrictions are often implicit, insinuated by their histories, exhibition practices, and architectural forms; even so, their effects are no less commanding than if all the rules were explicit. As the Guerrilla Girls have observed, only one woman had a solo exhibition at one of the big four New York galleries in 1985; by 2015 the situation had not much improved, with only five one-woman shows that year.[8] This problem is not unique to the visual arts. A 2014 American report that major films feature '2:1 actors to every actress'[9] spurred the UK movement ERA (Equal Representation for Actresses) to campaign for 'a 50:50 gender balance across our screens and stages by 2020'.[10] These inequalities of institutional and industry-wide gender representation are of course also problems for diverse representations across class, race, dis/ability, age, region, and more.

Institutional advantages

There is a lot I agree with in institutional critique, both in what I've outlined above and its broader arguments. Furthermore, this critique has been profoundly generative for Live Art, with many practitioners performing actions or events to resist producing commodities, and often practising in public spaces in order specifically to 'exit' or even negate institutions. But I also think that institutional critique runs some risks worth noting, and that innovative, self-reflexive institutions like LADA bear benefits worth preserving and celebrating.

As I indicated in my introduction, one of the biggest risks I see in institutional critique is what it shares with neoliberal deregulation. Both institutional critique and neoliberal capitalism distrust the rules and regulations of institutions, particularly those of governments in the case of neoliberalism. As institutional critique wants a world where institutions' oppressive rules are challenged and art can be more free and open, neoliberals want a deregulated 'free market' where trade (and profit) can be pursued without tariffs, taxes, or other forms of state intervention such as government ownership.[11] These approaches offer some advantages, as outlined above, but it's also worth bearing in mind what they put in jeopardy. Most importantly, neoliberalism's deregulation means not only the 'freeing' of (some) markets, but the risk of unethical, self-serving behaviour by some companies, alongside the reduction—or even desecration—of the kind of regulatory overview that protects workers, consumers, and the world. I'm thinking of regulations regarding health and safety, wages, hours of work, discrimination, environmental welfare, public infrastructures of social support like unemployment benefits but also healthcare and social care, and more.[12] Neoliberal capitalism uses pejorative rhetoric to bolster its cause, calling regulating (frequently left-leaning) governments 'nanny states' and, for example, a state-funded institution such as the BBC, 'Aunty'. The language is patronising, sexist, and ageist. Neoliberal deregulation's current rampant disavowal of all structures, including socially beneficial ones, reminds me that many institutional structures, run well, are hugely socially beneficial. Furthermore, as Johanna Linsley observes in her LADA Study Room Guide on institutions, *Dreams for an Institution*,

> We live in a time when many long-standing institutions are in a state of crisis, and precarity is becoming a normalized condition for vast swathes of the population. What kind of stance can a radical politics take towards institutions in these times? It doesn't seem sufficient to be simply anti-institution, however coercive or obstructive some institutions can be.[13]

For me, it is important to believe in the possibility of institutions that are not bureaucratic, self-interested, and exclusive, but well-managed, open-thinking, innovative, self-reflexive, generous, consciously ethical, and committed to supporting diverse practices.

Beyond the benefits of good institutions just noted, institutions have the kind of critical mass—and therefore power—that a solitary artist or marginal practice will seldom have, and that need not be exercised either unethically or selfishly. Furthermore, as Linsley observes, 'since it is difficult to imagine a present life separate from institutions, it may be even more important to think through how institutions might be challenged, re-made, or made new'.[14] Deployed benevolently, institutions' power can negotiate and advocate on behalf of diverse artists, audiences, issues, and the arts themselves. Institutions' critical mass means they can also provide services and resources that are helpful to individual artists but that artists couldn't afford on their own, such as support with research, fundraising, audience engagement, and other forms of professional development. Institutions can connect diverse artists and workers to help generate valuable learning experiences and collaborations. They can provide training and security. At their best, they stand for values that enable the diverse artists, employees, and affiliates who work for and with them. As I have argued elsewhere, I think it is a particular duty of large, well-resourced, institutions—especially those supported by the state—to do more for their communities, beyond

Right: Liberate Tate, *Human Cost*, Tate Britain (2011). Image Amy Scaife.

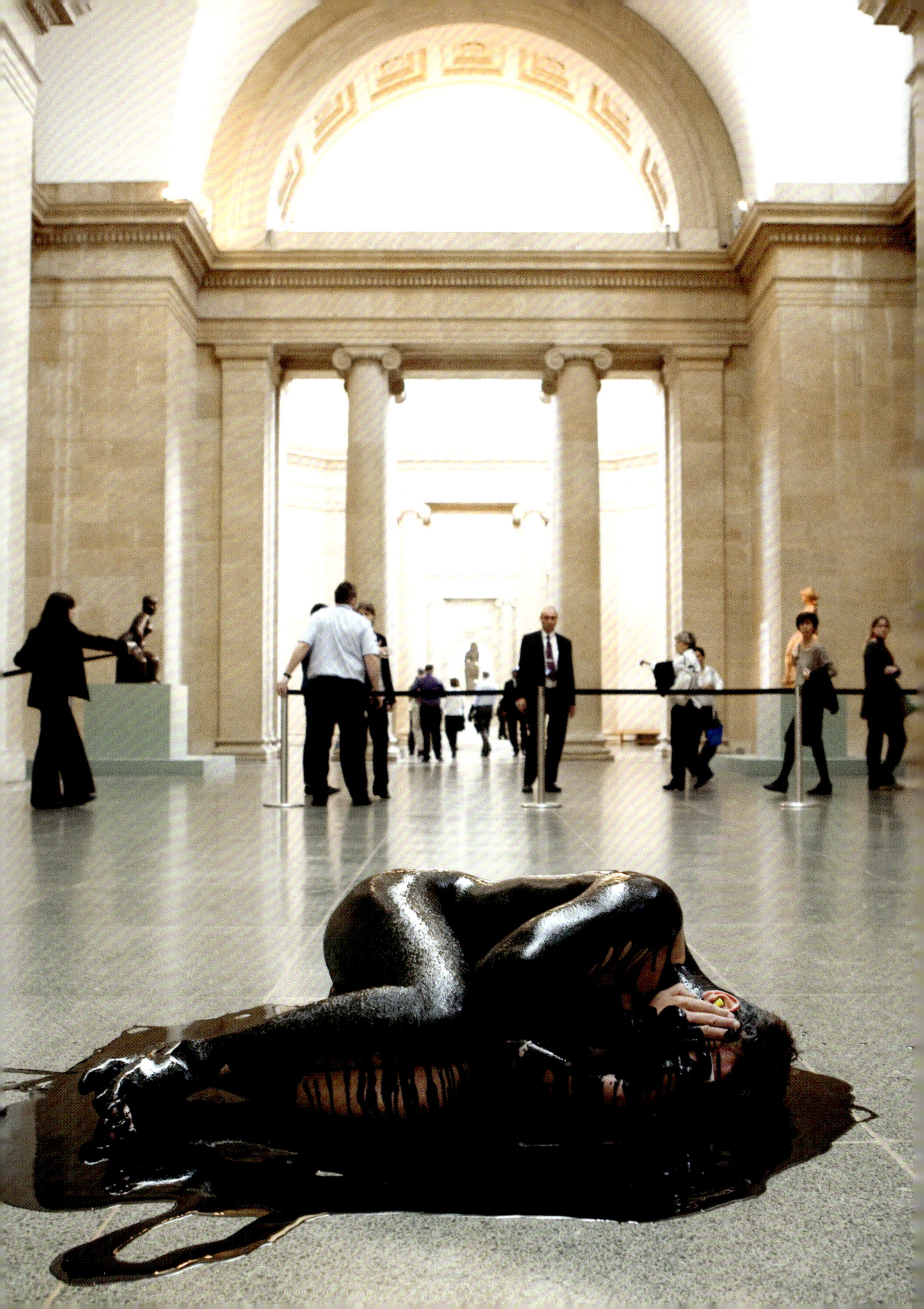

themselves, to serve their industry, its artists, and its audiences.[15]

Celebrating LADA

Institutions like LADA do the kinds of socially valuable and progressive things I've just noted. LADA provides services that are enabling, supportive, sometimes provocative, and often inspiring, including the Study Room, training programmes, publishing programmes, curated festivals, online materials, thinkers in residence, and more. LADA educates audiences, funders, students, researchers, and other artists about what Live Art is and what it might be. It actively supports the development of the next generations of live artists, audiences, and producers, for example, though its Next Steps Scheme for emerging Live Arts administrators and producers.

As a matter of principle, LADA does not hoard resources self-interestedly; it shares them, including its free-to-access library, and its funds, for example for publishing or artist-led artist development DIY workshops, which are free to participants. It works actively to extend its good practice of sharing resources beyond its own work, 'pioneer[ing] models of cooperation to pool resources and expertise'[16] in collaborations with other organisations in the Live Art UK network. Also on principle, LADA works to forge ethical practices in fundraising and to disseminate best practice in this area. It is dedicated to being Oil Sponsorship Free[17] and has a detailed funding policy that commits it to 'direct its fundraising efforts towards companies, organisations, and individuals whose work is in alignment with our values and aims, and/or makes a positive social, cultural or environmental impact'.[18] Furthermore, it aims to work with partners that share its values, and positively to influence others to adopt more ethical practices.[19] On principle, LADA consults about what it should be doing and how it should be doing it, using its resources to enable decision-making, but devolving engagement in decision-making to diverse 'stakeholders', especially artists (though I doubt LADA would ever use such bureaucratic vocabulary as 'stakeholders').[20] LADA *enables* many activities, but many of them are *artist-led*, not institution-led. In its introduction to its DIY scheme, for example, LADA notes that, 'Most professional development schemes are conceived by "arts professionals" and tend not to be geared to the eclectic and often unusual needs of artists whose practices are grounded in challenging and unconventional approaches, forms and concepts.'[21] By contrast, in LADA's DIY artist workshop scheme, 'lead artists self-determine and run their own projects, which includes defining the participants' application and selection process'.[22]

Through its many strategies for sharing knowledge—including the Study Room and online platform, artists' DIY workshops, and book publishing and launches—LADA works to collectivise knowledge, artists, and audiences. This is especially important in the context of neoliberalism, which does so much to atomise and disaggregate people, and to loosen bonds of social connection and social responsibility. It is a good example of some of the most important work LADA does now: working to recalibrate what arts, culture, and society value.

Crucially in this area of recalibrating social values, LADA is currently highly active in diversifying who works with Live Art and who watches it. For example, for the Next Steps Scheme for emerging Live Arts administrators and producers noted above, LADA particularly sought applications from people whose financial backgrounds might otherwise exclude them, either because so much early career work in this sector is underpaid or voluntary, and/or because they couldn't afford the formal education that would help them get arts work.[23]

Similarly, as coordinator of the Live Art UK network, LADA co-delivers the Diverse Actions initiative, which 'champions culturally diverse (BME: Black and Minority Ethnic) ambition, excellence and talent in Live Art' through supporting professional development, new work, leadership, and legacy.[24] These are examples of LADA and its collaborating institutions operating self-reflexively and with *self*-critique, recognising the ways they are currently socially exclusive and actively working to redress that problem.

Ultimately, LADA is asking questions and supporting learning not just about Live Art practices, but much more broadly about 'what it means to be here, now'.[25] LADA uses its critical mass, clout, knowledge, expertise, resources, connections, intelligence, ethics, creativity, and care to promote Live Art but, in doing so, to change the world, to make it fairer, while preserving its own capacity to take risks and to embrace change, and while devolving its resources to artists. LADA actively shares its power—its agency—with those whom big, conservative institutions would exclude, exploit, or simply fail to see. It demonstrates how a self-critiquing institution can operate, deploying its stability to do good work, while devolving its resources to open the field. LADA's work is a long way from the exclusivity, self-interest, bureaucracy, and conservatism of those worst kinds of institutions I discussed in the first part of this article. LADA is not an institution 'preserving the history of wealth & power', in the words of the Guerrilla Girls. LADA is an institution that deserves appreciation, not just for its own sake, but because it practices and promotes values that deserve celebration.

1. Live Art Development Agency <http://www.thisisliveart.co.uk/>.

2. Guerrilla Girls, 'Activist Work: Projects/Resistance: Posters, Stickers, Billboards, Videos, Actions: 1985–2017' <https://www.guerrillagirls.com/projects/>; emphasis in original.

3. Art Not Oil Coalition <http://www.artnotoil.org.uk/>; BP or not BP? <https://bp-or-not-bp.org/>; Platform <https://platformlondon.org/>.

4. Live Art Development Agency, '"Take the Money and Run?"–Documentation' [2015] <http://www.thisisliveart.co.uk/projects/take-the-money-and-run-documentation-from-an-event-about-ethics-funding-and/>.

5. Medeia Cohan-Petrolino, 'How To: Gallery Commission', *Artquest* <https://www.artquest.org.uk/how-to-articles/gallery-commission/>.

6. Hannah Ellis-Petersen, 'Tracey Emin's Bed Is Sold at Auction for over £2.5m', *Guardian*, 1 July 2014 <http://www.theguardian.com/artanddesign/2014/jul/01/tracey-emin-my-bed-sale-auction>.

7. Linda Nochlin, 'Why Have There Been No Great Women Artists?' [1971], in *Women, Art, and Power and Other Essays* (London: Thames & Hudson, 1989), pp. 145–78 (p. 150). Partially quoted in *Institutional Critique: An Anthology of Artists' Writings*, ed. by Alexander Alberro and Blake Stimson (Cambridge, MA: MIT Press, 2009), pp. 2–19. For more on institutional critique, see, e.g., *Art and Contemporary Critical Practice: Reinventing Institutional Critique*, ed. by Gerald Raunig and Gene Ray (London: Mayfly, 2009).

8. Guerrilla Girls, 'Activist Work' (a poster from 2015).

9. ERA (Equal Representation for Actresses) 'About Us' <http://equalrepresentationforactresses.co.uk/about-us/>. The inspiring report was Stacy L. Smith, Mark Choueiti and Katherine Pieper, *Gender Bias Without Borders: An Investigation of Female Characters in Popular Films Across 11 Countries* (Los Angeles: University of Southern California, 2014) <https://seejane.org/symposiums-on-gender-in-media/gender-bias-without-borders/>.

10. ERA (Equal Representation for Actresses) <http://equalrepresentationforactresses.co.uk/>.

11. Neoliberal deregulation does not totally deregulate; its regulations tend to give preferential treatment to corporations and the wealthy.

12. For more detailed examples in theatre and performance, see Jen Harvie, 'Neoliberalism, Theatre, Performance, Inequality, and Alternatives', lecture in print and online on *Digital Theatre, 4 x 45 | Theatre and Performance in a Neoliberal Age*, ed. by Andy Lavender (London: Digital Theatre and Routledge, forthcoming) <http://www.digitaltheatreplus.com/>.

13. *Dreams for an Institution: A Study Room Guide on Engaging & Challenging Institutions*, ed. by Johanna Linsley (London: Live Art Development Agency, 2013), p. 2 <http://www.thisisliveart.co.uk/resources/catalogue/dreams-for-an-institution-a-study-room-guide>.

14. Linsley, p. 12.

15. See, for example, Jen Harvie, *Fair Play: Art, Performance and Neoliberalism* (Basingstoke: Palgrave Macmillan, 2013), especially pp. 173–7; Jen Harvie, 'The Power of Abuse', in *The Routledge Companion to Theatre and Politics*, ed. by Peter Eckersall and Helena Grehan (New York and London: Routledge, forthcoming).

16. Live Art Development Agency, 'How We Work' <http://www.thisisliveart.co.uk/about/how-we-work/>.

17. LADA, 'How We Work'; and Oil Sponsorship Free <http://oilsponsorshipfree.org/>.

18. Live Art Development Agency, 'Ethical Funding Policy & Procedures' [2018], p. 5 <http://www.thisisliveart.co.uk/uploads/documents/LADA_Ethical_Funding_Policy_2018.pdf>.

19. LADA, 'Ethical Funding Policy & Procedures', p. 7.

20. For example, it regularly holds events with invited but numerous participants to discuss what it should do and how; I have recently participated in discussions about its publishing activities, and about specific artists' publications.

21. Live Art Development Agency, 'DIY' <http://www.thisisliveart.co.uk/opportunities/diy/>.

22. Live Art Development Agency, 'DIY 15: 2018–Call for Participants', <http://www.thisisliveart.co.uk/opportunities/diy-15-2018-call-for-participants-1/>.

23. See Live Art Development Agency, 'Job Opportunity: LADA Coordinator' <http://www.thisisliveart.co.uk/opportunities/job-opportunity-lada-coordinator>.

24. Live Art UK, 'Diverse Actions Awarded Arts Council England Ambition for Excellence Grant', 18 January 2017 <http://www.liveartuk.org/activities/diverse-actions-awarded-arts-council-england-ambition-for-excellence-grant/>.

25. LADA, 'What Is Live Art?'

Right: Mad For Real, *Soya Sauce and Ketchup Fight, You Are Here*, Liverpool Biennial (2002). Image Bluecoat.

Overleaf: Monica Ross, *Acts of Memory, Act 09, House of Commons* (2009). Image Bernard G Mills.

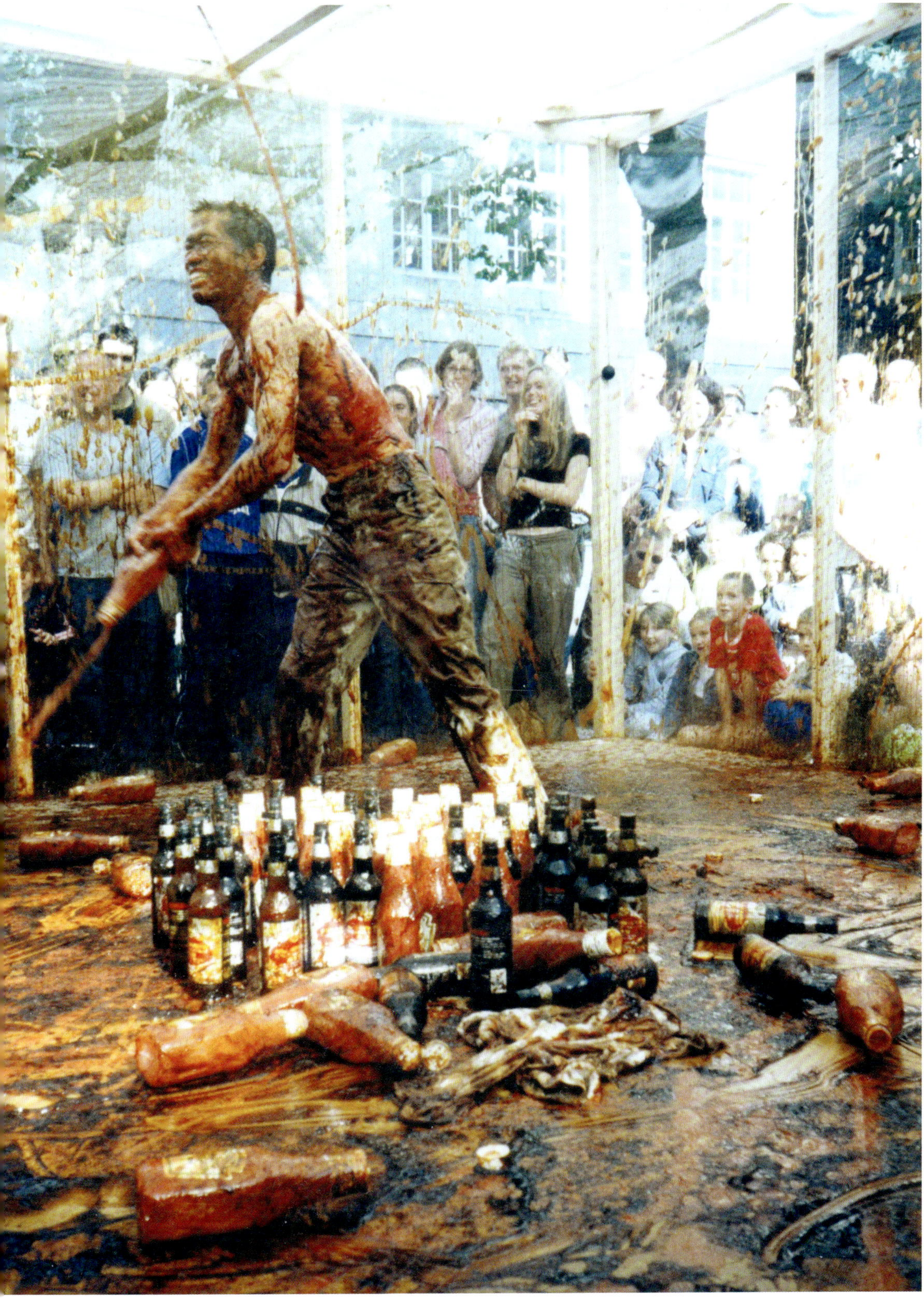

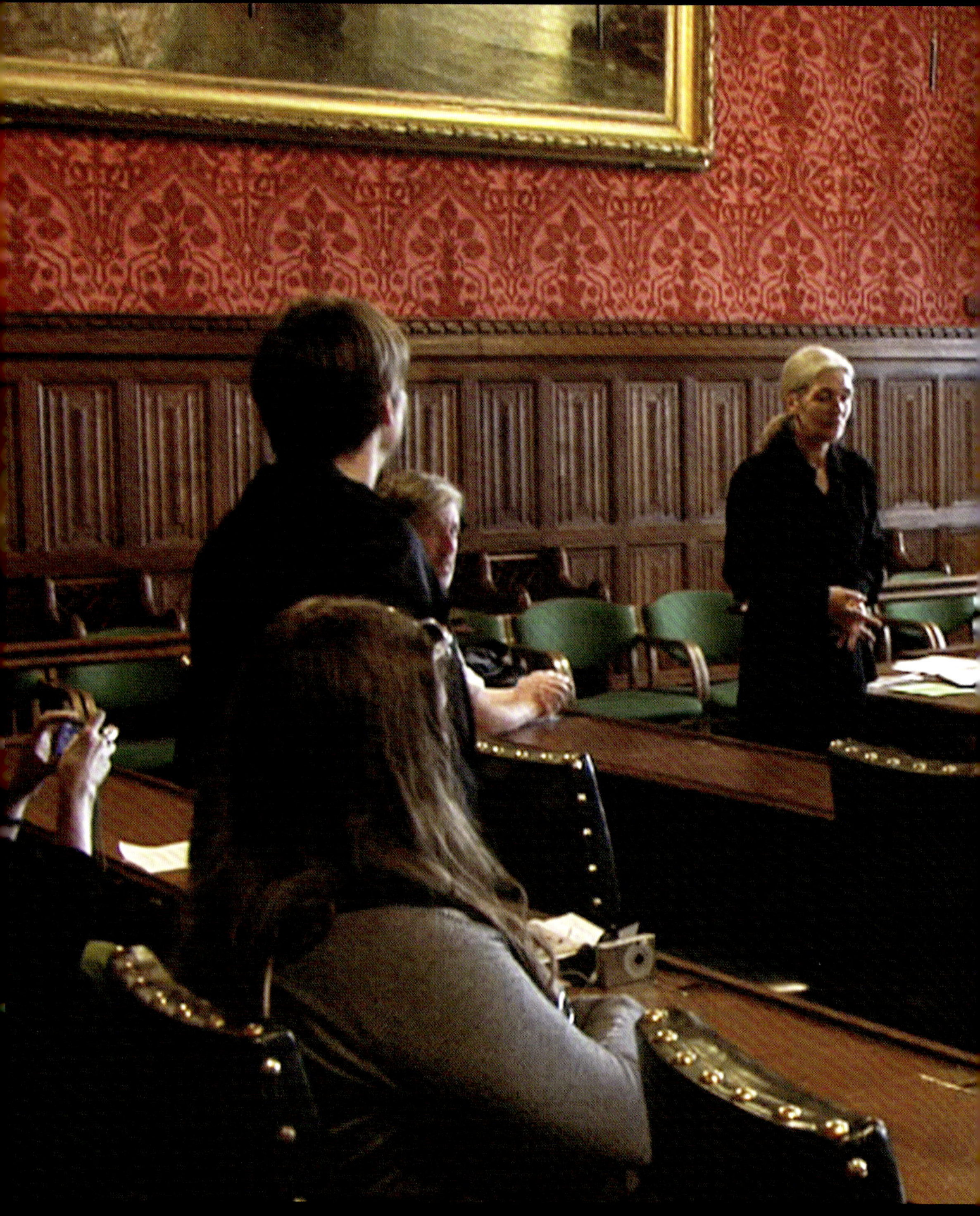

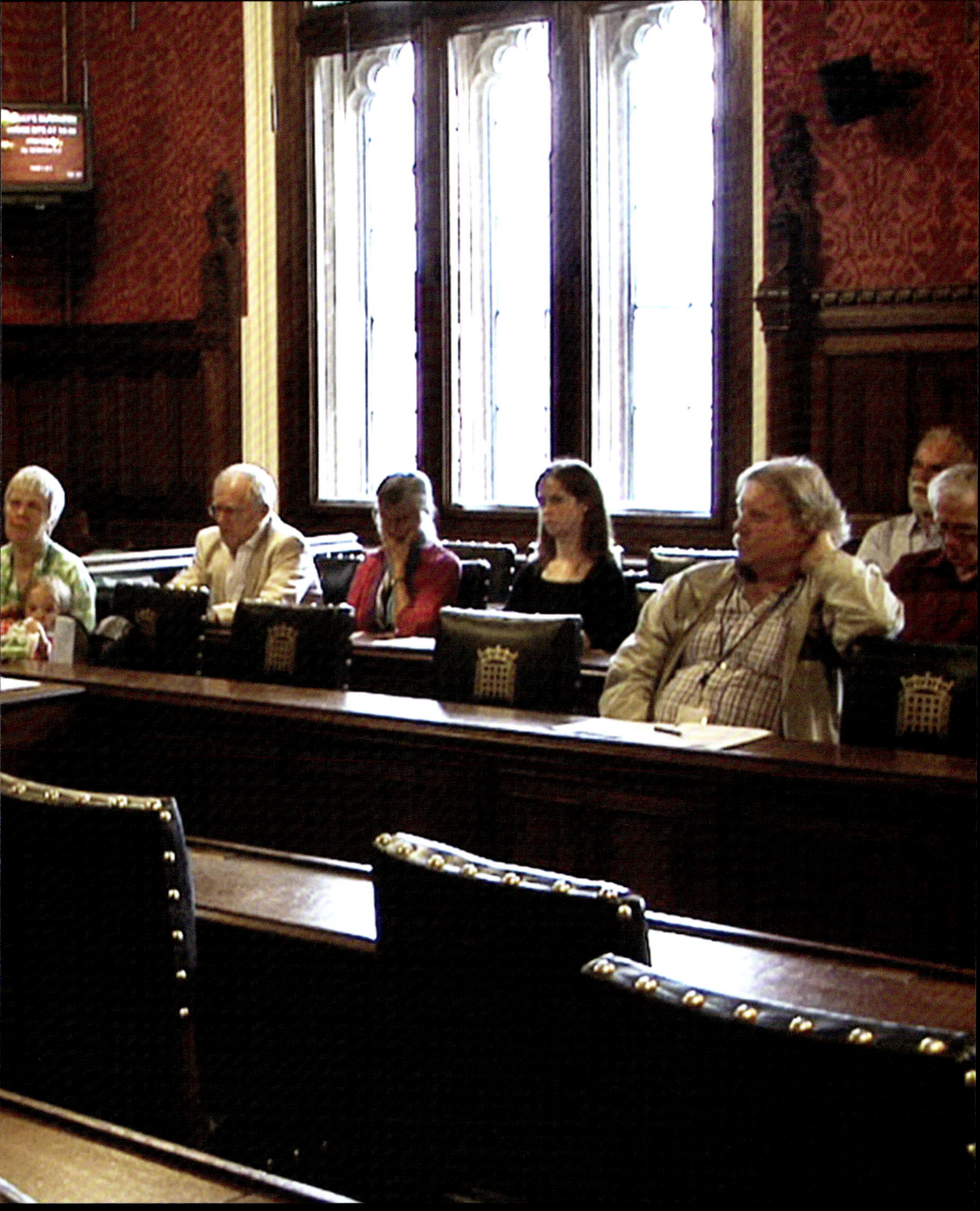

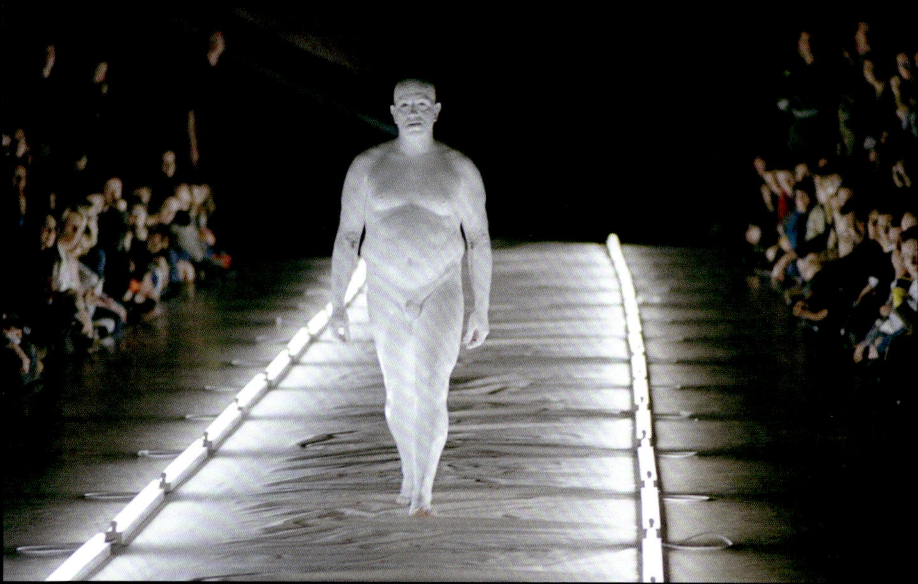

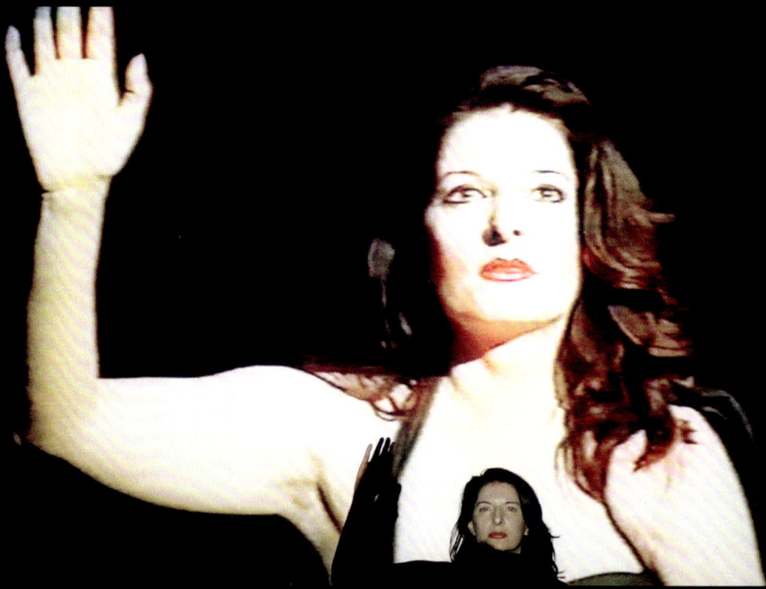

Top: Franko B, *I Miss You!*, *Live Culture* (2003). Image Hugo Glendinning.
Bottom: Marina Abramović, *Live Culture* (2003). Image Hugo Glendinning.

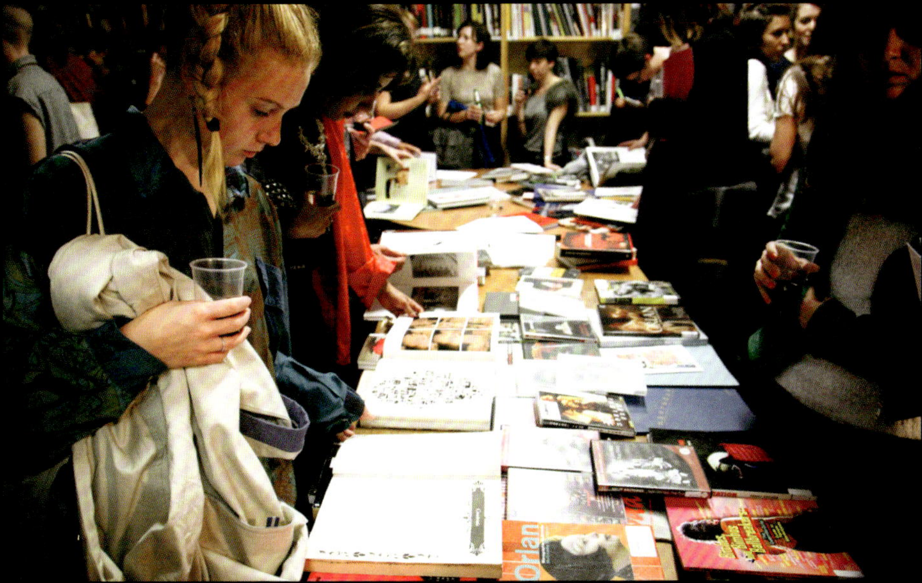

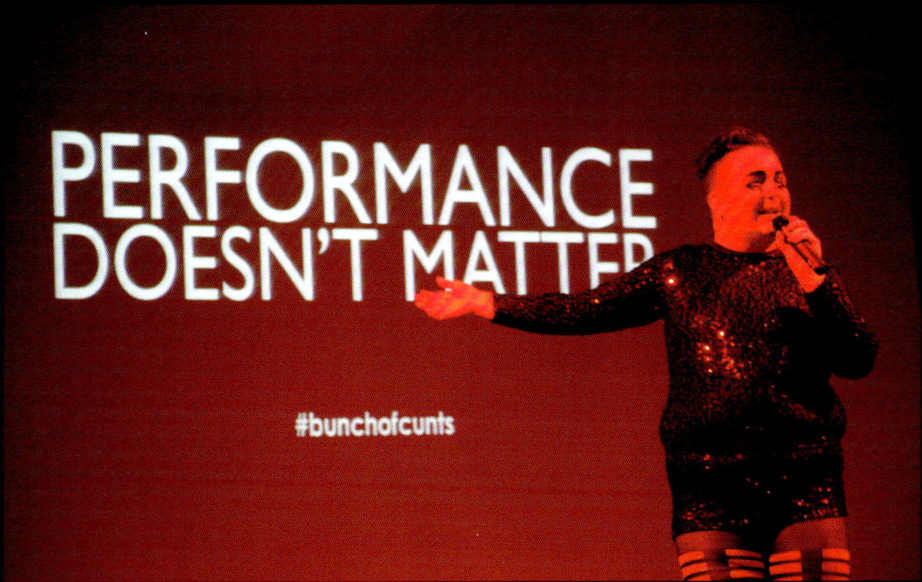

Top: LADA Study Room, The White Building. Image Alex Eisenberg.
Bottom: Scottee, *Performance Doesn't Matter, Performance Matters* (2011). Image Christa Holka.

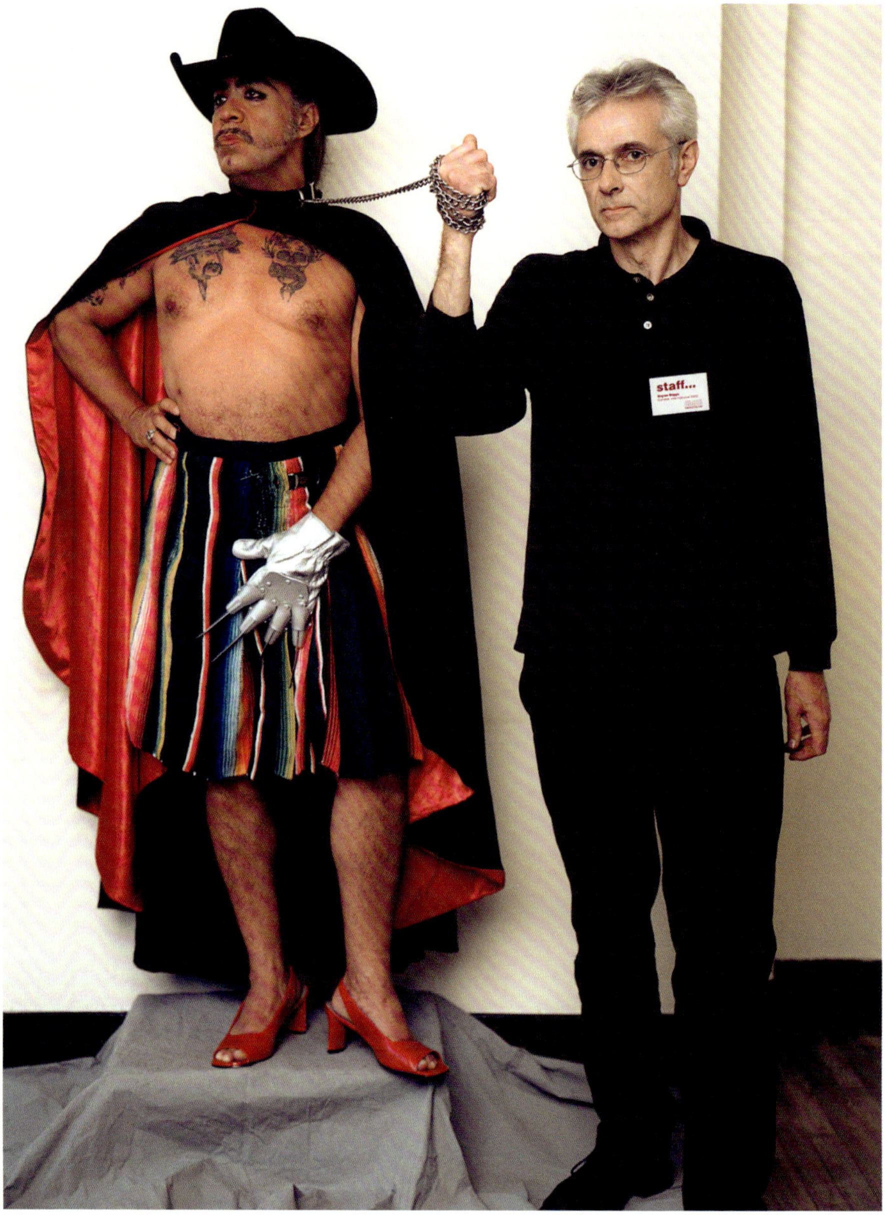

Guillermo Gómez-Peña and Manuel Vason (with Bryan Biggs), *Collaboration*, Tate Liverpool (2002). Image Manuel Vason.

COMMUNITIES

ANNE BEAN

SIMON CASSON

ALASTAIR MACLENNAN

JORDAN MCKENZIE

ALAN READ

RAJNI SHAH

THE VACUUM CLEANER

LOIS WEAVER

COMMUNITIES

One of the central questions of this collection has been not only what *is* Live Art, but also what and who is it *for*? As evidenced by the diversity of themes, forms, and ways of working described across this collection, 'Live Art' is less a description of a set of practices than a collection of concerns and preoccupations that are held by different people and practices at different times; and while LADA may have begun as an advocate for a distinctive sector in need of funding and support, this book also reveals that these twenty years have seen a wild proliferation across venues, institutions, and forms of engagement—reflecting not only various artforms, but also activities and domains not normally identified with 'art.' Arguably, this diversity is a source of vitality: as Jordan McKenzie observes in the conversation in this section, 'No one agrees on what Live Art is, and that's what makes it exciting and volatile. People are always prodding at it: I'm not sure it's this, and I'm not sure it's that, either.' Indeed, a recurring motif across this collection is a degree of circumspection from the artists in conversation about whether they even 'fit' within 'Live Art.'

At the same time, another thread is the recurrence across different conversations of connections between individuals who name each other as peers, collaborators, and friends. McKenzie invites French & Mottershead to the estate he is working on; Simon Casson recalls that it was an intervention from Joshua Sofaer that made him realise the precarious state he was in; Rajni Shah recounts the impact of working in the Open Doors project that emerged out of Curious' *(be)longing* project; and across so many of these conversations, we hear about Lois Keidan's commitment to these artists, not just as artists, but as people. What is being described, then, is a Live Art community—not so much a community of shared practice, but of affinity, of identification. It is a 'loose community,' perhaps, in the phrase Rajni Shah uses in her conversation, but one that can manifest in moments of solidarity—as in the farewell party for outgoing LADA Associate Director Daniel Brine, with which Lois Weaver begins her provocation. As Weaver observes, this is a community 'that allowed, even encouraged, its members to move, to come and go freely.' Though it may come together for moments of solidarity, she continues,

> it was neither necessarily rooted in a place of gathering nor in any sense of home or origin. Nor was the sense of community tied to rules of custom or consistency or even continuity. This was a group of people in motion who were making connections on their own terms and for their own reasons.

How do you support such a community of affinity? As evidenced by its two funding schemes that directly support individual artists, the One-to-One Artist's Bursary and DIY—workshops *by* artists *for* artists— LADA's approach has been one that encourages voluntarism and self-determination. The One-to-One Individual Artists' Bursary Scheme ran from 1999–2006, initially distributed by LADA on behalf of the Arts Council, and eventually fully delegated to LADA. Under this scheme, artists were invited to apply for £10,000 each, with the specific criterion that this was *not* for the development of an artistic outcome, but instead should support open-ended exploration and experimentation. Over its seven years, 52 artists were recipients of the award (including many who are contributors to the present collection), and uses of the award ranged from Helen Paris beginning explorations into 'body memory', including learning deep-sea diving to confront her fear of drowning; Rajni Shah developing forms of encounter in public spaces, as she describes in the conversation in this section; Robin Deacon testing new forms of documentary approaches to autobiographical performance; and Joshua Sofaer meeting another Joshua Sofaer living in the USA, which ultimately led to the work *Namesake,* as well as producing his 'infotainment video', *What is Live Art?*[1]

A 2004 evaluation by Salette Gressett identified self-determination, support for practice, and responsiveness to the sector as amongst the strengths of the One-to-One scheme.[2] Gressett also noted that the required consultation prior to application became increasingly important to the programme, something to which Shah refers in her conversation, and cites over 2,000 advisory sessions taking place over those first five years. In LADA's contribution to the report, they note, 'The consultation process has also proved to be a great mechanism for LADA to meet new artists and to develop relationships with them regardless of whether they receive a bursary,' but they also identify the shortcomings of a self-determining scheme, such as the small number of applications from artists of diverse cultures and backgrounds.

The One-to-One scheme ended in 2006 because an 'administrative error' by the Arts Council removed the funding, but LADA's other artist development scheme, DIY, continues to run. This programme invites individuals or collectives to propose an artist-led workshop for other artists; in general, selected projects receive £1,500 each, and the expectation is that the workshops will be free for participants. The programme began in 2002 in collaboration with Artsadmin and New Work Network and expanded in 2007 with the addition of partner organisations throughout the UK, each of whom contributes to the DIY budget and provides additional resources (such as

Right top: Nigel & Louise, *Probing Elvis*, DIY (2013). Image Greg Wohead.

Right bottom: Sheaf+Barley, *How To Build Boats and Influence People (To Build Boats)*, DIY (2017). Image the artists.

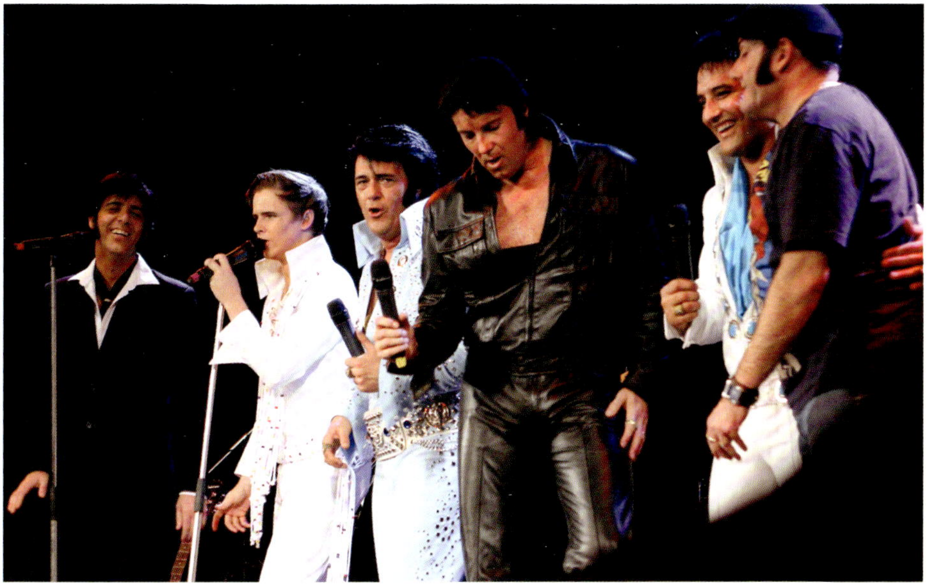

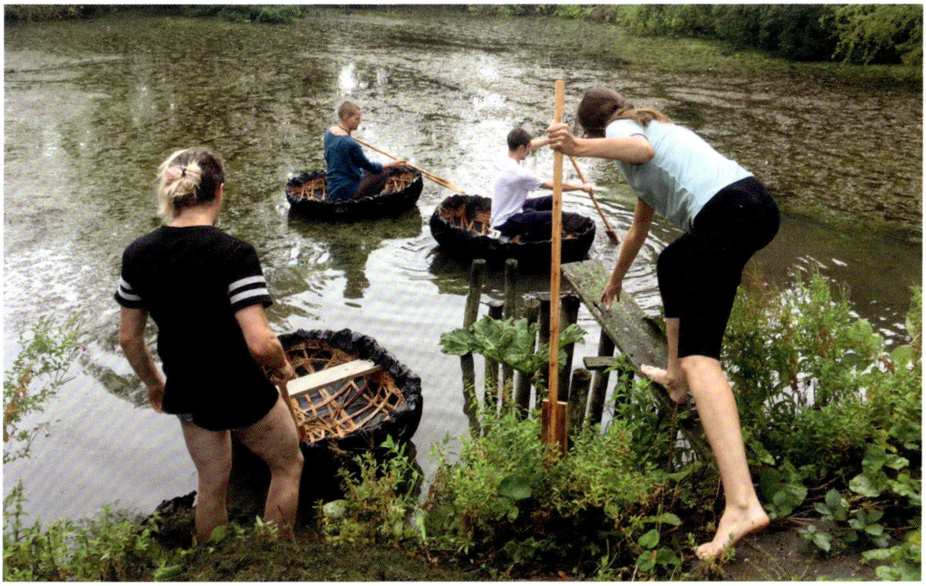

space) where possible. In 2017, 28 projects were supported in collaboration with 26 partner organisations.[3]

The self-determining nature of this scheme produces wildly diverse approaches to what counts as artistic research and development, and interaction with unlikely forms, locations, and communities. To illustrate just from artists contributing to this collection, these have included: Kira O'Reilly alternating grappling/Jiu Jitsu training with writing from exhaustion; Martin O'Brien following Dracula's journey to Transylvania (realised with additional funding through an expanded DIY+ scheme supported by Jerwood Charitable Foundation); Manuel Vason exploring the idea of the 'photo-performer', a hybrid mode between photographer and performance artist; a workshop in stealing other artists' ideas led by Andy Field; Joshua Sofaer inviting participants to engage with institutional logic through the form of the artist's proposal; Barby Asante and Teresa Cisneros (as Agency for Agency) exploring non-Western rituals; The Institute for the Art and Practice of Dissent at Home facilitating critical responses to Liverpool's 'Capitalism of Culture' (which led to the banner they describe in their conversation earlier in this collection); Helen Paris and Leslie Hill 's influential *Autobiology* workshop that laid the foundation for numerous artist projects; and *Look At The E(s)tate We're In*, a three-day symposium organised by Jordan McKenzie *on* a council estate about socially engaged practice.

Each of these projects creates a temporary community, and a number of them have a life that extends beyond the DIY timeframe: as Jane Trowell describes in the previous section, the Free University of Liverpool began as a DIY project; and John Jordan 's DIY that brought together artistic creativity with activist politics led to the formation of the Laboratory of Insurrectionary Imagination, which Jordan founded with Isabelle Frémeaux and James Leadbitter (the vacuum cleaner) .[4] As the contributions to this section remind us, the intersection of Live Art and community applies both to these deliberate acts of authoring community, as with Anne Bean's international coalition PAVES, or Simon Casson's 'good nights out', but also to the communities that form by accident of circumstance, or about which we might have no choice: McKenzie finding himself living on a council estate and becoming curious about his neighbours, MacLennan walking to art school across a divided Belfast, Leadbitter's lived experience of the insides of mental health hospitals. Following Alan Read's provocation, we might think of these as communities that are not so much imagined, but *performed*: and what is performed can always be performed differently.

1. See Joshua Sofaer, 'What Is Live Art?' [2002] <http://www.joshuasofaer.com/2011/06/what-is-live-art/>.

2. Salette Gressett, *Live Art Development Agency One to One Individual Artists' Bursary Scheme: An Overview and Findings of the First 5 Years (1999–2004)* (London: Live Art Development Agency, 2004) <http://www.thisisliveart.co.uk/uploads/documents/OnetoOneAppraisal.pdf>.

3. See <http://www.thisisliveart.co.uk/opportunities/diy/>.

4. The Laboratory of Insurrectionary Imagination <https://labofii.wordpress.com/>.

COMMUNITIES

CONVERSATION

SIMON CASSON

THE VACUUM CLEANER

DATE

07 JANUARY 2016

PLACE

LONDON

Simon Casson is Producer for Duckie, which he began with Amy Lamé in 1995 as a club night at the Royal Vauxhall Tavern in south London. For over twenty years, the weekly Saturday club night has continued as a platform for challenging contemporary performance, dancing and 'a good night out'. Duckie ran their infamous annual 'Gay Shame' event from 1996 until 2014 at various venues in London on Gay Pride Night. They have created unusual cabaret formats, Christmas shows, and other events for the Barbican Centre including *The Class Club* (2006), where punters received different experiences based on how much they paid. Duckie's current activities include *The Posh Club*, a tea time cabaret for older folk in five towns; The Slaughterhouse *Club*, an arts drop-in for homeless Londoners struggling with addiction and mental health; and *Palace of Varieties*, a dementia-friendly platform for care homes. Duckie have also partnered with LADA through the DIY scheme.

James Leadbitter makes work as the vacuum cleaner, which he describes as 'an art and activism collective of one'. Early projects included *Cleaning Up After Capitalism*, which made literal use of a vacuum cleaner; *The Church of the Immaculate Consumption* that gathered for religious worship in department stores; and various acts of guerrilla activism, including alteration of the Starbucks Coffee logo to read 'FUCK OFF', which led to a lengthy legal prosecution by Starbucks. James co-founded The Laboratory of Insurrectionary Imagination (labofii) with Isabelle Frémeaux and John Jordan, and was very involved in anti-capitalist activism. As he describes here, his recent work has focused on mental health, drawing on his own experiences, with works such as *Mental* (2013–present), an autobiographical performance that recounts his parallel experiences of surveillance by the police and the failing mental health care; and *Madlove: A Designer Asylum* (2014–present), which has been exhibited at the Wellcome Collection. With LADA, James has contributed to East End Collaborations; was one of the resident artists for Louder Than Bombs at the *Stanley Picker Gallery*; created *Everything for Everyone, Nothing for Ourselves* for the labofii's contribution to *Performing Rights*, an action that he repeated at ANTI Festival (Finland); and curated LADA's sell-out event *Last Night Art Saved My Life* (2018).

Simon and James had not met before this conversation.

James: When I was 19 I was sectioned under the Mental Health Act, and I was in hospital for over a year, and after that I was homeless for quite a while. So I feel like that was my education. I didn't say, 'I'm going to make some art'—I just started doing things that were a way to make sense of the world and my place in it. Then my friend Robert Walton said I should come to this thing called the National Review of Live Art. That was an amazing experience, because it felt like a lot of my experiences were validated in this space. After being in hospital and being told you couldn't do certain things, because it was self-harm or destructive behaviour, and then to realise that in *this* space, it is valid. It is aestheticised and not considered destructive behaviour. I didn't feel weird, or different, or mad.

Then I met Ange Taggart from My Dad's Strip Club, and she took me under her wing. She said, okay, you've been doing these things—have you thought about making a website? Do you want to do this under your name, or do you want to create a persona? She said if I was going to do things that are highly illegal, I shouldn't do it under my name. [*laughs*] So that's when I created the persona of the vacuum cleaner. It was also a good way for what I was doing to not be about *me*, but to be about the work.

At the time I had done *Cleaning Up After Capitalism*, where I went around the City of London with a vacuum cleaner, which was a chance to engage bankers and rub up against that environment. And I did *Prayers to Products*, that declared shopping was the new religion and so we should go into supermarkets and department stores to pray. Sometimes the police would be called, and we managed to shut down Selfridge's on Oxford Street for about half an hour. At the time, I think I felt like 'fuck this world that I don't belong in,' because I had been treated in such a violent way by the mental health system and because of being homeless.

And then I met people from the Live Art Development Agency, who invited me to this East End Collaborations thing and said they would give me £100. And I thought, '£100! That's like two weeks' worth of benefits!' But also, after the National Review of Live Art, to be 'formally' invited into this new community was amazing.

Simon: To be honest with you, I hardly ever mix with artists, and I don't really know anything about art. I don't really like it. But when I hear you talking about those experiences, I find that very meaningful.

I'm from a council estate in Hackney. When I was a kid in the 1970s and 80s, I was frightened and I was queer, which was a horrible thing to be at that time. I didn't want to be that. It was a very macho culture, and there was a lot of street violence, and I felt under threat all the time. That stayed with me, I think. That queerness stayed with me and made me vulnerable.

Because of my background I knew what ordinary working class folk want to do to have fun. When I was eleven, we used to go to the social club on the Nightingale Estate, and there was an Irish club behind the church where they would have bands every Friday night. That's where my mum and dad would go. Seven o'clock there's bingo, and at eight o'clock the cabaret and the music would start up. So I know what working-class entertainment is… and in a way I've exploited that, to be honest.

I started Duckie when I was on the dole. I was looking for a nice job in the arts, but no one would give me one because I wasn't qualified for one. I was also a pisshead, so I was completely useless. I worked with someone called Amy Lamé in a café, and she said, 'Hey, do you want to take me to the theatre?' We went to see Harold Pinter and neither of us understood it. So we got talking, and because I'd always been a big clubber—three times a week since I was fourteen—it just seemed natural to open a club. So we opened a club night. That was twenty years ago, and it still happens every Saturday. We had 26,000 punters last year. I just had to write it up for the Arts Council.

I feel very, very lucky to be able to do stuff. And I don't know, James, but I wonder if you didn't have that experience when you were nineteen, maybe you wouldn't have the power that you have now. I'm not saying those things should have happened, but if you never know bad then it's difficult to really connect with humans. Do you think there's any truth to that?

James: I think you have to be careful. People always ask me, 'Do you think your madness makes you more creative?' And maybe those experiences and that insight have allowed me to see things that other people haven't seen. But equally, when I go into my mental health hospital in Hackney, I see plenty of other people who will never be able to do that. I'm the only white guy on the ward, and none of them are going to be able to fly around Europe doing art gigs!

But I'm working a lot in mental health hospitals at the moment, and I feel so at home there. I had a hard time with the amount of privilege in the activist world. It's full of alpha males and females. When I was functioning well, it was fine. But if you're in the middle of a psychotic episode, or if you've got no money, or if you're not white or straight or from a privileged background, I think it can be quite unwelcoming. But at the moment, I'm working inside a high-security mental health hospital, and I feel like that's my place. Working with other crazy people and working in a completely different way is much more profound for me; but also in terms of trying to change something, it's much more effective. It's

Right top: Duckie, *The Posh Club*. Image Caroline Furneaux.

Right bottom: Lucy Hutson, Selina Thompson, Hana Madness, Ria Hartley, Daniel Oliver, James Leadbitter, *Last Night Art Saved My Life* (2018). Image Hana Madness.

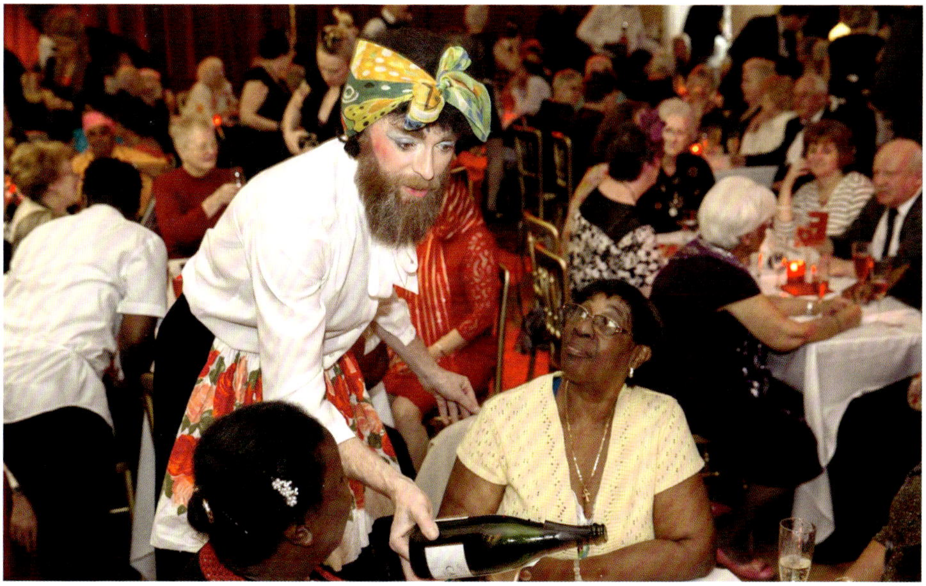

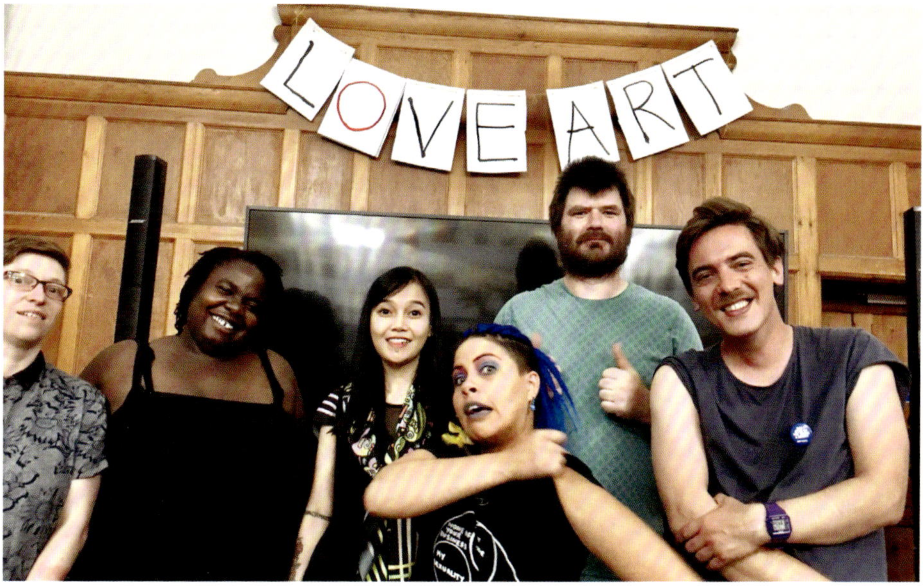
LOVE ART

not as spectacular as 'Let's shut down this power station in a really creative way,' or 'Let's stop this G8 meeting.'

Simon: What is it instead? Is it one-to-one?

James: It can be one-to-one, but it's much slower. I might be working with someone who has never been in the education system, who can't read or write, and has had the most horrific experiences you can imagine. And I have to create an environment where everybody's welcome, everybody can engage. That process of being genuinely inclusive, and trying to do something radical and interesting and beautiful, can actually create profound change for individuals—and also on a systemic level as well.

Simon: What are you making with them?

James: The project is called *Madlove: A Designer Asylum*, which is about making a utopian mental health hospital. We're getting people who have spent time in hospitals or have cared for family members, and we're asking them if they could design the perfect mental health hospital what it would be like. The idea is to get people with lived experience to really take ownership of these places.

It really comes out of my own experience. I was doing all this fun, creative, subversive stuff, and it was all going really well—and then I crashed in a major way. I was sectioned again, and homeless again, and I thought: hang on a minute. I've got these skills that I can use for myself. Can my creativity get me out of this situation? So I did a project called *The Ship of Fools* where I turned my council flat into a hospital, just by declaring it so, and I wrote my own Mental Health Act and sectioned myself with it, and then asked people come spend time with me. I was very distressed at the time, on a high amount of medication, and I was a danger to myself. So it was real, not pretend. I talked to Lois [Keidan] about it, and she gave me some amazing advice. She said, 'You have to do this, but be careful. If you kill yourself I'll be really angry with you!' [*laughs*] She laid it on the line in a really straight way.

And I came out the end of the project and realised that it had probably saved my life. And also that I had 'come out', in a way, because before that nobody knew about my mental health. On the back of that, other things happened. I did a test version of this hospital in Liverpool, and then I got invited to do a presentation at the Designing Mental Health Conference, which is an industry conference where all the big architecture firms are there, and the people that make anti-ligature doors, and so on. Afterwards someone came up to me and said, 'I really liked your presentation. It's really beautiful to see how you're giving all these people this agency to take control of their environment.' I said, 'Thank you. That's really kind of you to say that.' Then she says, 'But it's kind of meaningless, isn't it? Unless you can do it in the high-security hospitals it's just an art project.' I was like, 'Yeah, you've got a point. I can't argue with you on that.' And she said, 'Well, that's where I work. I run the arts program in a high-security psychiatric hospital. Would you like to come in?'

Simon: So you work as an artist-facilitator?

James: Yeah, but it's not necessarily just me as an artist. Like I was running these workshops recently with twelve-year-olds with schizophrenia and thirteen-year-olds with anorexia, and it was going really badly and it was just soul-destroying. They really didn't want to be there. And then I stop and tell them my story, and all of a sudden they go, 'Oh, he's like us.'

Simon: I think you've got to the absolute centre of this conversation, for me, which is about being qualified to do something, or being on the inside, and the only way you can really do anything is if you know about it. So, for instance, Duckie runs a project for addicts and alcoholics in the homeless hostel in Vauxhall and Battersea. I wouldn't have the audacity to set that up, or even the interest, if I hadn't have given a lot of deep thought to addiction. I'm an addict myself, and I've struggled for many years as an addict. And all of the men in my family have addictions.

That's what I meant earlier about things coming good. Because I spent enough time in my bedroom being frightened, shaking, nearly having a heart attack, going on the floor trying to get the tiniest flecks of cocaine or whatever. I was desperate for many, many years. About fifteen years ago, Joshua Sofaer said to me, 'Everyone thinks you're going to die.' And that was quite key. I think they call that rock bottom. If you're going to be punished like that, or if you're going to punish yourself for whatever psychological reasons you're punishing yourself, then some good's going to come out of that eventually. It must do.

These days I'm much more into making a difference in people's lives by making people happier, and more well, than I am interested in any notion of art, I'm afraid. I don't want to be disrespectful to art, but to me it's a tool to get people in a room together. To talk about what it is to be a human being, and what the point of life is—and to have fun, laugh, and cuddle each other. The really important things. I'm into letting all these different communities and parties of people off the leash, because I'm into being off the leash—you know, to really have genuine fun.

James: It's why club nights exist in the first place.

Simon: I remember being twelve years old and lying in my bed and reading about the clubs in London, and that sense of excitement of the night, that anything was possible. Rather than the domestic sphere. Go out and meet strangers. Go out and connect with someone you never met before. I wonder if that's my queerness that makes me want to do that, because it gives me a lot of pleasure to meet a new stranger, and to have a genuine connection. *Especially* if they come from outside your community.

We run this club in Hackney every Wednesday, called The Posh Club (because it's in Stoke Newington). And a big demographic are Black Caribbean women that are in their 70s, 80s, and 90s. Nellie is 104 and comes every week, and Irene is 107 and comes most weeks. These are people I might not normally have a relationship with, because how am I going to meet them? But if you put on a party for them that's designed to attract people like them, then of course you're going to meet them. And then you make these relationships with them, and I just think that is really what life's all about.

James: Do you feel more comfortable around working-class people?

Simon: As a worker, I suppose I do. I think I feel less comfortable servicing middle-class people. I supposed I don't understand them as much, and I'm not qualified for them. All of my friends are middle-class, to be honest, and I think they've got enough shows and events to keep them happy!

James: I guess I was asking that question because I spend a lot of time thinking 'I don't belong here.' I'm really lucky to travel, and I can live off a show for two months, but I walk in somewhere like the Kunstmuseum Luzern and I know this is not for me. I don't belong here. I feel really awkward. I'm touring this show *Mental*, which is an autobiographical performance staged in bedrooms. I first did it in my own flat and pushed really hard to get other crazy people in the audience, and it was electric, because all these people were looking back at me, like 'I know what you're talking about and you're giving me agency and making me feel less isolated in the world.' And then I was in a festival in Munich, and I was performing to international curators and critics—people who wouldn't say hello to me on the street—and it just felt weird and voyeuristic.

Simon: We've all been in those audiences where you see a performance art show where somebody really means it and you feel genuinely connected to yourself, to the world, to humanity. And you think some of the meaning of life is revealed to you. I think that's great.

However, I do think the whole infrastructure of the whole of the arts in the UK needs a complete kick up the arse. I just think the whole thing needs rethinking. This idea of Live Art is always meant to be thinking outside of the mainstream, and yet there is this quite nice circuit of things that people do for other people that like Live Art. There's nothing wrong with it, and I'm not going to attack it because there are better things to attack. It's just people doing interesting things with each other. I just don't operate in that world because it doesn't interest me.

I want everyone to be able to do something else, something genuinely creative and life-changing and revolutionary and exciting. Whether it's your mates where you grew up, James, or Nellie and Irene at The Posh Club in Hackney, or my brother-in-law, who's nearly on his knees with alcohol addiction and in desperate unhappiness, or just an ordinary person who works at the checkout at my local Sainsbury's. I won't be happy until I get that.

COMMUNITIES

CONVERSATION

JORDAN MCKENZIE

RAJNI SHAH

DATE

13 JANUARY 2016

PLACE

LONDON

Jordan McKenzie has worked across fine art, performance, and social practice. His early work queered legacies of minimalist art and drawing, which are themes to which he has recently returned with work such as *Public Triangles* (2016) and *Lewitt Lean* (2013) for the Yorkshire Sculpture Park. As he describes here, his experience of moving onto a social housing estate affected his practice, and he co-curated LUPA (Lock-Up Performance Art) on the estate from 2011–13. Supported by a DIY grant, he also ran *Look At The E(s)tate We're In*, a three-day summit on social housing and the arts, which took place on the estate itself. Recently he has directed *Shame Chorus* in collaboration with the Freud Museum in London, psychoanalyst Susie Orbach, and the London Gay Men's Chorus, which uses chorus members' anonymised memories of being shamed as the basis for original songs and choral works. Jordan has received a One-to-One Artist's Bursary, and LADA published *Jordan McKenzie: Occupations 1996–2013*, a DVD of Jordan's work.

Rajni Shah has worked collaboratively with a number of different artists, situating her practice between Live Art, Dance, Theatre, and Visual Arts. From 2005–2012, Rajni worked with a group of other artists to create and tour a trilogy of performance works exploring moments of cultural identity and alienation: *Mr Quiver* (2005–2008), *Dinner with America* (2007–2009), and *Glorious* (2009–2012). Alongside these larger performances, Rajni and her collaborators created a series of public interventions exploring the relationships between gift and conversation, which, as she discusses here, arose directly out of the research she began through her One-to-One Artist's Bursary. Initially entitled *small gifts*, this series culminated with two touring pieces made for public spaces: *give what you can, take what you need* which toured alongside *Dinner with America*, and *Write a Letter to a Stranger* which was at the core of *Glorious*. While she was based in London, Rajni worked closely with LADA in a number of different roles: she was the project director for RRR1 on Live Art and Race (2006–2008), culminating in *Documenting Live*, and worked as project consultant for RRR2 on Live Art and Disability (2009–2012); she led two DIY projects (2007, 2009); and most recently, LADA co-published the DVD/custom book *Dear Stranger, I love you: The ethics of community in Rajni Shah Projects' Glorious* (2013).

Jordan and Rajni knew of each other's work but had not spoken at length before this conversation.

Rajni: People have asked me about my choice to position my work as Live Art, and I would love to say that it was some kind of artistic vision that I had for how my work should be seen in the world. But it's really just that they're the only people who've supported me as an artist! I actually see myself much more as a theatre-maker or choreographer, if theatre or dance in this country looked anything like the work I make.

What happened was that LADA invited me to do a workshop with Guillermo Gómez-Peña. At the time I felt funny about it, because I had this sense that they didn't know my work and were just looking for brown people to do this project, and I raised that issue with them at the time. But interestingly, now I think of that project as very significant for me, in terms of getting to know other artists and finding something of a community.

And then in 2002 I worked with LADA on *Documenting Live*, which was looking at exactly these questions of artists who aren't 'white' and who aren't getting the attention that they should be, as part of their ongoing series *Restock, Rethink, Reflect*. And I think that whole series of projects is genuinely interested in opening up conversations. It's tricky, because it's a small agency, and so those projects are like: okay, for this year-and-a-half we will focus on *this*, and then we will have to move on to this other thing. But it was an important project.

As part of *Documenting Live* there were two roundtables: one group of artists who were predominantly making work in the 1990s, and another that was more my generation of artists. I wasn't part of the actual roundtable, because I was producing, but I felt those people [in the second roundtable] were my peers, and what was interesting was that we all felt that we didn't want to be labelled in terms of race or cultural identity—that this was not how we defined our practice. Whereas the 'older' generation *all* felt that this was exactly what they were looking for—and that initiatives that defined their practices through the lens of race helped them to have a voice, and to find peers and mentors.

I haven't thought about this until now, but it's interesting that this is shifting for me as I grow in my practice, in that more and more I *do* define myself as being 'of colour'. Or at least it's become important to me to not make that narrative invisible: the way in which 'success' is about a kind of passing, in many ways: as white, as educated, as straight, etc. I think that narrative is very deeply embedded and I'm more and more interested in calling it out.

Jordan: It's interesting that we've been put together in this conversation, because I feel we're kind of the same and very different. When I started involving myself with LADA I came from a position of real naivety. I was doing a degree in literature and critical studies, and I didn't really know that there was this thing called 'performance art' out there. Through working at Nottingham Trent University, I discovered that there was actually this rich space for these kinds of things in Nottingham. Robert Ayers was there at the time, and he was very invested in performance practice, and there was the NOW Festival—where Robert Pacitti was banned. Actually quite a few people have been banned from Nottingham! So Nottingham has a rich history that I was lucky to be part of.

Also there was an upsurge of very political work, mainly around HIV and AIDS, and there was a lot of body art and work addressing the body. But the thing with me is that I've always been uncomfortable about community. We need communities, and I like being part of them, but I never feel that I can be *fully* part of them. I have always been very suspicious of practices that proclaim truths, and I felt that 'the flesh' was being seen as something that was a kind of 'ground zero'—which I didn't really believe. So I started to do performances that played with the idea of body art, but they were always quite satirical: if artists were using blood, then I was using tomato ketchup. If it was hard core, then I'd do cabaret.

But then, just by virtue of where I moved, I've ended up making a different kind of work. Like you, I wouldn't say that my work is strategised. Sometimes it's just following your nose and saying, 'Oh, I'm here now. That's interesting.' I moved onto the Approach Estate [in London] and found myself living in a group of people in 'social housing', and as a result I've become very interested in that environment. And I've become interested in class, as well, because I don't think class is discussed that often. Unlike gender and various other identities, I think class is often swept under the carpet.

And LADA have been very supportive of that work. I think their strength is that they are flexible—that you can take something difficult to them, and they'll go, 'Yeah, great. That sounds really interesting. Let's look at that.' I think they follow their nose, too, rather than saying, 'This is our strategy for Live Art.' No one agrees on what Live Art is, and that's what makes it exciting and volatile. People are always prodding at it: I'm not sure it's *this*, and I'm not sure it's *that*, either.

Rajni: We're always encouraged to act like we know what we're doing, and not to own up to not-knowing. But that's not how I work. I don't think about a piece of work, then research it, and then know

Right: *Lock Up Performance Art (LUPA)* (2012). Image Jordan McKenzie.

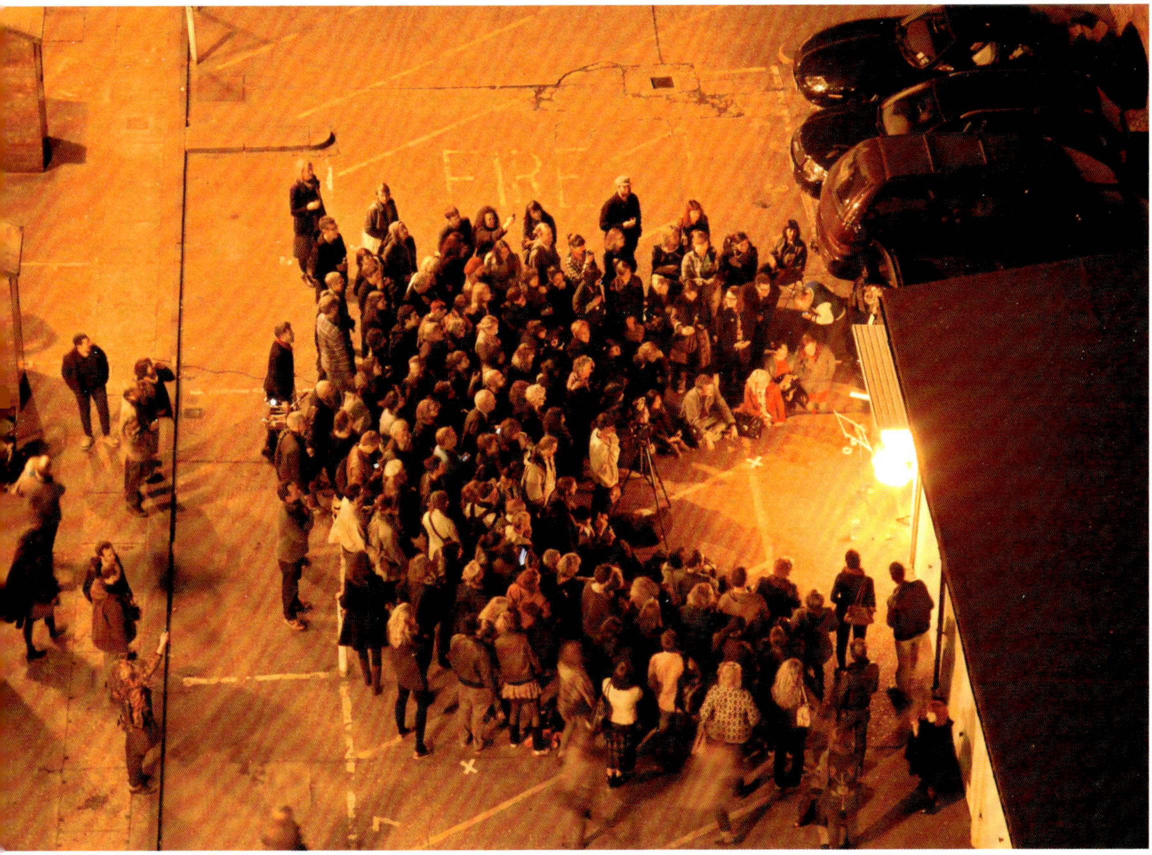
FIRE

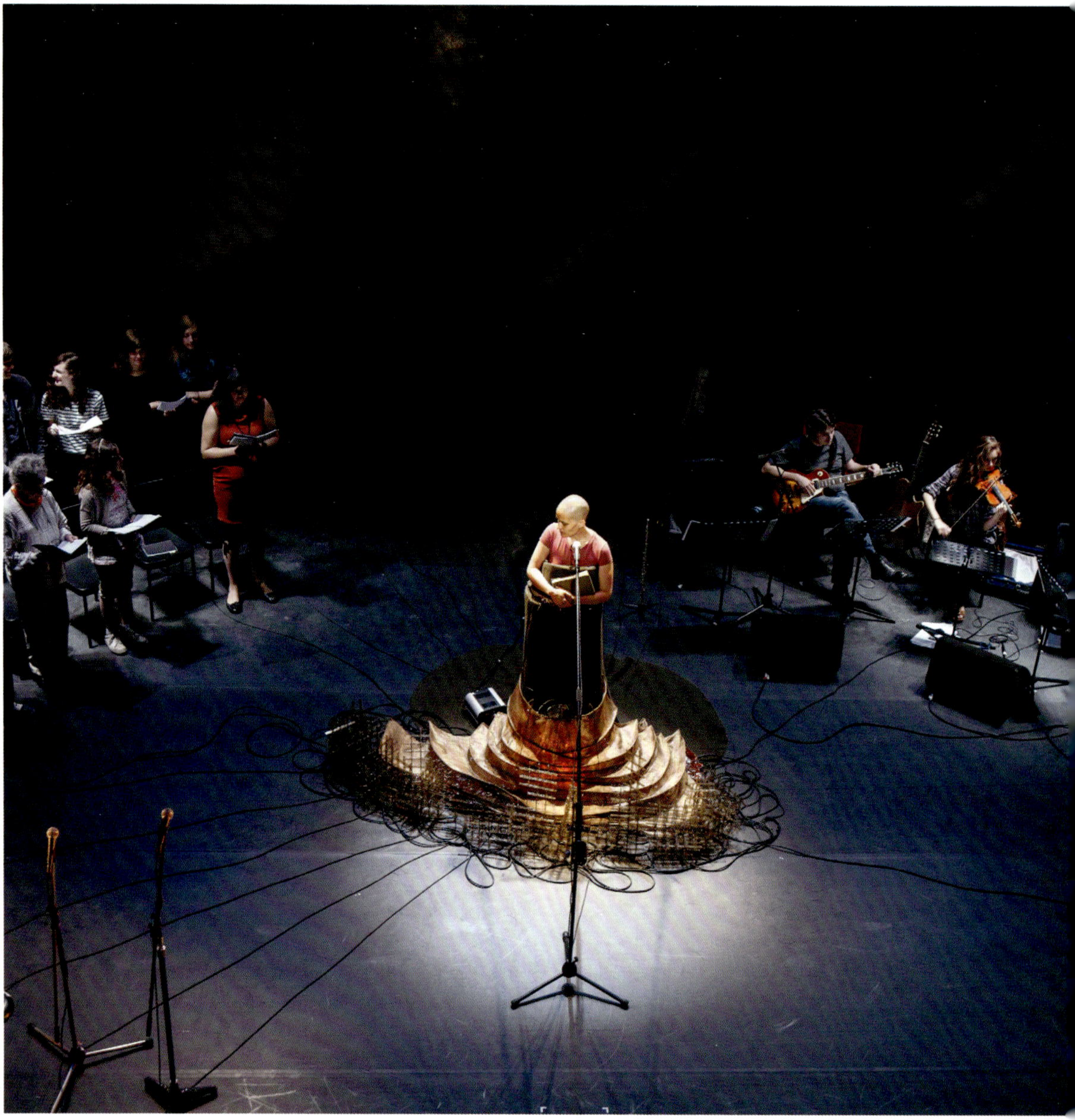

what it's going to be, and then make it. It's the other way around. Through the work I discover things, and then some time after I've finished making the work, *maybe* I can articulate what it was.

For example, I was recipient of a LADA One-to-One Bursary—I think it may have been the last year of that scheme. And it was just amazing to get that; I would say it was key to me being able to *be* an artist. And they insisted as part of the process that before you applied you came and had a chat with them. I remember sitting down with Daniel Brine, and we talked about making an application in a way that it wasn't about a finished thing, but about a problem or a question that felt important to explore.

I was really interested in looking at what would happen if I took my work out of theatres and out of institutions—because the Live Art scene had been very supportive, but I didn't want to make work just for other artists in the same scene. So my proposal was to take my practice into public spaces in cities I had never visited before—and they gave it to me, which was astounding! From that I developed this series of public interventions that gave me the courage to do the work I really wanted to do, which was about meeting people—meeting *anybody*.

And then I made *Glorious* as the culmination of the public intervention

Left: Rajni Shah Projects, *Glorious* rehearsal, Mons, Belgium (2012). Image Jonathan Brisson.

work. I wanted to ask the question, if I meet strangers on the street, can I then invite them to be on stage? Can we build a show where it isn't *about* the fact that we met people on the street, but that they become part of the fabric of the show? And it was also about a holistic vision of how touring might work, and how it could be about real relationships. It required months of build-up for just one performance, and the venue had to be really invested in meeting people in their community. That was very telling. There were some venues who would have a narrative about inclusivity, and meeting communities, and taking risks—but they were not prepared to follow up on that.

It's like what you were saying about being uncomfortable with the idea of community. What do we mean when we say community? It can often become over-simplified in a way that is only applicable to very particular circumstances: this idea of a tight community or an unchanging community. I feel like people in the arts still speak from a place where they don't include themselves when they're talking about community. They don't include themselves in it. Then you get venues and artists talking about whether they can get 'those people' to come see this work, or why don't 'those people' like what we like? And it starts to feel really dangerous.

I've been thinking recently about 'loose communities'—which is different from the idea that an artist parachutes in and then out, or however that's supposed to work—but about the fact that communities are always shifting and porous and overlapping. And what I can offer as an artist is to put something out there in public space and to be really clear about what the offer is—which means it *won't* be for everyone. I think clarity is the key to access, and you lose clarity as soon as you say, 'art for everyone'.

Jordan: That chimes on so many levels with my experience living on the estate. Suddenly I found myself involved in this tremendously complex place, which was a mixture of people that owned their flats and people in 'social housing'. My block has everything from a crack house to architects who had bought one of the flats on the top floor and converted it. There's so many ways that you could say there's a community there, but on another level there's more ways you can say there isn't.

And at the same time, it seemed like everything in performance and Live Art was about *venues*, and artists were worried about venues closing down or they were chasing pockets of money. And I thought, why do you have to go to those spaces to see the work? There's a garage down there. No one's using it. It's in a pretty grim car park space that is mainly used for drug dealing and people passing through, maybe having a bit of a fight occasionally, and it's a pretty ugly space. Why don't we just turn that into a performance venue once a month? So I started LUPA (Lock Up Performance Art) with Aaron Williamson and Kate Mahony.

I didn't particularly want to make work *about* the estate. The question was just what happens if performance art is on the estate? Rather than a specialised venue, what if it was just out there and people bumped into it? There were some concessions in terms of thinking about who would see this work: no nudity, no people shoving things in their orifices and then cutting themselves, etc., because I just knew it would polarise certain groups on the estate. But I was really interested in difference, and how people from radically different positions and different places communicate with one other. I didn't want to water down the work. I didn't want it to be 'understandable'.

We had one every month no matter whether it snowed, rained, hailed, whatever. It did attract an 'art' audience. But because it wasn't in a gallery with all their covert rules around audience and viewing, those who attended could get involved, talk, drink, mill about. And also, because of where the garage was, all the flats looked down onto it. So it meant that if people didn't want to join that crowd, they could stand on the balcony and have a look at it. There was a kind of comfort there that I was really interested in. And some of my neighbours would get some wine, or get the kids, and look at what was going on.

Rajni: I love that. It makes me wish I'd lived in one of those flats, and been able to pop out and have a look, maybe come down if I was free. Or not.

It makes me think of a part of my trajectory that's been really important in terms of my practice, which was the work I did with women who were sex workers as part of the Open Doors drop-in. It feels parallel in that it felt like getting to know my neighbours—but the neighbours that would never have been visible to me if I hadn't done that project. It was a project run by Emmy Minton, who I met working together on projects at LADA. Emmy worked with the NHS to set up a weekly arts drop-in (which came out of the project *(be)longing* that she worked on with Curious). The NHS workers would go out on night duty and tell all the women about it, and then we'd just see who showed up. And every week Emmy would curate it and work with Susannah Hewlett and Kaye Dunnings to make the hall incredibly welcoming—transforming the space—and bringing in quite amazing guest artists. And for the NHS it meant that they were seeing women they'd never been able to see before, because those women wanted to come in and do some performance art or do some weird project with George Chakravarthi or Bobby Baker—and the artists were really doing their practice, not changing it because it's a 'community project'. I think that's the reason that the women came back, because it wasn't dumbed down for them. And it took a lot of work, but it was also so cheap and so easy to run in lots of ways.

Jordan: Like with the Lock UP, we got a bit of dosh to pay for the garage and that was it. There was that necessity for it to happen, and it doesn't need to be in special places with people that have some kind of knowledge of it. It can operate on its own terms, and actually people from lots of different social spaces and backgrounds can have a relationship with it. I don't just want to make art purely for people 'in the know'.

We always made a physical newsletter, which was very accessible in terms of what people were going to see, and I would deliver it personally. I didn't know how important those newsletters were—I thought people just chucked them. But when French & Mottershead came, they said their piece *was* going to be about working with members of the estate. So we knocked on doors, and people were like, 'Oh yeah, LUPA. We read about your thing every time and we look forward to it.' It was a slow process over two years. I think this is similar to what you said earlier. I call it holding my hand out. You can shake my hand if you like, and it's equally alright if you don't, but it's there. Gradually people took it and they shook it. And the crowds got bigger.

And I'm part of that social housing, but I'm also different from some who live on the estate with me. I'm middle class, and white, and educated. And also, I'm an artist. I really like this idea from ethnography of the 'professional stranger'. What if I am the professional stranger who is part of something, but also acknowledges their difference in quite an overt way?

Rajni: The public interventions feel parallel in some way. I realised there is something really key about what happens when I'm able to do something as an artist. All I have to do is say, 'I'm doing this as an artist,' and suddenly I'm able to do a lot more than I would feel able to do otherwise. It's an odd switch to make, but I feel like I'm able to take responsibility, and to try something that is more aligned with my values and beliefs, when I've given myself permission to be an artist. This might sound a bit stupid, but I even think about that sometimes when I'm on the bus and I want to offer my seat to someone, and it feels like a big deal: how do I do that? But if I were thinking of myself as an artist, there would be no question about it. I'd just do the thing, and maybe we'd have a conversation.

Jordan: It's funny, isn't it? The playing and not-playing of yourself at the same time.

Rajni: More and more what I'm interested in is the declaring of a space, and seeing who comes to it. For me, how we hold those spaces open is the skill that defines being an artist. I believe that anyone can make art in some way if they want to. I believe that really strongly. But I don't believe that everyone wants to hold that space within which art can happen. The artist is the person who, at that moment, is prepared to hold the space.

COMMUNITIES
CONVERSATION
ANNE BEAN
ALASTAIR MACLENNAN
DATE
05 FEBRUARY 2016
PLACE
LONDON

Anne Bean has a diverse and multifaceted practice, often involving collaboration, such as the Bernsteins in the 1970s (which she describes here); her widely-known work with Richard Wilson and Paul Burwell as the Bow Gamelan Ensemble in the 1980s; and her multinational collaboration PAVES (also described here). She is one of LADA's patrons, was a recipient of an Artist's One-to-One Bursary, has led two DIY projects, and was one of the recipients (along with Tim Etchells) of the LADA/Tate *Legacy: Thinker In Residence* awards, with which she worked with Robin Klassnik and Richard Wilson on *TAPS: Improvisations with Paul Burwell* (who had died the previous year). Anne is the subject of the LADA/Intellect Live publication, *Anne Bean: Self Etc.* (2018).

Alastair MacLennan has created an extraordinary body of work over several decades, predominantly working with actions sustained over extended durations and slow tempo, sometimes up to 144 hours. Since 1975 he has been based in Northern Ireland, and in 1997 he represented Ireland at the Venice Biennale with intermedia work commemorating all those who had died as a result of the Troubles since 1969. He is member of the performance art collective Black Market International (BMI), and co-founder of Bbeyond Performance Art International. He performed as part of *Live Culture* (LADA/Tate 2003) and collaborated with Manuel Vason for *Encounters* (2007) and *Double Exposures* (2015). He performs globally, nationally, and locally, and is the subject of an upcoming Bbeyond-initiated publication on his work.

Anne: In thinking about this twenty-year timeframe, the first thing that comes to mind is the Whitechapel Gallery's series *A Short History of Performance* (2002), and the realisation that at that moment that performance had become *historical*. They phoned me up, and I remember their phrase, 'We would like to re-create iconic performances'—and I just had such difficulty with those words. My whole work is anti-iconic—not in a militant way, but in the way that it is all about process, through many works and collaborations. I don't feel that I've done any particular work in a way that is recognisably me. The work *is* the whole.

So for the Whitechapel I decided to revisit this performance from the early 1970s that I'd done with a group called the Bernsteins that existed briefly, when seven of us occupied a semi-squat in Mile End. For that piece we decided we would challenge each other to laugh for an hour, and see what would happen in the space between authentic laughter and hammy, theatrical laughter. Since then our lives have all dispersed form each other, so I thought for the Whitechapel we would gather together, having not all been in the same room since then, and come into the space and laugh for an hour *as* our first communication after thirty years.

Alastair: In Ireland there's a saying: '*same difference*'. There's sameness in difference and difference in sameness. You would have noticed this in the laughter piece.

Anne: Since then there's been this absolute avalanche of archive, legacy, document, interviews, etc., but I've always felt terribly uncomfortable about that. I wouldn't even have agreed to interviews until ten years ago or so, because I felt there was this danger of solidifying something—whereas the very reason for jumping into a space was its complete mystery: a shared space that was beyond words.

Alastair: What is Actuality, 'before' and 'after' language? It's performing without knowing what'll happen in the next second, without time to think, yet body/mind, in presence of others, can inter-link, inter-relate. Conceptual thinking can interfere. Through meditation I allow mind/body to interfuse. It's at the heart of performance practice I've been immersed in, for over 40 years.

I started out as a young academic oil painter, quite skilled in portraiture, but sensing something was missing.... And while still a young student, I was taking a painting, personally, by train, to be included in a prestigious art exhibition in England (quite an honour, I felt, for a young person like myself). On the journey, we had to change trains and wait for half an hour before boarding another. It was cold, so I entered a small waiting room. There was a tramp in one corner. People sat as far away from him as possible. He tried to communicate, but was rebuffed. His response was instructive. Though he'd lost 'everything', I sensed he was freer than any of us there (including me) with our hopes, dreams, aims and objectives, fashionable clothes and agendas, etc. This intrigued me and lingered on.... I realised how effective one person's 'presence' could be as a societal 'signal', and how an artist might use such (or other) 'mind/body' material, to convey political, social and cultural malfunction, in or as art.

Eight years later (at age 30), outside LA, I spent time with a Japanese Rinzai Zen Master, doing *sesshins* which would last a week or longer, for two years, with the *koan*, 'How do you realise your true nature while art making?' He wouldn't accept any answer for two years. The solution came when I gave up all concepts about art and just gave myself over to present-tense processing. He watched me closely and could tell if I was separating subject from object. He could tell from the fluency of bodily moves, wherein there's no separation between 'how' and 'what', self and other, subject and object.

I found this hugely beneficial for expanding art beyond any kind of conceptual frame. You realise the art 'canvas' is the time and space you have as a human being, alive, in relation to others. Where is the frame? *There ain't no frame*. It's 360 degrees in all directions. Art and life, life and art become one, *experientially*, not just conceptually, as in New York in the 1970s. One could use one's whole body/mind within the artwork of living. That's how I got into performance: how to 'perform' living?

Anne: There was a time when I was also a painter. I was doing painting and sculpture at Cape Town University in the late 1960s, and I didn't even know of this thing called 'performance'. It was the height of apartheid, and it became absolutely obvious that painting a still life, or life drawing, was just so at odds with this completely toxic situation. Art became so irrelevant and so *privileged*. I had to do something visual, and I remember doing this piece about these 'white only' benches, where I would paint my hands black and sit on a bench. I saw it as a *visual protest*, and separate from this thing called 'art'.

But then something happened, which was this mixed-race person asked what would happen if someone who was black painted themselves white and sat on the bench. Whereas I could get a slap on the wrist, or maybe even spend a night in prison, it would never be the same as would happen to them. That really brought me up *sharp*, and made me realise that I was part of the problem, and the only thing I could do was leave. I didn't know where to go with the *weight* of the feeling that art was so redundant—pathetic, maybe—in this all-pervading situation. So I came to England to go to art school.

One of my tutors at the University of Reading was Rita Donagh, who was a fantastic open-spirited woman. We did this project called *Three Weeks in May*, which was meant to be a life-drawing class, but we turned it into *drawing life*. The life model was recognised as a human being with a history, involved in this situation with us—rather than just a *body*. An extraordinary atmosphere arose in which we started to make all sorts of responses, such as 'life drawings' where we asked her questions and we wrote up the answers. And then the shootings at Kent State happened, and we brought in this awareness of what was happening around us, by drawing the bodies and blood stains on the floor of the studio. That project opened up so many possibilities of how one can engage as an artist. It solidified a notion of collaboration, and how one can enter spaces between oneself and other bodies. The assumption of that solid state human being disappears. It's a very permissive space to be.

Alastair: Seven years after I graduated from the MFA program at the School of the Art Institute of Chicago, I applied for a job at the art college in Belfast, Northern Ireland. During the interview a bomb went off. The sky blackened with flying pigeons. I was intrigued, so when the offer came of a Fine Art job I took it. I was living in a working-class area in East Belfast and at two or three in the morning you would hear bombs, shootings and army helicopters circling overhead. And in the morning I'd walk to work, up Royal Avenue, in the centre of Belfast, where the army was lodged, behind high, barbed-wire fencing. There were snipers, checkpoints, and army tanks in this area. I'd pass through every morning on my way to work. There was no way I couldn't acknowledge the devastating effects here. I'd somehow have to embrace it in my art.

After coming under 'direct' and indirect political pressure and threat from certain quarters in the city, I wrote a statement one night… how, if you make art with heart, it's worth dying for—in case I got shot the next day. I was young (age 32), writing a statement headed 'Art is skill in action, where skill is the resolution of conflict.' The following morning I walked up Royal Avenue wearing a large shooting target over my neck and chest. If you're being intimidated from conveying what's important to you in life, nature, and art, there's an obligation to stand by the principles underlying your practice.

I didn't get shot. In 1975, some Fine Art students and I accepted an invitation to contribute to Queens University Festival, in Belfast. At the time there were oppositional political marches up and down certain sections of the city, so (as part of our contribution) we decided to go as an 'art march' along certain routes. We walked along those, in line, wearing identical masks and white coats, with 'ART' printed over our coat backs. We wanted to experience the implications of taking art out of galleries and into public spaces, engaging (where possible) political-social-cultural inter-fusions and inter-relations… addressing 'same difference', sameness in difference and difference in sameness. Students were from different political-social-cultural backgrounds. We embraced *both and*, not *either or* thinking, to introduce performance art practice to the public in Belfast.

A few years ago there was a program addressing conflict resolution at the art college in Belfast, involving local and international artists and a variety of community workers. An observation from a local union rep resonated with me. He said, 'It's all well and good flying artists in from other countries to talk about conflict resolution, but then they fly off and away the next day.' What was needed, he said, was *direct*, ongoing, week in/week out, community involvement, over a number of years, showing *real* commitment by people in the arts, to facilitate genuine, experiential, cross-community healing.

Anne: It reminds me of being paid by the British Council to go to Kurdistan as an artist, which was a project initiated after meeting a young Kurdish Iraqi refugee named Adalet Garmiany who came to Hull. He was an admirable young man, and he said that he felt that bringing contemporary art to Iraq would give hope and permission to young people. He spoke to the British Council, who gave us 'protection', I suppose is the word, in that there were soldiers and weapons. It was all very strange and unreal—staying in these nice hotels while trying to engage with people who have been through the most devastating genocide. You don't know if you've got any right, or if you're doing *anything* at all. I worked with a lot of women on a big piece in an ex-Saddam Hussein jail, and they said to me that it was a really cathartic action. It feels so very *small*.... although Adalet has made a remarkable difference to many lives there...

... and I met this young woman, Poshya Kakl, who showed me this video of her making this protest action which completely blew me away. She was only seventeen. I thought: if I do nothing else I'm going to really support this young woman. I decided to bring together women from countries which have experienced political tragedy and conflict. I knew Vlasta Delimar from Croatia, who did incredible political actions in relation to former Yugoslavia. There was Sinéad O'Donnell from Northern Ireland, this vigorous force, who you know well, Alastair. And Efi Ben-David, a young Israeli woman who had done a lot of work with Palestinians. Together we were PAVES, after the first letter of each of our names. We decided that we would go to each other's countries and work.

The first place we were going to do it was in London, so everybody came—except Poshya, because at the very last minute her visa was refused. We were all artists who used our bodies in our work, so the work became about how we were going to enter space in a bodily way together despite difficulties. Poshya Skyped to us this astonishing piece of work she did with women who were burned—so-called 'honour killings'—for not going along with arranged marriages and

Right: Alastair MacLennnan, *Target*, Belfast (1977). Image the artist.

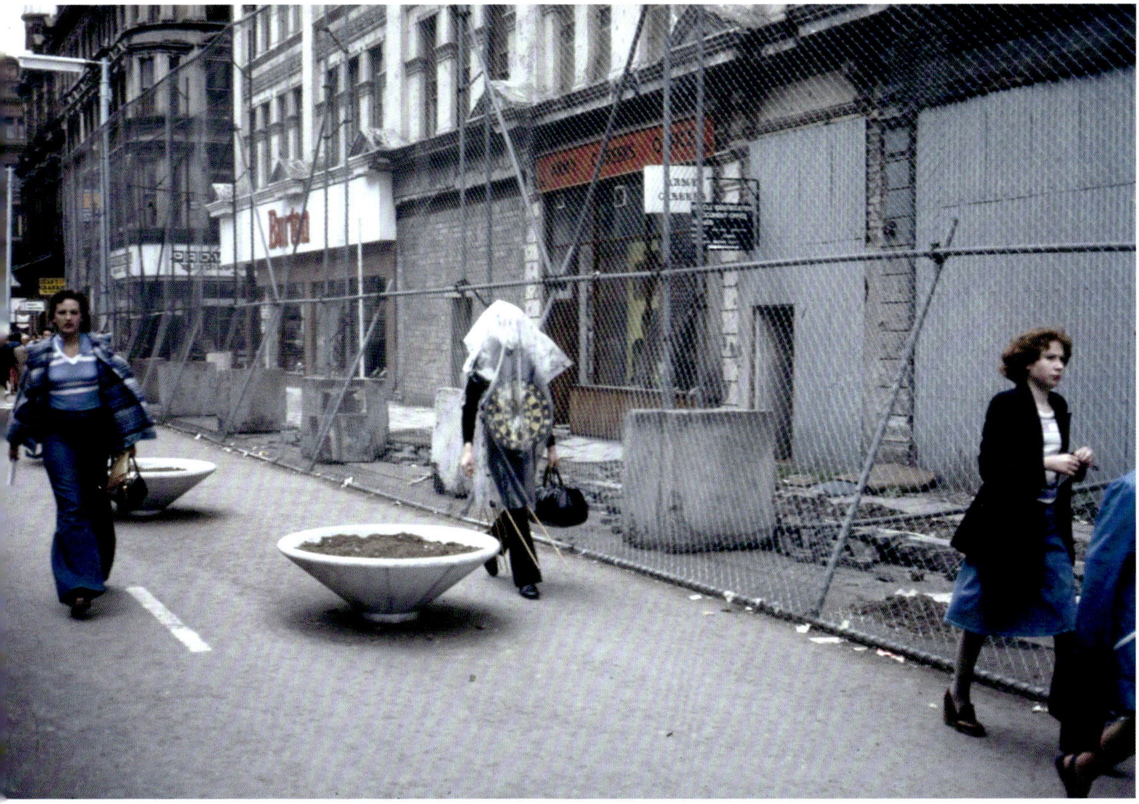
Burton

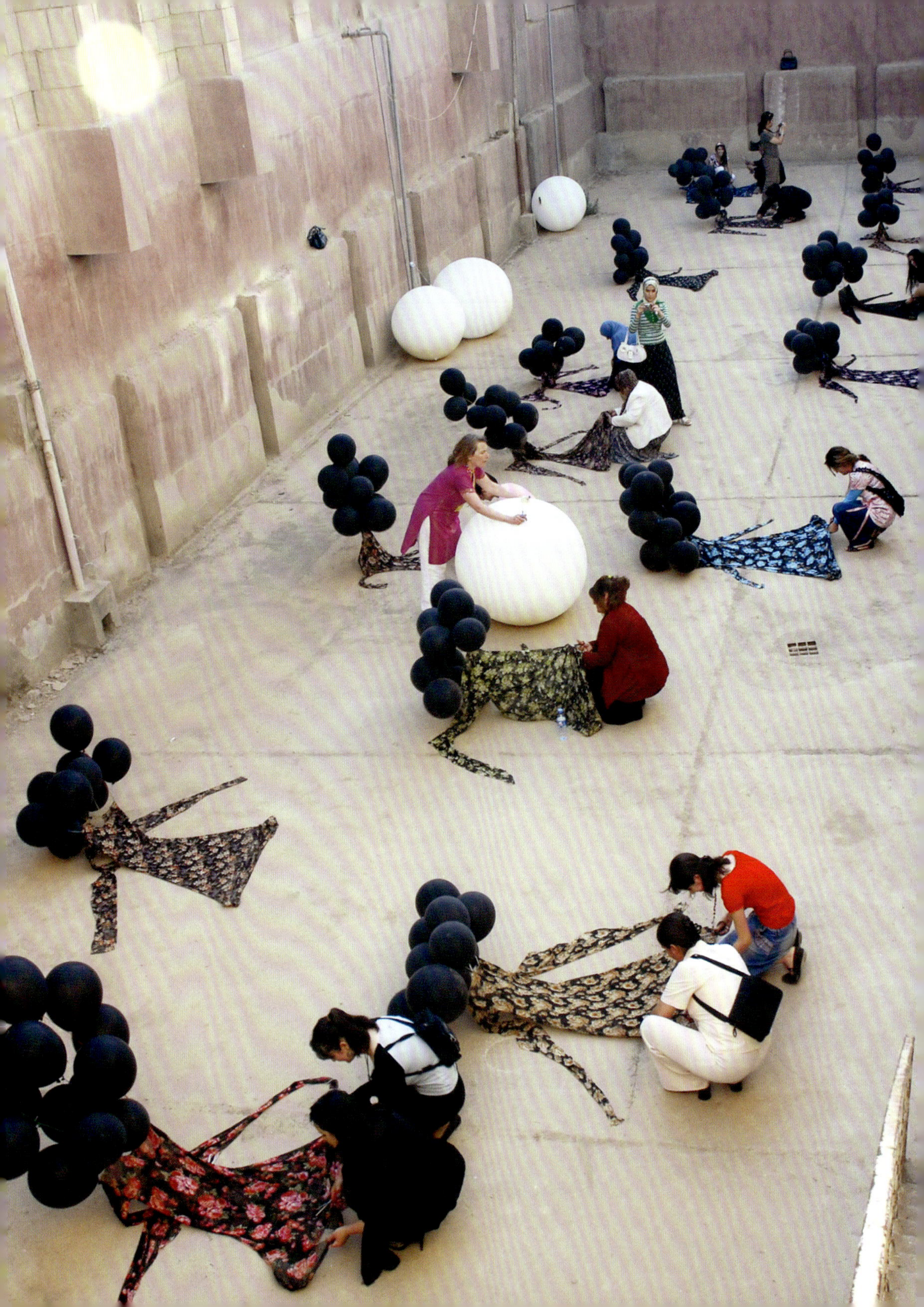

so on. It's just beyond comprehension. No matter how much you try and confront it, you just don't know to deal with it. I felt so overwhelmed by these images that I had this very immediate response to just bandage my computer, and then to bandage everything in the room. It was a very immediate sense of deep empathy—and at the same time knowing that you're almost not allowed the empathy because you couldn't possibly know. It was *beyond* moving.

Alastair: Something interesting happened a few years ago when Black Market International came to Belfast to give a BMI performance, solo performances, and performance workshops at Queens University. The workshop participants included artists, but also people from the diverse, locally divided communities. One participant had a 'severe' history during the Troubles, with terrorist/freedom fighter connections throughout. After the workshop public presentation at Queens, he said such workshop processes would work really well in resolving cross-community conflict.

BMI performances are 'meetings', or 'encounters'. Members (from several different countries) come with unknown materials to start things off. But what I've noticed, as a participant, in our longer performances of eight hours or so, is we 'exhaust' the items we've brought, so we 'drop' these and perform with what's left: our human inter-connectedness.

Left: Anne Bean, *MASS*, Iraq Kurdistan (2008). Image the artist.

Who needs a prop? We all carry our past and future in the Present. In the mutuality of trust within 'encounter', there is recognition of each person's autonomy, and validity, in being how he/she is in relation. You could even have people simultaneously screaming—but after a while we realise, 'same difference'... here we are, human beings, inter-fusing, together.

Maybe we've been over-manipulated by political, social, and cultural 'branding' systems... but one's own identity is more liminal, more fluid. Why be pigeon-holed? We don't need to be conceptually trapped. We can go out, come back, intervene, consider other contexts, hybrid combinations, etc. What intrinsic authority does any agency or entity have, for defining, rigidly, fixedly, who and what we are?

Anne: With regard to art and life, I think the most fulfilling piece I have done was the year and half where I simply changed my name, and I didn't take anything of my former life with me. The name was all I had as a being. It overwhelmed me, actually. It frightened me. I didn't know if I was experiencing my *life* or my *art*. Which looking back is pretty wonderful, but it was often a very uneasy space. I suppose it became more real than my life here. Of all the things I certainly didn't expect, I formed very real and profound friendships. I didn't know I would make art as Chana Dubinski, but I ended up doing it. It gave me permission to do the sort of art that I might think would be a bit over-the-top, or a bit questionable in one way or another.

Alastair: For the past forty years I've worn only black, as a visually 'invisible' performance art metaphor. As a former painter, I know black (or grey-black) is a result of mixing equal amounts of primary and secondary colours together, so black 'contains' the integration of all possibilities in painting. If I walk down the street, no one's aware of the metaphoric implications. But to me, a real question is 'How to "perform" living in everyday life?' People may not see it, because there's no 'frame' around it. It's not necessarily in an art gallery and doesn't need to 'look' like performance.

Performance art (and we need to be conscious of this) begins to 'look' framed itself... unless it becomes so fluently illusive and integrative we can look at, but not 'see' it (in a positive sense), any and everywhere, simultaneously. The term 'Live Art' postulates *dead* art, doesn't it? Maybe we need a term that embraces both.

Anne: Or we could pronounce it differently; instead of 'Live Art' it could be *live* art [as in '*to live*'].

Alastair: Or you could play with the letters and change them around: vile art!

Anne: Evil art!

[*they both laugh*]

COMMUNITIES

PROVOCATION

ALAN READ

TITLE

PERFORMED COMMUNITIES:
IMAGINING SOME RESEARCH
WORTH DOING

Alan Read is a writer and currently Professor of Theatre at King's College London. He was Director of the Council of Europe Workshop on Theatre and Communities, and Rotherhithe Theatre Workshop in the Docklands area of South East London, where over a decade of intense land speculation in the 1980s local neighbourhoods found resources for play, protection, and political resistance. Alan Read worked as a freelance writer in Barcelona and as Director of Talks at the Institute of Contemporary Arts in the 1990s at the same time as Lois Keidan was Director of Live Art. From 1997–2006 he was Professor of Theatre at University of Roehampton where he directed a five-year AHRC research funded programme on performance, architecture, and location exploring theatre and public ceremonial in rational housing blocks and council estates. At King's, in collaboration with the Centre for eResearch and King's Estates he conceived and developed the Anatomy Theatre and Museum on the Strand and the Inigo Rooms in the East Wing of Somerset House to provide King's with publicly accessible venues for performance and cultural practice. His books include *Theatre & Everyday Life: An Ethics of Performance* (1993), *Theatre, Intimacy & Engagement: The Last Human Venue* (2008), *Theatre in the Expanded Field: Seven Approaches to Performance* (2013) and Theatre & Law (2016). He is commissioned to publish a 25th anniversary rewriting of his first book, titled *The Dark Theatre: A General Economy of Performance*, due in 2020.

When you have been doing some work for a while, how do you take stock? What kinds of reflection are adequate to the complex experiences of that doing? The taking stock I am currently involved in considers what 'Performed Communities' might be. One way to describe the work, for the purposes of a research project for instance, though such limits are not exclusive, a lively *conversation* about what matters now would be an equivalent prompt, would be to call this 'doing' something like the following: a longitudinal study of live art and civic engagement in Europe between 1973 and 2023. The dates simply describe when and where I started doing this thing, and when I intend to end my own participation in this thing, at a date not un-adjacent to when I am of an age that others insist on describing as 'retirement' but I would prefer to call simply 66 (given that's the number of a lively Route out of a dead-beat town). Another way to describe it would be 'doing things with those who make a difference after another fashion' amongst whom I would certainly include each of those writing and speaking with whom I work alongside in this volume who in turn, not coincidentally, share an elective affinity with the profound influence if not the generative practice of the Live Art Development Agency. The research I now seek to do, and offer in this imagined proposal, would return to three questions, irritating them you could say. What *diagnostic* capacities do live arts offer the political agency of individuals within communities resisting threat to their existence and identities? What *heuristic* potential is evidenced by performance practices with regards to 'critical citizenship' and 'civic engagement' in these communities? Which institutions demonstrate a verifiable *innovating* role in the infrastructural support of socially engaged art in such precarious circumstances?

Why bother taking stock by way of research? It's not for everyone after all. In the early years of the twenty-first century the cultural claims for Live Art, performance and performativity, the social impact of theatrical practice and engaged art, and their potential for fostering community cohesion are widespread amongst practitioners, agencies, and institutions. Amongst those 'agencies' I would want, for homeopathic reasons, to foreground the Live Art Development Agency itself, now twenty years 'in the making'. From its earliest iteration gloriously led 'out' of the Institute of Contemporary Arts by the live art impresarios there, Lois Keidan and Catherine Ugwu, across a London-wide, national and increasingly international landscape, this celebration and support of artists' agency itself, appeared as a beacon whose guide others gradually followed. The LADA Study Room alone (for it is by definition unique), fostered in its most recent burgeoning form by Keidan, CJ Mitchell, and their curatorially inquisitive team, stands as a testament to just the kind of performed community and its archive that this short essay seeks to celebrate. But, LADA notwithstanding, as the Arts Council of England concluded in their major study on 'The Value of Arts and Culture to People and Society' (2014),[1] there is minimal long-term evidence as to the social efficacy of cultural practices of these performative kinds. Most problematically as the report states emphatically: *longitudinal studies* of any description are wholly absent from the record.

Now, this kind of work has always been undertaken cognisant of its loop-holes and lacunae, and LADA have been testament to precisely that kind of caring circumspection. Theoreticians in the international field, for example Claire Bishop,[2] have vigorously questioned such quantitative, or positivist attempts to measure cultural participation, sceptical of political instrumentalism (as I have been myself over 300 pages of my book *Theatre, Intimacy & Engagement*).[3] But sensible reservations about instrumentalism need not be an invitation to eschew empirically demanding diagnostic rigour. Indeed, work of the kind I am imagining should precisely meet Bishop's methodological challenge when she says: 'Each work needs to be judged on a case-by-case basis taking into account—and being read against—the dominant modes of participation in that culture as a whole.'[4] In just such historically material 'case by case' studies, my thinking about a research project called Performed Communities would have to go further and take up Janelle Reinelt's public challenge, addressed directly to me in a valedictory lecture to the discipline at the end of her long and distinguished career as a chronicler and critic of the social arts: 'Perhaps neo-liberal individualism [...] might yet be held accountable to a larger vision of collective organisation and struggle, imaginative in its transgressions but ordered or at least strategic in its actions.'[5]

To have any effect whatsoever Performed Communities would have to, perhaps unfashionably, return the question of community to the fore in Live Art, theatre, and cultural research. It would have to do so within very precise, and yes, definable, theoretical framings of communities of *interest*, and communities of *location and identity*. And it would do so wholly aware of the common characterisation of community as a 'fall guy' unworthy of serious attention (despite the evidence of publications such as this) and recently the subject of *ad hominem* attack. Suffering secondary status in political and cultural theory when placed alongside questions of equality, freedom, justice, and rights, 'community' for some appears to have become so contested as to be not worth the trouble, apparently at odds with the welcome sophistication of intersectional interests. And despite a plethora of publishing in relational, collaborative, and social fields of performance, the vocabulary and practices of 'community' have either been successfully concealed from view so as not to frighten the horses or elided from the discourse altogether over the last decade. But I want to insist here that the complex, half-century disagreements regarding 'the problem of community', (not to be confused with the movement of communitarianism), cannot anymore be taken as an excuse to circumvent its profound analytic and normative potential. The term community in its association with Live Art and theatre through the last five decades has, after all, allowed for a methodologically precise, socially inclusive range of performance practices to be theorised beyond the conventions of the written dramatic and literary canons, confidently placing practiced and embodied researches amidst social contexts at the centre of the performance studies field, including the fine work of Eugène van Erven, Helen Nicholson, James Thompson, Petra Kuppers, amongst many others.[6] Initially emerging from the mix of counter cultural, radical, and liberational theatres of the 1960s and early 1970s (in Latin America and North America, as well as Europe) community theatre movements, groups, and institutions valued (and still value) local narratives, participatory ethos, improvised methods, and social interventions as their modus operandi.

Tellingly, by 2007 Petra Kuppers' excellent *Community Performance: An Introduction* had retired theatre from the title page and emphasised the North American shift towards Performance Studies and its productive, intersectional critical modes. Performed Communities, an imagined research project, should welcome this shift without faddishly following its geo-specific orientation and problematic politics of disciplinary hegemony that often ties Performance Studies to the North American academy. This, in tandem with *The Community Performance Reader,*[7] are substantial achievements in a field light on theoretical underpinnings, and are widely used amongst undergraduate university courses. But, inevitably, and this applies to almost all projects subsequent to the 1980s, there is little or no feedback loop established in any of these researches with those with whom the work was *done*, despite the very best and inclusive efforts of a number of recent works from Shannon Jackson, Jen Harvie, Maria Hlavajova, and Ranjit Hoskote.[8] Even the most formative and canonical of 'community theatre' workers, amongst whom the Brazilian Augusto Boal might be taken as a fine exemplar,[9] were notoriously disinterested in any detailed analysis of quite what the work, whether that be 'Forum Theatre' or 'Theatre for Social Change', was actually changing. There is certainly no longitudinal evidence of this work.

A more recent major research event that reflects something of the ambition of my imagined project Performed Communities is the curatorial approach of the established Liverpool Biennial, with its serious regard for community concerns. Following innovative partnerships such as the community oriented *Visible Prize,* the Biennial turned its forensic attention to the bifurcation between community cultural practices of the 1970s and 1980s and more recent socially engaged art practices, for which a Biennial of this kind would commonly offer an international platform. The involvement of the architectural/artist practice Assemble, the recently celebrated Tate Turner Prize winning collective, working on housing with residents on derelict sites in Liverpool, amongst many others, brought international attention to the recovery of the term 'community' in the Biennial's agenda amongst this new generation of cultural producers who might previously have eschewed any such conceptual label for their work. I gave a keynote address at the Biennial 'Community Arts? Learning from the Legacy of Artists' Social Initiatives' working alongside others with whom, over the previous four decades, these questions of community and cultural production had been played out.[10]

How might our imagined research advance such state of the art enquiries? One focus, as the critiques of other projects above suggest, is with a far more fully-rounded and incisive theoretical and methodological framework for analysis. Both are critical to work of this kind and might be expected at the very least to clarify the critical status of *political agency* within marginalised communities. As the title of my imagined research project implies, Performed Communities would first adopt a theoretical perspective from Benedict Anderson's seminal work on nationalism, *Imagined Communities*, that changed the analytic ambience of everything that followed in the academic discourse. Anderson, as is less well known, took his own starting point from Hugh Seaton-Watson's work on nations and states: 'a nation exists when a significant number of people in a community consider themselves to form a nation, or believe as if they form one'.[11] Anderson 'translated' 'consider themselves' to 'imagine themselves' in a definitive attempt to shift from the implications of 'falsity', 'fabrication', and 'invention' carried over from the ideologically negative reading of Ernest Gellner, towards more constructive implications of 'imagining as creation'. As Anderson put it, foregrounding the potential for what he called 'horizontal comradeship': 'Communities are to be distinguished, not by their falseness/genuineness, but by the style in which they are imagined'.[12] The rhetorical move by Anderson here in the use of the word 'style', on behalf of analytic precision, a word that is central to the subsequent readings of 'communities' as pluralistic, contested manifestations of 'critical citizenship' as conceived by Pippa Norris.[13]

To ground and materially situate its analysis in the embodied subjects of communities, this imagined research project would now shift that qualifier another stage towards an agential conception of 'performed communities' drawing on the full methodological range that a two-decade legacy of the performative optic now offers us (from J.L. Austin to Judith Butler).[14] Where Seaton-Watson's community 'considered' themselves associated, and Anderson's 'imagined' themselves in 'comradeship', this project proposes communities are *performed*, engaged in processes of continuous creation of embodied subject-hood, agency, which by its very nature makes them susceptible to robust analysis through a performance research lens. Indeed this project would contest such identities are *only* comprehensible at any sensible level of articulacy through a performance oriented analytic frame. That is the unique offering of Performed Communities—indeed perhaps its only offering.

Beyond the neat symmetry of imagined and performed communities, the tougher, methodological motor of the project would then seek to deliver an ambitious and perhaps foolhardy promise: to *measure* the influence of cultural practice on political agency and social change. (The kind of claim that art historian Claire Bishop would resist at all costs.) Each definable community of location, interest, or identity potentially of central interest to the project has, by definition, already been put 'under threat' by evidential examples of precarious conditions of labour, health, environmental expulsion, or religious/sexual preference / gender / disabilities intolerance. Such threats to agency as widely documented in the archives of practitioners, in the LADA Study Room, and demonstrated in the practices themselves between 1973 and 2018 (at the time of the writing of this imagined project), demand a high-risk methodology that combines expectation of both critique *and* innovation. There can be little point in identifying such violences and cultural resistances to such violences without insisting on the responsibility of the researchers and researched to move from the description of practices to participation together within such struggles. It is only through such methodological alliance *between* researcher and researched that as Lea Ypi has suggested we might aspire to 'viable forms of resistance, and coherent discourses of political, social and cultural transformation'.[15] Thus *normative* principles and political agency would be methodologically central and of equal significance to work of this kind.

A normative understanding of methodological approaches is one that insists that explanatory perspectives are not sufficient alone. Normative models identify ideals as expressed within the communities in question, shared models of practice that are perceived as conducive to the most justice for the most people and especially judicious to the protection of precarious individuals and groups. Obviously the necessary subjective element of such normative principles means that they can be neither proved nor disproved, but they *can* be *weighed* and *judged* precisely through research, and I welcome that methodological challenge. Furthermore, work of this kind considers research to be a human right shared by researcher and *researched* in this significant sense. Unlike the low-risk, timid relativism of three decades of postmodern truth-questioning, we might insist that now, amidst the not-fake news of communities under threat, it is time to weigh and judge in defence of those most put at risk by neo-liberal forces, extreme exclusions, and expulsions. If one accepts that such normative perspectives are equipped to motivate necessary political agency in such precarious communities, then the heuristic role of cultural practices and their relations to conflicts within such communities can be tested to determine the degree to which they *improve* on their rivals' claims, (for instance social, political or bureaucratic solutions), with specific regard to problem diagnosis. The heuristic method is by definition one that is not optimal in such circumstances (urgency demands action), but is 'good enough' to guide political transformation given existing political structures. As I have made clear at length in *Theatre, Intimacy & Engagement*, it is unlikely that cultural practice, never mind Live Art or theatre practice, has the instrumentalism available to it to change political structures themselves. This does not mean for a moment, as Janelle Reinelt has suggested, that there is any less resolve (from me at least) politically to *challenge* those threats to the communities in question through diagnostic and critical force. But to guard against Pollyanna-ish voluntarism might be our most demanding mission. The dialectical method at work here, approaching normative questions in tandem with non-ideal case studies, allows for the focus to be not only around the *celebration* of particular affirmative practices within these fraught circumstances, (though the timely celebration of courageous live art acts attested to in this volume is right and *improper* as it should always be), but the tougher analysis of their moments of crisis. Agonism, after Chantal Mouffe and Christopher Balme,[16] informs any such methodological approach. Here the focus of the research is on reflecting critically on the kinds of *conflicts* such contestation within communities express, the different concepts and creative practices protagonists invoke to render such conflict meaningful, and the kinds of theories and interpretive paradigms that are deployed to explain the occurrence of the threat. Having taken account of such forces and the ways that cultural practices can offer *diagnoses* of them and for them, the descriptive exercise should offer heuristic resources to direct future actions by those put most cruelly at risk.

1. Arts Council England, *The Value of Arts and Culture to People and Society* (London: Arts Council England, 2014) <http://www.artscouncil.org.uk/exploring-value-arts-and-culture/value-arts-and-culture-people-and-society>.

2. Claire Bishop, 'The Social Turn: Collaboration and Its Discontents', *Artforum*, 44.6 (2006), 178–83.

3. Alan Read, *Theatre, Intimacy & Engagement: The Last Human Venue* (Basingstoke: Palgrave Macmillan, 2008).

4. Claire Bishop, 'The Myth of the Active Subject', in *Practicable: From Participation to Interaction in Contemporary Art*, ed. by Samuel Bianchini and Erik Verhagen (Cambridge, MA: MIT Press, 2016), pp. 797–98.

5. Janelle Reinelt, '"What I Came to Say": Raymond Williams, the Sociology of Culture and the Politics of (Performance) Scholarship', *Theatre Research International*, 40.3 (2015), 235–249.

6. Eugène Van Erven, *Community Theatre: Global Perspectives* (London: Routledge, 2001); Helen Nicholson, *Applied Drama: The Gift of Theatre* (Basingstoke: Palgrave Macmillan, 2005); James Thompson, *Digging Up Stories: Applied Theatre, Performance and War* (Manchester: Manchester University Press, 2005); Petra Kuppers, *Community Performance: An Introduction* (New York and London: Routledge, 2007).

7. *The Community Performance Reader*, ed. by Petra Kuppers and Gwen Robertson (New York and London: Routledge, 2007).

8. Shannon Jackson, *Social Works: Performing Art, Supporting Publics* (New York and London: Routledge, 2011); Jen Harvie, *Fair Play: Art, Performance and Neoliberalism* (Basingstoke: Palgrave Macmillan, 2013); *Future Publics (The Rest Can and Should Be Done by the People): A Critical Reader in Contemporary Art*, ed. by Maria Hlavajova and Ranjit Hoskote (Utrecht: Valiz and BAK, 2015).

9. Augusto Boal, *Theatre of the Oppressed* [1974], trans. by Charles A. McBride (London: Pluto, 1979).

10. Live recording available at Alan Read, 'Lay Theatre and the Eruption of the Audience', *Stages*, 5 (2016), <https://biennial.com/journal/issue-5/lay-theatre-and-the-eruption-of-the-audience>.

11. Seton-Watson quoted in Benedict Anderson, *Imagined Communities: Reflections on the Origin and Spread of Nationalism* (New York and London: Verso, 1983), p. 6, fn 9.

12. Ibid.

13. Pippa Norris, *Critical Citizens: Global Support for Democratic Government* (Oxford: Oxford University Press, 1999).

14. J. L. Austin, *How to Do Things with Words* [1955], ed. by J. O. Urmson (New York: Oxford University Press, 1965); Judith Butler, *Gender Trouble: Feminism and the Subversion of Identity* (New York and London: Routledge, 1990).

15. Lea Ypi, *Global Justice and Avant-Garde Political Agency* (Oxford: Oxford University Press, 2012), p. 3.

16. Chantal Mouffe, *The Democratic Paradox* (New York and London: Verso, 2000); Christopher B. Balme, *The Theatrical Public Sphere* (Cambridge: Cambridge University Press, 2014).

COMMUNITIES

PROVOCATION

LOIS WEAVER

TITLE

COMMUNITY—A CASE STUDY IN FOUR ACTS: THE BREWERY, THE CIRCUS, THE WICK, AND THE GREEN

Lois Weaver is a Guggenheim-winning artist, activist, writer, director, and Professor of Contemporary Performance at Queen Mary University of London. Her work centres on feminism, human rights, and possibilities for public participation. She was co-founder of Spiderwoman Theatre, WOW, and Artistic Director of Gay Sweatshop in London. Lois was named a Senior Fellow by the Hemispheric Institute of Performance and Politics in 2014. She has been a writer, director and performer with Peggy Shaw and Split Britches since 1980. Her experiments in performance as a means of public engagement Public Address Systems include the Long Table, Porch Sitting, *The Library of Performing Rights*, the *FeMUSEm* and her facilitating persona, Tammy WhyNot.

As she describes here, Lois has been closely involved with LADA since its inception and contributed to numerous programmes as an artist and facilitator. She was Director for *Performing Rights* at Queen Mary University of London and its subsequent iterations in Vienna and Glasgow; and she edited *Are We There Yet? A Study Room Guide on Live Art and Feminism* for RRR3 On Live Art and Feminism, and *Know How: A Study Room Guide on Live Art and working with older individuals and communities* for RRR4 on Live Art and Privilege. In 2015 LADA co-published *The Only Way Home Is Through The Show: Performance Works of Lois Weaver* as part of the Intellect Live series. Lois is one of LADA's Patrons.

I find talking about community difficult. Every way you look, the term is contested, celebrated, discredited, and overused. Before you can get an adequate description of a community's constituents and purpose down on paper, the community in question has often been reconfigured and reconstituted. Considering community in the context of Live Art is even more challenging, given that the practice itself is based on individual aesthetics, politics, and sensibilities, and the individuals who comprise the collection of artists that we might call a Live Art Community are fiercely and vocally independent. So what is community in the context of Live Art? And specifically, what is the nature of a community associated with the Live Art Development Agency?

An Introduction

> *Community is in motion.*
> *It lets go and lets leave.*

Communities are often associated with place, and I find I can most clearly see or feel a community when people gather in that place to celebrate a particular person or event. My first glimpse of a UK Live Art Community was in 2008 when the Live Art Development Agency (LADA) was already nine years old and I was invited to host a going-away event for Daniel Brine. Daniel had been an associate director with Lois Keidan since 2000, just after the Agency began, and was leaving London for Australia. Sending him off in the style of the TV program *This is Your Life* gave friends and family an opportunity to acknowledge Daniel's contributions and support. Moreover, it gave us a chance to revisit the important connections we had made during the last nine years. More than twenty artists, including Marcia Farquhar, Yara El-Sherbini, and Barby Asante, made surprise entrances through a makeshift glittery curtain and performed their goodbyes. As tributes gave way to mingling and some dancing, I sat on the couch with Daniel and realised how reassuring it was to be accompanied by these wildly diverse people in this wildly unpredictable world of Live Art. I recognised this sense of being in good company as community. Watching Daniel say goodbye, I realised something even more important: this was a community that allowed, even encouraged, its members to move, to come and go freely. Yes, the company, solidarity, and support was comforting, even essential, but it was neither necessarily rooted in a place of gathering nor in any sense of home or origin. Nor was the sense of community tied to rules of custom or consistency or even continuity. This was a group of people in motion who were making connections on their own terms and for their own reasons.

As I reflect on this way of constituting, or at least recognising, community in the context of Live Art, I think about LADA's constant motion. Lois Keidan and the ever-expanding LADA team have literally relocated premises four times in twenty years. Moving from a Brewery to a Circus to a Wick to a Green has fostered many of the complex aspects of community that are associated not only with this mobile collection of diverse artists, but also with the community, activity, and labour attached to each those named places. As a witness and occasional companion, I hope this map of motion will serve as a guide to thinking about the ways we find and lose, construct and leave community.

The Brewery

> *Community is intergenerational.*
> *It often situates itself in places of*
> *making, doing, and thinking.*
> *It sows and reaps and simmers and brews,*
> *sometimes sheltering in the shadows,*
> *sometimes bringing its business into*
> *the bright light of day.*
> *A community is visible.*

In 1999, Lois Keidan and Catherine Ugwu set up LADA in the Old Truman's Brewery off Brick Lane. This warren of dark brick buildings was one of the largest breweries in the world through the 19th century. At the end of the 20th century, it was re-emerging as a workplace for arts and culture. Down one of the alleys that led to the courtyard at the heart of this industrial site was a glass-fronted office where LADA began the process of boiling, soaking, and fermenting a support system for an underrepresented art form. Lois and Catherine, already known as advocates and friends to Live Art, set about acquiring the necessary equipment. Understanding that generational exchange was crucial for survival in any community, they quickly tapped into the existing structures of higher education and established a network of academics working in theatre, performance, and visual arts. Inviting people like Susan Melrose, Richard Layzell, Anna Birch, Jen Harvie, Shaheen Merali, and others working at the edge of these disciplines in London institutions, they set up the Live Art in Higher Education Forum. I was one of these drafted participants.

I remember sitting in the fading light with fading post-school-day energies, wondering how it would be possible to take on another set of responsibilities. However, those attending understood the importance and mutual benefit of this initiative. Our job was not only to document and critique an emerging field, but also to nourish and build the training and exhibition grounds for the future of the discipline. Slowly over the next few years, academic departments emerged, associations like Live Art UK grew, new public platforms for emerging performance like East End Collaborations and SPILL were established, and well-established platforms like the National Review of Live Art found new life. Opportunities for mid-career artists increased as they were invited into institutions as artists in residence or visiting lecturers. A community infrastructure emerged, and in this way and in this short time, LADA established a full line of manufacturing—from seeding and harvesting to brewing, bottling, and distributing.

For me this developmental stage has always been associated with the light and shadow of the Truman Brewery buildings. I think of walking down the alley off Brick Lane and heading toward LADA's office. On those Higher Education Forum afternoons, it was always a dark day. However, light always beckoned from that storefront at the end of the alley. It was a beacon reaching out to those searching for a home or community, but it was also a window in for the curious. The business of Live Art and of this fledgling community was conducted in full view. In fact, a lot of the business was conducted outside in the alley itself, or we met and plotted at tables in the nearby cafe. Perhaps this was the true business of what I am calling a Live Art community: to bring us out into the light where we might be seen and overheard; to make visible the work, the life of the work, and the workers' lives.

The Circus

> *A community is like a circus.*
> *It is various and flourishes under a big tent.*
> *It has a taste for spectacle, an appetite*
> *for risk, a threshold for chaos,*
> *a need for discipline,*
> *and an absolute dependency*
> *on collaboration.*

Circus is my go-to word for describing chaos and mayhem. LADA's next physical move was to Arnold Circus, which is essentially a bandstand in the centre of a tract of land located in London's East End. Arnold Circus had its own complex journey, moving from its designation as Britain's worst slum, to the honour of being the first site for social housing, to its current status as semi-gentrified neighbourhood and hipster destination. In 2004, LADA relocated to Arnold Circus and into a repurposed Victorian school building with all the energy and determination of a traveling show. Surrounded by the frantic frivolity of small fashion design companies also located in the school and nourished by the on-site bike shed canteen, Lois, Daniel, and an expanded crew including Andrew Mitchelson, Emmy Minton, Season Butler, and a line-up of others, set up their big top and got to work. Every circus metaphor I can think of applies to this stage of the LADA community building project: three rings, spinning plates, and a variety of acts.

In the centre ring, I watched a growing roster of artists whose work was being commissioned, installed, promoted and produced around the world with LADA's support. In rings flanking the centre were the growing partnerships with UK universities like Queen Mary, Goldsmiths, and Roehampton, who worked with LADA to produce festivals and initiatives like *Performing Rights* and *Performance Matters*, and collaborations with international organizations that host and advocate for Live Art, such as Kontejner (Croatia) and

Tanzquartier Wien (Vienna). All the while LADA kept the plates spinning backstage, devising safety nets for individual artists. They conducted surgeries; provided bursaries to assist artists in crucial points of their careers; developed research resources like the Study Room, an open access, on-site library; and launched Unbound, an online shop dedicated to Live Art materials. One of the strongest aspects of a circus is variety, and this kind of diversity of reach, resource, and representation became LADA's community-building priority.

Like in a circus, this amount of intense and simultaneous activity necessitated fierce discipline: discipline on the part of artists whose job it is to risk but not fall; discipline on the part of the workers who handle the setting up, breaking down and moving on; discipline on the part of the organisation whose art it is to collaborate with all these parts. LADA was the ringmaster of collaboration, and I had a ringside seat. From where I sat, I witnessed in-depth questioning, listening, and formulating with artists and communities on subjects of race and disability that manifested in projects like *Restock, Rethink, Reflect*, and I participated in multiple thorough and satisfying acts of collaboration myself. This rigorous commitment to collaboration was the rigging that kept the community secure.

Right: Lois Weaver, *Long Table* at LADA office, The White Building (2013). Image Alex Eisenberg.

The Wick

A community circulates its life source.

The 2012 migration to Hackney Wick was a challenge. A wick is an outlying farm or village, and the White Building, hugging the edge of the River Lea in East London, was certainly an outlying location. But 'wick' can also mean a material that draws by capillary action, which seems more apt for this point in LADA's history and this meditation on community. LADA created a destination, a home to the study and production of new practices that drew us out to the edge of Hackney, just as it drew us out to the edge of an art practice now beginning to establish itself in the centre. LADA in Hackney Wick was somewhat like what I enjoy about destination dining, a full menu of tasty and nutritious treats in an environment that makes you want to linger a while. Although actual good food was hard to find in the area, as Lois Keidan would often lament, a regular audience found they could feast on delicious on-site Study Room activities, like artist-curated screenings, which drew from the vast collections of performance documentation. Artist/scholar residencies designed to both catalogue and increase the collection of materials opened nourishing public dialogues on Live Art and feminism, class, privilege, childhood, and age. In addition, Long Tables, book launches, performance workshops, and artist presentations regularly drew many us to this riverside location.

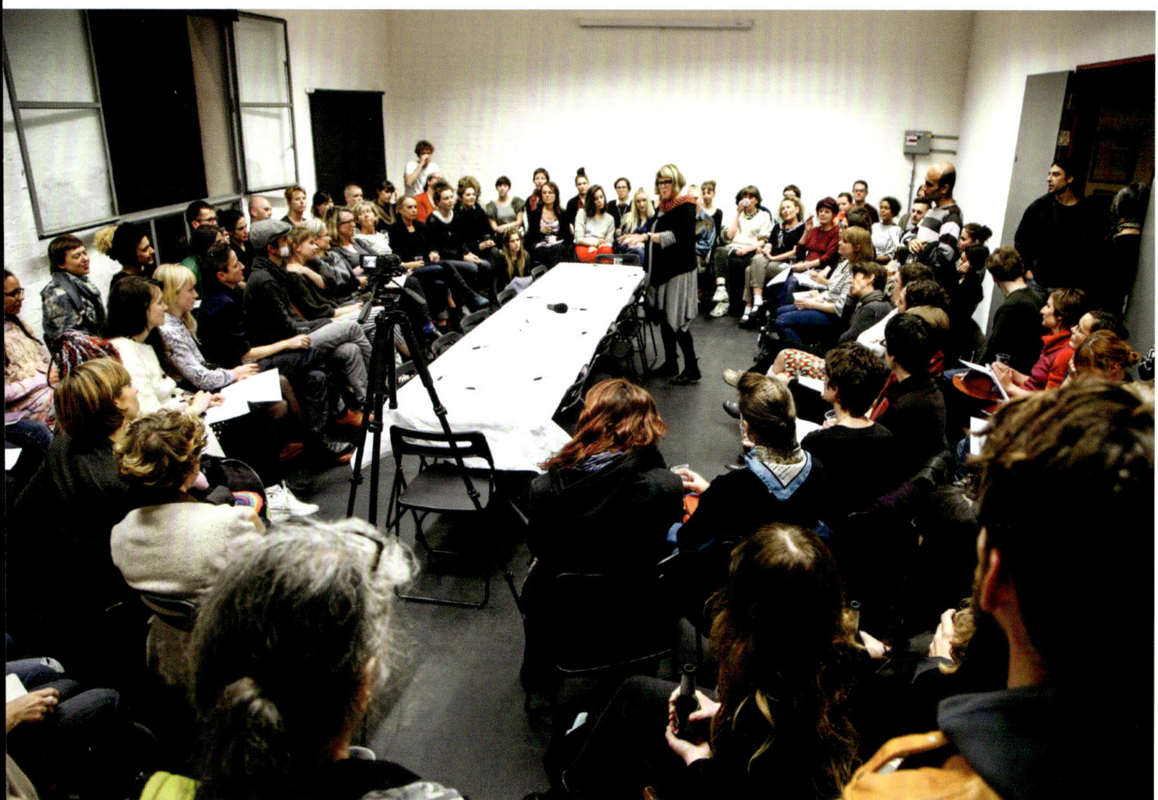

Yet capillary action is not necessarily a one-way system; it is a system of circulation. Live Art was beating in the heart of Hackney. It was also circulating through academic institutions, museum programming, and even on television. Despite this transfusion into the mainstream, Lois Keidan, CJ Mitchell and a continually growing team like Aaron Wright, Katy Baird, Alex Eisenberg—just to name-check a few—were still busy going out, rooting out the radical, representing the marginalised, and keeping the circle of circulation complete.

Taking circulation quite literally, they also expanded another life-giving project: establishing LADA as a significant publisher and disseminator of Live Art materials. Boxes of books both created and purchased for the Unbound bookshop, and boxes of new books commissioned and published in collaboration with Live Artists and thinkers like Ron Athey, Kira O'Reilly, and Adrian Howells began to flow through this 'wick', nourishing the community and this outlying field.

The Green

> *Community seeks common ground. It goes outside in bad weather, sets up in the town square and invites the neighbours to the party.*

In 2017, LADA took up residence at the Garrett Centre in Bethnal Green. For me, this move is a statement about LADA's current thinking on community and serves more as a gesture of hope for our collective futures than a case study on aspects of community built through time, task, and location. Garrett is a Centre committed to the arts and social action and rooted in the diverse communities of Bethnal Green. LADA'S partnership here seems to signal their own renewed commitment to art, action, and community at a crucial time.

A green is common ground. It is a public spot open to all and reserved, if not protected, for the occupations of sitting or meandering, proselytising or protesting, selling wares or exercising bodies and rights. It's a place to gather. And now is a time to gather, because these feel desperate and lonely times. Our world is on the edge of multiple divides: yes against no, leave against stay, science against humanities, and a host of fractures too deep and complicated to be represented in this binary list. Now more than ever, we need to have places, times, and methods for talking to one another. We need to find ways to come to the same table. We need to gather in halls, collect on the village green.

In this last move, LADA opened the doors to a wider public by creating a centre within a centre and making space for both local and global communities to engage with challenging art forms and the possibilities of what those art forms can achieve. It promises to be a site for generous exchange and meaningful partnerships where a diverse public can look at how the practice and methodologies of the arts, and specifically Live Art, can affect our ability to survive.

A Conclusion

> *A community can live long or it can live short. Some communities only live as long as it takes to read these words.*

I think community is best described using the definition of coalition: a group of people who come together for a certain amount of time to accomplish a certain goal. I wish I could take credit for this way of thinking about community, but I heard it first from feminist theorist Sue-Ellen Case at a talk she gave years ago somewhere in Texas. It's been my working definition of community ever since. I think it works especially in this context of Live Art practice, which, like a coalition, can be ephemeral, durational, task-based, and independent.

Community is not necessarily something we are born into. We don't buy it or subscribe to it. It could simply be the company we keep, the road map we use or the road itself. Or perhaps it's the tools and infrastructure that helps us get things done.

And engaging *in* (not with or for) community, even the temporary kind, is the only way we will survive.

Overleaf: Marcia Farquhar, *The Cabinet of Horribly Violent Glove Puppets*, Space Station (2006). Image Jem Finer.

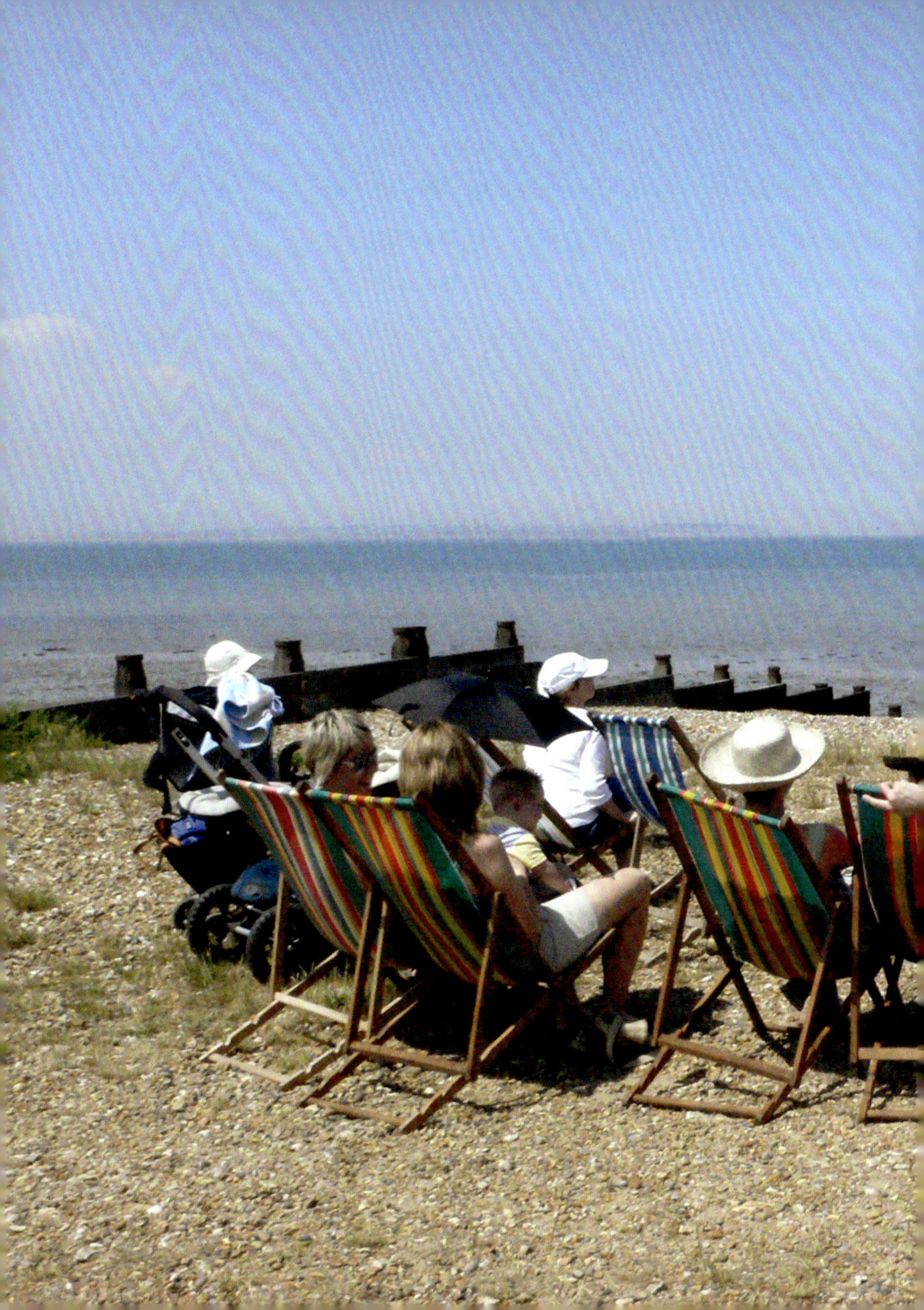

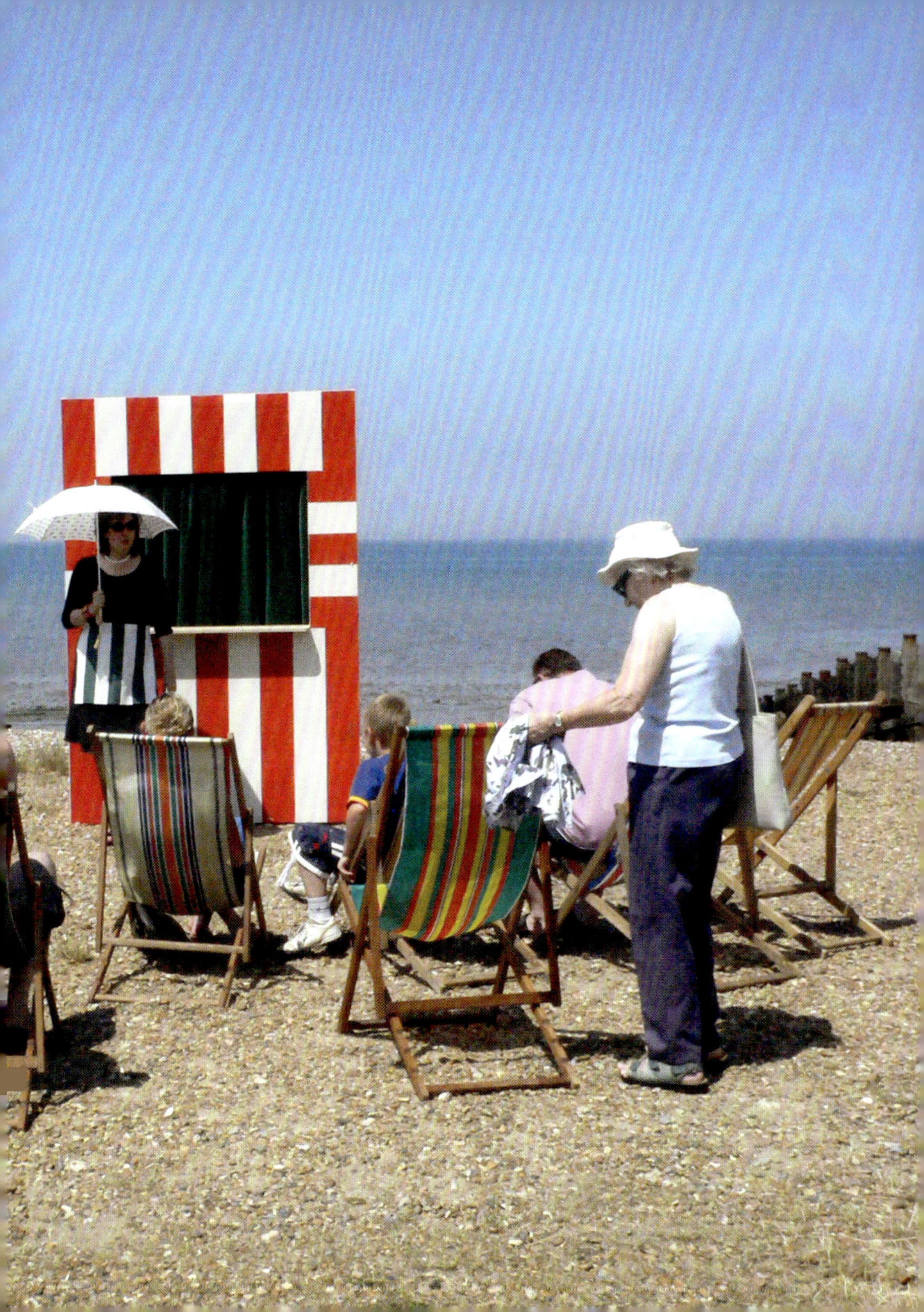

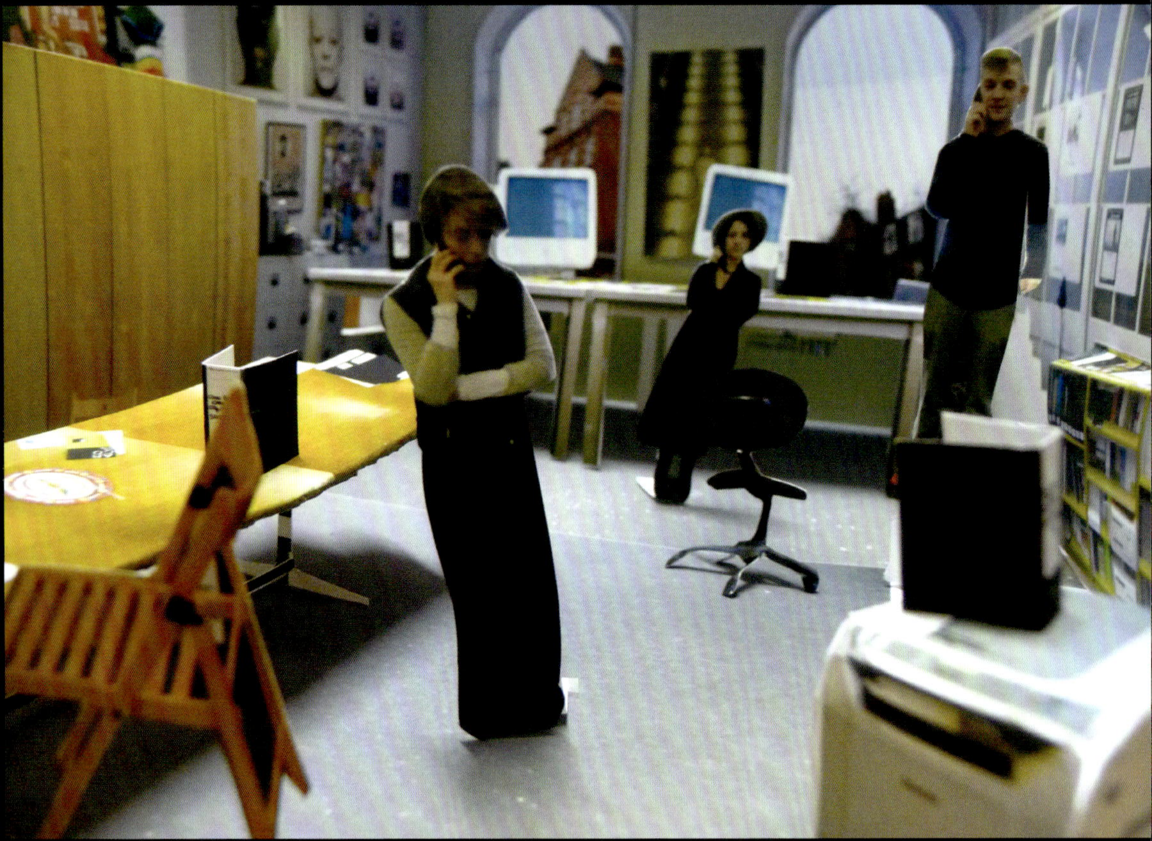

Richard DeDomenici, *Build Your Own Replica Live Art Development Agency*, edition for LADA 10th Anniversary (2009).

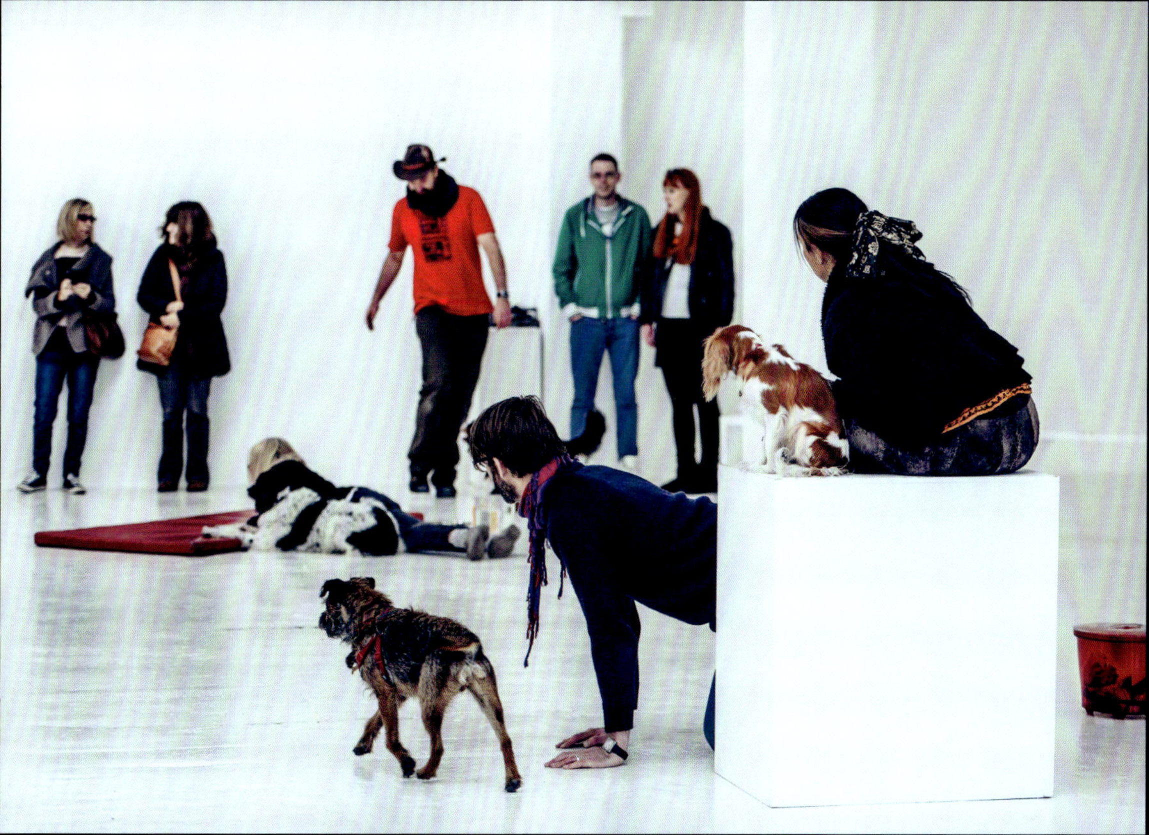

ngela Bartram, *Be Your Dog*, DIY (2016). Image Dom Moore.

verleaf: Dickie Beau, *The House of Strange Loops*, DIY (2014). Image the artist.

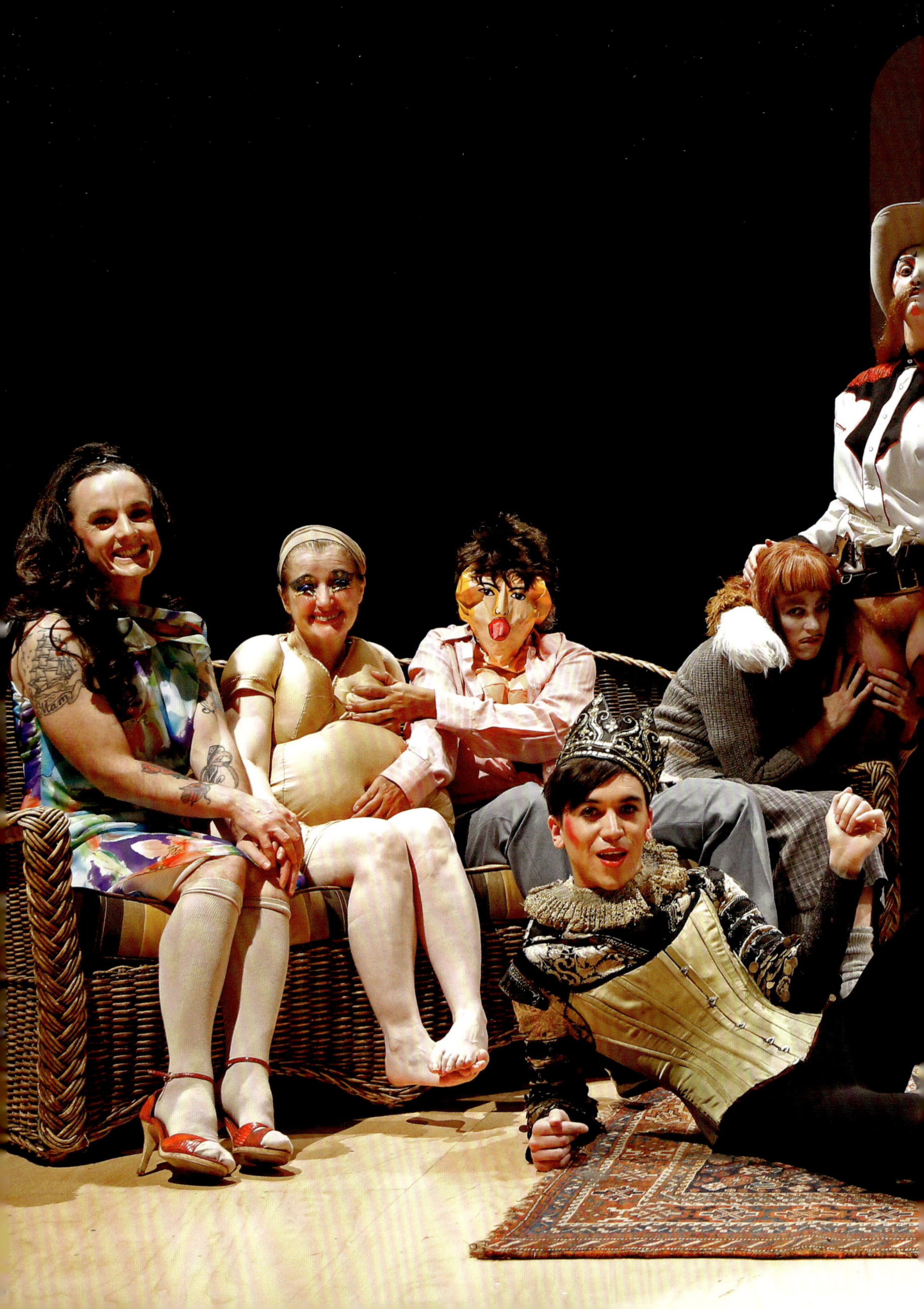

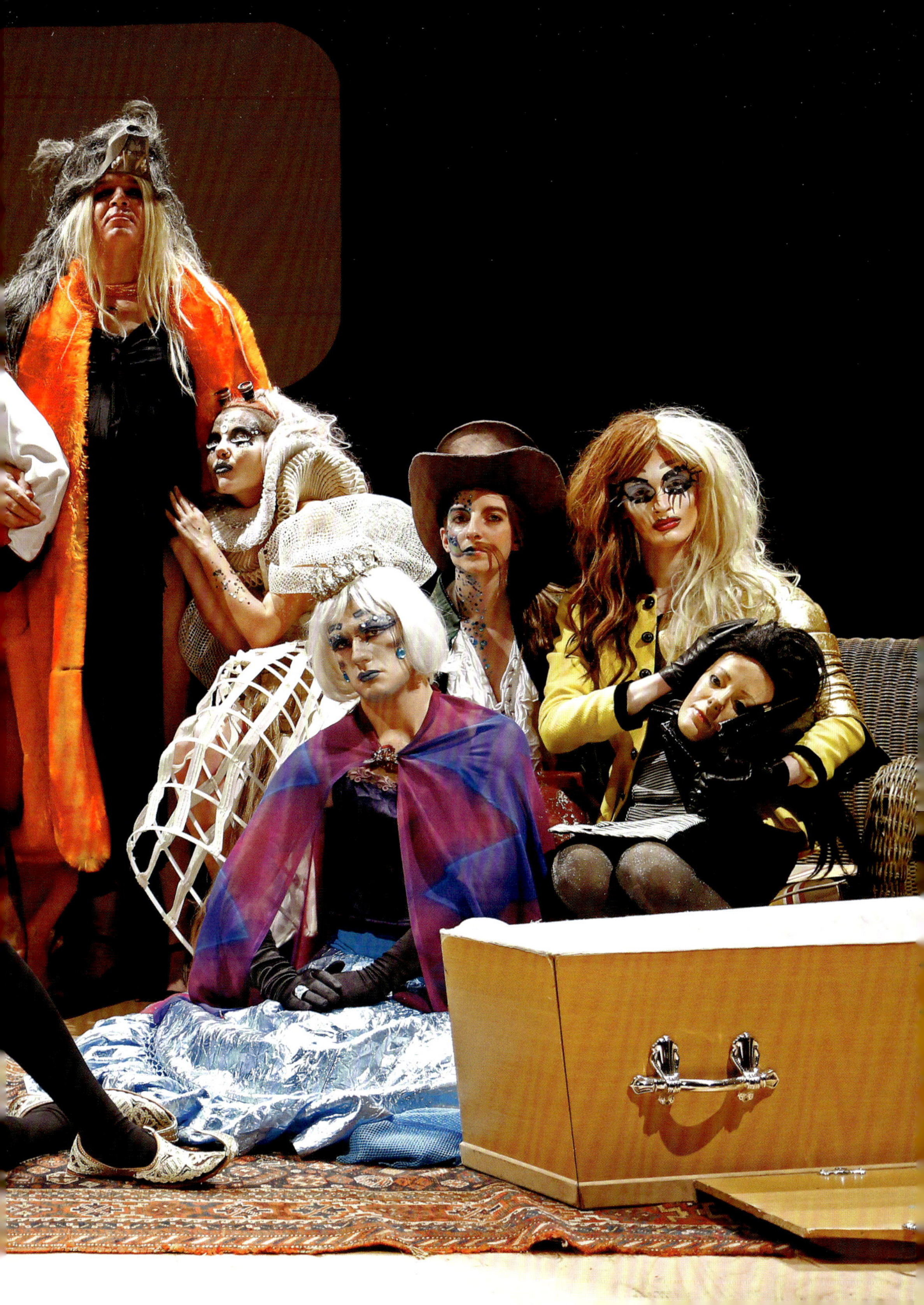

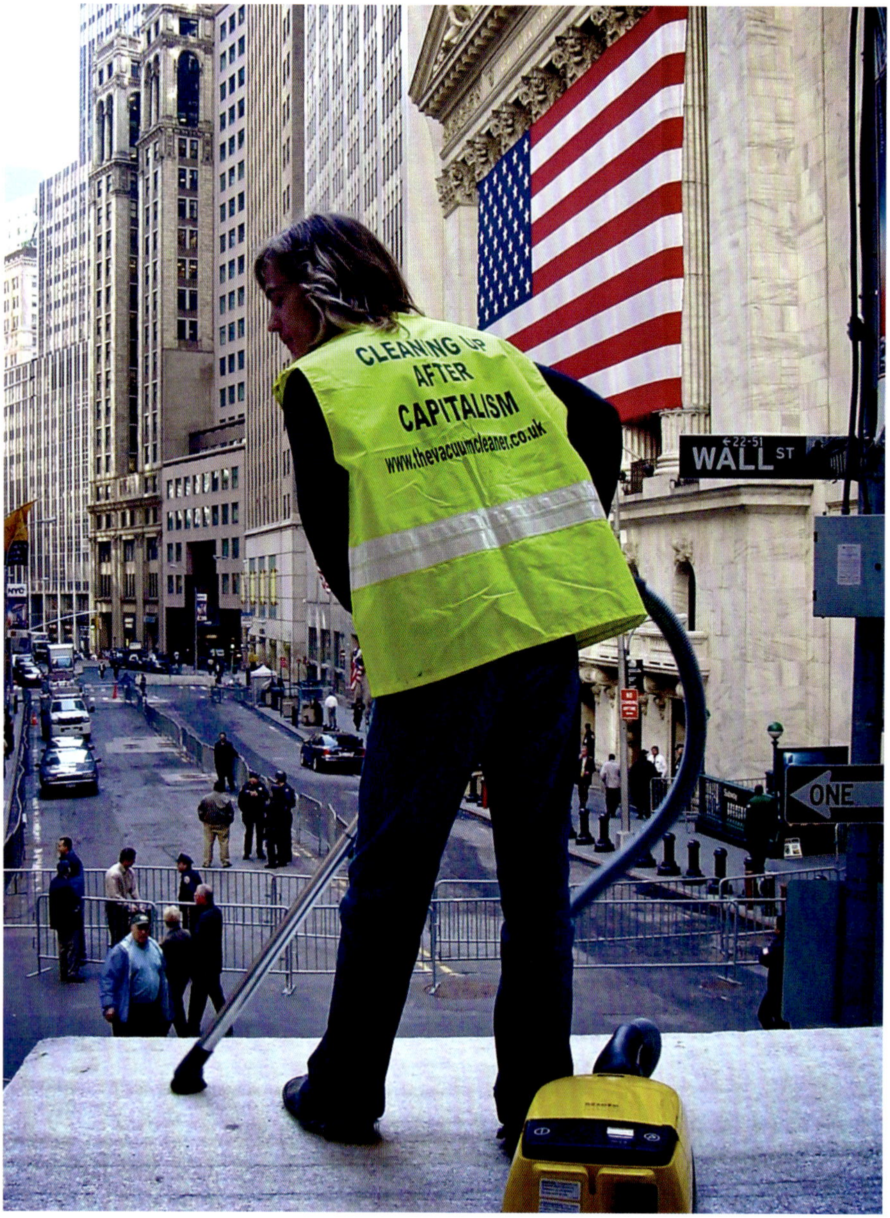

the vacuum cleaner, *Cleaning Up After Capitalism* (2003). Image the artist.

ACTIONS

KATHERINE ARANIELLO
BARBY ASANTE
RON ATHEY
DAVID A. BAILEY
CASSILS
RICHARD DEDOMENICI
GUILLERMO GÓMEZ-PEÑA
JOHN JORDAN
AARON WILLIAMSON

ACTIONS

'Did we ever say we're trying to make the world better?' asks Katherine Araniello of The Disabled Avant-Garde (DAG) in this section. 'Making the world better is not our objective, and never will be.' This section addresses relations between Live Art and forms of political action, but like Katherine, many of the contributors to this collection emphasise the indeterminate, the ambivalent, the space of potential: 'I don't want to fix things—like an activist wants to "fix" things,' comments Barby Asante. And Richard DeDomenici cites the LA Cacophony Society as a synopsis of his goal, to 'try to create the kind of uncertainty that leads to possibility.'[1] Rather than resolving the question of 'is this art?' or 'is this activism?', this very question, and the way it might produce a moment of hesitation on the part of the spectator or policing authority, is an opportunity to get away with what one is doing for a little bit longer: 'I'm interested in anything that will give you an extra five or ten seconds before someone comes and tells you to stop,' DeDomenici observes.

In this way the frame of 'art' can be a means of doing politics: 'In the name of art, people have crucified themselves as a form of protest, created fake corporations to denounce environmental injustice, and printed useless money and conceptual passports to invent their own countries,' writes Guillermo Gómez-Peña in his provocation.

This interventionist aspect of Live Art practices has been a theme throughout this collection, as artists have described their interruptions into the conventions and structures of power regarding bodies, spaces, institutions, and communities. And LADA's own projects often seek to intervene within the politics of the artistic sector as well as broader cultural issues. Some of these have already been discussed, such as the *Restock, Rethink, Reflect* series, in the way it focuses attention on issues of race and cultural diversity, ability and social disablement, gender inequity, and privilege and access; or *Take the Money and Run?* (on the ethics of arts sponsorship) and Live Art UK's Diverse Actions initiative, both of which are discussed by Jen Harvie in her provocation earlier in this collection. Another long-running project of LADA is *Performing Rights*, which began as a series of commissions to accompany the Performance Studies international (PSi#12) conference on the same theme, hosted by Queen Mary University of London in 2006, for which LADA was a cultural partner. Some of the actions presented in PSi#12's cultural programme included Leibniz's *Book of Blood*, in which the Universal

Declaration of Human Rights is transcribed by a calligrapher using ink made from drops of blood donated by visitors to the performance (carefully collected by a medical practitioner); *Everything for Everybody. Nothing for Ourselves*, in which the Laboratory of Insurrectionary Imagination turned their artist's fee into a pile of coins which visitors were free to take as they wished; Guillermo Gómez-Peña and La Pocha Nostra performing *Mapa/Corpo*, a living diorama in which audience members were encouraged to participate in a ritual enactment of the 'body politic'; and Richard DeDomenici's *Fame Asylum*, an attempt to form a chart-topping boy band out of people seeking asylum in the UK.[2]

Performing Rights was re-imagined in other formats by LADA and its collaborators for Vienna (2007), Glasgow (2008), Rio de Janeiro (2012), and Montréal (2014).[3] And from 2017, *The Library of Performing Rights* (LPR), initially created with Lois Weaver as an installation and resource for PSi#12, has expanded into a multi-faceted set of initiatives. Facilitated by Weaver, the artist and researcher Elena Marchevska, and The Study Room in Exile (based at the Institute for the Art and Practice of Dissent at Home in Liverpool), the LPR has been reconceived as 'a place of action, a place of knowledge exchange, a repository of experience, and a resource and a context that others can use to support and advance their own work.'[4] For example, in 2018 Marchevska held a LPR 'Open' event on US artist Aram Han Sifuentes' project *The Official Unofficial Voting Station: Voting for All Who Legally Can't*; and Barby Asante has been selected for the first of the LPR's annual commissions to develop her *Declaration of Independence* performances addressing Black death, racism and violence, and the present day legacies of slavery and colonialism. Other projects that LADA has supported with an explicitly activist or interventionist politics have included: *Louder Than Bombs: Art, Action & Activism* (2010), a collaboration with the Stanley Picker Gallery at Kingston University in London that invited seven artist/activists to occupy the gallery for a week each;[5] and *Awkward Bastards* (2015) and *Awkward Bastards 2* (2017), a series of mixed-mode symposia in collaboration with Disability Arts in Shropshire and mac, Birmingham, which advocated for an approach to diversity that is intersectional across a broad spectrum of disability, race, gender, and class.[6]

Live Art is part of a broader legacy of artistic and activist impulses that have engaged with the politics of everyday life, as John Jordan writes in his provocation describing his movement away from the 'zoo' of the 'art world'. But whereas these impulses can sometimes feel deliberately abstracted from lived experience, what is striking in Jordan's reflection on his participation in the utopian ZAD community—and also in the other conversations in this section—is the

Right top: Ansuman Biswas, *Present*, *Louder Than Bombs – Art, Action & Activism*, Stanley Picker Gallery, London (2010). Image Christoph Ferstad.

Right bottom: *The Library of Performing Rights*, Montreal (2014). Image Dexter Miranda.

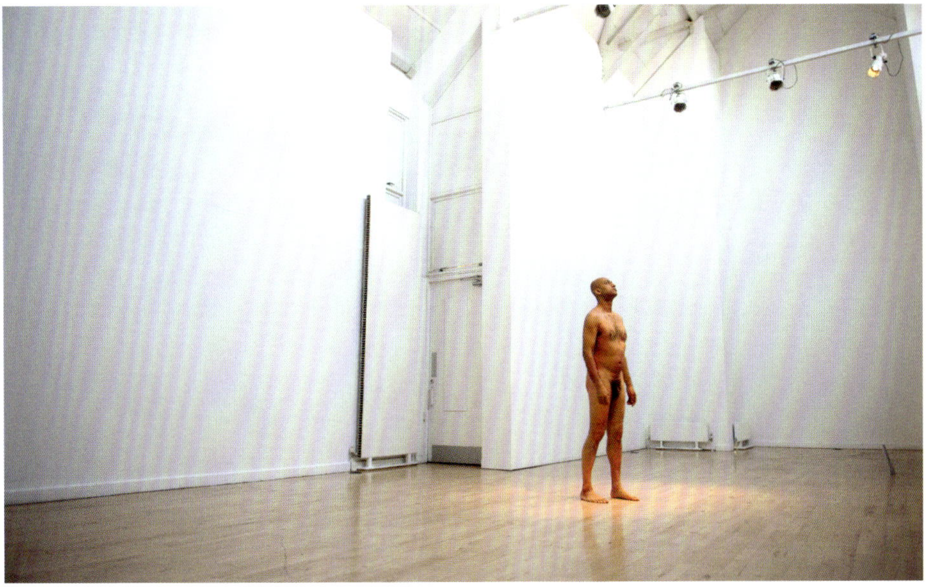

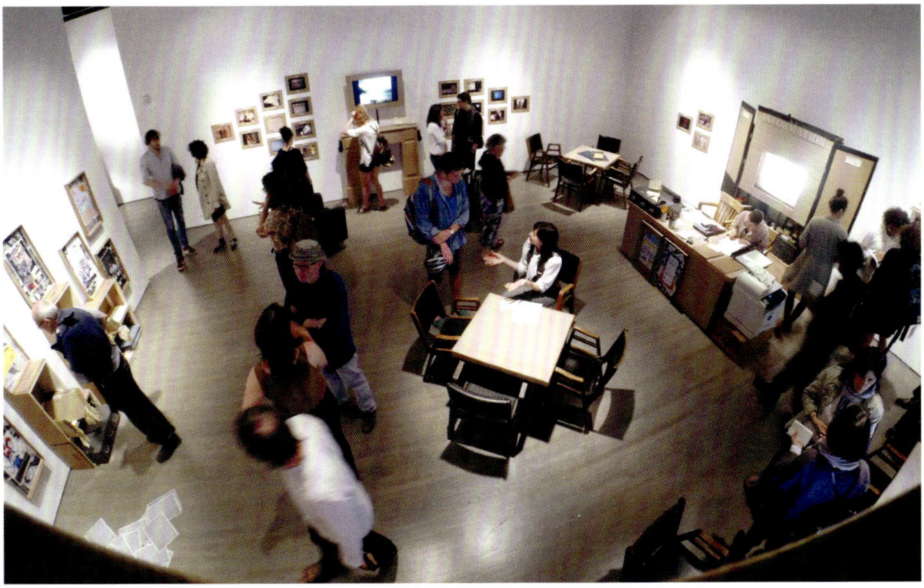

way in which these creative practices are intertwined with the material conditions of lived experience. When Jordan talks about care-giving and paying attention as elements of 'the art of life', he means this is in relation to the very real problems of daily sustenance (and sustainability) in a utopian community; and in the conversation between Cassils and Ron Athey, which took place just after the 2016 US election, you can hear the viscerality and violence of their experience of living within a 'machine [that] is trying to pulverise us to dust.' In the face of such machinery, Cassils observes, someone like Athey is 'a living example of resistance.' Or as Aaron Williamson of DAG puts it, 'What is avant-garde is the fact that we are making work!' If social support structures continue to be dismantled as the present UK government intends, he continues, 'we'd be the opposite of the Disabled Avant-Garde, and what's that? Just "disabled".' And so, in addition to supporting projects that have an explicitly activist or interventionist politics, addressing some external theme or issue, perhaps one of the most important actions that LADA undertakes is the continual and everyday support for the 'art of living' itself: caring for individual artists as much as for an artform and a sector, from the first few people to walk through the doors of LADA's Truman Brewery office in 1999, to the endless series of people passing through their doors on any given day to drop off a new artwork, plan a future project, use the Study Room or other resources, or simply be alive, together, finding agency in and with each other.

1. Deirdre Heddon offers an excellent analysis of the emphasis on 'potential' in Live Art discourse in 'The Politics of Live Art', in *Histories and Practices of Live Art*, ed. by Deirdre Heddon and Jennie Klein (Basingstoke: Palgrave Macmillan, 2012), pp. 175–205.

2. Performance Studies international, 'PSi #12: Performing Rights' [2006], <http://www.psi-web.org/past-events/psi-12-performing-rights/>; Live Art Development Agency, 'PSI#12 Performing Rights: London, 2006' <http://www.thisisliveart.co.uk/projects/psi12-performing-rights-london-2006>.

3. Live Art Development Agency, 'Performing Rights' <http://www.thisisliveart.co.uk/projects/performing-rights>.

4. Live Art Development Agency, 'Library of Performing Rights' <http://www.thisisliveart.co.uk/resources/collections/library-of-performing-rights>.

5. Stanley Picker Gallery, *Louder Than Bombs–Art, Action & Activism* [2010] <https://www.stanleypickergallery.org/exhibitions/louder-than-bombs/>.

6. DASH (Disability Arts in Shropshire), 'Awkward Bastards' [2015] <http://www.dasharts.org/projects/awkward-bastards.html>; Live Art Development Agency, 'ABsence: Awkward Bastards 2' [2017] <http://www.thisisliveart.co.uk/projects/awkward-bastards-2>.

ACTIONS

CONVERSATION

KATHERINE ARANIELLO
AND AARON WILLIAMSON
(THE DISABLED AVANT-GARDE)

RICHARD DEDOMENICI

DATE

10 FEBRUARY 2016

PLACE

LONDON

As the satirical organisation Disabled Avant-Garde (DAG), Katherine Araniello and Aaron Williamson create performance, video, and public interventions that intend to cause confusion and inspire debate through humorously distorting or subverting traditional stereotyping of disability. Some of the works they discuss here include *The Disabled Avant-Garde Today!* (2006), an exhibition of 'homages' to their (ironically) 'avant-garde' influences such as Tom and Jerry, Busby Berkeley, etc.; *Charity Stall* (2007, 2008) and the resulting film *Amazing Art*, where they sold badly-made art that they claimed was funding their 'art therapy'; and *Stage Invasion* (2011) where they invaded the London Mayor's Liberty Festival to challenge its 'feel-good' attitude toward disability. DASH (Disability Arts Shropshire) supported *Camp DAG* (2011), in which a dozen disabled people appeared overnight and set up camp in rural Wales, playing on fears of invading migrants; and DASH and LADA collaborated on *M21*, a collection of public interventions by DAG and several other artists over a bank holiday weekend as part of the London 2012 Cultural Olympiad. DAG contributed to RR2 on Live Art and Disability, leading up to *Access All Areas* (2012), and the *Awkward Bastards 2* symposium (2017). LADA released a DVD of DAG works titled *Bite The Hand That Feeds!* (2012), and have also supported Katherine and Aaron's solo practices, publishing *Aaron Williamson: Performance / Video / Collaboration* (2008) and Katherine's *The Dinner Party Revisited* (2015).

Richard DeDomenici makes absurdist interventions that, as he describes here, 'strive to create the kind of uncertainty that leads to possibility.' These actions include confusing the crowds gathered for the London 2012 Olympic torch relay by running moments ahead of the actual torch holding a homemade replica; giving out balloons in new shopping centres with 'Bored of Shopping' printed on them; and setting up a 'Pedestrian Congestion Zone' during the Edinburgh Festival Fringe (in reference to a controversial vehicular congestion zone proposed for the city). Documentation from these actions, alongside satirical mashups and fake songs, form the basis of solo shows such as *Popaganda*. His *Redux Project*, in which local participants re-enact movie scenes in the same locations as the originals were shot, has become very popular, happening over 70 times since 2013, including a commission for BBC4 as part of their programme *Live From Television Centre* (2015). In his first TV project *Fame Asylum* (2006), which was commissioned for *Performing Rights*, Richard created an asylum-seeker boy band called Status. LADA released Richard's DVD *Normalisation of Deviance* (2007).

This conversation was interpreted by Jeni Draper.

Katherine: When Aaron and I got together to form Disabled Avant-Garde, we were immediately on the same page, i.e. we were competent around disability-related issues, both politically and satirically. We were both already using subversive humour in our work, which was challenging and giving an alternative representation of disability.

Aaron: We each make solo work that doesn't necessarily engage with identity politics, but we formed DAG specifically as an outlet for that interest. I'd met other disabled artists, but there wasn't anyone I wanted to work with because I thought it was very po-faced and worthy, and I found that self-defeating in a lot of respects. But when I first met Katherine I was as much attracted to her punk identity as her disability, really—because I'm an old punk myself. There's nothing sacred. We're ready to attack, or to suffer, anything that comes along. Now, that's not specific to disability, but we filter it through disability.

Katherine: I don't give a shit how people see me. The worst they see me the better the art!

Aaron: I don't care, either. That's the flag we fly under: *we don't fucking care.*

Katherine: The thing about DAG is we're not being prescriptive. We're not interested in trying to teach people what it's like to have the disability I have, or what it's like for Aaron. I find that really boring. We're doing something that has more to do with social taboos, awkwardness, discomfort. We just put it out there and let people figure it out for themselves.

Aaron: When we started we were very much taken with satire and Jonathan Swift's *A Modest Proposal*—where he challenged the Irish people to solve the hunger crisis by learning to cook and eat their babies, and he played it deadpan. Some people got the satire, but some people thought it was a jolly good idea! DAG begins with that premise: putting something outrageous in the public domain and seeing what sort of reaction it will garner. Over the years we've been our own audience, in a way, because we've put ourselves in situations where it's been fantastically amusing and entertaining for *us* to watch how people respond.

We first called ourselves the Disabled Avant-Garde with an installation at Gasworks that paid homage to our version of the avant-garde, which included people like Simon and Garfunkel, Tom and Jerry, Busby Berkeley. We played it deadpan, and some people took that at face value and thought we really thought that Simon and Garfunkel were avant-garde artists! So already at that stage, we were amazed with what we could get away with.

Katherine: We realised after we started making work that we could really push the limits. We even filmed in Trafalgar Square, and we got away with it because all the people immediately moved on because I was disabled and Aaron can't hear. The work was affected by that, in a good way. Everything that happened we just integrated into the film.

Aaron: There's not a demarcation between when we're performing for the camera and when we're hanging out doing our thing. We've blagged our way into first-class lounges, we got a guy in Liverpool to pay for us all to have a champagne dinner, and I'm quite proficient at getting upgrades on airplanes! People want to help us, and so we let them get on with it… and then we make work about *that* as well.

Katherine: It says something about people's awkwardness around disability. They don't know what to do, so they give us some authority. And we use that to our own advantage.

Richard: I'm interested in anything that will give you an extra five or ten seconds before someone comes and tells you to stop—which DAG do by using people's weird expectations and pre-conceptions about being disabled. I stole a phrase from the LA Cacophony Society, who did great things like fill teddy bears with cement, put them back on the shelves of Toys R Us, and then try to purchase them. They said that they 'try to create the kind of uncertainty that leads to possibility.' It's all about creating moments of greyness.

But I've found it takes a lot of preparation to get away with things. You can't be reckless. Well, you can, but it often doesn't work! I tend to prepare for the worst and hope for the best, and normally the outcome fits between those two extremes. It took a while to figure out the right level, because it's easy to get arrested these days. That's not a challenge for me. I got arrested when I was still in art school because I tried to break into a prison, and I didn't even realise that just touching the prison walls constituted Aggravated Trespass. But what was interesting about that was that in the car on the way to the police station, the policeman was very engaged with the idea that what I was doing might constitute art—because I have a much more relaxed attitude than most people when it comes to this. He didn't believe me, but was intrigued, so he drove me to art school to see my tutor, Professor André Stitt, and luckily, André was in, and said, 'Yes, this is art!'—and so the policeman dropped the charges.

Aaron: We've found that we can't get arrested!

Richard: It's a hassle for the police to arrest you unless they really have to—even more so in a wheelchair. Do they have accessible police vans?

Katherine: They didn't, at least years ago when I was genuinely protesting to try to make buses wheelchair accessible. They wanted to arrest me, but I said, 'I can't get into your vehicle because it isn't accessible.' So they made me follow them to the police station in my wheelchair-accessible vehicle!

Aaron: The closest we've come to getting arrested is when we invaded the stage at the Liberty Festival. We were being quite aggressive, because we had a banner proclaiming 'Disability is dead,' and Katherine was using the PA to tell people, 'Go home!' We were wearing these death costumes and skeleton masks, and when the security came to chuck us off the stage, I said, 'I can't understand what you're saying. Can you go and get an interpreter?' That gave us an extra four or five minutes on stage.

Katherine: What usually happens in that kind of scenario is that rather than talk to us, they talk to the able-bodied person who they think is connected to us. They don't actually have a dialogue with us—and I go into this 'art mode' anyway, where I become oblivious and vacant in response to anything I'm asked.

Richard: I don't like to signpost anything I'm doing as art, because it's often easier to interpret a work of art if there are no signifiers to suggest that it's a piece of art in the first place. But sometimes it can get you out of tricky situations—like in Chicago in 2004, where I was walking around with a bag on my head to protest the use of hooding by coalition forces. Once people realise you're a *professional* weirdo—that you do it for a job and you've gone to school to learn it—they're less scared, and they might not, you know, want to shoot you! People's moods change, and they become much more friendly. But in Chicago, I only got away with that performance because I was a white English guy. It may have turned out differently had I been a local person of colour. So I'm aware of my white Western male privilege—but I try to use that to my advantage as well, in the same way that you guys might use your disabilities.

Aaron: Richard, in terms of using people's credulity, don't you find that if you're working with a camera crew that you can get away with a heck of a lot? We use a lot of hidden cameras, but we've also done that a few times where we have mics and cameras and sandwiches and all that.

Richard: Cameras are weird. They can be helpful in that they give a bit of legitimacy to what you're doing, and people are scared of cameras, and sometimes it's useful to have things documented, and someone to jump in if you get into trouble. But when I started making street performance, I would actively *not* have someone documenting, because that would be one of those signposts that what I was doing was art. So I was kind of against documentation for that reason—not because I was into the purity or the liveness of the piece, but because I didn't want the camera to signpost what it was.

But these days everyone has a camera, and often you don't even need to document things—you can just find footage afterwards that people have already put on Youtube—like much of the documentation for my Torch 2012 project, in which I ran around the UK, slightly ahead of the actual Olympic Torch, with a fake Olympic torch, to cause the kind of uncertainty that leads to possibility amongst spectators, organisers, and the police.

I don't know how exploitative it is to put footage of people's reactions online. It's fair use, I think, if it's in the street. A young man called Andrew was absolutely convinced that my Pedestrian Congestion Charging zone in Edinburgh was real, and was quoted in a newspaper saying as such, much to the hilarity of his friends. Some people are very imaginative and think that what I'm doing is real, and I don't think of them as being stupid or gullible, just as having big imaginations—and that's a good trait. The target in my work—if there is a target—isn't the spectators, but the bigger structures that the work is trying to critique.

Katherine: With *Amazing Art*, which was at the Southbank and also at the Brick Lane Car Boot Art Sale, we really played to people's ignorance. Everyone else had genuine stalls, but we were there creating a completely fictitious narrative. We weren't there to make money, but to observe, and to create a space for the punters to interact with us. We had all these bizarre things for sale, and people genuinely believed that we were trying to get money towards our 'art therapy'. So it was two different things: a performance that wasn't in the guise of performance, and then we turned the footage into a film.

Aaron: This must have happened to you, too, Richard, but what was interesting for us was that we leave the work open to reinvention as we're doing it. Because most people weren't interested in the boring ashtrays we were selling or whatever, but they wanted to stroke the chihuahua that Katherine had. Everyone who came asked to stroke the dog, so after a while we put up a sign: '50p to stroke the dog.' And in the last two hours we took about 20 or 30 quid from people paying to stroke the dog!

Katherine: We tried to create a formula in which anything might happen. In a sense, we are responding to our 'audience'. By the way that they react, they stimulate us into changing things. And from the feedback that I got, even people who knew all about disability just couldn't get it. It was totally confusing for them.

Richard: I think all work that we do in the street is participatory, even though a lot the participants are *unwilling* or *unknowing*. But I find it's getting harder to make work in the street, because subversive ideas quickly get co-opted by the mainstream, stripped of their radical intent, and imitated purely for commercial reasons. That's the nature of the avant-garde, I suppose. Good ideas will

Right: The Disabled Avant-Garde, Image the artists.

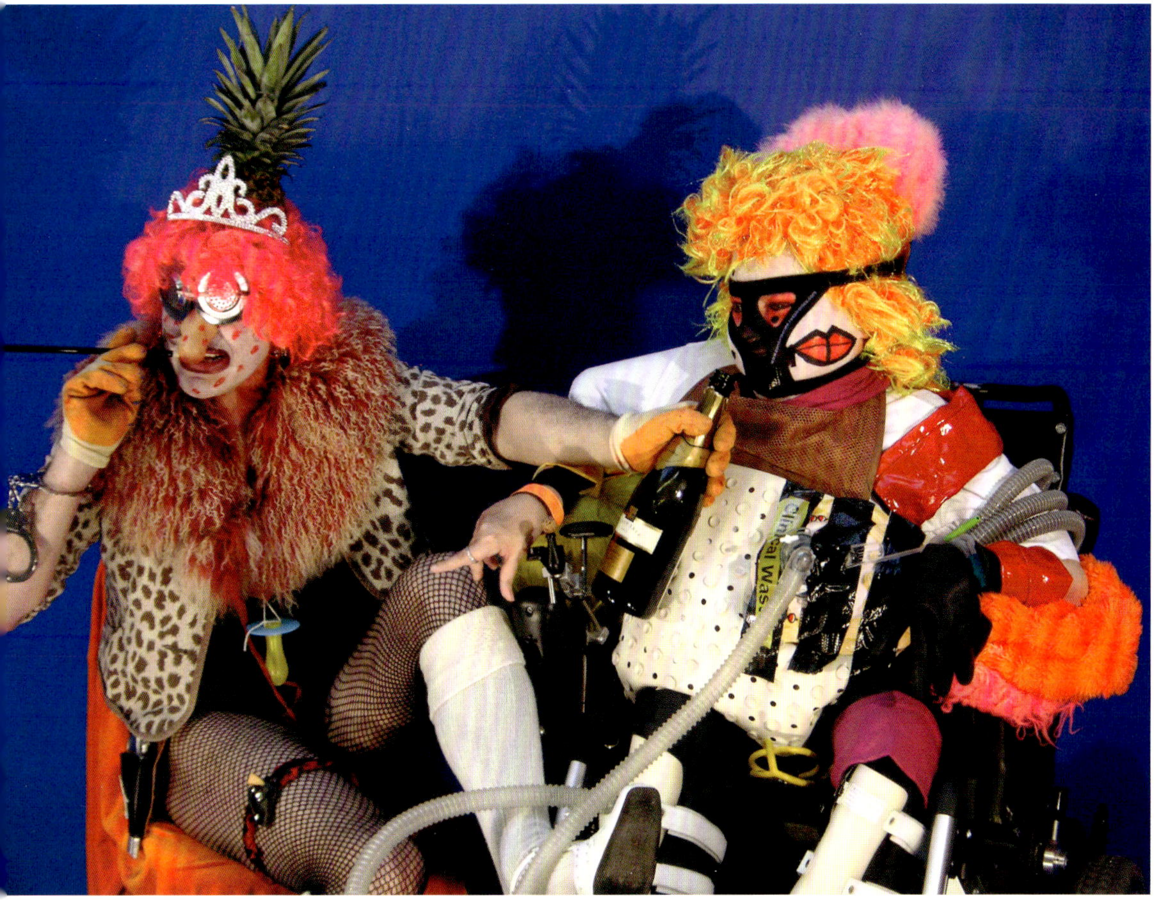

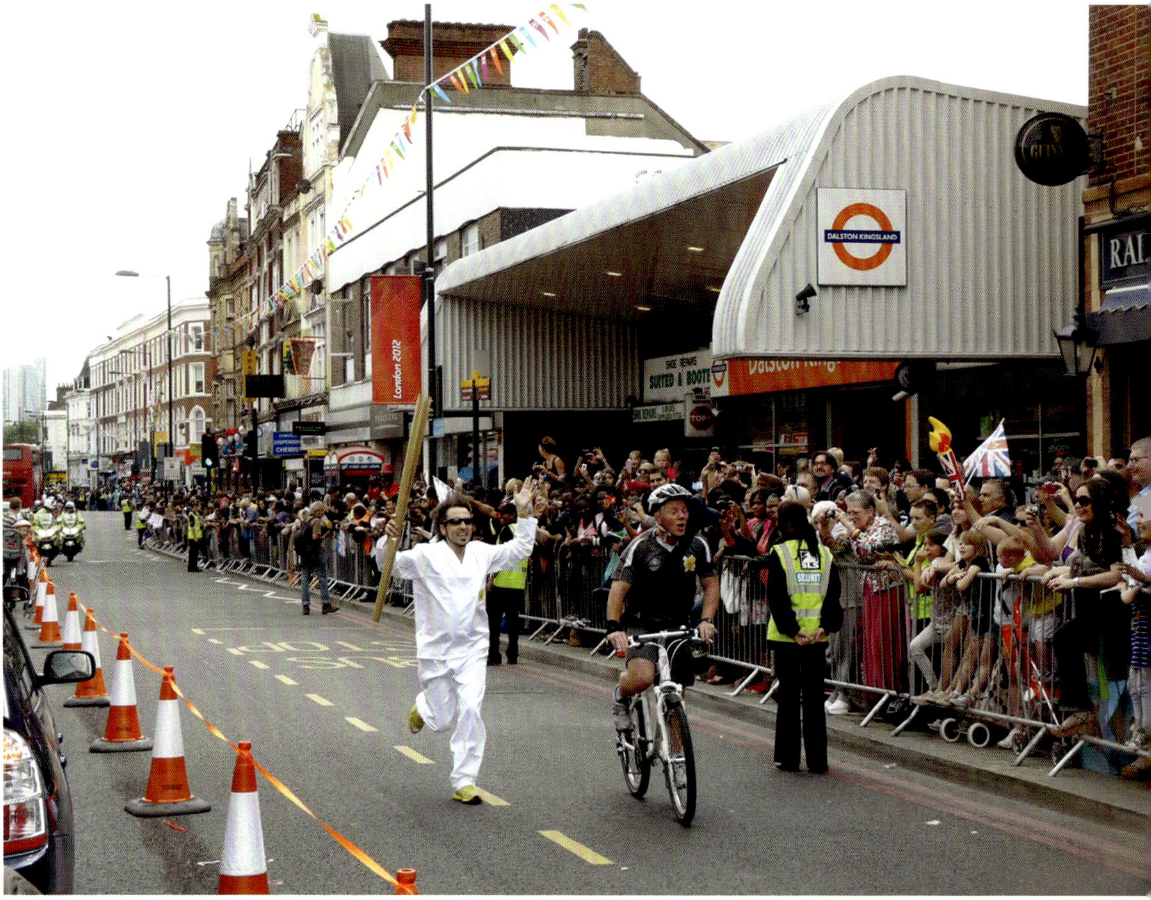

DALSTON KINGSLAND
London 2012

always get co-opted. But, if every invention eventually becomes convention, then it's the job of the artist to keep on innovating!

The Redux Project, in which I make low-budget shot-for-shot recreations of scenes from famous movies, in the original locations, with amateur local cast and crew, is probably my least subversive work, but it seems to be the most popular, and I blame audiences for that! [*laughs*] It troubles me that that everyone likes *The Redux Project* so much, but I'm able to use the fact that it's quite accessible to talk about other things—representation on screen, the imbalance of power in the entertainment industry—and it led to things like the BBC *Redux Project*, where I was able to talk about gentrification for several minutes on live television without anyone making me stop.

Aaron: It would be nice to be wanted. We've done a lot of things that are totally off-grid in terms of funding. We don't necessarily wait around for commissions to validate what we want to do. That's great because it means we can do whatever we want to do. But on the other hand, we wouldn't mind a bit more attention, would we? And we're an outsider in the disability movement, as well—they mostly hate us too!

Richard: I think the Disabled Avant-Garde are still ahead of their time. People aren't ready for you yet.

Left: Richard DeDomenici, *fake torch* (2012). Image David Altheer © LovingDalston.co.uk

Aaron: It's worth saying that the one organisation that has supported us consistently is the Live Art Development Agency. They've released our DVD and published my book which has a lot of DAG stuff in it.[1]

Katherine: And *Access All Areas* [*part of Restock, Rethink, Reflect*] was important because it managed to merge disabled and non-disabled artists tougher. It was an opportunity to take work outside the disability movement. And I think more people are saying that their work is informed by disability, maybe triggered by *Access All Areas*—people like Daniel Oliver, or Martin O'Brien.

Aaron: One of the things that came into play when working with *Access All Areas*, and LADA in general, is that it gives space for multiple identity positions, not just through the disability scene. People were coming from different identity positions and engaging with queer politics, feminism, etc.

Richard: I feel very lucky that I managed to make it this far, and it was due to the Live Art Development Agency. Really. Even the course that I studied, Time-based Practice at Cardiff School of Art, has been closed down. Lois [Keidan] noticed me blowing up balloons in a telephone box in Cardiff one day. I didn't know who Lois was, I didn't know what the Agency was—I didn't know what Live Art was! She said, 'Come and perform this at the National Review of Live Art'—I didn't know what that was either. So that was my kind of fairy godmother moment.

Aaron: Our country is incredibly short-sighted, not just in the disability frame, but in culture more generally. With the art schools being run down and the education system being increasingly privatised.

Katherine: Without funding I wouldn't be able to do my work. Everything I do is by employing a PA to assist me, so if that gets cut, then I am fucked. I require assistance in everything I do, and this includes making art. Without funding to employ PAs I would not be able to get out of bed or make art.

Aaron: We haven't won the Turner Prize, but we've made work for the Tate and we've had some degree of support. What is avant-garde is the fact that we are making work! If that's stopped because of cutbacks to our participation in society and culture, then we'd just be the opposite of the Disabled Avant-Garde, and what's that? Just 'disabled'.

Richard: I remain optimistic about the world. I think you have to be optimistic to be a live artist because it's such a weird way to try and make a living. If you're pessimistic you'd do something else. You have to be optimistic that your work has the potential to change something, anything…

Katherine: …Even if it's just nothing.

Richard: Even if it's nothing! Art that has the power to change nothing!

Katherine: I think we will always be able to make work that sits outside the norm. It's just too easy. Society is so restricted and conditioned in how it thinks, so as a positive I'm going to say that there will always be work.

Richard: You don't want to make the world so much better so that the Disabled Avant-Garde no longer need to exist. Then you'd be out of a job.

Katherine: Did we ever say we're trying to make the world better? [*laughs*]

Aaron: No, we want to make it worse.

Katherine: Making the world better is not our objective, and never will be. If the world starts to accept us then we'll change our discourse, and make sure that they spew us back up again.

1. Disabled Avant-Garde, *Bite The Hand That Feeds!* (Live Art Development Agency, 2012); *Aaron Williamson: Performance / Video / Collaboration*, ed. by Aaron Williamson and Oriana Fox (London: Live Art Development Agency and KIOSK, 2008).

ACTIONS
CONVERSATION
BARBY ASANTE
DAVID A. BAILEY
DATE
09 FEBRUARY 2016
PLACE
LONDON

Barby Asante is a London-based artist, curator, educator, and occasional DJ. Her work is concerned with the politics of place, space, identity, and the histories and legacies of colonialism, making work that is collaborative, performative, and dialogic. As she describes here, her trajectory has led from making autobiographical and autoethnographic works into participatory and social practices, with projects such as *The South London Black Archive* (2012), *Baldwin's Nigger RELOADED* (2014) with the collective sorryyoufeeluncomfortable, and most recently, *As Always a Painful Declaration of Independence : For Ama. For Aba. For Charlotte and Adjoa* (2017). This latest work was first shown at the Diaspora Pavilion for the 57th Venice Biennale, curated by David Bailey and Jessica Taylor. With LADA, Barby has contributed to RRR1 *On Race and Live Art / Documenting Live* (2008) and has led several DIY projects, including *To Gypsyland* (2013) with Delaine Le Bas, exploring the personal and political in performative, collaborative, and socially engaged practices; and *Bringing In the Directions* (2015), drawing on non-Western rituals. The latter was led by Agency for Agency, an ongoing collaborative project between Barby and Teresa Cisneros. Barby has also received a One-to-One Artist's Bursary, been LADA Thinker in Residence, and is the recipient of the first of LADA's annual commissions for *The Library of Performing Rights*.

David A. Bailey MBE is a photographer, writer, curator, lecturer, and cultural facilitator. David lives and works in London and Nassau, The Bahamas. David's practice is focused on the issues relating to black representations in the area of photography and artists' film. These interests informed his appointment as an advisor on the founding bodies that established Autograph (ABP) and the Institute of International Visual Arts (Iniva) in 1994. He co-curated the seminal exhibitions *Back to Black—Art, Cinema and the Racial Imaginary* with Petrine Archer-Straw and Richard J. Powell at Whitechapel Art Gallery in London (1995) and *Mirage: Enigmas Of Race, Difference & Desire* (on the influence of Frantz Fanon) at the ICA in London (1995). From 1996 to 2002, he was Co-Director of the African and Asian Visual Artists Archive (AAVAA) at the University of East London. Until the end of 2009, he was Senior Curator of Autograph ABP, and Curator of the organisation PLATFORM's *Remember Saro-Wiwa Living Memorial*. He is founder and director of the International Curators Forum.

This conversation took place the day after Beyoncé released the video 'Formation' and performed the song live at the US Super Bowl.

Barby: We're being asked to think about 'history' or 'histories', and the first thing to say is that's a very loaded question! History is alive and occurs in our every action. And to think about this fifteen–twenty year history of so-called 'Live Art'... well, I feel as if I've been 'adopted' by Live Art and by the Live Art Development Agency, and that's been really helpful for support and context, but I would also dispute my relationship with a thing called 'Live Art'. So what I would want to do now is to question my position within that history.

When I first started making art, I was exploring the anthropological or ethnographic image, and in a way 're-performing' these images. I was trying to find *my* image within the contexts of art school, or the library, or in gallery walls, and I didn't seem to find them. So it seemed appropriate to start using my body—in one of my first pieces called *Between a Mother and a Child*, for example, that was related to my experience of being a mother. And after college I started looking at ways to take images out of two-dimensions and start placing myself in public place. So I did *Wig Therapy* (2001), where I took on the persona of a wig therapy consultant at a hairdressing salon, and people could book appointments with me; or *I Accept Your Image, I Am You* (2001), where instead of putting work in the gallery that commissioned me, I made a series of public interventions. But I had no concept of this as a performance practice, or any sense of 'live-ness'. It just came out of my experience.

I was working at Mannafest in East London, around the corner from where the Live Art Development Agency used to be, and Lois Keidan made contact. I did master-classes with people like Desperate Optimists, motiroti, and Guillermo Gómez-Peña —and that's when I became aware of the idea of 'Live Art'. I got a lot from those conversations with Guillermo—not really about being as confrontational as in those performances that I took part in with him, but more this idea of how one might create forums or spaces to interrogate, to discuss, to propose, to re-perform....

But I still struggle with defining what 'Live Art' is. I've had conversations with a number of artists, many of whom were involved in *Documenting Live*, and we have this real *hunger* for a kind of criticality—like Catherine Ugwu did with *Let's Get It On* in 1995.[1] More recently I've led two DIY projects with LADA—with Delaine Le Bas and Teresa Cisneros —and those have been projects that have been really trying to look at how I fit within Live Art: *is* this what I do? [*laughs*] I described the feeling that I've been 'adopted' by Live Art, and, yes, it's nice to be adopted and to have a family! But that's not where you start. You are adopted *into* something, and the adopted child is very curious about where they come from. So the DIY project with Teresa was looking at ritual practices—which is something that's been coming up in my personal practice, where I've been working with Orisha ritual. I've been asking myself where my artistic practice and artistic voice comes from, looking back at my own family history.

David: I would imagine that growing up you would have gone to blues parties, and sound system events, and church. So you were already in an immersive environment, a pre- but highly modernistic live art space. What I am trying to say here is that we should not always look at the gallery or white cube spaces for traces of the emergence of a Live Art genre, but also spaces that tend to get neglected—like our own domestic spaces where we grew up, where there was a constant bombardment of music, visual culture, and performance.

Barby: Yes, I started going to carnival with my aunt when I was six, and I used to feel this *opening* in a very bodily way. Or when my dad would have family over, he would call on God and pour libations, so there would be this moment of *action* to mark something. To open the space to talk about something. There's a ritual of ceremony, and the space that you create then creates *dialogue*. And that history has certainly influenced things like the *South London Black Music Archive* (2012) in Peckham, an 'open archive' that mapped objects and places contributed by the public}, or *Barby's Karaoke* (2009), that used karaoke as a way for older people to tell their histories.

David: I would say we're very similar. We have these personal histories, and these professional histories—but neither of them are actually fixed. They're very fluid and complicated.

Barby: I think a lot of young artists and activists really struggle with the personal and the political. It's a struggle. I think it's that very action of being in a world where you're trying to be seen, or trying to write a history because those histories are not present. Or they're discounted, or they're not the ones you're allowed to speak. I see that more and more in my work.

David: Okay, so let's agree that Live Art is a genre, a particular practice. And it's like a Venn diagram—it emerges at the point where various things overlap. It doesn't come at the point when we're going to parties, and looking for set answers. And it doesn't come at the point moving forward when we're doing interventions and making our own work. It's an epistemological break.

An example for me is Isaac Julien 's *Looking for Langston* (1989), where he made this film that was a way to position an ambivalence around the role of photography and gay desire (as in [Robert] Mapplethorpe). But then from the film he extrapolated these performances, [*Undressing Icons*], first in King's Cross and then at Edge 90 —which was a great performance organisation [in Newcastle]. They're almost like live stills from the film, where he uses King's Cross and St Pancras cemetery as a place for cottaging. He recreates that as performance, so that people would walk through and come across these different scenes. Since then, Julien has moved onto making the kind of immersive installations with 15 different screens that he makes now. But those *moments*—that's Live Art. That's what I would define as Live Art. And I think that's why it's been difficult to archive those 1990s works, and why there seems to be no continuity, because *that* was the practice. It was discontinuous. It happens in this epistemological break. It breaks, and then suddenly it's gone.

Barby: For me, I can see performance in Chris Ofili 's painting, *Captain Shit and the Myth of the Black Stars*, which is this performance of male bravado that I think was like what was happening with hip hop, but in the art world. Or I think about Rashaad Newsome 's *Shade Compositions*, which uses the nuances of 'shade' and the performativity of a regular person on the street. Or Rashid Johnson, who made this work using shea butter, so when you walked into the space there was this particular smell. It was like a code that certain people would know, and other people wouldn't.

So I think performativity extends beyond the idea of a Live Art practice. It's also happening in the practice of popular culture. That's what happened with the Pier Kids and vogueing, where they were performing this critique of society. And although it's not how I would do it, it's happening now with Beyoncé. The political and the cultural start to conflate.

David: Yes, I think you're starting to distinguish between performance and post-performance or what could be defined as Live Art. I feel like Live Art has an attraction. The genre attracts people to expand the frame of cultural identity. And in this country in particular, there's been a surge from post-1990s to a current generation of particularly Black women, who are playing ambivalently around sexuality.

Barby: Yes, I think of people like Project O.

David: Then I feel we need to explore the idea that it is the art form itself that attracts people who want to develop a process that allows that, because it allows you to expand those cultural nuances—as in the example you just pointed out, where you can actually smell and taste the lingering of it. So why is that different from performance? It's because it's *live*. More than that: I think LADA should get rid of the 'E' and we'd call it *living*, because it's a living art.

I think that's why I've always had difficulty with the term 'Live Art', because it's not about 'live', it's about the process of living. The word 'live' is really a distinction about audience. It's a distinction in your Arts Council project funding: do you have a live audience, or is the audience coming via the internet? I mean, the Royal Opera House now performs 'live'—and you can watch it from the Odeon in Leicester Square!

But there's a paradox, too. You can be as expansive as you like in your practice—'I can do that! I can do this!'—but you can still be trapped within identity politics. The practice itself doesn't *expand* enough to deal with the complexity or fluidity of identification. Particularly if you're Black, if you're female, if you're gay, then *that* identity is your only avenue to be expansive.

Barby: Exactly! That's why I want to expand the notion of what performativity is, in terms of the working practices of artists. I hear some of the students I work with say, 'I work in Live Art practice'—but I would *never* want to be defined by that; I would never want to be limited. And the same with that other term, 'socially-engaged', which some people have called my work. You've got to be joking! I'm not here to be instrumentalised: 'Can you come work this particular community' or whatever. I ditched that.

So I started to create my own community, so to speak. They might exist *within* a community, like the events I've done in Brixton related to activism. Or they might live just for a little while. This is what we're doing with the work around *Baldwin's Nigger*.[2] The first time began with an invitation to around twenty young artists to work together to unpack the film—like opening up a box. This became the collective sorryyoufeeluncomfortable, and we created this live event [at Iniva] which was also a re-enactment, in a way, where we watched the film together and had questions afterwards. It was an action, an event, and [Horace] Ové was there. And there was also the *action* of taking over the building. We were very concerned about the state of Iniva at that time. Working with Teresa [Cisneros], we decided that we would secure the whole building, and we ended up bringing in 550 people—which was the most people they've had since it opened. So that was a living act, a kind of action/performance/conversation.

Since then we've re-performed that event in different contexts. If I can, I turn the space into a party, because Baldwin was really into parties—and I realise now that this goes back to what I was saying about my own family, and creating those convivial spaces for dialogue to happen. Each time it feels like it creates a community that speaks through Baldwin. Baldwin gives this call to action at the end of the speech that begins the film. He's basically saying, 'What should we do?' I think he asks that of each person in the world, and how we're taking responsibility for everything that's going in the world. It's quite an incredible thing to do.

David: I don't know if you knew this, but you and I have worked with the same material! But I did something completely different, and I think this is a perfect illustration of the difference between different generations and different practices—between a Live Art approach and a somewhat traditional curatorial approach. I also worked with Horace Ové, and *my* approach was: get his incredible photographs together; put together an exhibition at the National Portrait Gallery; develop partnerships with major photographic organisations such as Autograph who led on the touring aspect of show; and get him over to talk about the work and show his films.

Right: Barby Asante, *A Declaration of Independence* (2018). Image the artist.

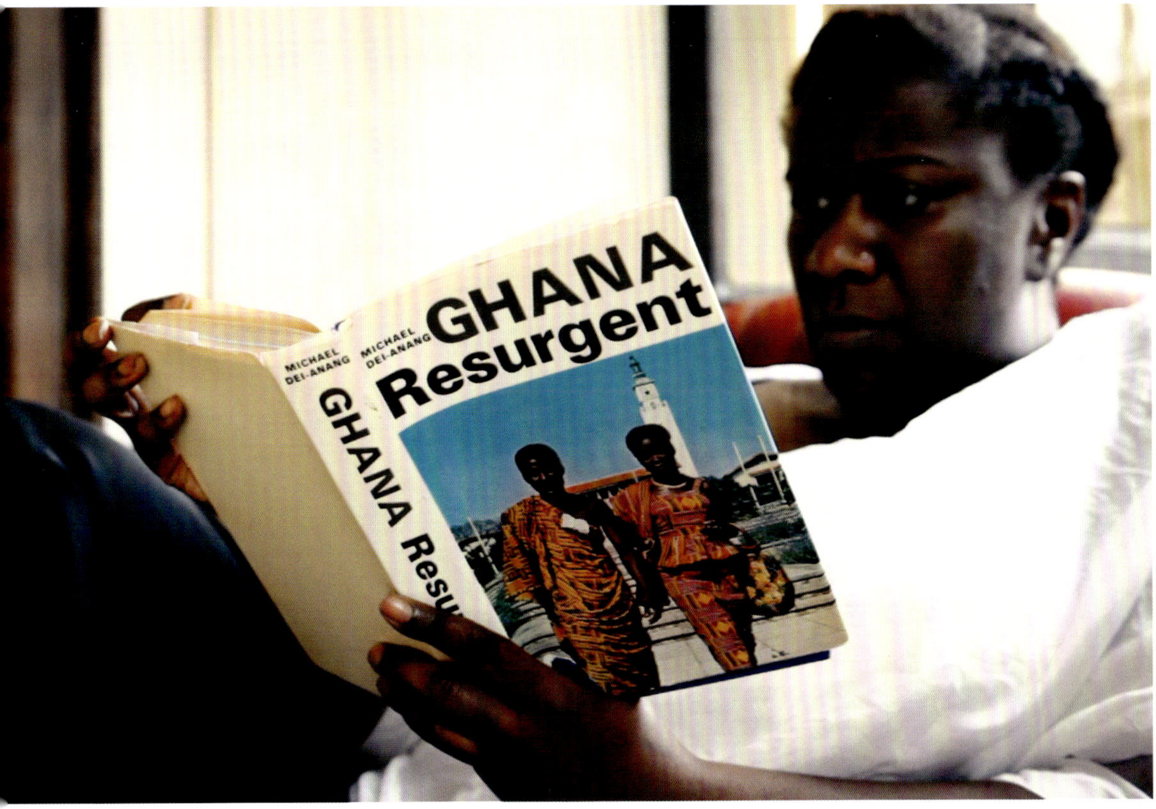
MICHAEL
DEI-ANANG
GHANA Resurgent
MICHAEL
DEI-ANANG
GHANA
Resurgent

My project was to canonise someone within the particular lens of the Western art world. *Your* project was to work within the Live Art genre: to answer the call that comes out of the work itself, to find a way to make the work relate to a younger generation of artists, and to create this living, performative event. If you want to see the difference between performance and 'living art', just look at how we both used that film and those artists.

Barby: Your approach was completely appropriate at the time, because you had Horace as a kind of living archive. But what happens when that actual, physical person is not around to present it? We need to think about other ways to activate that material. That's particularly important for Black people, for people of colour. There's this provocative question from a woman in the film, who asks, 'Mr Baldwin, where will the Black man be in fifty years' time?' That was in 1968, and we're nearly fifty years on, and actually Baldwin is being quoted a lot now in relation to police brutality and the Black Lives Matter movement.

David: The thing about Baldwin is that he is a precursor to everything. If you wanted to talk about people who were a precursor to Live Art, then you'd have to put Baldwin's name forward. He's there in the trajectory for people like Isaac Julien: the opening sequence of *Looking for Langston* is Baldwin's funeral, which Julien attended. But that only takes us so far—and here's that epistemological break again, when someone like you comes in, Barby, and says we need to take the *actual* Baldwin and the film and London, and take it to a younger generation in London.

It's a question of where agency comes in. For me, agency came from infrastructural and institutional structures: building new collections, or helping to found Autograph and Iniva . Whereas for you, the question is who's going into those buildings? What work is going to be there? What are the mechanisms and processes that allow that infrastructural agency to happen?

I'm really surprised. I came to this conversation thinking I would talk about *Mirage* [*the exhibition Bailey curated with Catherine Ugwu at the ICA*] and [Frantz] Fanon, or Ken Saro-Wiwa, and all that kind of stuff. But the more I think about it, this project—which is a project that we actually share, in a way—is a really good example of how to take the material of an artist who has lived through all these decades, and suddenly make that artist's work expand into a new genre: Live Art.

Barby: I am interested in proposals. I don't want to fix things—like an activist wants to 'fix' things. I'm interested in giving you questions. Could you develop this conversation? What happens if you do this? What *is* our agency? It's a question, rather than a fixed thing.

1. *Let's Get It on: The Politics of Black Performance*, ed. by Catherine Ugwu (London/Seattle: ICA/Bay Press, 1995).

2. *Baldwin's Nigger* (1969) is the first film by Horace Ové (who later made *Pressure* [1976]), which documents James Baldwin talking in London in 1968 with people from the British West Indian

ACTIONS

CONVERSATION

RON ATHEY

CASSILS

DATE

26 NOVEMBER 2016

PLACE

LOS ANGELES

Ron Athey is an iconic figure in the development of performance art and Live Art. Over several decades of work, he has pushed the boundaries of his own body and of performance, exploring themes of gender, sexuality, SM and radical sex, queer activism, post-punk and industrial culture, tattooing and body modification, ritual, and religion. He is one of LADA's patrons, and presented at the symposia for *Live Culture* (2003) and *Performance Matters: Performing Idea* (2010). *Pleading in the Blood: The Art and Performances of Ron Athey* (2013) was amongst the first publications in LADA's Intellect Live series.

Cassils is a performance artist, body builder, and personal trainer, whose work treats the body as a form of social sculpture. Cassils is gender nonconforming and trans masculine, and performs transgender not as a crossing from one sex to another but rather as a continual process of becoming. Supported by Los Angeles Contemporary Exhibitions (LACE) to make a work engaging with their archives, Cassils created *Cuts: A Traditional Sculpture* (2010), a response to Eleanor Antin's *Carving: A Traditional Sculpture* (1972), in which Cassils gained 23 pounds of muscle over 23 weeks. Again responding to an archive, Cassils created *Becoming An Image* (2012), which is described in this conversation, for the ONE National Gay & Lesbian Archives. Cassils performed *Inextinguishable Fire* (2015), using stunt techniques to burn for 14 seconds, at the National Theatre (UK) for SPILL Festival, and made the short film *103 Shots* (2016) in response to the nightclub shooting in Orlando, Florida. In 2014 Cassils was the first recipient of the ANTI Festival International Prize for Live Art, and is also the recipient of the United States Artists Fellowship (2018), Guggenheim Fellowship (2016), Creative Capital Award (2015), Artist Fellowship from the Canada Council of the Arts, and MOTHA (Museum of Transgender Hirstory) award.

This conversation took place in Ron's studio in Los Angeles, shortly after the 2016 US presidential elections.

Ron: When a work is on fire, I just gravitate toward it. It's hard to explain which work. The medium doesn't matter to me as much as the presence of the sublime, when an artist channels a situation, and some kind of spark happens.

Cassils: A state of urgency—that's how I would put it. A state of urgency, when it's absolutely necessary to communicate. It's so easy in the art world for things to become formal exercises for their own sake, or to become commodities, but I think you and I share a love for that work that feels driven and urgent.

Ron: It has a chemistry. Whether that's adrenaline or neurology, it's like actually taking it inside of you. Not sitting in a room being clever, but psychically entering that *panic state*, and from that state, giving back an image, an action, a thought. Something that's more than the headlines we're all reading.

Cassils: In relationship to all the insanity right now I've been finding it calming to return to Audre Lorde's work. She has this essay where she talks about the sacred space inside women, but I think she's really talking about the dark space inside oppressed people.[1] It's a space where there are no words, and there is this power—but it's a power we're taught not to value because we're taught that we need to be articulate in words. That's been true in the way I've been educated and institutionalised: 'What's the thesis? What does it mean? How does it relate to art history?'

Ron: I think that work comes from really different places. I started to realise that often I'm not performing what I *think* I'm performing. I can make all these grand statements at the beginning of the process, but that's just the entrance to the state of performing. I try to shed something within that state, so whatever the original intention is, I don't come out the other side and try to read it through that intention.

Cassils: For me it feels like there's this marriage between what I'll call 'the gut', for lack of a better term, and I'll call the other thing 'the puzzle'. The gut and the puzzle! [*laughs*]

Ron: That's a good one!

Cassils: For example, there's this piece I did recently for camera, *The Powers That Be*. It started coming together many years ago with you in the 'boot camp' you ran with Julie Tolentino. There were about ten of us together in the Mojave Desert for ten days and nights. It was intense. That's where I met Julie, and Empress Stah, and Manuel Vason, and Zackary Drucker—that was the chrysalis of our friendship. Each of us was tasked with coming up with a new performance, and it was over 100 degrees in the day so we were working at night, in this strange, altered state. I was bit blocked artistically, and you hypnotised me, Ron, and that's where I had this vision for the piece.

I had been to stunt school before that, learning how violent images are constructed, specifically through fight choreography, which is designed so that you never make actual physical contact, but the camera collapses three dimensions into two selling the contact and animating the action. One day my fight choreography partner wasn't well, so I performed my part without her, responding to invisible blows and throws as if she was there. When I looked at the documentation afterwards, it looked like I was battling with a ghost. I realised that I could create this phantom presence, and that's what I started working with in the desert, illuminated by car headlights. After that I came back to this image again and again, and I finally worked through it in a more developed way two years ago.[2]

But then recently I was talking about it with a client, and they said it reminded them of [Edward] Kienholz's *Five Car Stud* [1969–1972], which was this sculpture, a life-size tableau of a Black man being castrated by a group of white men, surrounded by cars, and the scene is illuminated by these car headlights. And I realised I had seen that work, maybe in an art history lecture as an eighteen-year-old. It's such a strong image that it had etched itself into my sub-conscious, and I was re-creating it without knowing it—but I was re-creating it for a reason that has to do with how things are now.

So it's the puzzle and the gut, not always one of them leading: sometimes one informs the other, and sometimes the other way around. In that essay Lorde writes, 'There are no new ideas. There are only new ways of making them felt.' That's the challenge for an artist: how to make contemporary iterations that speak to the current times.

Ron: It's true that images burn in people's heads. And sometimes after a performance, people will describe that image back to me and how they interpreted it. But that doesn't mean that the work is just that image, and that by minimalising and making it cleaner it would be stronger. That's the problem with live work: sometimes it's all the messy things that make this profound experience that leaves you in tears.

Like with your piece in the desert, where there was this desert sand blowing through, like a cyclone, and the headlights are hitting it, like stage lights but in a really crude, intense way. And there are things like smells, and grit in your eye, that would never get told back to you if someone were describing the image—and that you

Right: Ron Athey, *Solar Anus*, Hayward Gallery, London (2006). Image Regis Hertrich.

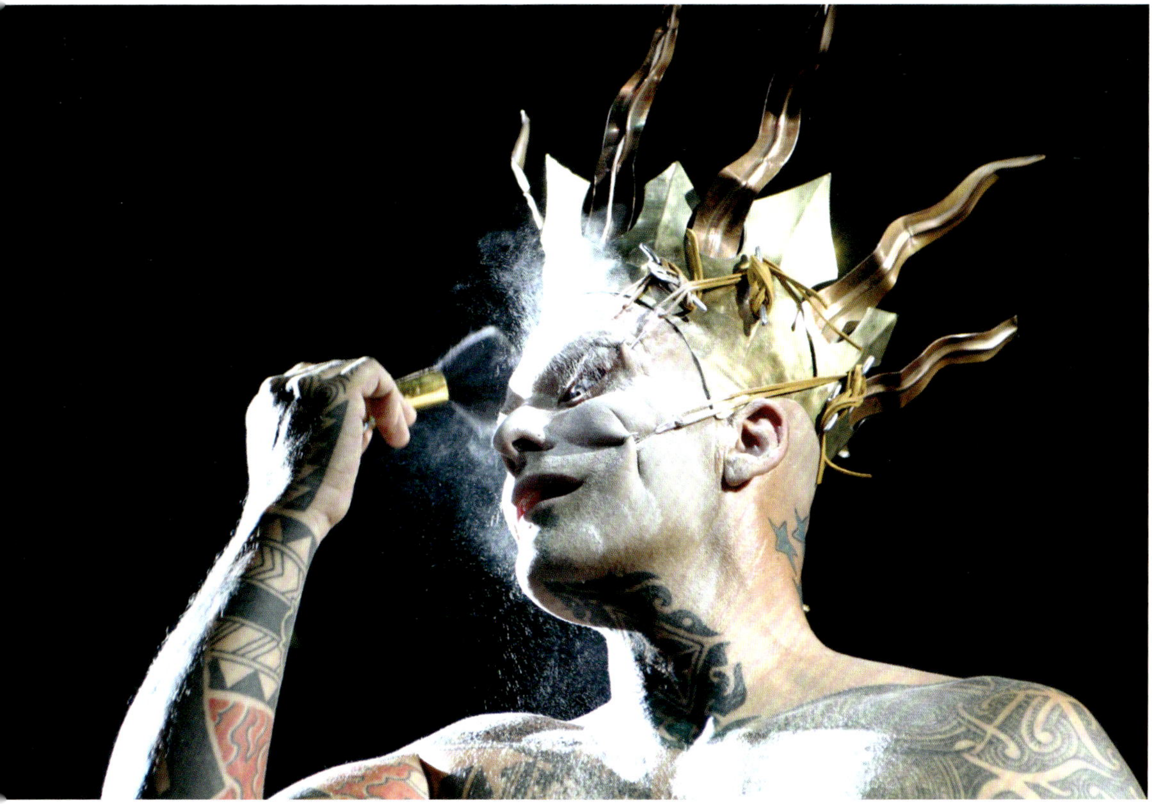

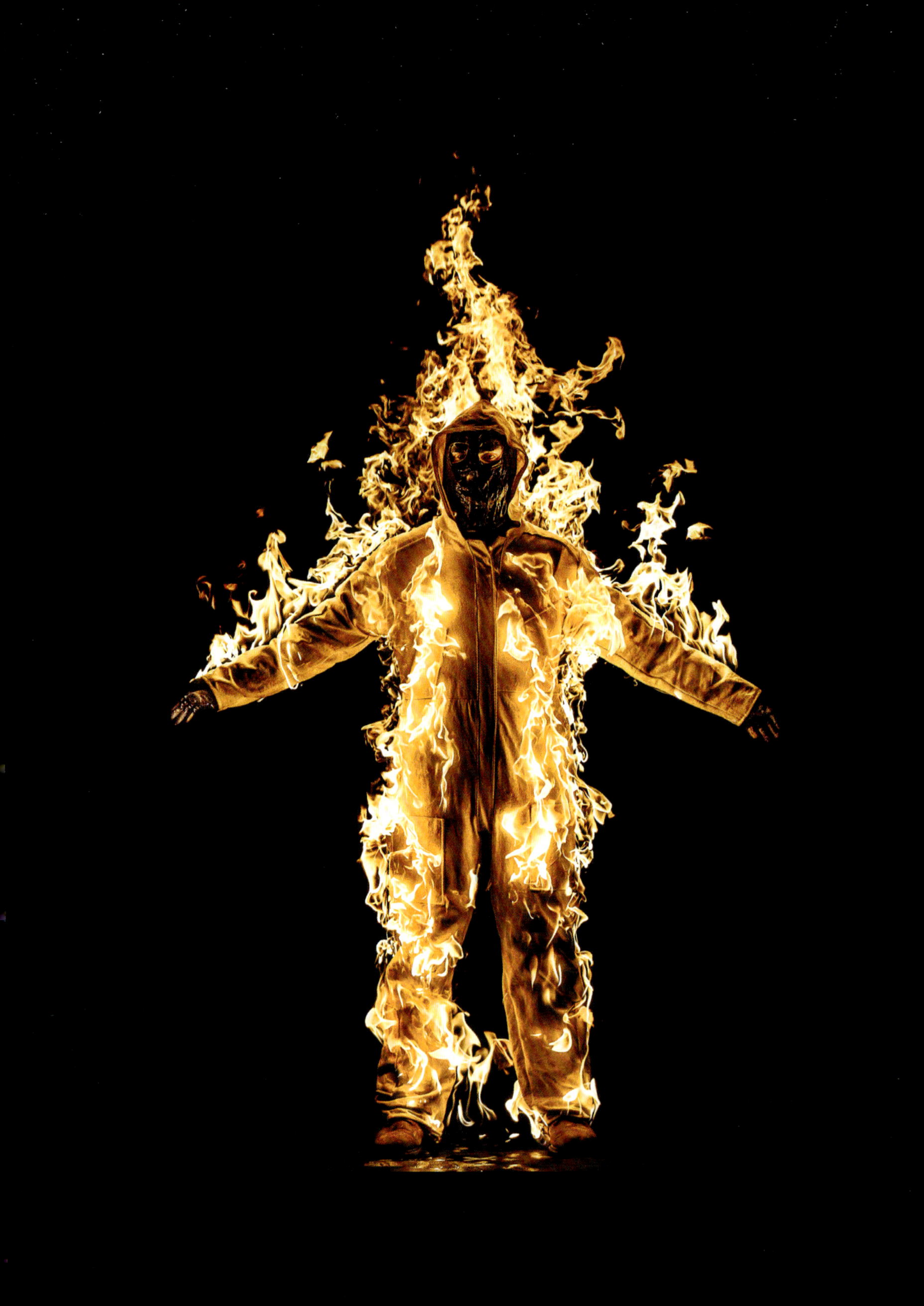

couldn't have in a museum. Or if you did it would be really overwrought.

Cassils: Yeah, 'Let's bring in the dust!'

Ron: It's not always easy to understand what brought the magic into the room. That's one of my goals, I guess: making magic with my work. [*laughs*]

I'm elderly now, so I can think about decades of past work. In the 1990s I worked with a company of the same group of people within this very narrow body-modification community. It was community work, in a way: body art *within* body art. I think we were sensing something about the queer body, just a tiny bit before that became an academic term. The queer body—not the perfect gay body, but all these different bodies. There's a way you can represent, without that being the *aim* of it. And I think that came out of the confidence that comes out of being inside a bubble—a counter-culture, an underground, a closed system that forms something powerful and then brings it back out into the real world. I've been thinking about that because I think that bubble has to be rebuilt now, *real strong*.

Maybe it's just my way of being political without realising it's political. In the past it was more overt, like when I publicly stated in 1985 that I was HIV positive. It was like 'Queer Nation! Fuck you!' That infected faggot perspective: I have AIDS and I'm angry. There was a charge to it. But there's such a difference between how that felt versus more recently, where I've had a recurrence of Hepatitis C and I've started taking HIV drugs, and this time it doesn't feel political. It's a different climate, or I'm in a different stage. It feels a little bit shameful now.

Left: Cassils, *Inextinguishable Fire*, SPILL Festival of Performance, London (2015), produced by Pacitti Company. Image Guido Mencari.

Cassils: Why does it feel shameful?

Ron: Maybe it's the element of aging that makes it feel disempowering to be sick—and I got talked into going on Triumeq, and then you enter this pharmaceutical world of $100/day for drugs, and waiting lists for new treatments, and so on. I don't feel like I'm fighting for my life and have this whole group spirit behind me. There was that frantic political spirit in the 1980s and early 1990s, ACT UP and all that coordination. But Hep-C has been this really quiet issue, because nobody wants another AIDS, so they just keep quiet around it.

Cassils: But it's also a product of it being not just HIV-positive faggots being denied healthcare. It's everywhere. Nobody has good healthcare. I feel like so much of our lives as queer people has been about tolerating being on a fringe, and a lack of acceptance—but now it's like, 'You too can have ridiculous healthcare and be abandoned by the system!' What is this bullshit?

One thing this moment has made crystal clear is that I feel very polarised. This risks sounding cheesy, but I think about a chosen family, the people who I trust. They may not have the same beliefs, but they have the same thing at stake, and the same frustrations with the way this machine is trying to pulverise us to dust.

Ron: Yeah, I've never thought that my one group was the centre of the universe. I don't think of people as queer and non-queer or non-whatever. The way I function in the world is pretty easy and fluid. This is a hard thing to articulate, but I actually don't like activism because it's absolutist. There's no room for dissent or half-measures. I think about the way that AIDS activists were appalled by how Susan Sontag wrote about AIDS in 'AIDS and Its Metaphors'.[3] That was a faux-pas? I can't be around that. Probably because I come from a Christian fundamentalist family, and I don't like fundamentalism. I don't have a vision that if everyone was just like me that we'd have a nice perfect world.

Cassils: Well, you're punk.

Ron: I'm punk, but I also believe in healing. I remember the time when everyone was dying, and there was this cooperation and communication—so that when the popular people already had too many people squeezing into their hospital rooms, you'd go visit someone a little funkier. I wear all of that on me, having lived through that time period.

Cassils: When you were talking about 'I'm infected and I'm angry,' I think there are certain aspects to the transactivist movement, and how quickly it has been picked up and commoditised. It's not as simple as representation giving power: the moment we have representation, we also have a commodity market. This intervening, over-arching aspect of capitalism usurps any critical distance.

I don't think my work is only about trans issues *at all*, but one thing I garner from it is the idea of indeterminacy, spasm, slipperiness. It's like what you were talking about, Ron, where the moment you have an absolutist position you start to build walls. So my political relationship to transness begins where my personal subjectivity comes up against this machine. For you it was being infected. For me it's being told that you can be who you want to be, but first you have to be evaluated by a psychiatrist, have your body amputated, and get hooked on Big Pharma for the rest of your life, even though there have been no long-term studies of the effects of testosterone. Why should I have to amputate my body? Why is my body the problem? Why isn't society the problem?

So I've been making work that pushes back. Like *Becoming an Image*, which uses this constantly malleable piece of clay, made from Walt Disney's animation clay, that is never fixed, and that is formed through acts of violence. I unleash an attack on this 2000-pound block, delivering a series of kicks and blows in complete darkness. It is illuminated only by a flash from a photographer's camera that burns the image into the viewers' retina, creating a 'live photograph' in their eyes. At the end you're left with a sculpture that is an index of every fist, elbow, knee—the formal shape of a violent attack.

For me, it speaks to the idea of absence, and the way there is power in absence. We talk about the empowerment that comes through being visible, and that's certainly true—it's important to have rights. But there's something about the over-arching mechanism of capitalism that makes me suspect of visibility politics. It makes me think about the importance of building a bubble, as you were saying. I would call it creeping into a shadow-land. That darkness offers protection of sorts, to come together and regroup.

Ron: I hear you. There has been this big trans wave, and it's bigger than us—it will envelop you, whether you want it to or not, whether you're obviously trans or you float in the middle. And I feel like if you re-confirm that and become part of that movement, it can become limiting. Rather than just representing one group, there's something more esoteric about making a living image—something that's out of history, that's out of a dream. It's why I'm not into the pop culture consumption of 'heavy images'—like Beyoncé referring to a Black Panther pose but still being all Beyoncé and fancy. It cheapens everything.

I think I'm still trying to understand what *time* we're in. Because the tone is so lowered, we actually live in a reality show. It's like beyond post-post-modernism now—it's like turned inside outside in. It's ridiculous. Last year I spent a week at a Methodist college in Shreveport, Louisiana. I was showing them really disgusting things—I was really fucking with them!—and everyone left horrified. But this one kid said, 'I think I get it—it's kind of like Shia LaBeouf'! [*laughs*] But you know, at least he had an interest somehow.

Cassils: These are things we need to think about. How can you make your voice heard amongst the insanity of all the clamour and all the white noise? What are the strategies for that? In relation to the way that images get picked up and circulated digitally and spat back out, what are the tools for creating a lasting rooted impact? I think that's where liveness become intrinsically important.

Ron: Performance works on a more neurological level—even a psychic level. I can still use the word 'ritual'. I've had the experience in intimate situations where I feel that I'm embedding myself *inside* the performance. I already have all the 'tags' inside me about how to move through the performance, but it has an extra intention. A few times I've almost had an out-of-body experience.

But I'm always aware of when we become de-sensitised to images and tactics, when we stop being affected. This frenzied consumption of images that we live in is too much. And it makes being an image-maker bizarre. Maybe this is the other side of being in the LADA Study Room is that I'm treated as source material for younger artists asking me about something, or who want to cite my work—which can make me feel like I don't exist, like I'm not alive and vital in the moment. I'm not source material! I'm a living artist! [*laughs*]

Cassils: We first met when I was working as your teaching assistant at CalArts, and it's been very affirming for me to have your example, as someone who has lived through this cultural dysphoria. You lived through a time that I couldn't touch, but we're close enough in age that I can still *feel* it. You come from a time before queer was commodified in the way that it is now, and you have stayed punk. You live and work by your principles: a living example of resistance.

1. 'For each of us as women, there is a dark place within, where hidden and growing our true spirit rises, 'beautiful/ and tough as chestnut/ stanchions against (y)our nightmare of weakness/' and of impotence.' Audre Lorde, 'Poetry Is Not a Luxury' [1977], in *Sister Outsider: Essays and Speeches* (Berkeley: Crossing Press, 1985), pp. 36–39 (p. 36).

2. See <http://cassils.net/portfolio/powers-that-be/>.

3. Susan Sontag, *AIDS and Its Metaphors* (New York: Farrar, Straus and Giroux, 1989).

ACTIONS

PROVOCATION

JOHN JORDAN

TITLE

PERFORMING UTOPIAS:
FOR A LIVE ART THAT
LIVES AND LETS LIVE

Labelled a 'Domestic Extremist' by the British police, and 'a magician of rebellion' by the French press, John Jordan has spent the last 25 years merging art and activism. Working in various settings from museums to squatted social centres, international theatre festivals to disobedient climate camps, social movements are his main material. John was a co-director of Platform (1987–1995), and co-founded *Reclaim the Streets* (1995–2000) and the *Clown Army* (2004–present), which developed via a LADA DIY project 'RESPONSE-ABILITY: Building bridges between art and activism' and became a global protest meme.

He wrote the LADA Study Room Guide *In the Footnotes of Library Angels: A Bi(bli)ography of Insurrectionary Imagination* (2005), co-edited *We Are Everywhere: the irresistible rise of global anti-capitalism* (2003), and co-wrote *A Users Guide to ~~Demanding~~ the Impossible* (2010) and the film/book *Les Sentiers de L'utopie* (2011). A senior lecturer in Fine Art, he deserted the academy to work on the film *The Take* with Naomi Klein in 2004. He now co-facilitates the Laboratory of Insurrectionary Imagination (Labofii), founded with Isabelle Frémeaux and James Leadbitter (2004–present). Infamous for fermenting mass disobedience on bicycles, throwing snowballs at bankers, launching a rebel raft regatta to shut down a power station, running workshops in postcapitalism and refusing to be censored by the Tate Modern, the Labofii now lives on the autonomous zone of the ZAD of Notre-dame-des-Landes, 'a territory lost to the Republic,' according to the French government.

It's raining. No, that's not the right word. It's more like drizzle, rather half way between drizzle and mist. Let's call it *mizzel,* a beautiful in-between state, between liquid and wind, vapor and fluid. My hands are wet; they slide on the handrails. I'm nearly at the top; there is a last little steel ladder to climb. But I don't want to get electrocuted. I should dry my hands before I flip the switch.

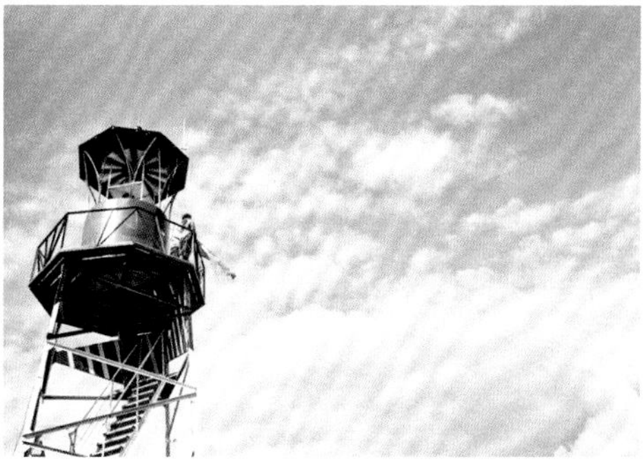

The lighthouse lamp begins to turn, and caught by its bright beam the *mizzel* begins to dance, white ghostly clouds of light swirling in the night. The beam turns faster than most lighthouses. But we are not on a normal lighthouse. In fact we are 50km away from the sea, 20m above an old stone farmhouse in the middle of 4000 acres of fields, forests and wetlands, in a place that French government called, 'the territory lost to the Republic ... the outlaw zone.'

Those of us who inhabit this land call it the Zone A Défendre, the 'Zone to Defend': the ZAD. Even the tabloid-like 24-hour French news channel BFMTV once called it 'a utopia that might be being realised'! To me it is home, a territory where I finally understood the force that comes when you dissolve the gaps between art, politics and everyday life. When you realise that the more you inhabit a place, the more it inhabits you.[1]

In the 1980s I deserted the theatre world for Live Art, because I wanted something more dirty, messy and free, closer to everyday life. But by the mid-90s I had deserted Live Art too, because I realised that despite all its claims, the art world felt equally enclosed. Of course, it claims to be risky, edgy, radical, but this felt like a posture. The discourse was of revolution, rebellion, even insurrection, and yet the reality was that it felt like a zoo: a place where life was put on show for a few but not lived to the full. It was a place to show the world not to change it. Suzi Gablik called the art world a 'prison',[2] but a zoo is worse: at least in a prison there is a chance of parole.

I had spent my youth enthralled by 1970s body art: Gina Pane sticking rose thorns into her arms; Chris Burden risking life lying down on the freeway wrapped in a tarpaulin; VALIE EXPORT offering up her breasts to strangers; the orgiastic mass therapy sessions of the Viennese Actionists. I loved the drama and the ritual. I loved the fluid boundaries between performance and everyday-life. But in a time of extreme ecological and social crisis, where the very foundations of life on this planet were being rapidly undone by the cancer like logic of capitalism and economic growth, it felt that to really act in the world was not to change art, but forms of life.

Rather than *live art* I chose the *art of life*. I did not give up art. I simply decided to let it free by breaking down the walls that separate it from worlds. I did not give up making the beautiful; it was simply realising that the most beautiful thing was trying to protect life itself. Art is so much wilder than the art world, and all of us who have been able to free the beast of art into the world know this. When you free it, it forgets its name. It becomes a force, not a thing; a means, not an end. It becomes a way of being in the world that erases the divisions between witness and actor, between spectator and performer. It re-injects sense into everyday life.

The avant-gardes of the 20th century had also been my teachers. DADA: 'Abolish art, individual genius, all limits and the audience.' Surrealism: 'We believe that the supreme task of art in our epoch is to take part actively and consciously in the preparation of the revolution.' Situationism: 'The suppression of art is its only realisation, don't feed the spectacle with culture but create playful participatory situations that spark insurrectionary desires.' From the mid-90s onwards I began applying creativity as an organiser and action designer within direct action movements, from Reclaim the Streets to the Clown Army, from the Global Anticapitalism movements to Climate Camp, and it enabled me to begin to realise Lefebvre's dream: 'Let everyday life become a work of art! Let every technical means be employed for the transformation of everyday life!'[3]

I was living in London and it began to seem impossible to lead a revolutionary life within the metropolis, where we are held captive by the commodification of everything. As artists we inevitably become part of a violent process of gentrification evicting the poor and destroying neighbourhoods. Seven years ago I moved to rural France and eventually ended up living on the ZAD. It was here that I realised what a world could look like when art becomes an ethos to be acted out in society, not something commodified by a museum or a gallery. Not the expression of a single atomised individual, but a way of living beautifully together, of paying attention, of crafting existence as if we were already free.

+++++

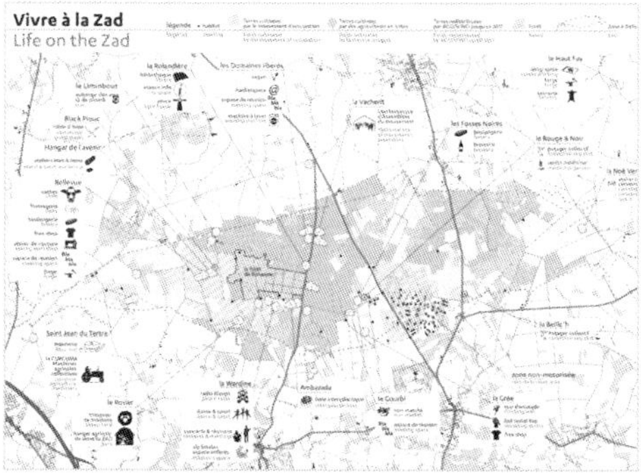

The lighthouse's beam sweeps across the forest of Rohanne, it makes me think of ghosts and the ghosts that I have felt in my life. You never see them, they are invisible, you simply feel them, sense them. This forest, like most, is haunted—or rather let's say inhabited—by two types of ghosts—or presences. One that gives life. Another that tried to take it away.

Since 1965, the year I was born, handfuls of men in government buildings and skyscraper headquarters have imagined an airport runway here. With their bulldozers they thought that they could destroy the complex relationships between the millions of beings that share the forest. The links between the crested newts and the pond plants whose leaves they use to wrap and camouflage their eggs, between the oaks and the mushrooms that share their minerals, between the clouds and the leaves that form their vapour. They wanted to replace all that with a lifeless strip of tarmac, three and a half kilometres long and 60 meters wide, just one of the two runways for the so-called 'green' airport for the city of Nantes. Another climate wrecking infrastructure, planned for a bygone age in which mobility was more important than inhabiting, for a world where people believed that existence was defined by identities rather than relationships.

But in January 2017, France's prime minister appears on live TV and announces the abandonment of the airport project, but in the same breath he says that all those illegally occupying land on the ZAD will be evicted by springtime. As the news comes in, the lighthouse becomes an improvised stage for TV cameras with their satellite trucks waiting below for the ZAD's reaction. Dozens of bodies light up bright red flares. Someone slices open a bottle of champagne with a machete and whilst dancing wildly they let a hand-painted banner unroll down side of the structure. It reads *ET TOC!*, which in French means *BAM! There you go! Put that in your pipe and smoke it*. That night the prime minister is interviewed on the eight o'clock news: behind him is a huge picture of the banner on the lighthouse.

Now when I cycle through the forest, I breath in the deep damp fungal smell of the place and begin to sense the presences of the other ghosts, the life-giving ones who have come to remind me of the resistance that took place here, and that ultimately led to the PM's announcement. In 2012, thousands of disobedient bodies put themselves in the way of the machines and the police who had come to build their airport. I sense the ghosts of the 40,000 people from all over France that returned to rebuild the farmhouses that were knocked down during the first days of eviction attempts. There are the ghosts of the bodies hanging in the trees to stop them being felled, of the farmers blocking the roads with their tractors, of the dozens of barricades each one built as a work of rebellious art.

Since that failed eviction attempt the ZAD managed to exist without police or any government officials for over six years. It has built a laboratory of commoning involving 80 different living collectives and over 300 people, all squatting the land and buildings, trying to live without domination—without bosses, gurus, or leaders, and free from the dictatorship of the economy. With its bakeries, pirate radio station, tractor repair workshop, brewery, banqueting hall, medicinal herb gardens, a rap studio, dairy, screen-printing atelier, vegetable plots, weekly newspaper, blacksmiths, flour mill, and library the ZAD has become a concrete experiment in taking back control of everyday life. When you no longer outsource your problems and needs, everyday life goes from being unthinking behaviour to being a question of technique: of art. For example, because we refused to let the police enter the zone, we had to design from scratch a system of communal justice to deal with conflicts. Experimenting new forms of life together is a messy difficult process, never easy but compelling in its intensity.

We need a technique of life, an 'art of living', claimed philosopher-activist Michel Foucault. Rather than 'something which is specialised or which is done by experts,' he asked, 'couldn't everyone's life become a work of art? Why should the lamp or the house be an art object, but not our life?'[4] For Foucault this was not about trying to be some kind of authentic, atomised self, but about pushing the boundaries of what that self can become in its interconnectedness with each other and worlds. During one of the many assemblies that organises life on the ZAD, one of the half a dozen farmers who refused the compulsory purchase of his farm for the airport said: 'Whether we like it or not we have become more than ourselves.'

But this kind of attitude requires a certain mindfulness and presence to worlds. It means learning to inhabit one's territory as much as one's body, knowing its stories, sensing the texture of things. This discipline of attention, this deep sensibility to doing and being, is in itself a form of care-giving. It requires presence, here and now, working with what is at hand rather than waiting for some moment of perfection. It means letting go of fixed ideologies in favour of sensing situations. Such presence means that we know where our food comes from, where the nearest spring erupts, what species of mushroom spreads beneath our feet. It senses the weather changing on our skin; it feels the tidal pull of the full moon on our bloodstream. A deep presence means that we notice when the local song birds fall silent, we mourn when butterflies no longer pepper the prairies, and we cannot just watch the bodies of migrants washing up on the shores of the Mediterranean. Paying attention is the essential ingredient of the art of life.[5]

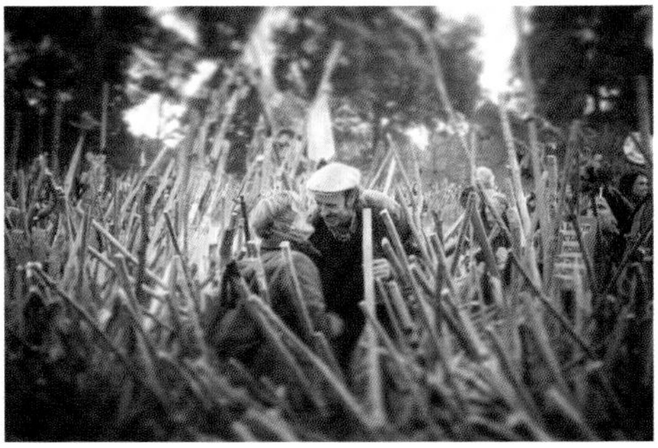

There was always a ritualistic essence in Live Art that moved me, but what was missing was the shared language of ritual, it always felt like the audience was watching someone else's ritual rather making their own.
On the ZAD, we try to reclaim ritual as a collective tool. Throughout 2016, then Prime Minister Manuel Valls declared weekly that he was coming to try again to evict us for the airport, threatening that up to two-thirds of the French Gendarmerie would be mobilised. Every night we would go to bed wondering if we'd be woken up by heavily armed cops breaking down our doors.

We responded with a ritual, co-designed during our assemblies and disguised as a demonstration. Just when the threat of evictions peaked, 40,000 people responded. They brought with them walking sticks and staffs, which they stuck in the ground making a pledge that they would return to defend the ZAD. 'We are here, we will be here!' they promised. As the tens of thousands of sticks were thrust into the soil, a cathedral-like medieval style oak barn, built during the summer by 80 traditional carpenters, was raised. The festivities continued late into the night. The magic worked. The government never came. That time, anyway.[6]

I began this piece up the lighthouse, switching the light on to mark the holding of the Assembly of the Uses, the entity where we organise the land as a commons outside of private property and the state institutions. We built a full-scale functioning lighthouse right on the site where the airport's control tower should have been. When we were building it, we did not know whether a few weeks later the bulldozers might come, making everything a ruin. Putting energy, time, and attention into building something when you know that it might soon be destroyed is a powerful experience, and perhaps the perfect metaphor for living in this strange end-time of the Capitalocene. You build as if you will be there for ever, but you face the possibility of losing everything tomorrow.

But inevitably spring came and the government's promise. At 3.20am on the 9th of April, we were woken by the gut-ripping roar of the police helicopter and 2500 gendarmes attacking the zone with armoured vehicles (APCs), bulldozers, rubber bullets, drones, 200 cameras, and 11,000 tear gas and stun grenades, injuring over 300 of us in under a week. It was France's biggest police operation since May 1968, all because, as anthropologist David Graeber wrote, 'the French state could not let an example of a place run without police, via bottom up forms of organising, against capitalism and the ravages of our natural world, continue.'[7] After destroying over forty of our living spaces a cease fire was negotiated, and we are now being forced to 'legalise' our farms and lives as private individual property. We are creatively hacking their bureaucracy, and fighting to keep the land as a commons.

Even if we lose this battle for the commons, the forest remains a forest. The airport will only be a ghost now. The ZAD has become an international icon of a Utopia in resistance. Countless people hold its picture in their minds, like one might carry the image of a great work of art: an image of hope in dark times. Holding back the monoculture machine, decolonising a place from capital, opening it up as somewhere that enables forms of life to flourish, connect, and differentiate: that is what is beautiful. That is the aim and aesthetics of an art of life.[8]

1. The Invisible Committee, *To Our Friends* (New York: Autonomedia, 2014).

2. Suzi Gablik, *The Reenchantment of Art* (New York: Thames and Hudson, 1991).

3. Henri Lefebvre, *Everyday Life in the Modern World*, trans. by Sacha Rabinovitch (New York and London: Continuum, 2002), p. 204.

4. Michel Foucault, *The Foucault Reader*, ed. by Paul Rabinow (New York: Pantheon, 1984), p. 350.

5. 'What if I were to think art was just paying attention?' Allan Kaprow, *Essays on the Blurring of Art and Life*, ed. by Jeff Kelley, expanded ed. (Berkeley: University of California Press, 2003), p. 202.

6. For updates in English on the situation at the ZAD see *Zad for ever* <https://zadforever.blog/>.

7. David Graeber in *Eloge des mauvaises herbes: Ce que nous devons à la ZAD*, ed. by Jade Lindgaard (Paris: Liens qui libèrent, 2018).

8. For a longer vision of the ZAD including writings by John Jordan, see Mauvaise Troupe and friends, *LA ZAD / THE ZONE TO DEFEND: A Liberated Territory Against an Airport and Its World* (Minneapolis: Canary Press, forthcoming).

ACTIONS

PROVOCATION

GUILLERMO GÓMEZ-PEÑA

TITLE

'PHILOSOPHICAL TANTRUM' #10: ON ART, IMAGINATION, DEMOCRACY, CENSORSHIP, HOPE, ETC.

Guillermo Gómez-Peña is a performance artist, writer, activist, radical pedagogue, and director of the performance troupe La Pocha Nostra. Born in Mexico City, he moved to the US in 1978. His performance work and eleven books have contributed to the debates on cultural diversity, border culture, and US-Mexico relations. His art work has been presented at over eight hundred venues across the US, Canada, Latin America, Europe, Russia, South Africa, and Australia. A MacArthur Fellow, Bessie, and American Book Award winner, he is a regular contributor for newspapers and magazines in the US, Mexico, and Europe, and a contributing editor to *TDR: The Drama Review* (NYU-MIT). He is a Senior Fellow in the Hemispheric Institute of Performance and Politics, and in 2012 he was named Samuel Hoi Fellow by USA Artists.

Guillermo is one of LADA's Patrons and has contributed to numerous LADA projects. With La Pocha Nostra he created *Ex Centris (A Living Diorama of Fetish-ized Others)* for You Are Here, the Live Art programme for the Liverpool Biennial (2002), and for *Live Culture* at Tate Modern (2003). *Mapa/Corpo* was presented as part of *Performing Rights* at Queen Mary University of London (2006).

The text presented here is adapted from Guillermo's keynote for Weathering the Storm, the 2015 Live Art UK gathering. A previous iteration was published in *TDR: The Drama Review*.

On democracy & art...

In the name of art, people have crucified themselves as a form of protest, created fake corporations to denounce environmental injustice, and printed useless money and conceptual passports to invent their own countries. In the name of art, people invent mysterious languages, religions, communities, and architectures that are more congruent with our needs and aspirations.

Artists & writers have envisioned a parallel universe in which our contemporaries can engage in meaningful forms of freedom and creativity. In this sense, true democracy can only exist in the imagination of art & literature.

Dear reader,

My only hope is in your eyes; because, as my distant companion, you are my salvation and source of hope, and together we can change the course of history, even if only for the duration of this text. Let us imagine a parallel world, just the two of us.

Snap your fingers with me.

I say...

In my world, there is food, clothing, housing, medical attention, and education for everyone.

In my world there's no difference between sameness and difference and borders are easy to cross, especially those from South to North

In my world, there are no 'illegal aliens'; no 'others'; no good or bad guys; there are no terrorists or crime cartels.

In my world, there are no guns, because there is no fear.

In my world there is a place for everyone, even if only for the duration of a performance.

I say...

In my world, people solve their disagreements through performance rituals and psycho-magic actions.

In my world the laws of poetry and quantum physics rule everyday life and all TV stations are run by artists and poets.

Beautiful statements, que no? But are they 'true'? In OUR world, they are.

But if I say, 'Art can save lives,' is this a correct statement? How so?

When a battered woman comes out of a performance determined to leave her violent husband, I'd say, art is working. When a gangbanger emerges from a performance thinking 'hey, symbolic acts can be powerful ways to express my anger. I'm exchanging my gun for a video camera,' I say we are definitely making a difference.

But let's face it: There are more efficient ways to save lives. What about volunteering for doctors without borders? Creating a citizen watchdog group to monitor police brutality with video cameras in your city? The fact is that first and foremost, we make art because we love it and doing good with it is an effect we welcome. But we don't like to talk about this because we badly want to believe that art is necessary… Is it? I think it is.

I think democracy cannot thrive without art; without the critical voice of the artist constantly testing its limits and possibilities… without the ethical mirror of art reflecting the distorted features of power. But do you think I am exaggerating?

The fact is that democracy, if done right, is the most difficult and painstaking form of government. It has to be a daily conscious project for every citizen, like Live Art is for us. Democracy is not working because most of us don't want to put the effort to have a democracy. So we mostly elect stooges; or don't vote at all; or allow ourselves to be tricked; or all of the above.

The question here is why is western society NOT listening to its artists? Why are so many artists and intellectuals, currently unemployed & uninsured like myself, or surviving from a job unrelated to our art? Why is this a much higher number than, say, unemployed doctors, lawyers, or computer programmers? Does this have anything to do with anti-intellectualism? Or with the death of democracy?

On censorship

The United States is no longer 'the land of opportunity' it once was, or the 'most advanced democracy' it claims to be. It is now the land of censorship, isolationism, xenophobia, and Puritanism; one of the most parochial places on earth; and perhaps the only Christian democracy left in the continuously shrinking 'free world' it claims to lead.

Our political class, like yours, is obsessed with closing our borders and keeping 'outsiders' from entering. Since 9/11, the USA's Immigration and Naturalization Service (the INS) has denied La Pocha Nostra (my company) dozens of visas to bring Mexican, Cuban, and Colombian artists to the United States to work with us. In this sense, the border has become another form of censorship, and cultural exchange is now a nostalgic project of the late 20th century. So far, what has saved La Pocha Nostra from closing our doors is international touring. Sixty percent of our budget now comes from other countries.

The imposed culture of panic, prohibition and high security permeating every corner of society—including our arts organisations—has created an incendiary environment for the production of critical culture. We are being offered budgets that are half what we used to work with in the pre-Bush era. As a result, we can only present small-scale projects in the United States, and under technically primitive conditions.

On hope...

The fact is... I don't believe in government. I don't think it is possible to correct 'the problem' from within the system. We've all tried. It doesn't work. The system is the problem, and politics is the art of manipulating the system to perpetrate problems. Being a 'radical' within the system is a mere prestidigitation act; part of the spectacle of radicalism that media consumers require to feel alive and authenticate their x-treme designer identities.

In my world, the vatos I would propose as political candidates are not even politicians. They are artists and literati, visionaries not functionaries. The country I would like to live in only exists in planet poetry, and planet performance, where imagination is the only law, art is part of everyday life, and everyone practices what they believe. Imagination is my nation; that's where I wish to live and die.

The crucial questions here are...

Where does one find the spiritual energy to continue when you don't believe in mainstream politics, and institutionalised religion gives you the creeps? What to do when you are too old to belong to a subculture and participate in the global rave, and too strange to get a chic job in academia?

Where do we locate our dissent when dissent is a corporate product, an HBO special, a perfume, the scent of dissent *(imagine a bad French accent)*, anarchic, extreme, suicíde... or when teens can simply wear a t-shirt that says, 'art *is* resistance' and think the job is done?

What to do when all the master discourses and epic narratives of hope are bankrupt? Which is the best energy drink? Do male enhancers really work?

Since 9/11, as my meta-horizons began to fade, I became obsessed with hope, with finding its spiritual source and location. Is hope a deep feeling of expansion located on the chest, the abdomen, or the sphincter? Is it a distant marker in the horizon that directs our actions, or a mysterious spiritual energy that propels you into the unknown against the laws of gravity? Is hope a matter of quantum theory? A form of poetic will? Is hope by definition illogical and unreasonable? Can hope be nurtured through art and education? Does hope put you at odds with the state?

Will I vote in the next elections? Unlike the presidential candidates, my hope is not connected to God, Country, or Economy. My hope is located... somewhere else; in obscure books, films, and performances;

in small communities that exist under the radar of the media; in the political streets of our cities; in the eyes of my students; in late night conversations at a bar full of outsiders; in animal species I've never seen; in the wisdom of indigenous cultures. My hope is always located on the other side of the border… or the mirror… or the page. In this very moment, my hope is located… in your hands.

Is love still an option? Love in times of war, disease, and global warming? Love amidst earthquakes and floods? Under red alerts and a suspicious purple moon coloured by smog and chemical waste? Is it possible to love as if 9/11 and the Invasion of Iraq never happened; as if our governments were true democracies and active members of the world community? Can we love as if the Earth wasn't mortally wounded? As if we had open borders and open hearts?

I think we can… Love can certainly help us continue but only so far, a few more miles, a couple of months, and then, we encounter yet another abyss…

And what about art? Is art our salvation?

In the past art has saved me from deportation, jail, and mental hospitals. True. Naming my anti-social behaviour 'art' has saved me from the jaws of the police & the border patrol. But I talk about art as critical thought and embodied theory, not as object or market. I talk about art as in uncompromising art practice, not as in 'the art world'.

The art world is full of compromises, humiliation rituals, and complicated power negotiations. It takes a special skill to survive it. If you comply too much you lose your voice, your sharp-edges, your *culo*. You become someone else you dislike. And one day, when you least expect it, they send you back to the margins where you wait and wait for a second chance that rarely comes…

…or should you succeed in preserving your ethics, uncompromised, you will eventually be rendered so marginal that no one will know that it was your choice to remain inconsequential.

And what if my art leads to my own death? What if I die in the service of art like the Italian live artist Pippa Bacca who was tragically murdered in Turkey a few years ago as she travelled across Eastern Europe as 'a bride for peace'?

So, between being an art world darling *culipronto* and being poor and bitter, I rather choose to be… an uncompromising dandy; an insider/outsider; a performing contradiction if you will.

Contra-dicción is the name of my favourite lotion. And my job as a performance artist is to avoid simplistic definitions, trends and adjectives, to remain slippery and evanescent, while I continue to ask irritating questions in original ways. What a bizarre job! And I get paid for it… kind of.

Merde, I'm so moody today, I feel like an existential wolf that went to sleep in the

Arctic Circle and woke up on the rooftop of a Manhattan skyscraper.

I wonder if community is still a source of hope?

Community is one of our obsessions. We all long to belong to a larger 'we' because we are obsessed precisely with what we lack.

But you know locas, communities of sameness drive me up the wall, conjure my asthma, give me acute vertigo and claustrophobia. My community is not confined by ideological, national, or ethnic boundaries. Mine is a community of difference, and therefore it is fragmented, ever changing and... temporary. And that's how I like it.

Besides, no one belongs to only one community, not even the Christian Right, not even my Chihuahua *Sigfrid ne Babalu*. He hangs out with rodents, marsupials, and ghosts.

Like Babalu's, my peers are scattered all over the pinche planet, howling outsiders jumping all over the planet. Some of you are my peers; others are total strangers in a virtual community of strangers. I long for my peers every night and hopefully, you long for me as well, and every now and then, when we get together, we lick each other's wounds and dance until the morning after like rabid kangaroos, and then we fall asleep in a circle of accidental bodies, and we dream of a better place and a better present.

In this imaginary place we dream about, artists and writers are actually needed and taken care of. We all have universal medical insurance, a decent low-rider car, and a great studio space in the bohemian hood of our choice. We don't have to write grants. And we get paid decently for what we do; and what we do matters. We make important decisions and fix concrete problems for society.

In this imaginary place we dream about, schools, hospitals, prisons, and even airports are re-conceptualised and designed by artists; the daily papers are written by philosophers, novelists, and poets. We have ongoing access to electronic media where we make people think, remember, imagine, and laugh. Politicians and religious leaders consult our opinions before making important decisions. We collaborate with progressive doctors, activists, educators, lawyers, priests, and socially-conscious scientists in the great project of co-imagining a better future for the borderless community of humankind.

Sounds so corny but so appealing, que no?

In this imaginary place we dream about there is a place for everyone.

Well... almost everyone...

Overleaf left: Áine Phillips, *Red Weight*, Galway (2006). Image Catherine Leanachain.

Overleaf right: Stacy Makishi, *Lifted* (2008). Image Vick Ryder.

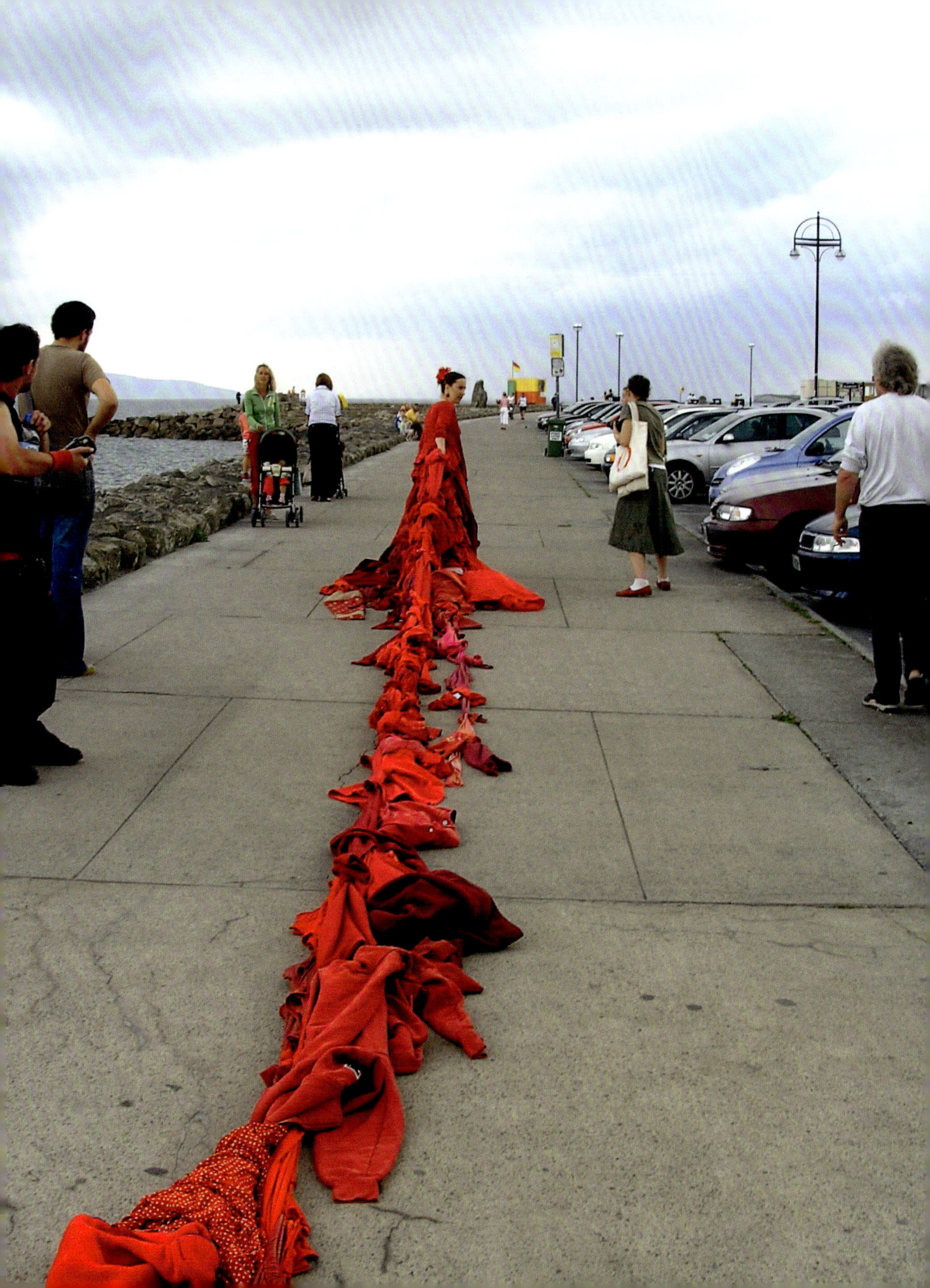

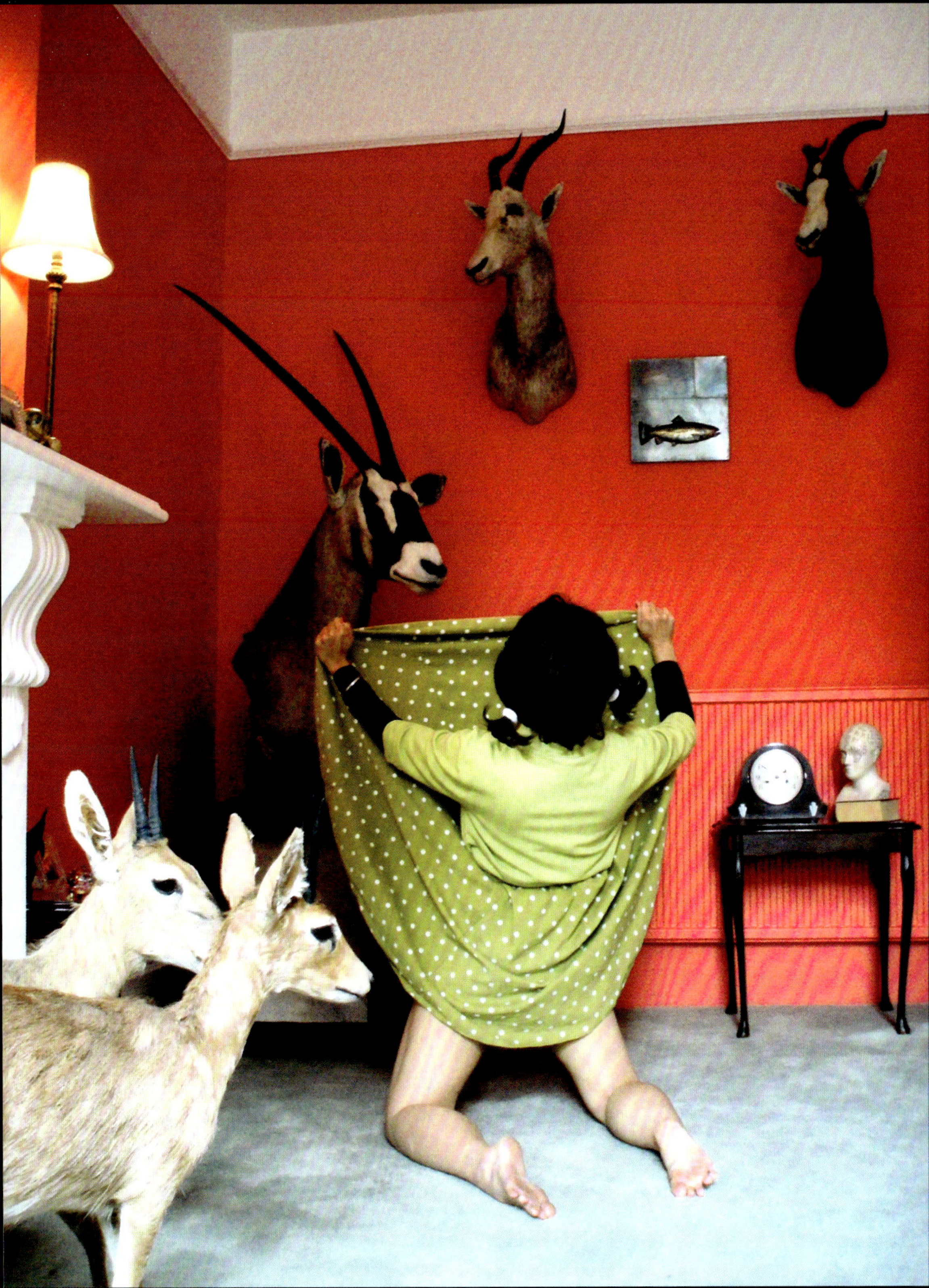

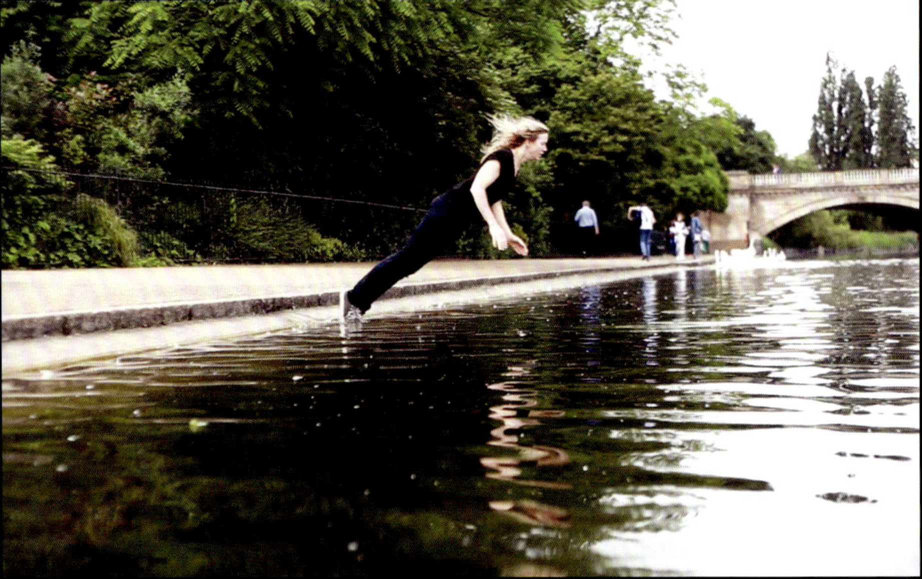

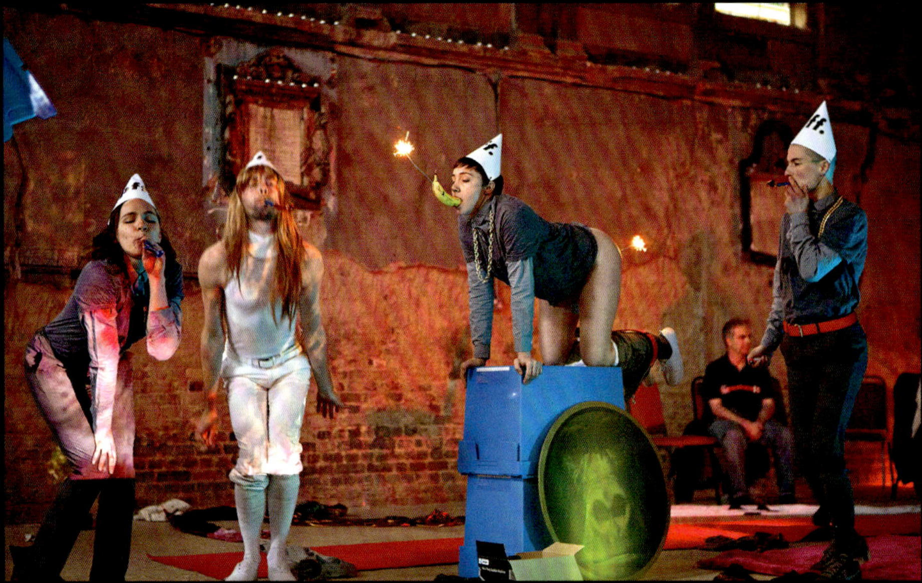

Top: Amy Sharrocks, *London Falling* (2013). Image Iris Long.

Bottom: Oreet Ashery, *Party for Freedom, Party for Hire*, performance still (2013), commissioned by *Performance Matters* and Artangel. Image Manuel Vason.

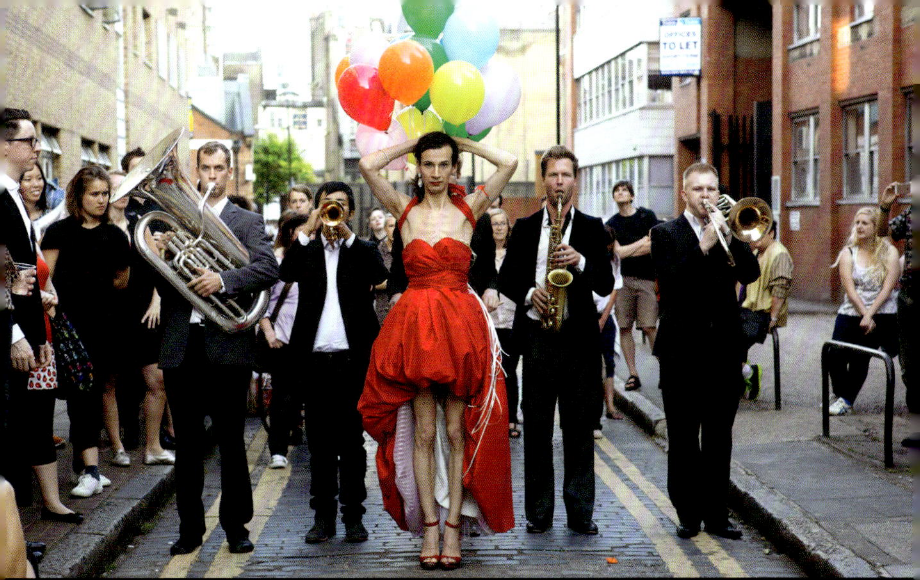

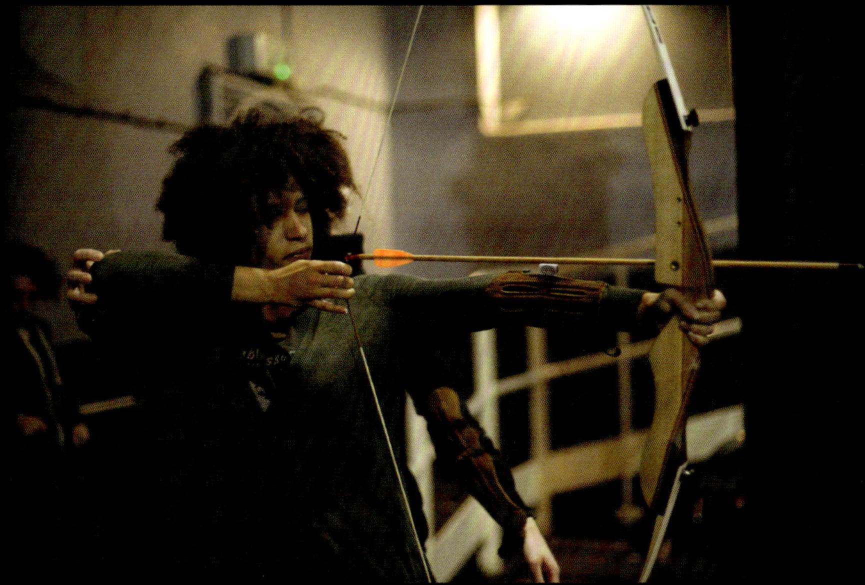

Top: Nando Messias, *The Sissy's Progress* (2014). Image Loredana Denicola.

Bottom: Tania El Khoury and Abigail Conway, *FAF (Female Armed Forces)*, DIY (2015). Image Tania El Khoury.

Overleaf: Nicola Hunter, *Raising The Skirt*, DIY, Newcastle (2014). Image by Dawn Felicia Knox.

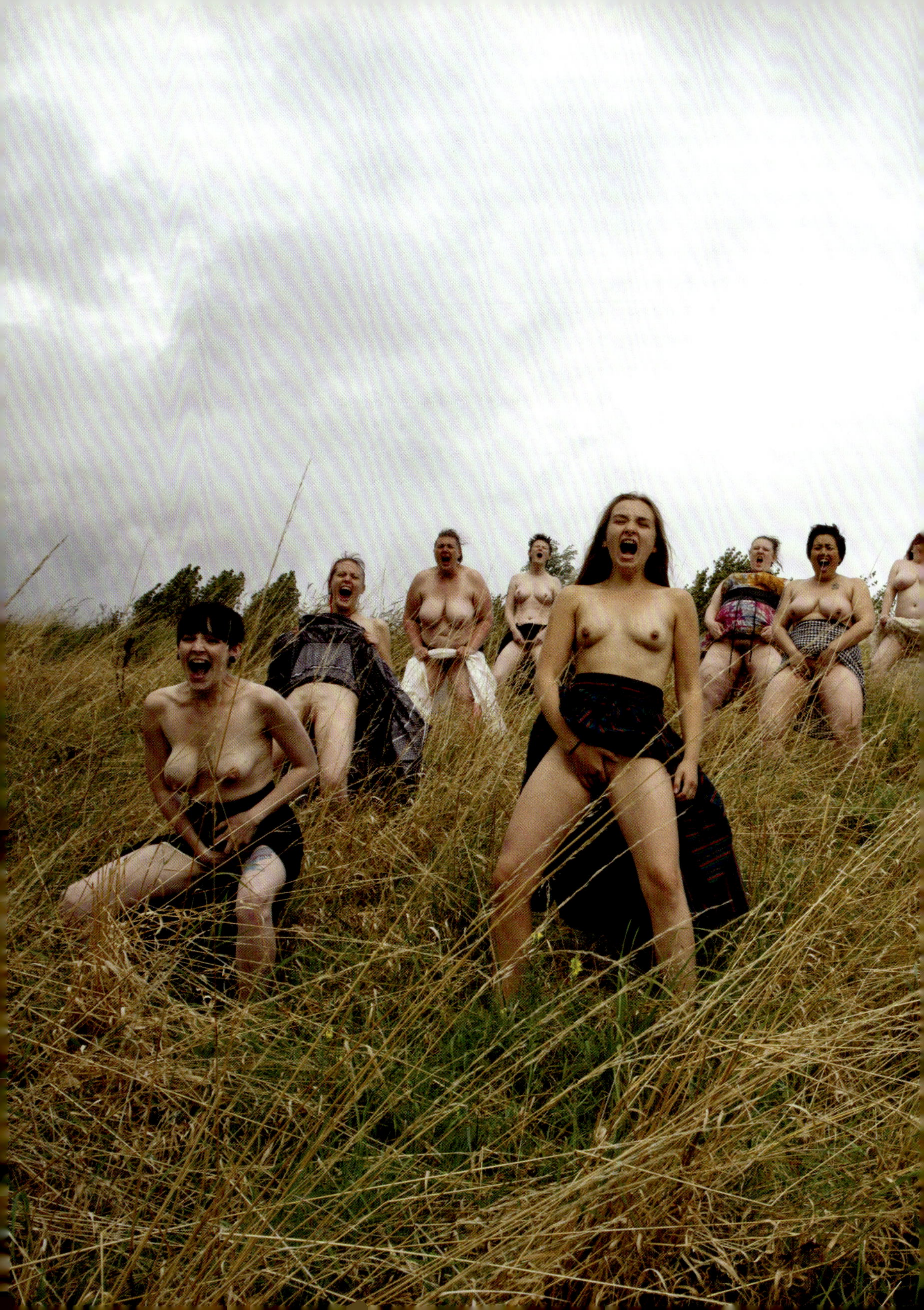

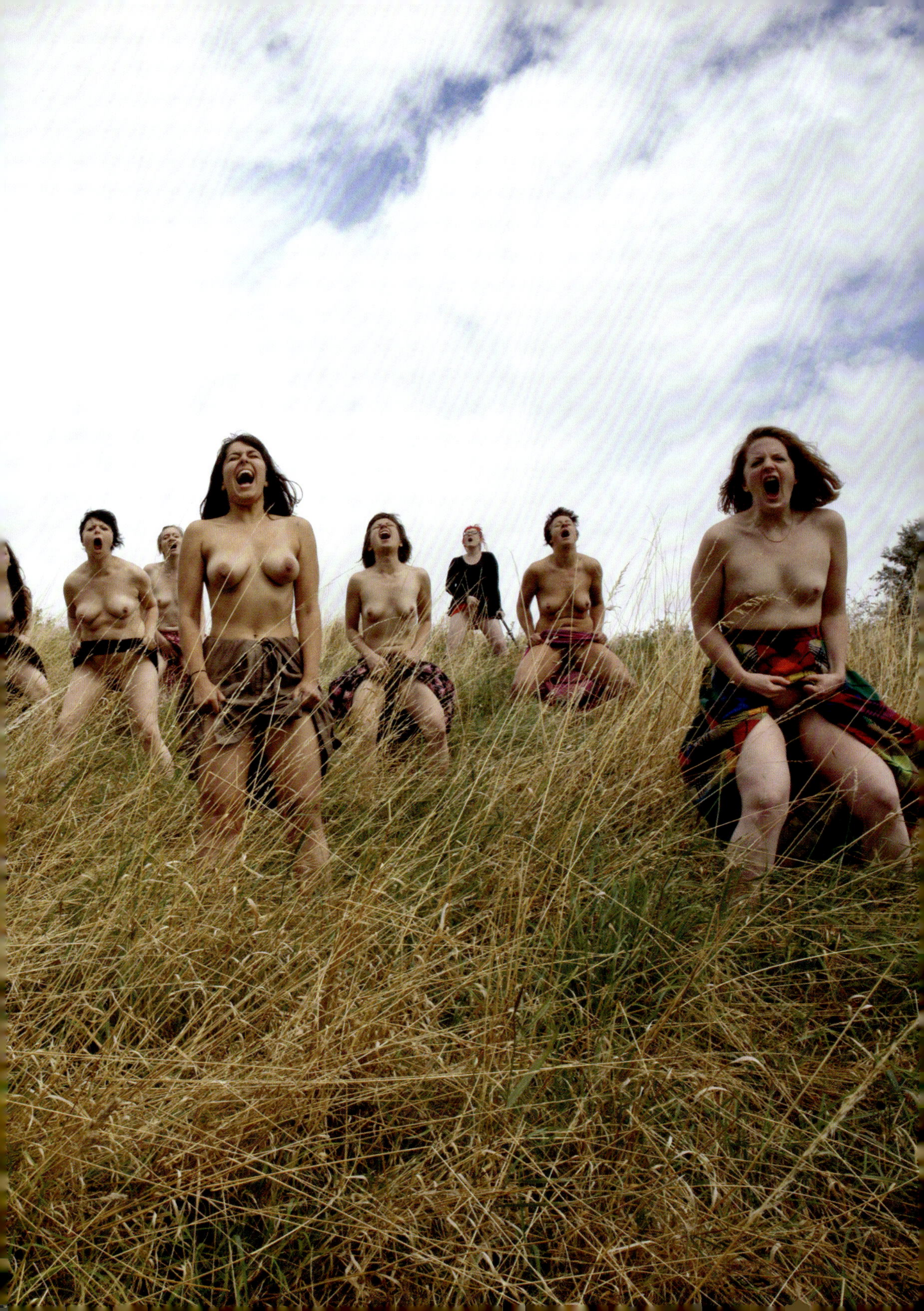

TIMELINE

1999

Lois Keidan and Catherine Ugwu launch the Live Art Development Agency as a London Arts Board Regular Funded Organisation

The first offices are at Truman's Brewery, Brick Lane, East London

PROJECTS

British Festival of Visual Theatre, Critical Practice 6 (with Total Theatre)

OPPORTUNITIES

One To One—Individual Artists' Bursaries in Live Art 1999/2000

Everything You Wanted To Know About Live Art But Were Afraid To Ask

East End Collaborations (EEC) Platform

2000

Catherine Ugwu leaves to work independently on large scale public projects; Daniel Brine joins as Associate Director

PROJECTS

x.trax, Green Room, Manchester

OPPORTUNITIES

One To One—Individual Artists' Bursaries in Live Art 2000/2001

EEC Platform

Everything You Wanted To Know About Live Art But Were Afraid To Ask

PUBLICATIONS

Adrian Heathfield, *Small Acts: Performance, the Millennium and the Marking of Time*, with Black Dog Publishing

2001

PROJECTS

EEC Platform

Everything You Wanted To Know About Live Art But Were Afraid To Ask

Ego, conversations between artists and scientists

Take 6, for Artsonline

OPPORTUNITIES

One To One—Individual Artists' Bursaries in Live Art 2001/2002

Focus Live Art

EEC Platform

Everything You Wanted To Know About Live Art But Were Afraid To Ask

Note: all London, unless noted otherwise

2002

PROJECTS

Liverpool Biennial: You Are Here, Bluecoat, Liverpool

Reading Performance Art From Then till Now, A Short History of Performance: Part One, Whitechapel Gallery

Marked, a season of work exploring the body as site, metaphor and material, Arnolfini, Bristol

OPPORTUNITIES

DIY:1, London—workshops *by* artists *for* artists

One To One—Individual Artists´ Bursaries in Live Art 2002/2003

EEC Platform

Everything You Wanted To Know About Live Art But Were Afraid To Ask

PUBLISHING

Documenting Live! moti roti's Wigs of Wonderment

Manuel Vason, *Exposures*, with Black Dog Publishing

2003

PROJECTS

Janine Antoni, Whitechapel Gallery

Live Culture, Tate Modern

OPPORTUNITIES

Thinker In Residence: Barby Arsante

One To One—Individual Artists' Bursaries in Live Art 2003/3004

EEC Platform

Everything You Wanted To Know About Live Art But Were Afraid To Ask

2004

LADA moves to Rochelle School in Arnold Circus, East London

PROJECTS

Activations, Tate Modern and Tate Liverpool

OPPORTUNITIES

DIY:2, London—workshops *by* artists *for* artists

Thinker In Residence: Maxx Shurley

One To One—Individual Artists' Bursaries in Live Art 2004/2005

Small Talk

EEC Platform

Everything You Wanted To Know About Live Art But Were Afraid To Ask

PUBLISHING

Joshua Sofaer, *The Performance Pack*

Adrian Heathfield, ed., *Live: Art and Performance*, with Tate Publishing

2005

Hannah Crosson joins as Administrator

PROJECTS

Variety Acts, De La Warr Pavilion, Bexhill-on-Sea

China Live, UK tour

OPPORTUNITIES

EEC Platform

Everything You Wanted To Know About Live Art But Were Afraid To Ask

Thinker In Residence: Manuel Vason

DIY:3, London and the South East—workshops *by* artists *for* artists

One To One—Individual Artists' Bursaries in Live Art 2005/2006

PUBLISHING

Daniel Brine and Shu Yang, eds, *China Live*, with Chinese Arts Centre and Live Art UK

2006

Hannah Crosson leaves to join New Work Network; Andrew Mitchelson joins as Company and Resource Manager

PROJECTS

Performance Studies International (Psi)12: Performing Rights, with Queen Mary University of London

Restock, Rethink, Reflect One: Live Art and Race

Liverpool Biennial: Liverpool Live 06, at Bluecoat, Liverpool

VITAL 06: International Chinese Live Art Festival, at Chinese Arts Centre, Manchester

OPPORTUNITIES

Thinker In Residence: FrenchMottershead

Thinker In Residence: Adrien Sina

Janice Antoni: Lore and Other Convergences

EEC Platform

Everything You Wanted To Know About Live Art But Were Afraid To Ask

PUBLISHING

Tim Etchells and Adrian Heathfield, *Somewhere Near Variety* DVD

2007

PROJECTS

Live in Prague

Live Art UK: *Check In/ Check Out* at The Great Eastern Hotel

SPILL Festival of Performance Symposium

Restock, Rethink, Reflect One: Live Art and Race

Performing Rights: Vienna

OPPORTUNITIES

DIY:4, national—workshops *by* artists *for* artists

EEC Platform

Everything You Wanted To Know About Live Art But Were Afraid To Ask

PUBLISHING

Joining the Dots DVD

Richard Dedomenici, *Normalisation of Deviance* DVD

Oreet Ashery DVD

Programme Notes: Case studies for locating experimental theatre

2008

Daniel Brine leaves to become Director of Performance Space Sydney; CJ Mitchell joins as Co Director; Andrew Mitchelson becomes Projects Manager; Maria Agiomyrgiannaki joins as Administrator

PROJECTS

Live Art Unpacked at Khoj Live 08, Delhi

Live Art Unpacked, Geneva

ARCO 2008—Trans:actions, Madrid

Restock, Rethink, Reflect One: Live Art and Race

Performing Rights: Glasgow

OPPORTUNITIES

DIY:5, national—workshops *by* artists *for* artists

Legacy: Thinker in Residence Awards, Tim Etchells and Anne Bean

EEC Platform

Everything You Wanted To Know About Live Art But Were Afraid To Ask

PUBLISHING

David A. Bailey, Lois Keidan, and Rajni Shah, eds, *Documenting Live*

Howard Matthew, *in practice* DVD

The Live Art Almanac

Aaron Williamson: Performance / Video / Collaboration, with KIOSK

2009

LADA celebrates its 10th anniversary

Maria Agiomyrgiannaki leaves to start an MA

PROJECTS

Tenth Anniversary Short Films and Special Events

Labour Practices: Ethics of Service and Ideas of Labour in Performance

Restock, Rethink, Reflect Two: Live Art and Disability

Legacy: Thinker in Residence Awards

OPPORTUNITIES

DIY:6, national—workshops *by* artists *for* artists

Thinker In Residence: Mary Paterson

Young People's Resource Pack on Live Art

EEC Platform 10th Anniversary

Everything You Wanted To Know About Live Art But Were Afraid To Ask

PUBLISHING

10th Anniversary Editions:

Joshua Sofaer, *Performance Artist Paper Doll*

Harminder Singh Judge, *For-Skin For-You-Ever*

Marcia Farquhar, *Rosebud Cupcake*

Tim Etchells, *Heroes & Heroines of Live Art (First 110)* Poster

Tim Etchells, *Heroes & Heroines of Live Art (First 110)* T-Shirts

Richard Dedomenici, *Build Your Own Replica Live Art Development Agency*

Anne Bean, *My Present in N O W*

Franko B, *My … hurts*

Manuel Vason, *10 Minutes For 10 Years*

Yara El-Sherbini, *Decision Maker Pen*

Áine Phillips, *Live Autobiography* DVD

George Chakravarthi, *unseen* DVD

Adrien Sina, *Farafin a ni Toubabou—black and white ethical projects* DVD

Everything You Still Wanted to Know About Live Art but Were Afraid To Ask DVD

Adrian Heathfield and Tehching Hsieh, *Out of Now: The Lifeworks of Tehching Hsieh*, with MIT Press

Oreet Ashery, *Dancing with Men*

Marcia Farquhar's 12 Shooters

Joshua Sofaer, *The Many Headed Monster*

2010

Season Butler joins as Administrator; Aaron Wright joins as Programme Coordinator

PROJECTS

Performance Matters: Performing Idea

Oreet Ashery and Larissa Sansour's Falafel Road Residency

'LOUDER THAN BOMBS' Art, Action & Activism, Stanley Picker Gallery

Restock, Rethink, Reflect Two: Live Art and Disability

Anne Bean, *TAPS: Improvisations with Paul Burwell*, Dilston Grove

OPPORTUNITIES

DIY:7, national—workshops *by* artists *for* artists

FRESH AiR

FRESH TIPS

PUBLISHING

Ron Athey and Lee Adams, *Visions of Excess* DVD

Ansuman Biswas, *Relics* DVD

Curious, *Gut Feelings Trilogy* DVD

In Time: A Collection of Live Art Case Studies, with Live Art UK

2011

Season Butler leaves to undertake a PhD

PROJECTS

Floating Cinema—Ian Giles, *A Smaller Sound, A Bigger Crowd*, with UP Projects

Joshua Sofaer, *Life Lecture*

PERFORMANSSI 2011, Turku, Finland

Access All Areas, Live Art and Disability

Performance Matters: Trashing Performance

Restock, Rethink, Reflect Two: Live Art and Disability

OPPORTUNITIES

DIY:8, national—workshops *by* artists *for* artists

FRESH AiR

FRESH TIPS

Legacy: Thinker in Residence Awards

PUBLISHING

Aaron Williamson, *Quick Clips and Short Cuts* DVD

Monica Ross, *Acts of Memory 2005–2010* DVD

Writing Not Yet Thought: Hélène Cixous in Conversation with Adrian Heathfield DVD

Mat Fraser, *Devolving the Mutant* DVD

The Live Art Almanac Volume 2

2012

LADA moves to The White Building in Hackney Wick, East London

Alex Eisenberg joins as Digital Manager; Aaron Wright becomes Programmes Manager; Katy Baird joins as Coordinator; Andrew Michelson leaves to pursue his own practice

PROJECTS

M21: From the Medieval to the 21st Century, Much Wenlock, with DASH

Performance Matters: Potentials of Performance

Restock, Rethink, Reflect Two: on Live Art and Disability

OPPORTUNITIES

SPILL National Platform 2012

DIY:9, national—workshops *by* artists *for* artists

PUBLISHING

The Disabled Avant-Garde, *Bite The Hand That Feeds!* DVD

M21: From the Medieval to the 21st Century, with DASH

Mikhail Karikis, *XENON* DVD

Poshya Kakil, *Knitting Iron* DVD

Brian Lobel, *CANCER, CANCER, CANCER, CANCER, CANCER* DVD

David Hoyle, *Revelations* DVD

Adrian Heathfield and Amelia Jones, eds, *Perform, Repeat, Record: Live Art in History*, with Intellect Books

Access All Areas: Live Art and Disability

2013

PROJECTS

Dangerous Border Crossings, in collaboration with Something Human

Floating Cinema–Tim Bromage, *It Could Only Happen Here: Jim Dahl's unreal Boat tour*, with UP Projects

Restock Rethink Reflect Three: Live Art and Feminism

Temporary?, on art and ethics

Just Like A Woman, City of Women, Slovenia

OPPORTUNITIES

(Re)Fresh

DIY:10, national—workshops *by* artists *for* artists

PUBLISHING

Gavin Butt and Ben Walters, *This Is Not a Dream* DVD

Mel Brimfield, *This is Performance Art* DVD

Oreet Ashery, *Party For Freedom* DVD

Adrian Heathfield, *No Such Thing As Rest: A Walk with Brian Massumi* DVD

Adrian Heathfield, *Transfigured Night: A Conversation with Alphonso Lingis* DVD

The Gluts, *Complete Works* DVD

Wrights & Sites, *4 X 4 SCREENS* DVD

Project O, *A Contemporary Struggle*

Maddy Costa, *I see a fake moon rising: Live Art in the public realm*, with Live Art UK

Jordan McKenzie, *Occupations 1996–2013* DVD

Forest Fringe, *Paper Stages*, with Live Art UK

Performance Matters Archive

The Live Art Almanac: Volume 3, with Oberon Books

Programme Notes: Case studies for locating experimental theatre, Volume 2, with Oberon Books

Dear Stranger, I love you: the ethics of community in Rajni Shah Projects' Glorious, with Lancaster University

Dominic Johnson, ed., *Pleading in the Blood: The Art and Performances of Ron Athey*, Intellect Live book series

Mary Kate Connolly, ed., *Throwing the Body Into The Fight: A Portrait of Raimund Hoghe*, Intellect Live book series

Tim Etchells, *While You Are With Us Here Tonight*

2014

LADA celebrates its 15th anniversary

PROJECTS

LADA at Venice International Performance Art Week

LADA 15th Anniversary, *ALAG: A Live Art Gala*

LADA 15th Anniversary, *15 Minutes With...* podcasts

Performance from the Edge, SPILL Festival, Ipswich

Remote Performances, in collaboration with London Fieldworks and Resonance FM

Performing Rights, Encuentro, Montreal

Floating Cinema—Leah Lovett, *Contraband*, with UP Projects

Zierle and Carter, *Between Lands: A Sense of Belonging Enquiry*

Access All Areas: Live Art and Disability (New York Edition)

Restock Rethink Reflect Three: Live Art and Feminism

2015

OPPORTUNITIES

DIY:11, national—workshops *by* artists *for* artists

Live Art Producer Residencies

FEM FRESH

PUBLISHING

15th Anniversary Editions:

- Hugo Glendinning, *Tea Break/Illusion*
- George Chakravarthi, *Barflies*
- Tim Etchells, *Look Away*
- Zierle & Carter, *Under Cover*
- Hugo Glendinning and Manuel Vason, *Double Exposures*
- Rosa Frank and Raimund Hoghe, *Throwing the Body Into the Fight*

Janez Jansa, *Life II [in Progress]*

HINCH: A film about Ian Hinchliffe DVD

Manuel Vason, *Double Exposures*, with Intellect Books

Bettina Knaup and Beatrice Ellen Stammer, eds, *Re.act. feminism #2—a performing archive*, with Verlag fur Moderne Kuns

LADA becomes an Arts Council England National Portfolio Organisation

PROJECTS

Through the Looking Glass: performances to watch and be part of, with Heart of Glass, St Helens

Double Your Money with Scottee, Royal Vauxhall Tavern

FANON Now, the legacy of 'Mirage Enigmas Of Race, Difference & Desire'

Old Dears, Chelsea Theatre

The Arthole Cockle Medal for Live Art Philantrophy, by Joshua Sofaer

Just Like A Woman: New York Edition, Abrons Arts Center

Just Like A Woman: London Edition, Chelsea Theatre

The Art of Noises: Where Live Art meets Music, Latitude Festival

dis/placed, with Counterpoints Arts

Performance and Politics in the 1970s, Whitechapel Gallery

Documenting Intimacy, with Brian Lobel and Marisa Zanotti

Awkward Bastards symposium: Rethinking Ideas Around Diversity, with DASH and mac

Weathering The Storm, Live Art UK Associates Gathering, Bristol

Take the money and run? on ethics, funding and art, with Artsadmin and Home Live Art

Restock Rethink Reflect Three: on Live Art and Feminism

LADA Screens

OPPORTUNITIES

The Arthole Artist's Award

DIY:12, national—workshops *by* artists *for* artists

FRESH AiR

PUBLISHING

Florian Malzacher, ed., *Not Just a Mirror: Looking for the Political Theatre of Today*, with House on Fire and Alexander Verlag

Bruce Gilchrist, Jo Joelson and Tracey Warr, eds, *Remote Performances in Nature and Architecture*, with Ashgate Publishing

Lois Weaver and Jen Harvie, eds, *The Only Way Home Is Through the Show: Performance Work of Lois Weaver*, Intellect Live book series

Katherine Araniello, *The Dinner Party Revisited*

Adrian Heathfield and Tehching Hsieh, *Out of Now: The Lifeworks of Tehching Hsieh*, with MIT Press (paperback edition)

Lois Weaver, *Are We There Yet?—a Study Room Guide on Live Art and Feminism*

Áine Phillips, ed, *Performance Art in Ireland: A History*, with Intellect Books

2016

Megan Vaughan joins as Programmes Manager; Amy Poole joins as Marketing Coordinator; Aaron Wright leaves to become Director of Fierce Festival, Birmingham

PROJECTS

Sibylle Peters, *PLAYING UP*, Tate Modern with Tate Early Years and Families

The Residents, The Wellcome Collection

Ouch: Pain and Performance screenings, London and Ljubliana

Restock, Rethink, Reflect Four: Live Art and Privilege

Helena Goldwater, *Glimpses of Before—1970s Performance Art in the UK*

LADA Screens

OPPORTUNITIES

Marcia Farquhar's Arthole Artist's Award

DIY:13, national—workshops *by* artists *for* artists

FRESH AiR

PUBLISHING

Elke van Campenhout and Lilia Mestre, eds, *Turn, Turtle! Reenacting The Institute*, with House on Fire and Alexander Verlag

The Live Art Almanac Volume 4, with Oberon Books

Dominic Johnson and Deirdre Heddon, eds, *It's All Allowed: The Performances of Adrian Howells*, Intellect Live book series

Sibylle Peters, *PLAYING UP: A Live Art Game for Kids and Adults*

2017

LADA moves to The Garrett Centre, Bethnal Green, East London

Finn Love joins as Coordinator; Katy Baird leaves to pursue her own practice

PROJECTS

KAPUTT: The Academy of Destruction, Tate Exchange, with Tate Early Years and Families

ABsence: Awkward Bastards symposium 2, with DASH and mac

Extravagant Bodies: Crime and Punishment, with Kontejner and KIOSK

Performance Magazine Online

Restock, Rethink, Reflect Four: Live Art and Priviledge

Afterlives, Queen Mary University of London

Blood Counts, Science Gallery, London

MAP 3: Archiving 'Asia', with Something Human

Ron Vawter's *Roy Cohn/Jack Smith* for World AIDS Day

LADA Screens

OPPORTUNITIES

DIY:14, national—workshops *by* artists *for* artists

Thinker In Residence: Claire MacDonald

Thinker In Residence: Hester Chillingworth

Diverse Actions Leadership Bursaries, Season Butler and Joon Lynn Goh

PUBLISHING

Harriet Curtis and Martin Hargreaves, eds, *Kira O'Reilly: Untitled (Bodies)*, Intellect Live book series

Mary Paterson, *Imagination and Potential: Cherophobia by Noëmi Lakmaier*

Florian Malzacher and Joanna Warsza, eds, *Empty Stages, Crowded Flats: Performativity as Curatorial Strategy*, with House on Fire and Alexander Verlag

Giulia Palladini and Marco Pustianaz, eds, *Lexicon for an Affective Archive*, with Intellect Books and NinA

2018

Anna R. Burzynska, ed., *Joined Forces: Audience Participation in Theatre*, with House on Fire and Alexander Verlag

Sibylle Peters, *Live Art & Kids: A Study Room Guide*

Sibylle Peters, *Performing Research: A toolkit on how to conduct research projects with kids and adults*

Lois Weaver, *Know How: A Study Room Guide on working with older constituencies*

Lois Weaver, *Action Recipes: A toolkit of methodologies for working with older constituencies*

Elena Marchevska, *The Displaced & Privilege (Live Art in the age of hostility): A Study Room Guide on working with the displaced*

Elena Marchevska, *A toolkit for itinerant artists on methodologies for working with the displaced*

Megan Vaughan leaves to undertake a PhD, Finn Love becomes Programmes Manager, Joseph Morgan Schofield joins as Coordinator.

PROJECTS

Barby Asante, *The Library of Performing Rights* commission 2018

The Library of Performing Rights Open, with Aram Han Sifuente

Sheaf+Barley, *Weeding* at LADA

Sheaf+Barley, *The Mansford Window*, The Garrett Centre Commission 2018

Scottee 10

LADA Screens

Kids, Families, Gender and Live Art

Prancing Poodles and Preposterous Pugs—Live Art and other animals

Restock, Rethink, Reflect Four: Live Art and Privilege

OPPORTUNITIES

Launch of MA Live Art with Queen Mary University, London

DIY:15, national—workshops *by* artists *for* artists

DIY in North America

Diverse Actions Leadership Bursaries, Victoria Sin and Zinzi Minott

In residence—Sheaf+Barley, Oozing Gloop, Áine Phillips

PUBLISHING

Marquard Smith, *Solitary Pleasures*

Martin O'Brien, *Survival of the Sickest: The Art of Martin O'Brien*

Curious, *The Artists' Borderpanic Compendium*

Tanja Ostojić, *The Lexicon of Tanjas Ostojić*, with Museum of Modern and Contemporary Art, Rijeka

Franko B, *Because of Love: Franko B's Story*

Jen Harvie, ed., *Scottee: I Made It*

Scottee, *The Outsider's Handbook*

Lucy Hutson, *Everything In My Head At One Time In My Life*

Lisa Alexander, ed., *To You To You To You: Love Letters To A (Post)Europe*

Rob La Frenais, ed., *Anne Bean: Self Etc*, Intellect Live book series

Kelly Green, *Let's Get Classy: A Study Room Guide*

Kelly Green, *Ways of Getting Classy: A toolkit of methodologies*

Learning in Public: transEuropean Collaborations in Socially Engaged Art, with Create and Collaborative Arts Partnership Programme (CAPP)

INDEX

2012 Olympic Games, 9, 74, 77, 260
Abramović, Marina, 51, 64n5, 188
Access All Areas; see *Restock, Rethink, Reflect*
ACT UP, 279
Agency for Agency, 196, 256
AN Magazine, 138
Anderson, Gary; *see* Institute for the Art and Practice of Dissent at Home, The
ANTI Festival, 73, 90–96, 104
Antoni, Janine, 132
Araniello, Katherine; *see* Disabled Avant-Garde, The
Arnolfini, 74, 100
Art Not Oil Coalition, 178,
Arts Council (UK), 6, 8, 10, 18, 46, 73, 91, 129, 158, 194, 200, 228, 269
Artsadmin, 77, 92, 166, 178, 194
Asante, Barby, 20, 196, 235, 251, 252, 265–72
Ashery, Oreet, 300
Athey, Ron, 23, 54, 58, 62–63, 65, 81, 133, 240, 254, 273–82
Autograph, 266, 270, 272
Ayers, Robert, 208
Bailey, David A., 20, 265–72
Baird, Katy, 240
Baker, Bobby, 4–5, 213
Baldwin, James, 270–72
Barbican Centre, 198
Bartlett, Neil, 122
Bartram, Angela, 245
Battersea Arts Centre, 77
Bauhaus, 113, 170
Bausch, Pina, 82
BBC (British Broadcasting Corporation), 180, 256, 263
Bean, Anne, 133, 146, 196, 215–24
Beau, Dickie, 246–47
Ben-David, Efi, 220
Bethnal Green Working Men's Club, 130
Beyoncé, 266, 269, 281
Biggs, Bryan, 155–64, 190
Birch, Anna, 236
Biswas, Ansuman, 253
Black Market International, 216, 223
Black Mountain College, 113, 148
Blast Theory, 158
Block Universe, 154
Bluecoat, 156, 157–158, 159, 164, 185, 190
Boal, Augusto, 229
Boliver, Rocío, 56, 68–69
Bourdieu, Pierre, 62, 63
BP (British Petroleum), 73, 178
BP or Not BP, 178
Brett-Bailey, Christopher, 82
Brexit, 117, 119
Brine, Daniel, 9, 23, 31, 32, 33, 74, 98, 99, 193, 211, 235, 237
British Council, 9, 220
Brook, Peter, 85
Brookes, Mike, 118
Brown, Paula, 9
Burden, Chris, 81, 285
Buren, Daniel, 177
Butler, Season, 237
Butt, Gavin, 7, 130
BUZZCUT, 77
CalArts, 282
Cape Town University, 218
Cardiff School of Art, 263
Carnesky, Marisa, 91
Case, Sue-Ellen, 241
Cassils, 96, 254, 273–82
Casson, Simon, 193, 196, 197–204
Chakravarthi, George, 17, 29–38, 213
Chapter Arts Centre, 23, 74
Charmatz, Boris, 151
Chavkin, Rachel, 85
Cisneros, Teresa, 196, 266, 267, 270
Clapham, Rachel Lois, 133, 136, 142
Clarke, Gillian, 118
Climate Camp, 284, 286
Clown Army, 284, 286
Colchester Arts Centre, 74
Compass Live Art, 74
Contact (Theatre), 74, 116, 119–20
Conway, Abigail, 301
Corrieri, Augusto; *see* Deer Park
Costa, Maddy, 136, 138, 143
Curious, 89–96, 193, 213
Damian (Martin), Diana, 136, 138, 143
Dance Theatre Journal, 138
Dartington (College of Arts), 24, 74, 82
DASH (Disability Arts in Shropshire), 77, 256
de Certeau, Michel, 82
Deacon, Robin, 194
DeDomenici, Richard, 159, 244, 251, 252, 255–64
Deer Park, 82
Delimar, Vlasta, 220
Descartes, René, 59
Desperate Optimists, 267
Disabled Avant Garde, The (Katherine Araniello and Aaron Williamson), 18, 77, 151, 251, 254, 255–64
DIY (workshops by artists for artists); *see* Live Art Development Agency
Djurberg, Nathalie, 153
Documenting Live; see *Restock, Rethink, Reflect*
Donagh, Rita, 219
Drucker, Zackary, 275
Duckie, 77, 198, 200, 201, 203–204
Dunnings, Kaye, 213
East End Collaborations, 90, 98, 129, 198, 199, 236
Edge, 268
Edinburgh Festival, 42, 73, 80, 83, 256, 260
Eisenberg, Alex, 240
El Khoury, Tania, 301
El-Sherbini, Yara, 235
Emin, Tracey, 178
Empress Stah, 275
ERA (Equal Representation for Actresses), 179
Etchells, Tim, 73, 77, 79–88; *see also* Forced Entertainment
European Capital of Culture, 156, 158–59, 163, 196
Exeunt, 138
Exhibit B, 42–44
Fanon, Frantz, 266, 272
Farquhar, Marcia, 235, 242–43
Field, Andy, 73, 77, 79–88, 196
Fierce, 74, 91, 92
Finley, Karen, 91
Fischer, Ernst, 17, 32–33
Flanagan, Bob, 17, 25–27, 54
Fluxus, 157
Flynn, Madeleine, 96
Forced Entertainment, 80, 81–82, 83, 84, 85, 147, 158
Forest Fringe, 9, 73, 74, 77, 80, 83, 86, 88
Foucault, Michel, 288
Frankfurt School, 169
Franko B, 17, 23, 24, 30, 38, 55, 56, 77, 188
Fraser, Andrea, 177

Fraser, Mat, 66
Free Home University, 173
Free University of Liverpool, The, 134, 156, 163, 165–74, 196
Frémeaux, Isabelle, 196, 198, 284
French, Rebecca; *see* French & Mottershead
French & Mottershead, 73, 77, 97–106, 193, 213,
Fry, Roger, 157
Garmiany, Adalet, 220
Gasworks, 257
Girls, The, 67
Gluts, The, 98, 105
Goldberg, RoseLee, 113, 129, 145–54
Goldsmiths, University of London, 7, 130, 237
Gómez Peña, Guillermo, 73, 93, 190, 207, 251, 252, 267, 291–297; *see also* Pocha Nostra, La
Grosvenor Corporation, 158
Guattari, Félix, 159, 160
Guerrilla Girls, 177, 178, 179, 183
Haacke, Hans, 151, 177
hÅb, 74
Hartley, Ria, 201
Harvie, Jen, 11, 175–84, 229, 236, 251
He Yunchang, 51
Heart of Glass, 77, 136
Heathfield, Adrian, 7, 14n15, 58, 129, 130, 132
Hemsley, Alexandrina; *see* Project O
Hendricks, Jon, 151
Henri, Adrian, 157
Hepatitis C, 24, 279
Hewlett, Susannah, 213
Higginson, Steve, 158
Hill, Leslie, 93, 91, 196; *see also* Curious
HIV/AIDS, 24, 208, 279
Hoghe, Raimund, 66, 133
Home Live Art, 166, 178
Howells, Adrian, 133, 240
Humphrey, Tim, 96
Hunter, Nicola, 302–303
Hutson, Lucy, 201
Hsieh, Tehching, 81, 123
ICA (Institute of Contemporary Arts), 18, 23, 32, 73, 83, 91, 99, 266, 272
Immigration and Naturalization Service (US), 294
Impact Theatre, 82
In Between Time, 30, 74, 77, 90, 91
Iniva, 266, 270, 272
Institute for the Art and Practice of Dissent at Home, The, 134, 155–64, 196, 252
Invisible Flock, 41
Johnson, Dominic, 12, 17, 47–56
Johnson, Rashid, 154, 269
Johnson-Small, Jamila; *see* Project O
Jonas, Joan, 150
Jones, Amelia, 17, 20, 25, 57–64
Jordan, John, 133, 196, 198, 252, 254, 283–90
Judge, Harminder Singh, 70
Julien, Isaac, 268–69, 272
Kakl, Poshya, 220
Kaprow, Allan, 157
KAPUTT: The Academy of Destruction; *see* Tate
Keidan, Lois, 6–9, 10, 18, 23, 31, 32, 33, 36, 73, 91, 99, 130, 193, 202, 226, 227, 235, 236, 237, 238, 240, 263, 267
Kienholz, Edward, 276
Kingston University, 252
Kleiman, Gillie, 45
Kontejner, 237
Kulik, Oleg, 77
LA Cacophony Society, 251, 258
La Ribot, 147, 152
LaBeouf, Shia, 281
Laboratory of Insurrectionary Imagination, The, 196, 198, 252, 284
LACE (Los Angeles Contemporary Exhibitions), 274
Lacy, Suzanne, 151–152
Lakmaier, Noëmi, 123
Lamé, Amy, 198, 200
Lancaster Arts, 74, 77
Layzell, Richard, 77, 236
Le Bas, Delaine, 266, 267
Leadbitter, James; *see* vacuum cleaner, the
Leckey, Mark, 151
Leibniz, 251
Lennon, John, 157
Lewis, Isabel, 151
Liberate Tate, 73, 98, 105–6, 124–25, 166, 181
Liberty Festival, 256, 259
Library of Performing Rights, The, 234, 252, 253, 266
LIFT (London International Festival of Theatre), 77
Live Art Bistro, 74
Live Art Development Agency (LADA)
  DIY (workshops by artists for artists), 22, 30, 40, 77, 80, 90, 94, 98, 136, 156, 160–61, 166, 167, 182, 194–96, 198, 206, 216, 245, 246–47, 266, 267–68, 284, 301
  Next Steps Scheme, 182, 183
  One-to-One Artist's Bursary, 30, 90, 98, 194, 206, 211, 216, 266
  Restock, Rethink, Reflect; see *Restock, Rethink, Reflect*
  Study Room, 7, 9, 18, 74, 98, 109, 133, 156, 180, 182, 189, 231, 234, 238, 252, 254, 281, 284
  Unbound, 133, 238, 240
Live Art in Higher Education Forum, 7, 236–237
Live Art UK, 8, 10, 77, 80, 116, 120, 133, 136, 182, 183, 236, 251, 292
Diverse Actions, 183, 251
Live Culture; *see* Tate
Liverpool Anarchist Communist Sunday School, 157
Liverpool Biennial, 156, 185, 229–230, 292
Liverpool School of Language, Music, Dream and Pun, 163
London Fieldworks (Bruce Gilchrist and Jo Joelson), 122
Lorde, Audre, 275, 276
LUPA (Lock Up Performance Art), 206, 209, 212–13
mac, 252
MacLennan, Alastair, 38, 83, 196, 215–24
Mad for Real, 185
Madness, Hana, 201
Mahony, Kate, xx
Makishi, Stacy, 299
Manchester International Festival, 64n5, 74, 116, 119, 120–21
Manifest, 267
Manning, Chelsea, 118
Marchevska, Elena, 252
Mauss, Marcel, 62
McCall, Anthony, 150
McGrath, John E., 73, 115–21
McKenzie, Jordan, 193, 196, 205–14
Melrose, Susan, 236
Merali, Shaheen, 236
Merleau-Ponty, Maurice, 60
Messias, Nando, 301
Minton, Emmy, 96, 213, 237
Mitchell, CJ, 9, 227, 240
Mitchelson, Andrew, 98, 237,
Moten, Fred, 132
motiroti, 267
Mottershead, Andrew; *see* French & Mottershead
National Portrait Gallery, 270
National Review of Live Art, 12, 31, 74, 83, 106, 130, 138, 199, 236, 263
National Student Drama Festival, 82
National Theatre Wales, 74, 116, 117–18
New Work Network, 99, 194
Newman, Hayley, 73, 97–106
News from Nowhere bookshop, 170, 172
Newsome, Rashaad, 269
Nigel & Louise, 195
Nottingham Trent University, 208
NOW Festival, 208
O'Brien, Martin, 17, 18, 21–28, 49, 52–53,

196, 263
O'Donnell, Sinéad, 220
O'Halligan, Peter, 163
O'Reilly, Kira, 17, 21–28, 38, 51, 54, 59–60, 61, 63–64, 93, 126, 129, 133, 196, 240
Ofili, Chris, 269
Offeh, Harold, 67
Oil Sponsorship Free, 182
Oldenburg, Claes, 150
Oliver, Daniel, 201, 263
One-to-One Artist's Bursary; *see* Live Art Development Agency
Ono, Yoko, 60, 150, 156, 157, 158
Open Doors, 96, 193, 213
ORLAN, 23, 51
Ové, Horace, 270–72
Pacitti, Robert, 208
Pane, Gina, 285
Paper Stages, 80, 85
Paris, Helen, 194, 196; *see also* Curious
Paterson, Mary, 129, 133, 135–44
PAVES, 196, 216, 220–22
Pearson, Deborah, 80, 82, 83
Pearson, Mike, 118
Performa, 129, 146, 153–154
Performance Matters, 7, 130, 131–32, 189, 237, 274, 300
]performance s p a c e[, 77, 130
Performance Studies international (PSi) 7, 176, 251, 252; see also *Performing Rights*
Performing Rights, 7, 90, 176, 198, 234, 237, 251, 252, 256
Peters, Sibylle, 8, 77, 108, 109, 112
Phillips, Áine, 12–13, 297
Pier Kids, 269
Piper, Adrian, 60
Platform, 166, 167, 178, 284
Playing Up; *see* Tate
Pocha Nostra, La, 149, 252, 292
Pope.L, William, 51
Princesse, La, 158
Project O, 19, 20, 39–46, 269
Queen Mary University of London, 7, 48, 129, 130, 176, 234, 237, 251, 292
Rancière, Jacques, 168, 172, 173
Rauschenberg, Robert, 148, 150
Read, Alan, 73, 82, 91, 110, 196, 225–32
Reclaim the Streets, 284, 286
Restock, Rethink, Reflect (*RRR*), 18–19, 22, 30, 206, 207, 234, 238, 251, 263, 266
  RRR1: Documenting Live, 18, 19–20, 30, 206, 207, 266, 267
  RRR2: Access All Areas: On Live Art and Disability, 18, 22, 27, 52–53, 136, 256, 263
  RRR3: Live Art and Feminism, 18, 30, 234
  RRR4: Live Art and Privilege, 18, 234
Rivero de Beer, Lorena, 77, 163
Romero, Mandy, 163
Roms, Heike, 13, 77, 107–114
Rose, Sheree, 18, 22, 25–27, 49, 52–53
Ross, Monica, 186–187
Royal Opera House, 269
Royal Shakespeare Company, 17, 30, 36, 178
Royal Vauxhall Tavern, 27, 77, 198; *see also* Duckie
Saatchi, Charles, 178
Salle Gaveau, 113
Saro-Wiwa, Ken, 266, 272
Schneemann, Carolee, 60
School of the Art Institute of Chicago, 219
Science Museum, 136, 139–142
Scottee, 189
Serota, Nick, 100, 105
Shah, Rajni, 18, 77, 136, 142, 193, 194, 205–14
Sharrocks, Amy, 300
Sheaf+Barley, 195
Sheen, Michael, 118
Shephard, Tom, 159
Sifuentes, Aram Han, 252
Sifuentes, Roberto, 93
Šimić, Lena; *see* Institute for the Art and Practice of Dissent at Home, The
Smith, Jack, 150
Smith, Patti, 49
Snapper, Julianna, 62–63
Sofaer, Joshua, 129, 133, 135–44, 193, 194, 196, 203
Sontag, Susan, 280
sorryyoufeeluncomfortable, 266, 270
Southbank, 260
SPILL Festival of Performance, 30, 74, 130, 138, 154, 236, 274, 278
Sprinkle, Annie, 23, 91
Stanley Picker Gallery, 198, 252, 253
Steakhouse Live, 77
Steinhauser, Sven; *see* Deer Park
Stelarc, 23
Stevens, Gary, 81
Stitt, André, 258
Swift, Jonathan, 257
Taggart, Ange, 199
Take the Money and Run?, 98, 136, 166, 178, 251
Tanzquartier Wien, 238
Tate, 7, 8, 73, 77-78, 80, 90, 98, 100, 105–6, 109, 112, 124–25, 129, 130, 136, 146, 147, 150, 151–53, 158, 178, 181, 216, 229, 264, 284, 292
  Early Years and Families Programme, 8
  KAPUTT: The Academy of Destruction, 8, 78, 108, 109, 112, 136
  Live Culture, 7, 77, 90, 98, 129, 136, 147, 149, 152, 188, 216, 274, 292
  Playing Up, 8, 77
Tate Liverpool, 158
Tate Modern, 7, 73, 77–78, 98, 105–6, 109, 112, 124-125, 130, 136, 146, 151, 284, 292
Tate Tanks, 7, 150, 151
Turner Prize, 229, 264
Thomas, Dylan, 118
Thompson, Selina, 17, 39–46, 201
Tolentino, Julie, 275
Total Theatre, 138
Turner Prize; *see* Tate
Trowell, Jane, 165-174, 196
Tryst, 96
Ugwu, Catherine, 6, 9, 10, 18, 73–74, 227, 236, 267, 272
Ukeles, Mierle Laderman, 177
Unbound; *see* Live Art Development Agency
Universal Declaration of Human Rights, 251
University of Reading, 219
University of Roehampton, 7, 130, 226, 237
University of Wales Institute, Cardiff, 23
vacuum cleaner, the, 196, 197–204, 248
VALIE EXPORT, 60, 285
Vason, Manuel, 17, 29–38, 52-53, 55, 65, 66, 67, 76, 149, 190, 196, 216, 275, 300
Venice Biennale, 216, 266
Wagstaff, Sheena, 147
Walton, Robert, 199
We Need to Talk about Live Art, 138
Weaver, Lois, 7, 8, 18, 92, 129, 131, 133, 176, 193, 233–41, 252
Wee, Cecilia, 9
Wellcome Collection, 40, 78, 198
Whelan, Gregg, 93
Whitechapel Art Gallery, 130, 217, 266
Whitehead, Simon, 96
Whitworth Art Gallery, 59, 61
Williamson, Aaron, 212; *see also* Disabled Avant-Garde, The
Wilson, Louise, 118
Wood, Catherine, 129, 145–54
Women's Library, The, 95–96
Wright, Aaron, 240
Wright, Fiona, 23
Writing from Live Art, 133, 136, 137, 138
Wunderbar, 77
Yard, The, 130
ZAD (Zone A Défendre), 252, 284–290
Zierle & Carter, 76, 77

WORKS CITED

All websites current as of time of publication.

Alberro, Alexander, and Blake Stimson, eds., *Institutional Critique: An Anthology of Artists' Writings* (Cambridge, MA: MIT Press, 2009)

Anderson, Benedict, *Imagined Communities: Reflections on the Origin and Spread of Nationalism* (New York and London: Verso, 1983)

Art Not Oil Coalition <http://www.artnotoil.org.uk/>

Arts Council England, *The Value of Arts and Culture to People and Society* (London: Arts Council England, 2014) <http://www.artscouncil.org.uk/exploring-value-arts-and-culture/value-arts-and-culture-people-and-society>

Ashman, Lydia, 'Live Art Development Agency: New Space Provides a Context for Collaboration', a-n The Artists Information Company [2017] <https://www.a-n.co.uk/news/live-art-development-agency-new-space-provides-context-collaboration>

Augsburg, Tanya, 'Orlan's Performative Transformations of Subjectivity', in *The Ends of Performance*, ed. by Peggy Phelan and Jill Lane (New York: New York University Press, 1998), pp. 285–314

Austin, J. L., *How to Do Things with Words* [1955], ed. by J. O. Urmson (New York: Oxford University Press, 1965)

Bailey, David A., Lois Keidan, and Rajni Shah, eds., *Documenting Live* (London: Live Art Development Agency, 2008)

Balme, Christopher B., *The Theatrical Public Sphere* (Cambridge: Cambridge University Press, 2014)

Barad, Karen, *Meeting the Universe Halfway: Quantum Physics and the Entanglement of Matter and Meaning* (Durham: Duke University Press, 2007)

Bennett, Jane, *Vibrant Matter: A Political Ecology of Things* (Durham: Duke University Press, 2010)

Bishop, Claire, 'The Myth of the Active Subject', in *Practicable: From Participation to Interaction in Contemporary Art*, ed. by Samuel Bianchini and Erik Verhagen (Cambridge, MA: MIT Press, 2016), pp. 797–98

———, 'The Social Turn: Collaboration and Its Discontents', *Artforum*, 44.6 (2006), 178–83

Boal, Augusto, *Theatre of the Oppressed* [1974], trans. by Charles A. McBride (London: Pluto, 1979)

Bourdieu, Pierre, 'Structures, *Habitus*, Practices' [1980], in *The Logic of Practice*, trans. by Richard Nice (Stanford: Stanford University Press, 1990), pp. 52–65

BP or not BP? <https://bp-or-not-bp.org/>

Brine, Daniel, ed., *The Live Art Almanac* (London: Live Art Development Agency, 2008)

Brine, Daniel, and Lois Keidan, eds., *Programme Notes: Case Studies for Locating Experimental Theatre* (London: Live Art Development Agency, 2007)

Bronfen, Elisabeth, *Crossmappings: Essays Zur Visuellen Kultur* (Zürich: Scheidegger & Spiess, 2009)

Butler, Judith, *Gender Trouble: Feminism and the Subversion of Identity* (New York and London: Routledge, 1990)

Butt, Gavin, Adrian Heathfield, and Lois Keidan, 'Performance Matters: Gavin Butt, Lois Keidan and Adrian Heathfield in Conversation', *Contemporary Theatre Review*, 24.1 (2014), 102–14

Cairncross, Frances, *The Death of Distance: How the Communications Revolution Will Change Our Lives* (Boston: Harvard Business School Press, 1997)

ten Cate, Ritsaert, 'A Home for Working and Living', ed. by Vertaalbureau Deceuninck and Martine Bom, *Theaterschrift*, 2 ('The Written Space') (1992), 48–57

Clapham, Rachel Lois, ed., *(W)reading Performance Writing : A Study Room Guide* (London: Live Art Development Agency, 2010) <http://www.thisisliveart.co.uk/resources/catalogue/wreading-performance-writing-a-study-room-guide-2010-by-rachel-lois-clapham>

Cohan-Petrolino, Medeia, 'How To: Gallery Commission', Artquest <https://www.artquest.org.uk/how-to-articles/gallery-commission/>

Connolly, Mary Kate, ed., *Throwing the Body into the Fight: A Portrait of Raimund Hoghe* (London and Bristol: Live Art Development Agency and Intellect, 2013)

Coole, Diana, and Samantha Frost, eds., *New Materialisms: Ontology, Agency, and Politics* (Durham: Duke University Press, 2010)

Costa, Maddy, ed., *I See a Fake Moon Rising: Live Art in the Public Realm* (Bristol: Live Art UK and In Between Time, 2013) <http://www.liveartuk.org/uploads/documents/ibt_lauk_publication_website.pdf>

Curtis, Harriet, and Martin Hargreaves, eds., *Kira O'Reilly: Untitled (Bodies)* (London and Bristol: Live Art Development Agency and Intellect, 2018)

DASH (Disability Arts in Shropshire), 'Awkward Bastards' [2015] <http://www.dasharts.org/projects/awkward-bastards.html>

DASH (Disability Arts in Shropshire) and Live Art Development Agency, *M21: From the Medieval to the 21st Century* (London: Live Art Development Agency, 2012)

Descartes, René, *Discourse on Method and The Meditations*, trans. by F. E. Sutcliffe (Harmondsworth: Penguin, 1998)

Edmunds, Becky, Elizabeth Lynch, Mary Paterson, and Rajni Shah, *Dear Stranger, I Love You: The Ethics of Community in Rajni Shah Projects' Glorious* (London and Lancaster: Live Art Development Agency and Lancaster University, 2013)

Ellis-Petersen, Hannah, 'Tracey Emin's Bed Is Sold at Auction for over £2.5m', *Guardian*, 1 July 2014 <http://www.theguardian.com/artanddesign/2014/jul/01/tracey-emin-my-bed-sale-auction>

ERA (Equal Representation for Actresses) <http://equalrepresentationforactresses.co.uk/>

Evans, David, ed., *Manuel Vason: Double Exposures–Performance as Photography–Photography as Performance* (London and Bristol: Live Art Development Agency and Intellect, 2015)

Foucault, Michel, *The Foucault Reader*, ed. by Paul Rabinow (New York: Pantheon, 1984)

Franko B, 'I Feel Empty', in *Live: Art and Performance*, ed. by Adrian Heathfield (London: Tate, 2004), p. 226

Free Home University <https://musagetes.ca/project/free-home-university/>

Free University of Liverpool, The, *Foundations* (Liverpool: FUL Press, 2012) <https://www.thisisunbound.co.uk/products/foundations>

———, <https://thefreeuniversityofliverpool.wordpress.com/>

Gablik, Suzi, *The Reenchantment of Art* (New York: Thames and Hudson, 1991)

Goldberg, RoseLee, 'Hidden from History: Performance Art and the Imagination', in *Art, Lies and Videotape: Exposing Performance*, ed. by Adrian George (London: Tate, 2003), pp. 20–24

———, *Performance Art: From Futurism to the Present* [1979], revised edn (London: Thames & Hudson, 2001)

Goldwater, Helena, ed., *Glimpses of Before: 1970s UK Performance Art* <http://1970s.thisisliveart.co.uk/>

Gressett, Salette, *Live Art Development Agency One to One Individual Artists' Bursary Scheme: An Overview and Findings of the First 5 Years (1999–2004)* (London: Live Art Development Agency, 2004) <http://www.thisisliveart.co.uk/uploads/documents/OnetoOneAppraisal.pdf>

Guerrilla Girls, 'Activist Work: Projects/Resistance: Posters, Stickers, Billboards, Videos, Actions: 1985–2017' <https://www.guerrillagirls.com/projects/>

Harvie, Jen, *Fair Play: Art, Performance and Neoliberalism* (Basingstoke: Palgrave Macmillan, 2013)

———, 'Neoliberalism, Theatre, Performance, Inequality, and Alternatives', in *Digital Theatre, 4 x 45 | Theatre and Performance in a Neoliberal Age*, ed. by Andy Lavender (London: Digital Theatre and Routledge, forthcoming) <http://www.digitaltheatreplus.com/>

———, 'The Power of Abuse', in *The Routledge Companion to Theatre and Politics*, ed. by Peter Eckersall and Helena Grehan (New York and London: Routledge, forthcoming)

Harvie, Jen, and Lois Weaver, eds., *The Only Way Home Is Through the Show: Performance Work of Lois Weaver* (London and Bristol: Live Art Development Agency and Intellect, 2015)

Heathfield, Adrian, ed., *Live: Art and Performance* (London: Tate, 2004)

Heathfield, Adrian, and Tehching Hsieh, *Out of Now: The Lifeworks of Tehching Hsieh* (Cambridge, MA and London: MIT Press and Live Art Development Agency, 2009)

Heddon, Deirdre, 'National Review of Live Art: The 30th Edition', *Contemporary Theatre Review*, 20.3 (2010), 386–88

———, 'The Politics of Live Art', in *Histories and Practices of Live Art*, ed. by Deirdre Heddon and Jennie Klein (Basingstoke: Palgrave Macmillan, 2012), pp. 175–205

Heddon, Deirdre, and Dominic Johnson, eds., *It's All Allowed: The Performances of Adrian Howells* (London and Bristol: Live Art Development Agency and Intellect, 2016)

Heddon, Deirdre, and Jennie Klein, eds., *Histories and Practices of Live Art* (Basingstoke: Palgrave Macmillan, 2012)

Heddon, Deirdre, Jennie Klein, and Nikki Milican, eds., *The National Review of Live Art 1979–2010: A Personal History (Essays, Anecdotes, Drawings and Images)* (Glasgow: New Moves International, 2010)

Henri, Adrian, *Total Art: Environments, Happenings and Performance* (New York: Thames & Hudson, 1974)

Higginson, Steve, and Tony Wailey, *Edgy Cities* (Liverpool: Northern Lights, 2006)

Hlavajova, Maria, and Ranjit Hoskote, eds., *Future Publics (The Rest Can and Should Be Done by the People): A Critical Reader in Contemporary Art* (Utrecht: Valiz and BAK, 2015)

Invisible Committee, The, *To Our Friends* (New York: Autonomedia, 2014)

Jackson, Shannon, *Social Works: Performing Art, Supporting Publics* (New York and London: Routledge, 2011)

Johnson, Dominic, *The Art of Living: An Oral History of Performance Art* (Basingstoke: Palgrave Macmillan, 2015)

———, 'Psychic Weight: The Pains and Pleasures of Performance', in *ORLAN: A Hybrid Body of Artworks*, ed. by Simon Donger and Simon Shepherd (New York and London: Taylor and Francis, 2010), pp. 84–99

———, ed., *Live Art in the UK*, special issue of *Contemporary Theatre Review*, 22.1 (2012)

———, ed., *Manuel Vason: Encounters–Performance, Photography, Collaboration* (Bristol: Arnolfini, 2007)

———, ed., *Pleading in the Blood: The Art and Performances of Ron Athey* (London and Bristol: Live Art Development Agency and Intellect, 2013)

Johnson-Small, Jamila, and Alexandrina Hemsley, *A Contemporary Struggle* (London: Live Art Development Agency and Project O, 2013)

Jones, Amelia, *Seeing Differently: A History and Theory of Identification and the Visual Arts* (New York and London: Routledge, 2012)

———, '"The Artist Is Present": Artistic Re-Enactments and the Impossibility of Presence', *TDR/The Drama Review*, 55.1 (2011), 16–45

Jones, Amelia, and Marin Blažević, 'The Voice of Death, Rupturing the Habitus', *Performance Research*, 19.3 (2014), 140–43

Jones, Amelia, and Adrian Heathfield, eds., *Perform Repeat Record: Live Art in History* (London and Bristol: Live Art Development Agency and Intellect, 2012)

Jordan, John, *In the Footnotes of Library Angels: A Bi(bli)ography of Insurrectionary Imagination* (London: Live Art Development Agency, 2006) <http://www.thisisliveart.co.uk/resources/catalogue/study-room-guide-in-the-footnotes-of-library-angels-a-bibliography-of-insur>

Kaprow, Allan, *Essays on the Blurring of Art and Life*, ed. by Jeff Kelley, expanded ed. (Berkeley: University of California Press, 2003)

Keidan, Lois, *Discussion Document: Live Art* (National Arts and Media Strategy Unit, Arts Council [UK], 1991), P218, Live Art Development Agency Study Room

———, *Vision Paper: A Question of Live Art* (Live Art UK, 2004) <https://www.liveartuk.org/uploads/documents/Live_Art_UK_VISION_PAPER.pdf>

Keidan, Lois, and CJ Mitchell, eds., *Access All Areas: Live Art and Disability* (London: Live Art Development Agency, 2012)

Klein, Jennie, 'Developing Live Art', in *Histories and Practices of Live Art*, ed. by Deirdre Heddon and Jennie Klein (Basingstoke: Palgrave Macmillan, 2012), pp. 12–36

Kuppers, Petra, *Community Performance: An Introduction* (New York and London: Routledge, 2007)

Kuppers, Petra, and Gwen Robertson, eds., *The Community Performance Reader* (New York and London: Routledge, 2007)

La Frenais, Rob, ed., *Anne Bean: Self Etc.* (London and Bristol: Live Art Development Agency and Intellect, 2018)

Laboratory of Insurrectionary Imagination, The <https://labofii.wordpress.com/>

Lefebvre, Henri, *Everyday Life in the Modern World*, trans. by Sacha Rabinovitch (New York and London: Continuum, 2002)

Lessing, Gotthold Ephraim, *Laocoön: An Essay upon the Limits of Painting and Poetry*, trans. by Edward Allen McCormick (Baltimore: Johns Hopkins University Press, 1954)

Lindgaard, Jade, ed., *Eloge des mauvaises herbes: Ce que nous devons à la ZAD* (Paris: Liens qui libèrent, 2018)

Linsley, Johanna, ed., *Dreams for an Institution: A Study Room Guide on Engaging & Challenging Institutions* (London: Live Art Development Agency, 2013) <http://www.thisisliveart.co.uk/resources/catalogue/dreams-for-an-institution-a-study-room-guide>

Live Art Development Agency <http://www.thisisliveart.co.uk/>

———, 'ABsence: Awkward Bastards 2' [2017] <http://www.thisisliveart.co.uk/projects/awkward-bastards-2>

———, 'DIY' <http://www.thisisliveart.co.uk/opportunities/diy/>

———, 'Ethical Funding Policy & Procedures' [2018], <http://www.thisisliveart.co.uk/uploads/documents/LADA_Ethical_Funding_Policy_2018.pdf>

———, 'How We Work' <http://www.thisisliveart.co.uk/about/how-we-work/>

———, 'Job Opportunity: LADA Coordinator' <http://www.thisisliveart.co.uk/opportunities/job-opportunity-lada-coordinator>

———, 'Library of Performing Rights' <http://www.thisisliveart.co.uk/resources/collections/library-of-performing-rights>

———, 'Performing Rights' <http://www.thisisliveart.co.uk/projects/performing-rights>

———, 'PSI#12 Performing Rights: London, 2006' <http://www.thisisliveart.co.uk/projects/psi12-performing-rights-london-2006>

———, '"Take the Money and Run?"–Documentation' [2015] <http://www.thisisliveart.co.uk/projects/take-the-money-and-run-documentation-from-an-event-about-ethics-funding-and/>

———, 'What Is Live Art?' <http://www.thisisliveart.co.uk/about/what-is-live-art/>

———, ed., *In Time: A Collection of Live Art Case Studies* (London: Live Art Development Agency and Live Art UK, 2010) <https://www.liveartuk.org/uploads/documents/In_Time_complete.pdf>

Live Art Development Agency and Eleanor Roberts, 'Live Art and Feminism in the UK', *Google Arts & Culture* <https://artsandculture.google.com/exhibit/1gLSx6pobvq_Ig>

Live Art UK, 'Diverse Actions Awarded Arts Council England Ambition for Excellence Grant', 18 January 2017 <http://www.liveartuk.org/activities/diverse-actions-awarded-arts-council-england-ambition-for-excellence-grant/>

Lorde, Audre, 'Poetry Is Not a Luxury' [1977], in *Sister Outsider: Essays and Speeches* (Berkeley: Crossing Press, 1985), pp. 36–39

Mauss, Marcel, 'Techniques of the Body' [1934], *Economy and Society*, 2.1 (1973), 70–88

Mauvaise Troupe and friends, *LA ZAD / THE ZONE TO DEFEND: A Liberated Territory Against an Airport and Its World* (Minneapolis: Canary Press, forthcoming)

McMillan, Michael, *Cultural Grounding: Live Art and Cultural Diversity: A Report for the Visual Arts Department of the Arts Council of Great Britain* (Arts Council of Great Britain, 1990), P1703, Live Art Development Agency Study Room

Merleau-Ponty, Maurice, *Phenomenology of Perception* [1945], trans. by Colin Smith (New York and London: Routledge, 2002)

———, *The Visible and the Invisible* [1964], ed. by Claude Lefort, trans. by Alphonso Lingis (Evanston, IL: Northwestern University Press, 1968)

Messer-Davidow, Ellen, 'Acting Otherwise', in *Provoking Agents: Gender and Agency in Theory and Practice*, ed. by Judith Kegan Gardiner (Urbana, University of Illinois Press, 1995), pp. 23–51

Moretti, Franco, *Distant Reading* (New York and London: Verso, 2013)

———, *Graphs, Maps, Trees: Abstract Models for a Literary History* (New York and London: Verso, 2005)

Morris, David B., *The Culture of Pain* (Berkeley: University of California Press, 1991)

Mouffe, Chantal, *The Democratic Paradox* (New York and London: Verso, 2000)

Newman, Hayley, *Common* (Isle of Wight: Copy Press, 2013)

Nicholson, Helen, *Applied Drama: The Gift of Theatre* (Basingstoke: Palgrave Macmillan, 2005)

Nochlin, Linda, 'Why Have There Been No Great Women Artists?' [1971], in *Women, Art, and Power and Other Essays* (London: Thames & Hudson, 1989), pp. 145–78

Norris, Pippa, *Critical Citizens: Global Support for Democratic Government*

(Oxford: Oxford University Press, 1999)

O'Brien, Martin, and David MacDiarmid, eds., *Survival of the Sickest: The Art of Martin O'Brien* (London: Live Art Development Agency, 2018)

Oil Sponsorship Free <http://oilsponsorshipfree.org/>

Paterson, Mary, and Theron Schmidt, eds., *Getting It Out There: The Future of Touring and Distribution for Contemporary Theatre and Live Art* (Lancaster and London: Live at LICA and Live Art UK, 2013) <http://www.liveartuk.org/uploads/documents/giot.pdf>

Performance Studies international, 'PSi #12: Performing Rights' [2006] <http://www.psi-web.org/past-events/psi-12-performing-rights/>

Perry, Grayson, 'Yes, Performance Art Is Extreme and Silly, but It Does Have a Point', *The Times* (UK), 22 March 2006, p. 16

Peters, Sibylle, *Playing Up: A Live Art Game for Kids and Adults* (London: Live Art Development Agency, 2016)

Phillips, Áine, ed., *Performance Art in Ireland: A History* (London and Bristol: Live Art Development Agency and Intellect, 2015)

Platform <https://platformlondon.org/>

Rancière, Jacques, *The Ignorant Schoolmaster: Five Lessons in Intellectual Emancipation* [1987], trans. by Kristin Ross (Stanford: Stanford University Press, 1991)

Raunig, Gerald, and Gene Ray, eds., *Art and Contemporary Critical Practice: Reinventing Institutional Critique* (London: Mayfly, 2009)

Read, Alan, 'Lay Theatre and the Eruption of the Audience', *Stages*, 5 (2016), <https://biennial.com/journal/issue-5/lay-theatre-and-the-eruption-of-the-audience>

———, *Theatre in the Expanded Field: Seven Approaches to Performance* (London: Bloomsbury, 2013)

———, *Theatre, Intimacy & Engagement: The Last Human Venue* (Basingstoke: Palgrave Macmillan, 2008)

Reinelt, Janelle, '"What I Came to Say": Raymond Williams, the Sociology of Culture and the Politics of (Performance) Scholarship', *Theatre Research International*, 40.3 (2015), 235–249

Roms, Heike, *What's Welsh for Performance? An Oral History of Performance Art in Wales 1968–2008, Vol.1* (Cardiff: Samizdata, 2008)

———, *What's Welsh for Performance? Beth yw 'performance' yn Gymraeg?* <http://www.performance-wales.org/>

Schneider, Rebecca, *The Explicit Body in Performance* (New York and London: Routledge, 1997)

Schneider, Rebecca, and Lucia Ruprecht, 'In Our Hands: An Ethics of Gestural Response-Ability. Rebecca Schneider in Conversation with Lucia Ruprecht', *Performance Philosophy*, 3.1 (2017), 108–25

Smith, Stacy L., Mark Choueiti, and Katherine Pieper, *Gender Bias Without Borders: An Investigation of Female Characters in Popular Films Across 11 Countries* (Los Angeles: University of Southern California, 2014) <https://seejane.org/symposiums-on-gender-in-media/gender-bias-without-borders/>

Sofaer, Joshua, *The Performance Pack*, numbered edition (London: Live Art Development Agency, 2004)

———, 'What Is Live Art?' [2002] <http://www.joshuasofaer.com/2011/06/what-is-live-art/>

Sontag, Susan, *AIDS and Its Metaphors* (New York: Farrar, Straus and Giroux, 1989)

Stanley Picker Gallery, *Louder Than Bombs–Art, Action & Activism* [2010] <https://www.stanleypickergallery.org/exhibitions/louder-than-bombs/>

Stiles, Kristine, 'The Story of the Destruction in Art Symposium and the "DIAS Affect"', in *Gustav Metzger: History History*, ed. by Sabine Breitwieser (Vienna and Ostfildern-Ruit: Generali Foundation and Hatje Cantz, 2005), pp. 41–65

Thompson, James, *Digging Up Stories: Applied Theatre, Performance and War* (Manchester: Manchester University Press, 2005)

Thompson, Selina, 'Exhibit B' [2014] <http://selinathompson.co.uk/exhibit-b/>

Tiller, Chrissie, and Patrick Fox, eds., *Praxis Vol 1: Of People, Place & Time* (St Helens and London: Heart of Glass and Live Art Development Agency, 2017)

Triscott, Nicola, 'Trust and the Taste of Flesh: The Ethics of Martin O'Brien's Zombie Performance' [2015] <https://nicolatriscott.org/2015/12/15/trust-and-the-taste-of-flesh/>

Ugwu, Catherine, ed., *Let's Get It on: The Politics of Black Performance* (London and Seattle: ICA and Bay Press, 1995)

University of Liverpool and Liverpool John Moores University, *IMPACTS 08: European Capital of Culture Research Programme* [2010] <https://www.liverpool.ac.uk/impacts08/>

Van Erven, Eugène, *Community Theatre: Global Perspectives* (London: Routledge, 2001)

Warr, Tracey, and Amelia Jones, *The Artist's Body* (London: Phaidon, 2000)

Weaver, Lois, Eleanor Roberts, Alex Eisenberg, and Jen Harvie, 'Editing Ourselves into History: A Live Art and Feminism Wikipedia Edit-a-Thon', *Contemporary Theatre Review* [2015] <https://www.contemporarytheatrereview.org/2015/editing-ourselves-into-history/>

Williamson, Aaron, and Oriana Fox, eds., *Aaron Williamson: Performance / Video / Collaboration* (London: Live Art Development Agency and KIOSK, 2008)

Wollaston, Sam, 'Last Night's TV', *Guardian*, 15 March 2006 <http://www.theguardian.com/media/2006/mar/15/broadcasting.tvandradio>

Wylie, John, 'The Distant: Thinking toward Renewed Senses of Landscape and Distance', *Environment, Space, Place*, 9.1 (2017), 1–20

Ypi, Lea, *Global Justice and Avant-Garde Political Agency* (Oxford: Oxford University Press, 2012)

Zerihan, Rachel, ed., *Study Room Guide on One to One Performance* (London: Live Art Development Agency, 2009) <http://www.thisisliveart.co.uk/resources/catalogue/rachel-zerihans-study-room-guide>

AGENCY: A Partial History of Live Art

First published in the UK in 2019 by

Intellect, The Mill, Parnall Road,
Fishponds, Bristol, BS16 3JG, UK
www.intellectbooks.com

and

Live Art Development Agency
The Garrett Centre
117 Mansford Street
London, E2 6LX, UK
www.thisisLiveArt.co.uk

First published in the USA in 2019 by

Intellect, The University of Chicago Press,
1427 E. 60th Street, Chicago, IL 60637, USA

Edited by Theron Schmidt

Designed by David Caines Unlimited
www.davidcaines.co.uk

Printed and bound by Gomer Press, UK

ISBN: 978-1-78320-990-3

ePDF ISBN: 978-1-78938-030-9

ePUB ISBN: 978-1-78938-029-3

Theron Schmidt and LADA would like to thank all the artists, producers, scholars, and writers for their generosity in contributing to *AGENCY*, and to all the photographers who have given permission to include their extraordinary images in this publication.

Additional thanks to UNSW School of the Arts and Media for financial support for interview transcription; Phoebe Patey Ferguson and Laura Dee Milnes for further help with transcription; Mary Paterson for feedback on the initial book concept; and Rajni Shah for their careful reading and reflection throughout the editing of this collection.

A catalogue record for this book is available from the British Library.

Live Art Development Agency

intellect publishers of original thinking

LOTTERY FUNDED Supported using public funding by ARTS COUNCIL ENGLAND